Out of the Cocoon

Rethinking Our Selves: An Introduction to a New Future

JOHN WILLIAM KUCKUK

iUniverse, Inc.
Bloomington

Out of the Cocoon
Rethinking Our Selves: An Introduction to a New Future

iUniverse books may be ordered through booksellers or by contacting:

iUniverse
1663 Liberty Drive
Bloomington, IN 47403
www.iuniverse.com
1-800-Authors (1-800-288-4677)

ISBN: 978-1-4697-4514-5 (sc)
ISBN: 978-1-4697-4516-9 (hc)
ISBN: 978-1-4697-4515-2 (ebk)

Printed in the United States of America

iUniverse rev. date: 03/27/2012

TABLE OF CONTENTS

ACKNOWLEDGEMENTS

This is the work of a lifetime. Providentially, as it developed I remembered many precursors of my thoughts. After finishing it I continue to uncover forgotten authors who long ago began my train of thought. One of these was Robert Heilbroner's *Worldly Philosophers*, a singlular acquaintance with economics. I was set in motion early in the years of my career by Orion Hopper, Phil Park and their crew of able young Presbyterians in an audacious project of the Presbytery of Detroit under the leadership of Kenneth Neigh and Matthew Thies. In addition to such as these, there are many who have helped me while I wrote this book. Three whose sharp minds were most helpful in launching it were Gene TeSelle, Jean Marlowe and Reid Huntley who read some of the earliest drafts, made suggestions, and saw more than I did some of the opportunities ahead.

After I had gained some confidence, I began sharing early drafts with colleagues and a number of them read enough to become excited about the end product – which most of them, understandably have been waiting for in print, being of my own (print-focused) generation: George Mehaffey stands out for his persistent encouragement, Gerry Gregg, Ken Wilkinson, Lynn Wybrew, Rawley Boone, and my special friend, Keene Lebold. Going through a severe downgrade in sight did not prevent Keene from engaging in long conversations from which many pieces of the manuscript benefited.

Others engaged faithfully in grappling with authors behind my writing, some of them quoted in the text. At The Ohio State University a weekly discussion during school sessions included George Smith, Martha Davis, Mervin Muller, Paul Andrews, Jacques Zakin, Rolf Barth and Andrew Oldenquist. Edson Lewis deserves special note, perhaps most responsible for the forty year history of this "Theological Discussion" group, who read the entire manuscript and spent hours with me in discussing points of concern. Another OSU oriented group of similar longevity has included such people as James Kraus, James Miner, Lesley Stansbery, David McCoy and Richard Trelease. Like Bill Lewis, Robert Russell, the inimitable kingpin of this Friday morning discussion group, has been responsible for the maintenance of the group over a similar span of time. Bob also introduced me to Joan Huber who reviewed early work. Shall we not note that these virile intellectual communities span a spectacular instant in the revolution described in *Out of the Cocoon*? It has been a privilege to be part of them for a few years. The dedication of all of these and many others are woven in the fabric of my life, all of them seeing and seeking beyond the usual attention of our time.

Though the pressures of life persistently reduced the time I spent readying over my career, a few people enabled me to maintain my intellectual awareness and accumulate a small library of important books. College professors Jacob Van Tuinen and Viola Wendt became dear friends throughout life. Bob Yolton and Kathy Doctor sustained me through a professional career in a tumultuous period of Presbyterianism. There were many, many others, but I name particularly my sisters, Janice Minardi, and Gail Baptist, and my wife, Jane Wiley Kuckuk, who bore the weight of two final edits. Jane's skills in forty years as editor and executive secretary of the Delta Omicron International Music Fraternity were applied once again in this task. Such indebtedness never ends.

PERMISSIONS

I am grateful to the following for permission to use materials from publications indicated:

Leslie Brothers, *Friday's Footprint: How society Shapes The Human Mind* (1997), by permission of Oxford University Press, Inc.
Sarah Coakley, "Evolution and Sacrifice" by permission of *Christian Century*, Oct. 20, 2009.
Robin Dunbar, *Grooming, Gossip, and the Evolution of Language* (1996), by permission of Harvard University Press.
Michael Gazzaniga, *Human: The Science Behind What Makes Us Unique* (2008), 224, 235, 240, by permission of HarperCollins, Inc.
Arthur Herman, *How The Scots Invented the Modern World* (2001), by permission of Crown Publishers, a division of Random House, Inc.
Serene Jones, *Calvin and the Rhetoric of Piety* (1995), by permission of Westminster John Knox Press.
Victor Lowe, *Understanding Whitehead* (1962), 34ff, 38,40,45 by permission of The Johns Hopkins University Press.
Daniel Maier-Katkin, *Stranger from Abroad* (2010) by permission of W. W. Norton & Company.
Nelson Mandela in Sen Amartya, *Identity and Violence* (2006) by permission of W. W. Norton & Company.
Fareed Zakaria, *The Post-American World* (2008) by permission of W. W. Norton & Company.
Daniel L. Pals, *The Victorian "Lives" of Jesus* (1982), Trinity University Press, by permission of the author.
Frans de Waal, *Our Inner Ape* (2005), Riverhead Books, by permission of the author.

ೋ

The author welcomes dialog at
jkuckuk@copper.net

OUT OF THE COCOON
RETHINKING OUR SELVES: AN INTRODUCTION TO A NEW FUTURE
© 2012 John Kuckuk

PREFACE

The beginnings of these paragraphs go back to my emergence into adulthood when I began to develop my capacity to think. Based on a thinking childhood that was, nonetheless, perverted by an antiquated and didactic culture, during my years in higher education I established a thinking posture that persisted in exploring the best thought available to me. In college I found my attraction to the social sciences to be a dead end but gradually absorbed philosophy and a penchant for history which waited for graduate school. There I was pushed to the limit, and in the years which followed I grasped at intellectual lights but found myself much too busy to pursue them.

This book began, then, as a sort of instinctual expression of my learnings over 15 years since I retired. To paraphrase J. B. Priestley, this is not a work of scholarship.[1] If it had been, it would not carry my name, for I have no allusions about my qualifications. If I had followed the usual path of men of my age, I would relax, read, and enjoy the sun. But I could not have written it when I was younger, because these years of relaxed reading have given me a whole new sense of the order of things. As a young man the nature of a "true" humanity haunted me in the face of what appeared as a culture full of confusing images. Reading kept reinforcing a recurring concept of the evolution of the human self. This concept of self has been a conundrum for a long time. The Roman god Janus, the "god of beginnings," looking forward and backward, may have been an early expression of our sense of history, of being connected to past and future. We have come a long way since then conceptually. Recently a variety of brain scans has been used to identify some aspects of the operation of the brain contributing to the evidence in recorded history of the progressive development and persistent correction of our confidence in understanding.

My observations are derived importantly from learning to read again. With reading problems that were not noticed in my childhood, I worked hard for my academic achievements. In spite of my problems I developed a love of learning. I read deep stuff constantly, probably because I could enjoy thinking while my slow reading gave me a habit of reflective reading. I remember struggling in high school through Sholem Ashe's *The Nazarene* (1939). Short devotional books like *Brother Lawrence* delighted me. I took speed reading courses twice during my career. Still reading remained a demanding discipline. When I retired, I was determined to surmount my difficulty, and largely have done so. Though I now read only three or four times my speed in school, I also have more control over it that allows me to comprehend more deeply and with better recollection than before. Reading is for me a greater pleasure than ever now that I am no longer distracted by earning a living -- for whatever encouragement that might be to all slow readers . Distractions are to be overcome!

My retirement has allowed me the freedom to follow my nose through book reviews, library stacks and my own small library, to update my lagging acquaintance with our intellectual world. As I read, the difference the past sixty years have made in our world became strikingly clear. Our world today is very different ! There is no adult who cannot identify some of the changes – but few understand the speed and extent of these changes in the history of humanity. I sometimes wondered at the changes my parents witnessed during the first half of the twentieth century, but the immensity of the changes in the second half of the century dwarf those. These changes are not consistently embodied in any one population. No one fits the "normal" exactly, though occasionally we are surprised by a close fit. So it is quite unlikely that the ideas I express here will be universally agreeable. There will be many different reactions to most of my assertions (which are many – the habit of making assertions hangs on among us).

Many readers will need to set aside preconceptions to follow the argument. This is philosophy, I suppose, perhaps philosophic anthropology, or cultural anthropology. But it is religious in substance. With such lights as Wittgenstein I see things through a religious prism. While he worked in the midst of the scientistic period, our culture allows us the liberation of the sea-change in our own century. I believe this to be a coming to terms with two distinct attributes of our culture. The first is a culture which has had a very long history of preoccupation with divinity. The second is a basically human view that is substantially an awareness of human finitude. The first of these cannot be erased, in spite of efforts to do so by persons who would like the concept of divinity to disappear. The second has required a long, arduous struggle to achieve a workable equilibrium in Western culture.[2]

Our new world at the beginning of the twenty-first century is so different from only fifty years ago that we cannot escape the sea-changes we are witnessing. The reader might think of being the captain of a World Cup sailing vessel. Sea changes have to do with such navigational problems as the ocean currents and winds. They can totally change sailing strategy. So the sea-change we are now experiencing in Western culture requires us to apply our human capacity for adaptation with a fresh determination. Though I have tried to see beyond, the only culture with which I am intimately familiar is our own, the United States. My capacity for transcending this culture was first signaled when I excitedly shared with a college professor a now lost print of a painting of cane-cutters in the fields of Cuba. When I later discovered Marcel Duchamp's "Nude Descending a Staircase," I realized that such art was "speaking" what was not yet broadly perceived, indeed, an early twentieth century signal of the sea-change.

As writing styles have changed, so ours are changing today. I have found myself using expressions which I myself regard as archaic, because I am a child of the middle of the twentieth century. That was a time of striking changes. With the help of Jane Wiley Kuckuk, my wife who had years of editing experience, the text has become much clearer. She had some difficulty with George Steiner's quote (VII B) which I find delightful. Since many readers will agree with her and most also are more familiar with other styles, I ask you to remember your superb human capacity to listen carefully, to adapt, and try to grasp the intent rather than to interpret writing literally. The tendency to literal interpretation, of course, is something we inherit in the West. I remind you that words are slippery and so I occasionally provide definitions. One of these words is "religion." Still I continue to use it quite freely of a basic human orientation and I do not claim to have defined it to everyone's satisfaction!

It is important to understand this book in terms of common life. It does not address moments of catastrophe nor other extremities. Natural disaster, fire, hurricane, and similar events are the subjects of other books. Here, we pay careful attention to the realm of common sense. Common sense tends to be conservative. In all the changes of the past, common sense has contributed some stability. But in the emerging mind which I urge upon you this does not need to impede change, only to assure that we give to our own past due credit for the common sense embodied in it – and utilize it wisely. This "new mind" could be said to be the middle way. Currently, the word "conservative" has been captured to designate a particular and reactionary mindset. This work argues from beginning to end against that point of view. But this does not mean I support what is currently called "liberal." The reason is that our common life always contains its own aberrations, its own errors of orientation, and its own blatant mistakes. Human life is the fantastic capability to weigh things carefully, to correct past mistakes to our satisfaction and to forge ahead creatively for the good of all.

A few suggestions to readers may be in order. One is that this narrative does follow an overall historical order, but makes many leaps back and forth in time and also in location of attention. Ancient is constantly compared with Medieval, and Medieval with Modern. European is compared with Mediterranean and American with European. Think nimbly! Fixing dates in mind is helpful. I have added a chronology to make the relation of one time with another, one person with another easier to identify. Beginning your own listing of the dates you find useful will make it easier to develop your critical faculties. Please keep in mind that we are talking here about the West. A view of this development from the East, even if Christian, will be different. I must speak from where I stand.

The formation of the violent world culture which issued in the genocide of the twentieth century is the focus of the first three chapters. Chapters IV through VI pay attention to the recovery of the human self, our growing self-consciousness, and the revolution in government demonstrated by the emergence of the United States. In chapters VII through IX we explore the emergence of a modern self consciousness which is evidently producing a "new mind." Chapters X through XII describe the shape of a new culture in which a practical philosophy and popular piety prevail. And the remaining chapters identify some issues we need to address in the twenty-first century. From time to time the reader will be subjected to a review of the past from different points of view. One might hope that the direction suggested here will substantially reduce if not eliminate characterization of our culture as violent and replace this sobriquet with "kind" and "compassionate." The issue before us is to contribute as well as we can to future generations enjoyment of their humanity.

Finally, we want to remind you that though many people are noted, there is no way we could pay attention to all the voices which have contributed to our culture. The number is immense, probably incomprehensible to all of us, just as the over six billion people on the globe today defy our grasp. We no longer relate only to family and a few beyond it as the earliest human species did. We must expand our sense of others to the limits of our imaginations if we are to begin to grasp the rich tapestry forming our new world culture.

The reader should be alert to the many astute authors of analyses of the evolution of our culture. Their number has burgeoned since the 1940s when nineteenth century geological stratigraphy was generally adopted by archaeology. Nuclear physicists had discovered radiocarbon dating, using the decay of unstable carbon isotopes in bone, charcoal, and other organic materials to tell how old the objects were. The dating of ancient artifacts took on some rationality. I have not only not read all of these authors, many are beyond my competence. I learn from each one into which I dip my attention. But I do want to mention that Scot Atran, a professor of Anthropology at the University of Michigan, in my opinion has written the definitive work on "the evolutionary landscape of religion," which is the subtitle of *In Gods We Trust* (2002). I am indebted to him and others for many insights and much information.

A further word about dates. From this point of view, most dates are relative approximations. But I have neglected one common use of dates. The dates used in end notes are conventionally the date of publication of the reference used. But in this book, I have attempted to use the date of first publication, in other words the date after which the reference could impact the culture. In this exploration it is of no help to see that a book published in English in 1934 by Walter Bauer (1877-1960) was republished in 2000. We cannot ignore those seventy years. This may be disconcerting to some readers, but since we are tracing the changing influence of human thinking on the way we have lived and live today, the logic should be clear enough. A danger to which I often succumb is to apply late labels to thought patterns I attribute to particular thinkers. Hobbes falls victim to this, but this does not diminish his role in development of modernism. My critiques are not intended nor should they be used to whitewash anyone. Everyone's contributions are important. I am accustomed to use words with the suffix "ism" to denote extreme and generally consistent ideational fixations. Such thought structures seem to me mistaken. Thus I write "rationalism" as most unfortunate while "rational" is not demeaned.

And a word more about words. Many words that have been misused (emotion, spirit, God) still play important parts in our talk. You will find me using words I dislike and too many words which some readers will find unfamiliar. But that is simply the result of a lifetime of deep reading. May I urge the reader to sit both critically and loosely with words, making good use of the reader's handbook, a good dictionary? Some words that appear here are in quotations, the usage of the authors. Let us note in passing, that much of our language has been borrowed and this is evident in this work. My sources are most often secondary since it is there that I have found evidence of the development of the human being's mind. These many secondary sources are themselves evidence of the evolution of the mind. And the writers, we hurry to say, were and are also human beings of their own place and culture as I also am.

The mention of culture prods me again to note the amorphous nature of culture and also of the "periods" we use to provide hooks for the major cultural changes of the Western world. Not only do these periods fade out and into one another, but they apply largely to the Western world. By West we mean essentially Europe and the Americas.[3] My view is sadly truncated by background and learning and makes only occasional references to Asia, Africa, and the Americas outside the United States. We sincerely hope that others better informed will continue elucidation of the notion of the evolution of the human self in other cultural contexts.[4] Perhaps eventually we will see our evolution clearly! Mistakes found here will then sift themselves out of the picture. Together we seek the truth of who we are. Who we are includes the unique inheritance of each of us from the past.

INTRODUCTION -- MAYBE A NEW BEGINNING

A. THE CRUCIAL ROLE OF PRINT MEDIA

Perhaps my struggle with reading helps me to be sympathetic with the Medieval people whose world was transformed by Gutenberg's moveable type. It is probable that Koreans and Chinese had already done this. Gutenberg applied the idea to the Western invention of the alphabet. His reinvention opened a flood of print on a population just discovering how arresting symbols on paper might be. People who could read had grist for their daily conversations with neighbors. With pamphlets flowing through the population of Europe after the Renaissance reading became a leisure time preoccupation. It gave a new dimension to the age-old practice of gossip.[5] Printers sprang up everywhere, and gave Europe hundreds of printed single books of the Christian scripture for broad distribution to people increasingly hungry to exercise their minds. But complete books were written also, and Erasmus changed Europe with his excellent Latin translations of the Greek manuscripts newly available from the East.

The Reformation freed the people to pursue the reading of scripture using their own minds to seek the revealed truth long published and protected by the established church. There is little doubt that freedom to use the vernacular removed a long-standing roadblock to intellectual development. Scribes had from very early times been essential and privileged parts of the culture. Their compilations of laws favored their status as well as arbitrary authority by oligarchs. Roman law was part of a quite amazing cultural advance. Latin, with its origins among the ancient peoples in northern Italy, served its purpose as a common language for the aristocracies of the new European world. In the Roman world writers had produced a linguistic excellence. In the first century BCE Cicero produced a quality of writing and literary expression which guided the education of Europeans for centuries and has stood to the present day challenging every intellectual to master his tongue. The same standards of excellence pushed intellectual development through refinement and precision of expression ultimately embodied in the multiplying volumes in European libraries. It was a quality of writing and literary expression which has stood to the present day. While emerging Europe built a new order, it did so on the base of the old.

Of course vernacular versions of scripture feared by the Church contained many errors, but so did Jerome's Latin text of the fifth century which was the church text for centuries. A primary inheritance from the ancient world was the cultural arrogance of aristocrats in the power structures inherited from oligarchs. It is fascinating that in spite of awareness that writing could contain errors and mistakes as well as misinformation, language, words, speech, and writing commanded increasing prestige and centrality in our culture century after century. In the Medieval church nothing was more fearsome than the power of words in the mouths of heretics. The increasing complexity and breadth of human language persistently grew, faster as it broke the constraints of the religious hierarchy.

Throughout the Middle Ages, the Church maintained its authority to control the thinking of the people. It began with the vacuum in the Roman period in which second and third century bishops of the church felt responsible to assure the correctness of the gospel as they had inherited it from those who had walked and talked with Jesus. They shaped Christian orthodoxy believing the gospel as they inherited it reflected accurately the life and teaching of Jesus. It was Constantine himself, eager for the unifying power of religion in his faltering empire, who established the pattern of collegial authority in the Church. He called the first church council of bishops in Nicea in 325 CE. There, some two to three hundred bishops established the root of orthodoxy in the divinity of Jesus and his equality with God. This was its answer to a threatening Christian named Arius who espoused one of the alternative understandings of the Gospel.[6] The Trinity gradually gave Christendom a unifying concept of God embodying the concepts of distinct identity and sociality. The extensive and perpetual arguments about this doctrine over the centuries provide a rich demonstration of the capacity of Christianity to accommodate the variety of human opinions. Already the writings of the major players in shaping the early Church are crucial.

In the short term this unity of words provided a base for the more or less common religion and culture of Europe, In the early Middle Ages the church battled an array of unacceptable views, but by the Renaissance there was a palpable unity of religion. It did not interfere with the conflicts between powerful people, however, and religion was sometimes the excuse for war. The persistent expectation that the ordinary people would defend their rulers kept the people under the thumb of oligarchy until growing literacy broke the dominance of Latin, the province of the Church, At that point the minds of people of all classes were freed of their subservient prejudice and opened to a new intellectual freedom. People were beginning to recognize that their minds had not just popped into existence at some distant time in the past, but were emerging from their captivity under the constraining aristocracies of the past.[7] The Latin which unified Europe also demeaned the people whose languages we call "vernacular." With print in their own tongues, the people gained a new measure of self-confidence.

The worst fears of the intellectual aristocracy were realized. Humanism emerged very slowly as an intellectual justification for human intellectual freedom. Humanists were generally faithful church members – as church critics were generally -- though no more than others strictly orthodox. The Protestant Reformation produced a growing literature encouraging people to think. Misunderstandings flourished along with the increase in knowledge. The futile attempt to burn heretical vernacular versions of writings out of existence with their errors hardly slowed the miraculous change in the human mind produced by this vast increase in the exercise of speech through print.

The origins of talk communication are lost in the mists of the ancient world tens of thousands of years ago. Perhaps it began as sign language and with shouts to other hunters sharing in the dangerous task of killing a large animal. Or perhaps it began long before that in dancing and singing celebrating a plentiful harvest. Man-who-speaks (*Homo loquens*) has dominated the world landscape ever since. The written language has long served the purpose of stabilizing the ancient oral languages of human beings and thus also their culture. It also makes possible building on an extensive past.

B. ACCELLERATING CULTURAL CHANGE

My introduction to cultural evolution were the words of the mid-century historian, Arnold Toynbee. In his succinct post-career summary he shared a growing fear of human beings loosing control of the technology which snowballed after World War II. But in the same breath he noted that we have control over the future by exercising our freedom of choice. It is our contention that this freedom is best maintained by attending to our natural human propensity to engage one another in conversation.

People had over thousands of years perfected their independent family life. They had been free beyond any later form. But as the population increased and people found the pleasures of association, they also began a process of socialization. And social life introduced the constraints of relationships. Languages developed and enhanced their involvements with one another producing tribes and villages. Late in the Stone Age their settlements became cities, and soon the process of socialization mutated into the process of developing ways of governing their increasingly numerous interrelationships. So the ancient period began. It was a time of glacial change, or so it seems to us.

Toward its end, the culture moved imperceptibly from a still-oligarchic mentality when the people were leaving their sheep-like orientation behind to introduce a culture in which each one was increasingly expected to think of his or her own welfare in the stream of life as they had done quite naturally before socialization had begun. As social life developed in growing cities, ordinary people had become part of the mass, controlled by leaders who had found their exceptional ability to lead people on a path to power. Under their leadership, the people built dykes and walls and irrigated fields for the community, and erected the monuments of the emperors. The fields for cultivation were well developed and each hovel had its fireplace and place to sleep. But the only way such leaders could control the inevitable tensions that develop among people in the cities was to exercise their authority as leaders. And so leaders accumulated power, and the oligarchic form of government emerged in civilization.

The early adoption of maternal-paternal roles was very likely the first demonstration of human's organizational genius. Surely extended families had become a common human pattern.[8]. About one hundred thousand years ago, the movement of human beings out of Africa into the endless world became the Great Migration. Crowding in over-used locales was unnecessary – move on! Long before the emergence of cities, people were organizing themselves for various purposes. The first changes humans effected in their world may well have been the depletion of the easiest prey in the neighborhood. Traveling further and further to hunt, men found new valleys and caves to encourage a move. Women going further and further to gather the more edible grains discovered lush valleys full of their favorite foods Mastery of child nurture produced larger families, and in the last three or four millennia BCE the population grew from family units to small villages, then to large villages and early cities, from hundreds to many thousands.

"Explosive" is a word cherished by the young for their fascination with the immediate. It is a very long road they have to travel to begin to understand just how miraculous our life is. But not miraculous in that sense. The miracle of modern humanity was shaped over an extraordinarily long period of time – not centuries but tens of thousands of years, and even, if you will stretch farther, hundreds of thousands.

Life is a miracle to most of us, even the destitute generally cherish the life they hold. This is a built-in instinct: to love life and to extend effort under extraordinary circumstances to meet its challenges is instinctual. But we have been given creativity in addition. For a very long time we applied ourselves to survival and procreation. We were the most successful of all animals. But we have long proved ourselves superior to every other life form, not only in reproduction but in every other dimension of change. Wooden spears found in Germany long preserved in water have been dated 400,000 years ago, a clear indication of the lengthy path to civilization. And no less than 800,000 years ago at the time when a large meteorite impacted the earth *Homo erectus* should be credited with sophisticated stone tools discovered in southern China.[9] Apparently, if we accept the African origin of *Homo sapiens*, we must also recognize a curiosity and sense of adventure that were evident in our widespread earlier ancestors.

The two words "miracle" and "explosive" are so much alike and yet so different. Miracle has been taken to refer to an event which happened in the present without due process. In that sense most of the miracles of human life are overlooked, because paying attention with thoughtful awareness is difficult for us; it is an acquired skill but one we began developing very early. Focusing is innate; most animals survive by focusing on food sources. But we humans have minds that are so expansive that we are easily distracted. There are selfish distractions and creative distractions. There are so many possibilities that it takes us years of self-discipline, building on the learnings of our culture, to develop skills matching the most demanding foci of our highly technical world. Still, human beings have long been able to manage the intricacies of interpersonal life, the uncertainties of economy and commerce and all forms of survival. Today we see that the complexities of social life get more complex with every hundred-thousand increase in the population. World-wide these two forces, complexity of life and size of population, have already begun a period of severe tension with each other. Our long history of adaptation and problem-solving might lead us to hope that out of the complexity – and the maturing mind of *Homo sapiens* – will come humane and compassionate solutions to overpopulation. We have adapted so successfully to life on this planet that we have begun to test our global limits.

It is the focusing of our attention that has given us all the innovations of human beings during tens of thousands of years. Stop and think of a single thousand years if you can. That is nearly impossible except for the few of us who have not forgotten the importance of history. Just one thousand years takes us back to the end of the ancient world and the beginning of the Middle Ages. For a long time, it seemed to Western people that not much happened then – we called them the "dark ages" because so much happened since then that we have been consumed with modern pride – "The Enlightenment." Perhaps that signals the end of the ancient mythology of a cosmic battle between light and darkness[10] And now that the twenty-first century has begun, we are in danger of ignoring how and why we must reshape ourselves so as not to repeat again the errors of the past and also to solve problems the past has left to us. And there are many signs in our life that we are ready and able to step out of our preoccupation with the present into a future which, like the past, is really our present.

That is a stretch! But now stretch back just seventeen centuries to the thoughts St. Augustine (emphasis on the second syllable, please: "au GUS tin") thought about God having only the present, but a present that included the past and the future. In God's time, then, Augustine said, there was a past-present, a present-present, and a future-present. So much for that! If you can, begin now to think of yourself as a human being who learned to make stone axes, a human being who first learned to save seeds and till the soil for farming, a human being who dressed and moved huge stones to create pyramids and other gargantuan monuments, a human being who drew on a cave wall his story of hunting herds of large animals. Are you with me? And we humans were learning through all this time to sing, tell stories, play drums, and dance! All these skills and more began to define our culture, clearly differentiating us from other animals. And we learned eventually to organize ourselves in cities (and work gangs and armies) and to build institutions and empires, to write and build libraries, and eventually to build universities and governments that are learning to exist together peaceably. We are all these and more.

Not long ago the people we revered were either members of our extended families or further extensions to heroes of our culture: national heroes, predecessors in our professions, religious saints. We used to include military heroes and great conquerors with pride. Even then we discovered "black sheep" in our families and kept them in closets. But whatever they did they were part of our past along with numerous others.

All those millions of people over tens of thousands of years were building the world we live in. We could not enjoy our sophisticated twenty-first century lives if generations upon generations had not learned to nurture children, pay attention to food sources; if they had not learned to live together to enhance the life of all, to sing in choirs and read and write all kinds of literature. Without the laborious development of an immense array of skills, we would not have stable governments gradually learning to avoid conflict among themselves, colleges and universities teaching and extending our knowledge, and libraries, hospitals, and dozens of other institutions. That is to describe our society. But we should extend it to ourselves.

In a word, all those many predecessors of ours prepared us to use our brains with thoughtful awareness. We have often thought of history as a succession of nations and empires, of great rulers and outstanding intellects. But we often overlook the contributions of brilliant ancient Persians to astronomy and mathematics, of the Egyptians to bureaucracy and organization, and the immense achievements of the Chinese people. We remember the Greeks and the Romans, but forget the countless people who discovered the wisdom of a revolutionary justice that put behind us "a tooth for a tooth" justice system still followed by some peoples. There were ancient thinkers unknown to us, besides Confucius, the Buddha and Hammurabi, Moses and Isaiah. With all these and many others we clearly see astounding evidence of human development.

With the intellectual culture of the Greeks and the open-mindedness of the Romans we entered the new world in which we live, though it took another two thousand years to achieve the opportunity we face in the twenty-first century. That was at the time when Greeks, Romans, and Jews came into a creative political mix at the end of the ancient period. This was the seedbed of the new Western culture we enjoy: we call it Europe. The twenty-first century will summarize the fruit of that culture and give us footing to jump into the future.

But while you have stopped to think about it, remember that no one knows how all this history could come together in the beautiful life of *Homo sapiens*. Our usual analyses revolve around political and economic realities which are, of course, real enough. The striking omission in them is the multitude of others who give our world its rounded richness. Culture is created by millions of people living out the persistent but constantly changing character of life. Culture is not only battles and each leaders' prowess or blunder. It is finding food and feeding families. It is singing and laughing. It is the wonderful mixture of activities of lively and intelligent human beings. Ordinary people raise kids and teach them how they have learned to thrive.

Far longer than ten thousand years ago, some one realized that we humans are different from the other animals in that we have the capacity to be wise, thoughtful, caring, and loving. Some person, perhaps a bit brighter than most others, enlisted neighbors to help care for a sick woman with tiny children when a man was killed while hunting. A hundred scenarios can easily be drawn that might have exposed the earliest leaders of tiny communities. People assumed leadership at critical moments, seeing what needed to be done for others in sickness, trouble, and sorrow. Neighbors followed their pointing and their early articulations of maladies and needs to protect, support, to supply and to assist in the growing number of ways people interacted. The variety of capabilities always present among people stimulated native leaders here and there, and others learned emergent ways to live.

Our fantastically sophisticated lives make such elementary living almost beyond our imaginations. Novelists serve well in reconstructing the past to remind us of earlier times. Some use too much imagination where a bit of contemporary sleuthing would uncover surprising discoveries by archaeologists and anthropologists. That some of us never become capable of the elementary acts of care and kindness of primitive people indicates the poverty of our own culture. Frequent references to Charles Darwin have preoccupied us for over one hundred years as an answer to "how" this culture came to be. We forget that our culture is built on the learnings of thousands of years of human life. And each generation passed on what it had discovered to build this sophisticated edifice we call civilization.

Such bursts of creativity are seldom isolated, however, and the idea of evolution had been floating around Europe for many years. Nonetheless, Darwin marks an intriguing contribution to our understanding of ourselves and our world. If we think about it, it does take us back to the earliest times even before higher animals came into the picture, when only the laws of reproduction and of tooth and claw preserved a species. We realize how much the present emerges out of the past and builds upon it. And the future will continue this pattern. The idea of change that emerges from Darwin's thoughtful observation of plants and animals in the past applies also to our social life in which each of us is inevitably wrapped up. We call it evolution although we must realize that we use the term almost as a synonym for progress, not as Darwin used it. We shy away from "progress" because some of our characteristically imaginative predecessors recently perverted this idea of building on the past into an overarching ideology. There is more to say about all of these things, of course. Here we simply note our use of "evolution."[11]

Now we are faced with a task as monumental as Darwin's. We have proved to ourselves that many egotistic paths of the past were mistaken. But almost every one did in some way contribute to the forming of our present culture. One of these paths ferreted out and appropriated by human beings over the whole extent of human evolution points away from our preoccupation with human achievement to a more human world. That is the path of cooperation. All advanced animals have made progress along this path, separating primates and many other groups from the almost insensate existence of lesser life.

In order to grasp the task we face, we must review for our cultural awareness the troubling history of progress – of evolution – as far back as we are able to see. In it we find many ups and downs. But every time a particular view has become overpowering it has been demonstrated to be inadequate. We have named recent ones: Rationalism, Romanticism, Scientism, Populism, Socialism, Communism and Militarism. One might want to include others. It might be that we will be able to agree eventually on a common path. Accelerating change will be increasingly evident in our relatively stable culture.

It seems to me at our own very intermediate junction, that the path ahead is like one repeated often of the past. We saw it in the early migration during which we learned to adapt to all climates and locales and in the age of oligarchy during which we learned something of our great capacity for self-discipline. This was confirmed in the Middle Ages and we added to it a self-conscious awareness of the value of reflection. (Reflection, unnamed, was previously just taken for granted as part of life.) We recognize it in the surprising and fortuitous expansion of knowledge and self-awareness of the modern era. The path ahead will be a path in which the word cooperation is central, the word accommodation is persistent, and the word love expanded. The path will be wide and the variety of human minds stretching into the perennially new future will work, side by side, with joy and appreciation for one another. We will build a rich new world of cooperation in which we strive together, mutually supplementing our somewhat puny individual contributions.[12]

Concretely, as we say, this means that our society will change in unexpected and surprising ways. Some have the freedom and sophistication to grow intellectually to immense heights. Some people will so develop their cultural understandings to command insight into the mind and spirit. Those whose self-development has lagged behind will find it irresistible to grow.

C. IN THE BEGINNING

Hardly any words can compare with the simple directness of the first words of the Christian Bible: "In the beginning." The story form is right to the point. All history is a story of sorts, interpretation of the way the past has appeared to us. As with all stories the composition of the Bible was dependent on the persons who were moved to crystallize their understandings. As we have already noted, writing developed differently in various locations just as language itself had done earlier. We had become aware of how fragile memories are (a recurring insight) and eventually learned to record a great variety of matters which seemed to us important, always in the familiar language. In ancient times scribes developed skill in doing this. Scribes became part of the elites.

People with insight found scribes to record their thoughts or themselves wrote.[13] They were not strangers to politics and people, though our modern categories had not yet been invented. Nonetheless, they were limited by all the usual human constraints. They were first humans, born of mothers who nursed them and taught them to care for themselves as all people learn the elementary lessons of life. They lived in their particular times and places. The question of beginnings may have bounced around in fireside talk for many generations and become a part of the narrative inheritance behind the insights and stories they wrote. The earliest stories we have are interpretations by the writers of those stories.

None of us can really understand what the life of the earliest Homo sapiens was like – it was long before writing. That was only more or less 100,000 thousand years ago. But they did not start the human episode on the face of the earth. In the previous hundreds of thousands of years, human beings' limited self-consciousness did not allow for much questioning. But recently even our primate cousins have been observed marveling at exciting natural phenomena. Jane Goodall has reported on more than one occasion observing chimpanzees massed together quietly watching a beautiful waterfall after a session of calling to one another and dancing.[14] Chimps regularly call to one another. Similarly, it is possible that long before humans could grasp anything like an abstraction they, too, wondered at the power of nature in many manifestations and made various noises to communicate with one another. We can count it as the elementary beginnings of human reflection: These early predecessors, too, probably danced and sang for many years even before the larynx was transfixed to connect the trachea and the throat in preparation for speech – even before the mentality for thinking was in place.

As these gifts developed into new human capacities, we can surmise that people developed drumming, dancing, and singing as early arts and probably exercised them as group activities. It is more difficult to guess when such activities might have taken on a religious character. But early, primitive expressions of awe, of wonder, of surprising excitement undoubtedly provoked thinking. When thinking began, of a sort that we could call "religious," we will assume that rudimentary reflection was already operative, perhaps something like a later stage of the awe of Jane Goodall's chimps. Anything we would today call "religious" must have an intellectual component, and when religious expressions first occurred they utilized whatever forms of expression had emerged in their cultures. No doubt that included the familiar group singing, dancing and festive group activities.

Homo sapiens appeared in Europe in the late Stone Age or Upper Paleolithic period of the last Ice Age perhaps 38,000 years ago.[15] The Ice Age ended about the time of the Agricultural Revolution about 10,000 years ago. During the Ice Age the people in the area of France and northern Spain managed quite well in south-facing caves warmed by the sun in winter. Here artists depicted every one of the 30 species of animals and plants of that period and these are organized into complex compositions not found elsewhere.[16] The artists knew every anatomical detail and behavior of the animals. The Ice Age hunters had applied their minds to careful observation and firmly planted the details in their memories. These were not simply illustrations. They played a role in ritual, stories and ceremonies of various kinds, perhaps a curing ceremony, or to celebrate the coming of spring.

This surely is evidence of substantial progress in self-consciousness as well as in application of imagination to use natural materials for marking symbols and drawing figures with coloring appropriate to each. Acute awareness of seasonal differences in the animals suggests that these artists were drawing symbols of observed processes of nature – rutting, butting, and bellowing; licking insect bites in the summer; the hooked jaw of salmon in migration upstream. The chance is that expectations for the hunt had been mythologized by the end of the Stone Age. But we may be looking at very early depictions of scenes like Isaiah's Holy Mountain since we know that few of the animals depicted in the caves were hunted. Were seasons and behavior being linked in some sort of early human exploration of nature? Was this possibly an early examination of the religious question of origins and how grateful we are for life?

From this point of view, "In the beginning, God..." is a very late conceptual development in the human experience. But this still means so far back in time that we have trouble conceiving of people with so primitive a culture that a knowledge of God was not common. By our analysis of primate and pre-*Homo sapiens* life, we may be confident that the emotional content of wonder, of being impressed by our perception of something, is not the first component of a religious sense. Our early ancestors knew nothing of the institutionalized character of religion as we understand it. They surely did react with horror at great volcanoes, immense fires, and earth quakes. Many powerful phenomena contributed to their persistent wonder at nature. But even before that, I think, they explored the circumstances of their lives, the geography we would say. They learned when and where to expect their favorite foods to appear. There can be no doubt that they found good crops and good hunting seasons times to celebrate. On into the biblical period, the harvest festival acquired almost mythic status among the Jews.

Eventually, ancient people did attach these celebrations to gods, usually specialized for the various challenges and problems of life. Out of this, polytheism surely developed, perhaps as tribes joined together in villages and villages in cities. Hindu writings called the Vedas gathered from many tribes represent the varied notions of gods familiar to ancient people in the Indus valley of Pakistan. For us, "religion" suggests a sense of power or control which is beyond even our own impressive intelligence. It is this high view of God which has misled some to identify God with anything we cannot thoroughly understand. At each intellectual discovery, such a view of "religion" is challenged. Religion must have more to it than that, or more people would have given up on it when awareness of the total human achievement mounted. Humans, after all, are very impressed as a rule by their accomplishments. But in fact the great intellects of the West have regularly espoused religion for much better reasons, though sometimes they were critical of aspects of Christendom. Those who exhibited undue pride in their own intellectual products have always been subject to correction by others who see beyond them.

The question of the beginning is part of such seeing. There are elements in it of "vision" which is sensory but there is more to seeing with our eyes. It is an intellectual extension of the function of memory.   Some would insist on calling this sense "spiritual" and that may be helpful. We are aware, however, that failure to recognize such vision as a function of our minds has led to a variety of errors reflecting on "religion." Recognition of the importance of mental constructions is fairly new.   Since all language is metaphor, we understand that a variety of constructions we have named have often been thought of as if they were realities in themselves. Let us note that while abstractions are reductions, separations from something, visions are constructions, assemblies of our thoughts and ideas. People have found both in reflection. And sometimes abstractions from great visions have distorted the vision. Especially in modernity we have extracted slogans from visions; in other words we have reduced grand visions into words that cater to popular and usually overly simple concepts.   Slogans usually pander this way, like the perennial apocalypse).

Visions which surpass common understandings are as a rule bright and fresh interpretations of a variety of ideas. They are constructions, but unlike emotion (a physiological construction revealingly analyzed by Leslie Brothers in Friday's Footprint) the visions with which we are concerned generally are oriented to our society.   These are truly intellectual constructions, the products of extraordinary reflection.

We have only slowly recognized religion as a human construction. But this does not mean, as many in our human "enlightenment" have thought, to be simply imaginary. In the "religious" patterns of expression we find ways of relating to life which open us up to possibilities that are beyond us. In our intellectualization during the modern period we have thought to credit great music, art, and other talents to the brilliance of individual persons. That was part of the dualism Descartes crystallized in the sixteenth century. We are periodically confronted by an unusually humble artist who admits to wonder at the creativity which flows through him or her. This humility should be emulated by many, we might say, *all* people in all disciplines: mathematics, physics, philosophy, and the rest.

Creativity, was labeled by Whitehead as the elementary force in all matter out of which evolution flows. It is a wonderful and wondrous aspect of our existence, and none of us can account for it with equanimity. But one thing is currently very clear: this creativity is not solely the product of individuals. No intellectual, no artist, no scientist is independently creative. In every case each bright individual who creates something of note is the product of earlier generations, and he or she will likely be the a parent and influence hundreds of others. The gifts that enable me to make a "creative" contribution are complex products of the creative forces in nature, people, and culture. No one creates anything *de novo*.

Pondering such realities as these, reflective people for thousands of years have felt themselves to be in touch with powers beyond their senses. The most persistent of them now and then would perceive such power everywhere, all around them. In the Middle Ages, immense effort went into attaining such spiritual states as to feel themselves to be in touch with God. To prehistoric people in their polytheisms, as well as among more recent human beings, it was always comforting for people to feel themselves specially connected to such "supernatural" power.

The problem that evolved in the late ancient period and multiplied as it became increasingly uncertain, was that this sort of "religion" quickly became self-serving. Except perhaps for a variety of saints, the human ego expected special privileges which might follow a perceived connection. The Gnostic religions which threatened Christianity for hundreds of years, beginning before, but notably, with Pythagoras' religious construction, used the ancient device of secrets to hide the essentials of their religions from outsiders. This never threatened the Jews as it did the Christians because the Jewish religion was solidly based on the concept of God as creator and people as God's creation. Knowledge of God was not secretive, but outspokenly vocal. It was not based on continued revelation so much as Christianity has been, but on the historic acts of God. However wonderful human creations may be, however perfect their mastery of complex poetic conventions, and however fluent their use of words, no one was more "in the know" than another. All were "God's children."

The real bugaboo in resistance to submitting to being "faithful" is not unreadiness to submit to social conventions, but the pride which separates us from one another, in which we claim superiority to others. Knowledge, religiosity, and skill all tempt us to neglect our human obligation to share as human beings, to help others enjoy freedom, to be creative and to be responsible. Over thousands of years, the wisest of wise people have grown beyond such selfishness and the bounds of ritual and dogma, to embrace what we generally call "a religious orientation." Gradually, we have discovered, that means living for others.

The real, consistent and powerful aspect of Christian religion is faithfulness. The Jews were reminded again and again that God is faithful and they, too, should be faithful. That is a matter of personal, individual self-discipline instructed by many. Each of us makes choices daily which reflect our values. If we are compassionate, choices reflect compassion. If we exploit other people's weaknesses (take advantage of them), we are not faithful. The rule is simple but demands the persistent attention we call self-discipline. "Should" is a religious term!

Often "seers" themselves considered their visions and religious constructions (rules, laws) to be messages from another world.[17] Today we can grasp that this interpretation of visions was part of the struggle of human beings to understand themselves. The cultural bias in those years (we can say) was governed by a demeaning view of human ability. In the Mediterranean world, after centuries of repression, it is easy for us to see how people would have found it difficult to think of humans as capable of faithfulness except in the sense of obedience. That much self-discipline was a gift of the

16

early cities. Sin was the universal human character, and it was understood as built into us. True seers, I think, while taking that seriously, understood the amazing ability of people to surmount most impediments to being human beings. This was not a perpetuation of paternalism, but an implementation of their belief in a graceful creation.

Before people were sufficiently self-confident to understand such things as Aquinas' natural theology such vision could not be understood as the result of thoughtful putting-together of the realities of life. Some will consider this statement as a denial of revelation, a contradiction of the direct communication of God to people. It need not be so understood. The human mind has been capable of so much more than we could grasp that we have forgotten that from the beginning we have regularly interpreted our world in terms of our current grasp of it – always limited by the conceptual extent of current vocabulary. There are no new words until someone discovers the necessity for them.

Still, our ancestors lived in patterns which allowed much more time for reflection than we allow. They walked and ran everywhere – good think time. They constantly met in ordinary commerce – good times for passing pleasantries and information. They had long evenings for talk and celebration. And for the many herders, there were infinite hours of minimal involvement watching for predators and managing frolicking adolescent sheep and goats from getting in trouble. David was understood as a poet. Pan pipes typically have been pictured as instruments of shepherds. When farming began, people began to learn of the tedious, repetitive mundane work of civilized life which required them to pay attention to tasks. In reflection, people explored themselves and their world at length.

That early Europeans increasingly used their heads is made evident in the sophistication of Ice Age art. At the beginning of the twentieth century Abbe Breuil put together a rough chronology of Ice Age art. It included an early style and a late style and identified almost every technique of artistic expression possible at that time including carving in the round and bas relief in stone, bone, ivory, and clay and engraving or line drawing. Painters used many techniques including mineral crayons, brushes of hair and fiber, and blowing paint through a hollow bird bone. There was polishing of stone and firing of clay; a prehistoric kiln for firing clay statues of animals and females has been found in Czechoslovakia – a considerable distance from the art of France examined by Abbe Breuil. These techniques and the sophistication of the art testify to mental capacities as "advanced" as those in today's schools of art.[18] This is not to say that we have learned nothing in the intervening thousands of years, but rather that the human mental capacity in which we take great pride in modernity is not new. It is what we have done with our minds that makes the difference. How we do that depends on our grasp of the contributions of those who preceded us. That we call culture.

That there always seems to be something yet to be discovered has surprised many a sophisticated person who thought that humans had mastered all knowledge. This misconstruction of human intellect hit a high point in the eighteenth and nineteenth centuries, the age of Rationalism. In the twentieth century, erudite intellectuals have thoroughly debunked that notion, but our culture is just now catching up to this vision of limited human mental capacity. Rationality was supposed to displace the human emotions with cold, hard facts. But the wholeness of humanity includes the emotional as well as the rational. We are unequivocally part of this physical world. One might say that up to now many intellectuals abdicated their humanity to enslaving knowledge. Humanity is now coming to the jumping-off place in reining in our immense human knowledge, the experience of innumerable generations, and the insights of seers of all ages. At this juncture we have the privilege to choose to share in building a more balanced culture to hand on to the next generation. Recognizing our humanity, the choice is ours.

Are not Jane Goodall's reports of chimpanzee enthrallment at a waterfall evidence that there are primitive roots of emotional reaction to the power of nature? The strength of animals (it would take several strong modern humans to physically constrain a single adult chimpanzee) put together with the growing awareness of people of their superior intelligence, surely made them wonder how they could be in the same world! But we are. General awareness of our superior intelligence must have been one of the factors in the confidence early *Homo sapiens* showed in the Great Migration out of Africa 100,000 years ago. It has given us an endless stream of decisions to make.

It is my guess that our brains were particularly good at "putting things together" very early in our evolution. Reading popular (though scholarly) reviews of current brain research leaves me guessing that this is the basic activity of the brain. The specialized brain areas scientists are uncovering are not for the most part "hard wired" interactions of neurons but simply a way the brain developed to reduce the path to much-used senses and thought processes. The persistent play of the brain among its millions of neurons has been organized by the ingenious brain to utilize functionally specialized parts of the brain. That some memory of life is engraved in these neurons is part of the mystery being untangled, but that all animals pass on to their progeny some such learnings is probably what allows evolution of culture to to go on forever. It is the amazing and persistent growth in human self-consciousness which most concerns us in this exploration. This growth seems to occur continuously, in spite of difficult and harsh life conditions. Such challenges have probably been among the many stimuli to change.

I believe that "putting things together" constitutes one of the earliest aspects of human thought. Again, evidence among the primates indicates primitive thinking abilities which have been part of the human being as early as five or six million years ago, when our common ancestry with the chimps and bonobos ended. But there is general agreement that somewhere in that dim, distant time the human being underwent an evolutionary sea-change. Like the phase shift from vapor to water, or water to ice, the change in appearance and characteristics is total; yet the molecules are the same, still hydrogen and oxygen. Human beings began to think in very different ways from other animals. The parts of the human brain include many if not all the same parts as that of a bonobo, but their functions and operation are excitingly different.[19]

Such observations point us to the truth of what modern Christian theologians call "natural theology." This is the view that evidence of God is everywhere in the natural world, and that rational humans can arrive at the concept of God quite easily from this evidence, although many people ignore or resist it. The concept of natural theology was definitively formulated by Aquinas in the thirteenth century when our sense of self was rapidly developing and the intensive theological effort of Scholasticism was in full flower.

But in the growing skepticism and new rationalism of the eighteenth century, this concept was severely criticized, and in the nineteenth century popular understanding of Darwin's theory of evolution further undermined it. Recent refinements have again made it respectable. Here we will not engage the argument, but only point out that such sophisticated thinking is a very, very recent human achievement. We may well appreciate the foresight of Aquinas, one of our forebears whose prescience is quite evident.

But we may speculate as to when humans started "putting together" their grasp of superiority to other animal life, their wonder at the awesome forces of nature, and the idea of a superior controlling force. We had begun to understand that our own human intelligence could change our environment, the very shape of the world. Perhaps the thought occurred to someone who began to think of what we call "intelligence." Perhaps an early village leader began to assume authority and do things with initiative. Acting out of a sense of power derived from a position given by the people would have been a personalized departure from all previously known leaders. It would not have been recognized as power derived from the people, but credited to the leader's inborn capacity. This happened over and over in many villages. Each such leader seemed to the people to be superior to others. It may have been the earliest manifestation of hierarchy and the institution of government.

We are free to guess that at some point in very ancient life some bright person or persons began to think there must be a person-like being outside our worldly realm who, with even greater intelligence (and power) than our own, would rule the world. It is quite unlikely that ideas of God leap into existence overnight. Along the way the most primitive indication of abstraction may well have been the reality of impressive experiences with the notion of spirits in such ethereal things as clouds of steam from holes in the earth, volcano, or clouds. Whatever stimulated the insight, it was obviously attractive and the recognition of human superiority over the beasts and birds (and increasing experience with others people and their leaders), would most naturally be expressed in the language they had developed, mostly about the natural world but even more about themselves. Anthropomorphism we call it, putting this early abstraction into meaningful terms.

In gestation, no doubt such thoughts encompassed only the world familiar to given people. But that world had a way over centuries of expanding. The number of people gathering in the villages kept growing. Explorers and adventurers kept wandering farther and farther. They found people who held religious ideas different from their own. And the ideas of god became associated with their origins, with the people who used a particular set of religious terms. As years passed, people who gathered came to accept many gods.

An honest and wise ancient observer might have noted that the growing power of leaders could be both privilege for the leader and provide effective leadership in the village. How much more would a superior being outside the world be an effective governance in it? Or perhaps not. Perhaps some who conceived such an idea over the years (especially after truly oligarchic cities emerged) might conceive of such a superior being as totally self-indulgent, producing "god" concepts such as proliferated in early Hinduism and later Greek religion.[20] But growing sensitivity to self and others produced new behaviors.

We know that by the time of the Neanderthals, there were funeral rites among humans. Death was a serious loss. Perhaps the veneration of deceased elders was an early religious act.[21] Death of a person may have been accompanied by communal mourning, even as various animals gather around a corpse until the stench becomes unbearable. But successful gathering of sufficient food to tide them over until Spring was worthy of a the festival. This was enlargement of the common gathering of people living in an area, probably originated a bit later in harvest celebrations. By the time people in the mid-east began gathering in large super-villages and the first cities began the crystallization of urban culture, neighbors' common notions of who they were and where they had come from were probably celebrated regularly.

About ten thousand years ago, people began farming. They had learned to save grain for planting, to till the soil, and to channel water to their crops. They learned how to save grain in various ways, having long since invented clay and grass pots, to prevent animals from scavenging their food and seed grain. Large and effective granaries were organized in the cities, no doubt the earliest sort of productive social organization. As chiefs achieved power over cities, securing the granaries and organizing the best hunters to control ravages of animals, they also became stronger than shamans and priests (whatever leaders of celebrations might be called). These chiefs undoubtedly gained power in the eyes of the people – by making alliances with shaman's early knowledge of migrations and seasons and the positions of stars in the sky. No doubt that was the beginning of aristocracy subsequently to be indelibly identified with power.

Aristocracy is deeply rooted. Dominance hierarchies are easily observed in the primates. Our automatic facial expressions carry numerous signs of the length and depth of dominant oligarchies. Christopher Boehm suggests that perhaps in the old stone age ("paleolithic") humans lived for hundreds of thousands of years with "reverse dominance hierarchies." That is the assumption that the innate dominance of males was controlled by the formation of coalitions of the weaker people against any indication of dominance.[22] It is one of the indicators of early animal cooperation. Daniel Lord Smail tells us that with the agricultural revolution (10,000 BCE) the dormant dominance instinct returned with a vengeance. People exercised the appropriate "anger, fear, contempt, disgust, pity, and embarrassment and advertised their submission with the many facial expressions that carry political overtones."[23] Overcoming these expressions is a primary requirement today in our business community, only partially achieved in most cases, as the remnants of aristocracy persist in our culture.

Anywhere aristocracy reared its head, the number of people defending the status quo multiplied. And these same people were always the ones most empowered by human creativity. Aristocracy was soon fixed firmly in the culture securing its own privileges. But – just as critical a social reality for the rest of ancient history – it appropriated the long-existing religious impulse. With appropriation of religious expression oligarchs obtained for themselves a mystical power beyond the value of any governance achieved for the people. Feathered ancient Inca leaders appeared bigger than life itself on their high thrones at their engineered popular celebrations and religious rites. It was a pattern repeated over and over right into modern times.

People for generations had allowed brighter and stronger people to lead them in common activities. They did not object when such leaders passed their authority on to a son and began the insidious addition of nepotism to the growing corruption of the people's authority over their own lives. With the power of the hunters at their command, the early oligarchs could control disagreements that arose among the people as well as repel enemies. Lewis Mumford suggested that this concentration of power is the origin of aggressive warfare. Naturally, as inventions of warfare were made, it was the citadel which was first equipped. And the pattern was appropriated over and over into modern times. Today, the United States spends more every year on armaments than all other nations combined.

While human conflict must have been part of the picture of human life from the earliest times, long before the development of cities, Mumford's observation bears attention. War may well have begun in raids of hungry people suffering starvation on the food stores of neighboring villages whose crops had not been ravaged by drought – or perhaps these communities had better food management in difficult times. Avarice, differential in wealth, and simple egotistic leadership may have extended the use of existing power against others and forcibly produced the first kingdoms by extending rule over several cities. Such power first consisted of numbers of fierce people bearing their hunting instruments, daggers, spears, clubs. But as human ingenuity produced bow and arrows, leather armor and then swords in all their forms, and metal armor, the outfitting of armies came to reflect the wealth of the oligarchs thus linking wealth with war. Smelting of bronze and then of iron both occurred in the ancient period each increasing the cost of warfare. Fortified citadels, originally intended for granaries and shrines, became the storehouses of wealth and armaments much of it plundered from other cities. The ostentation of leaders was demonstrated first in their own finery and elaborate and aggrandizing ceremony, but soon in stele and other forms of monuments describing their powerful rule. These were intended to impress ordinary people nearby and distant leaders by the spread of reputation.[24]

This pattern exhibited the power of the oligarch. Within severe limits it assured his safety from those who aspired to replace him. But the form of social organization it epitomized was both insecure and destructive, always subject to defeat by superior force. It is no wonder that petty kings gave way to stronger tyrants and emperors. Functionaries of past aristocracies learned to ingratiate themselves to new rulers if they were not slaughtered. It was a thoroughly unstable culture.

Thus the beginnings of our civilization are hardly fortuitous. What might have been from the beginning a generous, magnanimous, compassionate civilization has spent its resources largely on violence. Nonetheless, our amazing brains have enabled us to learn from our errors, to recognize the failure of our ways, and to seek better ways to live. That is what culture is about.

D. THE OPENING OF EUROPE: EARLIEST STEPS

The miracle of Europe begins with a remarkable culmination of the ancient world in the incipient Roman Empire at the moment when Jesus of Nazareth was transforming Judaism into a world religion. This is to credit Rome with adopting the Greek culture and eventually also the emergent Christian faith, not in any way to demean any one of them. The historical fact is, that is what happened. All three, Greece, Rome, and Judaism left indelible marks on Europe. The long glorification of ancient empires is over now – though it hung on in our culture for many centuries. The isolation of the Jews in Palestine was destroyed. But the way it happened is a tale in achievement of the human spirit.

We humans began our long journey of the past eight or ten thousand years as largely isolated, individualistic solitary persons living in groups no larger than families and small villages. Families could sometimes reach forty or fifty people and retain their identity. Villages usually did not exceed two or three hundred. As the city struggled to emerge, some villages probably began the expansion under the leadership of rare chiefs who could cooperate with others and lead their people into larger associations. Like Moses many years later in the Sinai, these leaders found their hands full adjudicating the normal squabbles that occur between unreconciled people. Moses learned from his father-in-law Jethro to appoint respected elders to share that task, and that probably eventually happened at various times in many communities. With that necessary and fateful step, the function of a privileged authority structure over the people got started. In the Bible they came to be called judges.

This elementary structure was not yet a hierarchy. Accrued privileges were minimal, just an early step in the long process of socialization. Depending on the way in which players exercised their authority, however, privileges accrued to novice aristocrats. It could not be many years before the hunters who were being called to fend off marauding beasts and persistent scavengers would be assigned such tasks on a constant basis. It was necessary from their point of view, and beneficial to the community. It was also another step toward an urban culture. In another respect, however, from our point of view, it was also the fateful step of adding to the incipient hierarchy an armed wing. The best of the hunters naturally became the chief of armed men, a powerful and symbolic addition to an emerging aristocracy.

Thus the organizational structure of the city took shape to meet the needs of a growing population. The growth of population would mark human pre-history just as it has marked recorded history. As the cities grew they approached several thousand people, places of immense human interaction and social learning. In the preceding Ice age, art and music had emerged, and undoubtedly singing and dancing were of even longer standing. It was early evidence to our eyes of the instinctual creativity of human beings. In the cities there was need for architecture, and water-use projects like dykes and dams, ponds, and irrigation ditches. These were projects for work crews. Someone conceived of building huge walls filled with dirt on which the granary would be built free from all threats. When this was done, further storage problems became more evident, of course, not only the perennial mouse, but bugs and rot which know height as no problem. Perhaps such walled cores were built self-consciously to be above expected floods, some of which would be very high. They were, after all, living on the deltas of huge river systems (like the Tigris and Euphrates in Iraq). Raising the granaries high above the fertile alluvial plains may have contributed to controlling rot by its dryness There were pluses and minuses in almost every step of our emerging civilization.

We humans began claiming our social nature as we came together here in the early cities. Having spent literally thousands of years building the basic skills of survival the city put us to work enjoying human companionship and growing in skills of common life. This "socialization" has been a long and difficult process. In it the capacities for language, for ceremony, for governance, and many of the attendant institutions and talents of modern civilization took form. Today, in the face of catastrophes, human beings still find difficulties almost beyond their strength, certainly "beyond their arm's length" as the mass of people expanded incrementally. The skills involved touch us today and we may be grateful for them as, when the magnitude 9.0 earthquake devastated Japan in 2011, the people managed to keep living, helping one another, seeking solutions to life's puzzles.

Looking back we see how primitive egotistic self-consumed leaders turned the potential for the common good of the city into war machines. Violence bred more violence and invention turned innovations into the coercive instruments of oligarchy. Cities produced kingdoms and kingdoms became empires. In the process, the individualistic primitive person became a sheep-like being, obedient to overseers and commanders. People learned to obey at the threat of the whip, and in the process self-discipline grew in them deeply. It was a bit like the domestication of animals. The native sense of self was submerged in presumptions of stupidity on the part of individuals themselves, and, of great consequence, on the part of persons whose social role was to be leaders of people. These shaped society into a slave culture. The nature of aristocracy perverted the human role of leader and also the role of follower.

These roles, we must remember, follow on the very nature of human difference. Only recently we have discovered the depth and extent of its basis in the DNA structure of our physical being. The combination of chromosomes in the reproductive process assures that no two persons will be the same. In addition, for well over a century, bright people have identified how each person is individually affected by his or her society, and no two of us has exactly the same combination of social experience. Therefore each of us has both different inherited capabilities and different growing up influences. The great sea-change among primates in the forest some five and a half million years ago produced a human being which eventually evolved into *Homo sapiens* – a creature with the capability to make decisions.[25] Thus from the first moments of life each of us begins a life-long process of choosing what person we shall be. No longer chained by nature to instincts, each person shapes his or her own self. Even in identical twins raised together, this significant operation means that each will be his or her self.

This imponderable diversity of people is indicative of the amorphous nature of culture. Culture is one of those catch-all words, a construct that embraces so much and so little at once that academicians have a difficult time pinning it down. But when we realize that the culture of any given group of people is the sum total of their several lives, the way which characterizes their life, we find its constantly changing character easier to grasp. It is unfortunate that facile descriptions of minor fads and characterizations of sub-groups that take place constantly among us are often called "cultures."[26] This is partly a result of our loquacious nature. We love to name things and claim that therein we know or understand them. The thousands of words of elucidation provided by the media does not demonstrate understanding, but characterization. Understanding comes from careful inquiry by a variety of minds, not by a pundit's quick insight, though persons engaged in popular descriptions do make a contribution which we do well to acknowledge. Our point is that our understanding of culture is not well-served by such snapshots.

Our examination is of the emergence of the new culture in Europe during the Common Era (CE). It is the product of thousands of years of prior civilization already sketched. The rich contributions of those earlier people cannot be discounted in understanding our culture today as we move into another major sea-change in the life of *Homo sapiens*. This is not so simple as it may sound. Keep in mind that the diversity of people alive at any moment is probably equal to the total diversity of human kind over a vast span of time. There have been brilliant people in every century since *Homo sapiens* entered the scene. Some few have become noteworthy by their wisdom or their innovations. But all together they have produced the *cultures* of their time and contributed to the *culture* of their future.

We begin with an exploration of the nature of the human self. The beginnings of the concept of self are obscure. It seems evident that at least the more self-conscious of ancient people were aware of themselves over against other people in much the same sense as we are. Yet their self-image, their sense of who they were, was limited by the human experience before and around them. In those times it appears that what psychologists today might call "hysterical contagion" was a common phenomenon. Surely this happened among people by the time of the early city when people were learning to live together with many others. They brought with them into the city many signals for danger of various kinds. We are, after all, what we make of ourselves on the basis both of inherited capabilities and on what we learn from experience. Perhaps hysterical cries had helped to scare off predictors, and so some cultures incorporated them in story and dance.

Hysteria is a form of mimicry, the most common form of animal learning in the world. Scholars are rapidly uncovering the complex operation of the brain and its many parts. Brain neurons use chemical and electrical communication to deliver messages internally almost instantaneously. Just what enables us to choose one path rather than another, to recognize ourselves and others, and to form our character as we make decisions day by day remains mysterious. But over thousands of years, people have found themselves capable of controlling almost every animal behavior. In recent years we have recognized that hysteria is not unlike the instinctual group reaction of chimpanzees to a cry of danger. Their immense chattering alerts all to the danger, but serves chiefly to excite them. So we see that hysteria, which has often swept through crowds in modern times, now becomes a behavior we can essentially do without. It can be dangerous

This is blatantly evident in the culture of violence which has prevailed world-wide for perhaps four thousand years. Today we have failed to progress much beyond the war-training of the Medieval world in teaching males macho habits from birth through maturity. In the same way the West is only beginning to get a grip on its sexist nature. The signs of this problem are mounting rapidly. This problem is constantly aggravated by the entertainment industry, by the media, and by politicians who exploit it mindlessly and constantly in drafting the laws of our nation. But even bonobo apes have transformed their sex play to produce social peace. There is no reason why we humans cannot in the twenty-first century conquer both these bad habits – war and sexism – often mistakenly excused as instincts.

In review of the development of our European roots we are surprised to find that some beliefs have hung on far into the modern era which are essentially the residue of our past. One of these, obvious after the disastrous twentieth century genocides, is the self-defeating belief in the value of warfare. Many people have long thought we humans should free ourselves of this plague. But it has hung on through the nihilism of the mid-century "world war" and into the persistent inability of a variety of different peoples to solve their social problems peaceably.[27] These are not limited to "less developed" nations. The highly developed West spends more than anyone else on armaments!

War, I believe, is not instinctual. Aggression is not war, and aggression can be controlled also. It has served its purpose often, but it is not often a necessary behavior in our society. We pay considerable attention to controlling it. Aggression, like sex, has instinctual roots. Monogamy and marriage are two approaches to providing for sexual expression in our society. But evidence of pedophilia and pornography alone are calling us to teach our young men and women much earlier how to control themselves, how to enjoy the fruits of self-discipline. Early grasping of self-restraint is essential to accomplishing social goals. Is this not the same problem as nurturing in our young people the ability to seek more productive solutions to anger than aggression? It is demonstrable that such learning can begin at a very early age. In fact, it must be learned early when children are ready to expand their view of themselves, because if not, they are doomed to wrestle with such basic drives all their lives. A new culture has become a necessity.

I want to emphasize one thing: Citing entertainment and media should not be taken as a puritanical regression into early twentieth century prohibitions. Nonetheless, exploitation of sex and aggression for profit is not necessary to making economic sense of these industries. They have taken the easy way, the most easily profitable paths in their pursuit of their objectives. However astute they may appear, the entertainment moguls have failed to seek more sensitive insights. The claim that they are satisfying their public is pandering. Like other super-capitalistic industries, too often they have made "the bottom line" their prime objective. We desperately need better use of our creative talents. Others should listen and take note, also. Life is not as easy as they wish it to be.

In every period of human existence which we can examine, there are examples of human effort which have contributed to a more human existence. That is what the rest of this book attempts to show. It progresses from the early cities to the achievement of intellectual prowess attributed to the Greeks. Beginning with the Jews, people in the Mediterranean basin began to learn to leave the repression of the ancient world behind. Over a millennium later Erasmus and medieval compatriots shined brighter than the creative turmoil of the Renaissance. Then the error of proud adoption of rationality was thwarted by the very critical thought in which it reveled.   Now the residue of many such forces are playing themselves out in the American experiment as we shape the startingly new culture of the twenty-first century. The speed of change in the Enlightenment era is apt to double in this dynamic new century. It seems to me that this vast panorama must leave us with hope and a happy disposition to move on into a future in which the diverse human family can learn to share in fulfilling life everywhere. Proof of the capacity of socialized human beings to rise above nonsense is evident to all with eyes to see and ears to hear.

I. THE SOCIAL SELF

A. OUR PERSPECTIVE ON TIME

Many schemes for reviewing the history of civilization have been proposed. We will not review them. In 1966 Arnold Toynbee began his modest effort to find precedents in history in *Change and Habit* with observations of our short memories and habitual patterns. But he adds that it is in times like our own that the human capacity for choice operates to change habits. He reminded us "The light derived from experience is...the only guide [we have] for dealing with the future...." "Adults can choose what they will transmit and what discard, and a rising generation (can to a degree add its mind to the evolution of society)." "History," he says, "is the process of change and Time-Spirit is the 'humming loom of Time' (Goethe, *Faust*)."[28]

Douglas John Hall brought to light one of the most provocative insights in modern times, the notion of "the end of Christendom." Hall extended the view of many Christians from a very short modern period to encompass the end of the history of Rome and its influence on the present shape of Christianity in the West.[29] "Christendom" was dominated by medieval institutions, but its influence extended past the Enlightenment.

Hall's focus is still narrowly on Christianity in North America. His humility in recognizing the difficulty of speaking sweepingly about world Christianity reflects the new world. It is a world in which we are not so apt to speak in absolute and global generalizations as our predecessors. We are bit more circumspect and considerably more analytical in talking of culture and belief. Hall is a "Reformed" theologian; the Reformed branch of Protestant Christianity is directly related to Calvin just as Lutheranism is a child of Martin Luther. The Reformed branch has always been "rational" in the best sense of the word, emerging in a world in which specialization of knowledge had not yet torn apart the wholeness of human perception and experience. Life was still more whole than we know today. The erudite Calvin's iconographic representation is a flaming heart, denoting love and compassion.[30] The rational element in the Reformed world is strong but always balanced by a fresh new sense of humanity, a key element in the new Protestant view of Christianity.

Hall also reflects the new mind increasingly evident in our culture in his careful, contextual, dialogical treatment of Christian theology. We will be more brazen and extend our time frame far beyond Hall's because many recent developments seem to point in the direction we will explore here. And an urgency has arrived, which Hall sensed, in the condition of human life which calls for our attention.

What the forerunners of our culture could not see clearly was the struggle of the human spirit at the end of the Middle Ages to free itself from a very long period of repression. They were aware of the role of slavery in ancient times, but had no sense of a humanity extending back tens of thousands of years. There was as yet no sense of geologic time. For them slavery was one of the many "sins" from which in their day

Christianity was understood to free individual people. One's private "self" saved from sin was closely identified with the "soul." This soul was treasured in the dualistic Medieval Church as a part of the person which was the object of salvation. The Reformation highlighted the basic unity of the person in the Judeo-Christian faith. One of the results of this was the identification of "the priesthood of all believers" – a democratization of the medieval church. This ended one of the remaining vestiges in their lives of oligarchy (and the self-image of sheep-like slaves) and enabled people to recover their self-confidence.

Many Western Christians have limited their historic sensitivity to the Christian period. Its beginning is universally defined by the dating mechanism we all use, now "CE" for Common Era, and "BCE" for Before the Common Era. Both periods begin with the year one, CE is positive, BCE is negative. The trouble with this mechanism is two-fold. First, the known history of our Western civilization (and most of the world) goes back much further "BCE" than we have come in the period "CE." The earliest cities probably took form between 5000 and 3000 BCE in the Indus valley of the northwest Indian subcontinent we call Pakistan and in Mesopotamia (Iraq). Judging by our best archaeological evidence, civilization began in these cities.

And before that, we are aware of the beginnings of modern agriculture as early as 10,000 BCE. This is the time of the great Agricultural Revolution in which human beings began the transition from hunter-gatherer life to settled farming and herding. But that is not really "the beginning," either.

The second problem is that we humans left Africa at least 100,000 years ago, and were evolving in Africa for perhaps five million years before that. It is a very long "history." Most of the really old skeletal remains of humans have been found in Africa. They include predecessors to *Homo-sapiens* (our species) as early as 200,000 years ago when a woman scientists called Eve lived. She may have been the progenitor of all current people. But she was far from the first of our ancestors. Just a few years ago, fossil remains of a child who died 3.3 million years ago were the first complete remains of a child of our ancient ancestors we have found. The child was of the same species as "Lucy," a woman who died only 150,000 years later. Evolution is a very slow process.[31]

After such a glance back to the earliest beginnings, the earliest known people in our own species may sound rather close, more within our comprehension. The earliest *Homo sapiens* probably lived about 200,000 years ago, with a brain about the size of ours. Still, it was more than another hundred thousand years before our ancestors began moving in great numbers from Africa into Eurasia. By 45,000 years ago there were numbers of us in Indonesia, Papua New Guinea and Australia, but it was probably only 35,000 years ago that Europe was largely settled. We are told that Americans are all descendants of the same African woman and most Americans came from this immigration into Europe. This short period of human history (for the mathematically inclined) is just one one-hundredth of the time since the earliest known human child lived. And in these 35,000 years, only one-seventh are within our documentable "history."

Yet in this brief period, *Homo sapiens* has transformed human life. Our journey began with a very small view of our world. It has come, now, to encompass a view beyond the extent of the heavens visible to the eye, to celestial structures billions of "light-years" from us. A light-year is the distance light can travel in a year at 186,000 miles per second – 3,100 million miles per minute. The numbers in this vastly expanded universe quickly became truly "astronomical" as astronomers from earlier times, like Kepler and Galileo, began pushing the boundaries of their sight with primitive telescopes. Before that star gazing was pretty much unaided. Glass making and grinding of lenses advanced rapidly in medieval Europe.

But there is something now within sight that has been as hidden from us as the outer reaches of the universe. It is the evolution of the human self. While the brain enlarged throughout the evolution of animals until it reached a size appropriate to each species, the human brain is actually smaller than that of the predecessor to our species, the Neanderthals.[32] This surprising fact leaves us. Why should Homo sapiens, with a lighter frame and a smaller brain, have replaced the Neanderthal, which is exactly what happened before 25,000 years ago? The probable answer is that Homo sapiens' size required less food – and that was the ice age. We could survive with less time foraging and more time to spend on other pursuits like making finer tools. Neanderthal people never achieved much finesse in producing their stone tools. But during the Old Stone Age, Homo-sapiens forged ahead to invent civilization.[33]

B. THE EMERGENCE OF CULTURE

Gathering in the first cities probably stimulated the emergence of the self-consciousness by which we call ourselves Homo sapiens. Farming had increased our ability to produce food and people began to use their time more creatively. Animals are surely aware of themselves in a very elementary sense; instinct guides them to seek food and shelter though in recent years observers have discovered among some of them indications of sympathy and similar human traits. Their instincts prepare them to evade predators, and to reproduce and, in the higher species, nurture their young. But we have limited evidence of a self-consciousness in them like that of human beings.

The huge growth of the brain and the emergence of Homo-sapiens from previous species may have accompanied the harvesting of sea life. Beginning about 80,000 years ago, seals and seafood may have been a nutritional trigger which provided the rich diet needed to fuel big brains and active life.[34] Large brains enabled Homo sapiens to react creatively to innumerable stimuli. Early people apparently were expert at finding and constructing suitable natural shelters wherever they went. But for long millennia they continued to live in very small enclosures used mainly for sleeping.

They spent their time alone seeking food and in family and small tribal groups. Many animals have lived among others in groups for a very long time. Bees and ants are the animal kingdom's most social creatures, living a totally hierarchical existence throughout their lifespan. In our lengthy pre-historic period, though some important changes in human behavior took place, the stimulation to encourage human social development was limited. In larger villages and eventually in the new phenomena we call cities, people developed patterns of life they shared with one another – the elementary marks of social culture.

From the earliest times, people grew in their self-awareness. They increasingly recognized that each one of them was different. That is a consequence of the way DNA is replicated from generation to generation. Eventually they became aware of their habits of social interaction. As cities grew and time passed, social interaction produced numerous complex patterns. In each social grouping many of these were totally integrated into their way of life. We ourselves are no longer self-conscious about many habitual responses. It is quite amazing that even jumping to the aid of a person in danger may be given no thought until after the emergency. When this occurs it merits newspaper coverage, and the actor often tells us he or she never thought of their own safety in the process.[35] Our sophisticated sense of ourselves and how we are related to innumerable others has grown in us gradually.

During the very long period before the city, literally tens of thousands of years, people were developing the extraordinary capacity of human beings for social interaction. For example, the ability to read one another's facial expressions grew with the growing musculature of the human face. This probably began long before humans started speaking words, and they had already become proficient in reading facial and body expressions which are still important today.[36] The growing ability to decipher anger, pleasure, and many other facial expressions is obvious in very young children. In our primate cousins this is a skill limited to little more than the extremities of snarling and squeaking, both as much aural as visual. But humans expanded that limited range and then added the capacity to talk in vast numbers of tones, volumes, and distinct sounds. A great array of facial expressions accompanied their words. This occurred as people became increasingly aware of themselves.

It is hard to imagine the story of the emergence of Western civilization without the lengthy, slow evolution of the human self. The people who lived for tens of thousands of years in their tiny family and tribal groups could not have been as self-conscious as we are today. They spent almost all their time foraging and, later, raising crops, and hunting. But when those small groups gathered in larger and larger settlements, and eventually in cities of thousands, they were energized by their interactions. They carried their earlier creativity forward by leaps and bounds. It was like the awakening of the brain, and it signaled a massive change in the ways people lived.

From this time forward we are able to find increasing signs that seem to give the idea of culture meaning. We maintain that those who lived earlier also chose ways of living that must be considered their culture. There had been much "progress" in the Ice Age preceding the Agricultural Revolution. Before the city emerged, people perfected stone tools in the late Stone Age or Mesolithic Period. Some have said that the advent of the city was the moment when civilization itself began. We know enough about the development of urban life to allow the city to function as the beginning of the rise and shape of our civilization. It is a period of only five to six thousand years – a small sliver of the evolution of our human species. But we always have a view of a much longer prior period of human life in which "culture" really "began."

C. THE NATURE OF CULTURE

We use the term "culture" now to mean the accumulated social life of a people. It is a very amorphous term, hard to pin down, defying definition. We can identify differences in cultures of different small groups and any group at different times. Cultures change constantly, the product of the way the people in any group live. We may talk about sub-cultures and cultures within cultures. Scholars have spent many pages trying to define culture without much success. About all they can do is to describe a culture at one point in time or another and perhaps to compare differences. But University of California (Los Angeles) School of Medicine's Leslie Brothers explains why narrative has become an analytical tool recently – because we have come to realize how we ourselves have been shaped both by our parents from birth and by the culture, the context, in which we were raised.

In the stories of people we have found how the "social order is continuously invented and reworked." Stories tell how people narrated the essentials of their lives, what was important to them, what preoccupied their attention, how they viewed existence. The predecessor to the story is daily conversation, the anecdotes we share with one another, the incidents that animate us. Storytellers skillfully weave people's face-to-face communication (talk) into sophisticated tales of their realities. And from such narratives we construct our views of the cultures of past societies. Their technologies have been the focus of our views of culture; these are but tools of in the lives of the people. Gradually, archeology and anthropology are becoming more sophisticated in their grasp of the signs of how people who invented the technologies lived, and more importantly from our point of view, how they thought since without thinking we do not create civilization. Brothers says,

> ... we are adapted not only to form the concept of person, but also as receptacles both for communal stories and for performances of what it means to be a person — and what a person in one's culture or one's family should do, think, and say. Moreover, we are highly flexible in this regard, even eager to redefine ourselves and each other through our interactions. The brain's social functions are relatively new to neuroscience. In contrast, the idea that people make social realities through their interactions has long been articulated by philosophers and workers in the social sciences....[37]

Understanding their social interactions only gradually became the center piece in our understanding the lives of human beings. In distant pre-history after the larynx was reshaped by evolution to connect esophagus and trachea, people must have found their elaborate sound-making capacity a major addition to the primate ability to relate to each other. Singing, probably in guttural and screeching tones, may have preceded speech by thousands of years. They had probably already been inventing many hunting techniques and discovered how to use fire. With their exploration of oral communication they slowly began to invent society.

Dr. Brothers names George Herbert Mead, John Dewey, and Ludwig Wittgenstein, among those who have significantly reshaped our understanding of communication in the past century or so. Such thinkers used to argue about whether human subjectivity is inborn or learned. These particularly recognized that it is our brains operate in a society, and it is this juncture which, as Mead and Rom Harre [a social psychologist] imply, each human being generates a self-consciousness. Within its first four years, the child normally establishes the elementary sense of self that identifies him or her among other people..[38]

Brothers' extensive analysis of autism demonstrates that neither a "social field" nor a brain is enough to enable us to make self and neighbor our own. The brain must have a capability to leap out of the instinctual life patterns of other primates. And "Society must provide the brain with specific forms of self and person, just as it provides the particular language that the brain's language-making capacity will take up and reproduce." Words are the vehicles we use to socialize human beings. Or we might say that our culture enlarges our self consciousness through language. Thus our selves and our social context are linked in ourselves. Our choice of words reflects our culture but also identifies us as distinct from others. And our words contribute to the shape of our culture. Like ourselves, culture is not good or bad, but the rich and complex interaction of all its elements.

One of the most dangerous aspects of language, however, is our capacity for turning our word constructions mentally into real things. This can be done with "culture." Our belief in emotions, Brothers makes clear, is one of those constructions. A certain kind of intensity seems to be associated with the word "emotion." "Feeling" is our way of talking about this intense reaction. For many years "emotions" were spoken of as if they existed in themselves. Brothers has demonstrated that emotions are simply bodily reactions to often-repeated circumstances which were long ago engraved in our old brains and have been passed on to us in our DNA. "Emotions" are the product of a variety of messages our brain sends to prepare our bodies for the eventualities which stimulate them. Both the circumstances which for thousands of years called these forth for survival reasons and their effect on us are usually archaic, of little consequence to us today. Sometimes we have used our emotions as excuses. This is true of many verbal constructions. Our responsible use of them will avoid blaming them for our problems or irrationalities.

Our concern should be with how we manage these messages. "Emotion" is a very useful word. Now, even though we know that when we feel excited it is because our brains have sent messages to tell our bodies to pump adrenalin into our blood stream, we will utilize the results to help win a race or to be alert. We will continue to use the concept of emotion because it is handy. However, perhaps we will not misconstrue it as has been done regularly in the 20th century. We also have feelings which we ourselves construct from our life experience. We apply the concept of emotion to simplify talking about it. Brothers goes on to remind us to be alert to our language, since scientists

> ... have discovered that the reality of socially constructed categories is underwritten by circular logic: Their factualness is presumed while, at the same time, inherently ambiguous events are brought to bear as evidence of them. This...is in fact the pervasive logic of everyday thought. ....Belief in underlying categories is only strengthened, never weakened, by actual events.[39]

One of the reasons why we convert complex behaviors into simple word concepts is to simplify language. It is easier to say "emotion" than it is to describe a complex set of feelings and an event that triggered them. But this sort of imprecise speech permits us to escape the discipline of thinking carefully when we speak, and we often call into our service words which only fit approximately, if at all. This is so easy to do that we normally make allowances for such slips as we listen. But we can turn such mistaken use of language into rationalizations. One of our twentieth-century learnings was the ubiquity of "rationalization." Sometimes this is a matter of outright obfuscation. But giving overly simple reasons can be useful in cases when a full really rational explanation would be counterproductive or, perhaps, beyond our ability. This is undoubtedly one of the best learned mental tricks of humanity which enables us, if we choose, to avoid responsibility. We "rationalize" instead of thinking carefully. "Circular logic" is deceivingly persuasive!

Part of the reason for sloppy speech is that we tend to be lazy. Some school children take on "vocabulary building" as an unhappy task. But, if in those very early marvelous word-finding experiences parents helped children to enjoy adding words to their vocabularies, we might make of them word-users as avid as the explorers years ago who found new islands. As exciting tokens of skill and openness, words might go with children through life, empowering them to speak with greater precision and ease.

But we shall probably always have to make allowances for the speech of older friends and family because over many years words acquire new meanings. Meaning is a social product meant to enable us to communicate. A word may mean to us privately something that no listener would supply in hearing or reading it. Such words are often literally private, like a conversation inside one's head. But high school and college students wean themselves of many such words or suffer the consequences. Teachers are notoriously picky about words -- for good reason. Our culture persistently allows us escapes from the conventional constructions of our time. Fortunately or unfortunately, rationalization is endemic among us.

D. EMERGENCE OF MODERN CULTURE

For a couple of hundred years, the English language was sufficiently stable to enable several generations of educated people to use language with fairly clear understanding of its meanings. This may be the elephant in the room when we think historically. From about 1600 to about 1850 the language of England and America sounded a little more like Shakespeare (1564-1616) and the King James Bible (1611)than it does today.[40] American Protestantism institutionalized similar language in the influential, basically Reformed, Westminster Standards. They were prepared by a group of British clergy meeting from 1645-1647. Revised in the twentieth century these Christian "standards" have played a substantial role in our Western culture. This would have been impossible without Gutenberg's moveable type (1436), Erasmus' translations of new Greek manuscripts to Latin, the development of liberal thought, and a host of new minds bursting the rigid bonds of the Middle Ages. Their influence is a perfect illustration of the stabilizing roles of language and religion in the midst of immense cultural change.

To us, any English that sounds like the "King James" would be considered antique. Though the English language remain fairly stable for a while, the human mind was striving to be free of the Middle Ages. The rate of change in Western culture increased incrementally and has been fast and furious during the modern period. We have just noted the movement culminating the Renaissance. Just before the germinal thought of Descartes (1596-1650) came to attention, a variety of other progressive people emerged in Europe. One of the most famous of these was John Calvin (1509-1564).

Calvin was a bright lawyer and preacher who saw beyond the prevalent culture (in which common people were still servile) to a new people self-consciously worshiping God unmediated by priests. We remember that the increasing formalization of religious practices in the very early city may well be the context of the emergence of "priests." In each age, those who best internalized the current practice naturally became leaders and teachers and led the celebrations in which rituals developed. Calvin followed Augustine substantially. But he conceived of the roles of clergy and laity in an equality of power. It was a revolutionary point of view. Since he advocated a church under the control of lay people, we might wonder why, in the mode of the time, he did not establish a national church. Shall we guess that the independence of cities at that point in Western development made that unlikely? Change was in the wind, and the people were gaining control, perhaps a little jealous of that independence. Nonetheless, Calvin has influenced more Christians than any other of the Reformers. Presbyterians and Baptists especially, but many others in addition became "Calvinists." Calvin's Augustinian roots led him to produce a stringently orthodox theology, embodied early in his career in *Institutes of the Christian Religion*[41] and perfected throughout his life.

John Knox was one of Calvin's students, and he is largely responsible with George Buchanan for the demonstration of democracy in the Scottish church. Calvin was austere, but Knox was harsh. He rid Scotland of Roman Catholic churches and thus of the only substantial institutional residue of the oligarchic history of Europe. Knox's "cleansing" destroyed priceless icons as Sir Walter Scott lamented. Perhaps his most important contribution was to establish a school beside every church. Well over 100 years before the French established a public school system, Scots were reading the Bible in every home, and each one had a couple of books in addition. Before long the English followed suit. By the time the French moved to catch up, there was a bookseller in almost every town in Britain. Knox's austerity fit the remnant sheep-like culture of the time, but had within it Calvin's vision of a responsible humanity.

No doubt the culture this produced, evident in an educated populace, is responsible for the immense importance of the British in the American experiment. It is a miracle that what Arthur Herman calls "The True Story of How Western Europe's Poorest Nation Created Our World and Everything in It" is, indeed, the way it happened -- not without other contributions, of course. The institution of schools by John Knox, the practical theologian of Reformed Protestantism, directly followed the hope of John Calvin for all Christians that they might read the Christian Scripture for themselves. No intermediary is needed to follow Jesus the Christ.

Literacy paid off for the Scots in the eighteenth century in the burst of creative energy they displayed in many fields. In the nineteenth century the inventiveness which brought the Industrial Age to full fruit in the United States was actually managed by many Scots who had migrated to the New World.[42] It is this personal industry which led the industrialization of America -- the practice of industriousness which settled on the Scots with the Protestant revolution. Americans no longer just learned the skills of their fathers. Their fathers had learned to live out their independence from autocratic authority. They applied their minds, exercised their imaginations, read up a storm and understood their world better than most people worldwide.

So John Calvin deserves some credit for the open-mindedness which has been the fountain of American freedom from its beginning. Presbyterians, Baptists, and most other Protestant Christians can thank Calvin for much of the strong base of their faith. Let us remember that Calvin was a well-educated intellectual. Anti-intellectual tendencies in America have sometimes twisted his teaching and contributed to a century of American confusion. Calvin would not only have approved of the evolution of his teachings over the centuries, he is at their center in encouraging and providing for the expression of basic humanity in the church. It is fortunate that he lived at a time when this creative humanity was showing itself in many of his peers. All over Europe, the spirit of reform had been boiling for many years, largely beneath the surface of repression.

It happens that this spirit of independent thought is a remainder of primitive human individuality disciplined under worldwide oligarchy to submit to autocracy. The primitive individuality had been sustained much longer in Northern Europe (and the northern part of Britain), largely outside the spreading aristocracy of the rest of the European culture of the Middle Ages long concentrated around the Mediterranean Sea. In the north, reformers found receptive people. In some fortunate ways they had become part of the increasingly literate European bourgeoisie. But they brought into European development a strong residue of that primitive individuality. Northern peoples had not been under the thumb of empire for thousands of years, but only for a few hundred at most as Rome extended its domain. Among them the indomitable spirit of early human beings still triumphed over the broken submissiveness of the ancient oligarchic heritage. Rather than obedience, they understood faithfulness.

The fortuitous timing of the opening of the Western Hemisphere to immigration provided for incubation of a distinctly new culture. By the seventeenth century Protestantism had triumphed in Britain. The Scottish Enlightenment had begun. The transition to modern farming produced the infamous "clearings" which dispossessed vast numbers of Highlanders many of whom emigrated to North America. Permanent settlements of English and Scots were well established along the eastern seaboard of the Americas, and the number of people immigrating was substantial. The spirit of independence grew as Britain's burgeoning empire also grew. The American war of independence was a relatively small blip in British empire building; it quickly made up for its loss elsewhere in the world. But that war, won by the American "proletariat" (with French help), spelled the end of the world-wide assumption that oligarchic population control was necessary.

Authority was accepted as necessary, yes, even by the Scots. Humanity had learned the value of social organization and the place for social control. But animosity for monarchy was only heightened by its persistent problems and these seemed to get worse in the eighteenth century. The Ulster Scots (from Northern Ireland), were fiercely independent and constituted at least a third of the Continental Congress, assuring that the new nation would not forget the people. Their spirit persists still, 200 years later. And the nation forged by all the forces of the past demonstrated resilience and vigor uncommon since the longest lived of the empires.

The twenty-first century presents a unique opportunity for the population of the West. We presume Europe and its environs have been moving for a long time in this direction, too. In the United States, the combination of education, self-governance, and the emergence of a new sense of self, exuding humble confidence, public piety,[43] personal alertness, self-discipline, compassion and common sense, give Americans today leverage never before available. With care and attention we are in a position to create a society of peace, liberty, hope, justice and satisfaction only dreamed of in the past – the achievement of this socialized self.

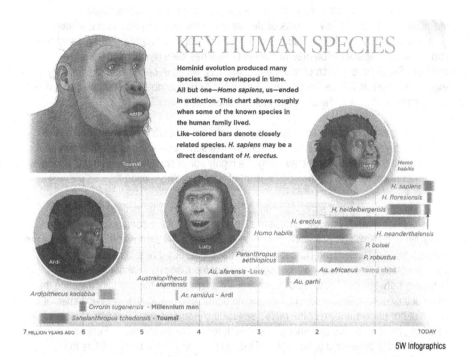

KEY HUMAN SPECIES

Hominid evolution produced many species. Some overlapped in time. All but one—*Homo sapiens*, us—ended in extinction. This chart shows roughly when some of the known species in the human family lived. Like-colored bars denote closely related species. *H. sapiens* may be a direct descendant of *H. erectus.*

Toumaï

Homo habilis

H. sapiens

H. floresiensis

H. heidelbergensis

H. erectus

Homo habilis

H. neanderthalensis

P. boisei

P. robustus

Lucy

Paranthropus aethiopicus

Ardi

Au. afarensis -Lucy

Au. africanus -Taung child

Australopithecus anamensis

Au. garhi

Ardipithecus kadabba

Ar. ramidus - Ardi

Orrorin tugenensis - Millennium man

Sahelanthropus tchadensis - Toumaï

7 MILLION YEARS AGO   6   5   4   3   2   1   TODAY

5W Infographics

II. SELF DEVELOPMENT -- TRANSCENDENCE OF INSTINCT

A. The Extent of Our Ape Connection

"Vive la differance!" says the voyeur. But in this context the difference is not gender but something more intrinsically *human*. Whereas our original human progenitors probably had very little sense of self, we have grasped the emergence of our self-consciousness with both hands and wrung it into an exalted shape. Since identifying ourselves as human beings, we have come to understand the extraordinary capacity and infinite variation in human persons. Every one of the earth's seven billion people is an individual self. It is the human "self" sets us apart from the highest form of animal life, the apes. Like them, we are all primates; but Oh, what a difference!

We have found in very recent years that categories for classifying ourselves as distinct from other animal life were simply not adequate any longer. We said that humans use tools that animals do not. But we discovered, among other things, apes using grass like straws to draw ants out of their holes in the ground. We have found that various animals care for their young for years as we find it necessary for us to do before setting our offspring on their own. And behaviors resembling empathy and commiseration are observed among the primates. So they use rudimentary tools. And they respect differences among them.

Now we understand and can be thankful that our genes carry forward in our individual "old brains" many aspects of life that we share with animals. Some animal "instincts" we have learned to control, some we have yet to overcome. Our gradual rise into our whole capacity to be mature human beings has seen us conquer one after another. Since the evolution of many basic instincts, we have been given the capacity to explore our past as well as the present. Leslie Brothers describes a neuroscientist's view of our transcendence of the animal kingdom. She calls it "mind":

> A great cognitive divide separated us from our ancestors and separates us yet today from our nonhuman counterparts. At some period in our evolutionary past, as a result of our brains evolving in a highly social environment, humans added a conceptual level to (their perception) of a fellow being -- mind.[44]

After enjoying and experimenting with voice and song, our earliest humanoid ancestors had already become proficient at reading much of the complexity of human social life and moved on past early use of gestures and facial expression. Our children are not born with all these mental capabilities. But when we observe a female baboon carefully grooming a young male *out of the sight of the ruling male of her group*, the boundary between her "mind" and ours blurs. This female had the capacity to sense the limits of the ruling male's vision, in the light, no doubt, of a previous angry encounter. It is a sign of her understanding of the male's self distinct from her own. She was calculating in satisfying her own desire to demonstrate her interest in the young male. Further, her mind was sufficiently developed to be aware of the risks she took. No tiny child has that sensitivity. But it starts developing almost immediately.[45]

> Sometime after the divergence between humans and other primates, it appears that our ancestors took off on an evolutionary trajectory leading from extensive sociality to theory of mind and the concept of person. Their socially responsive brains evolved to yield new high-level descriptions linked with a social order -- descriptions of mind and person. Like the bones of the reptilian jaw, socially selective neural ensembles in primates were rearranged to produce something new.[46]

Our memories are, perhaps, not different from many other creatures, but certainly more extensive, which has in itself made us *different* . Certain animal-rights activists keep reminding us that we should not assume that animals do not suffer. Nonetheless, the food chain itself seems to witness to the appropriateness of feeding our energy needs on meat as well as plant. In any case, our ability to ask such questions demonstrates our human capacity to adapt our animal heritage to another level.

We have spoken of transcendence largely in terms of perceiving supernatural understanding, but we might well stop a moment and consider that we are able to so far *transcend* our animal nature as to consider such supra-physical concepts as heaven, hell, eternity, divinity, government, science, mathematics, music, and philosophy, to name a few. All are abstractions. Our world in the twenty-first century is characterized by metaphors and by our named constructs. We are no longer dependent on animal instincts though these are still embedded in our old brains.

We have jumped to the conclusion that all animal life is bereft of sensitivity, only to discover a bonobo ape trying to help a starling that flew into a glass wall and fell, stunned, into the bonobo's enclosure at a zoo. It helped the bird, attempting to make it fly by releasing it carefully from a high tree. This shows a developed sense of self. We were startled to find another form of ape, a chimpanzee, helping a child which fell down from a wall into its enclosure. The chimp returned the child gently to zoo keepers who rushed to its doorway. This event was captured by a video camera and the tape was seen world wide. So we understand ourselves to be the animal capable of recognizing our intimate ties to the world beyond ourselves, as well as the world in which we must survive -- with a mind that seems to be able to grasp the whole world.

We also tend to be quite impatient. Like the apes, our immediate attention is now. But transcending that present has enabled us to dominate the world as well as understand it. The earliest rather complete skeleton of a human predecessor is named "Ardi" for short. Anthropologists' initial study of the Ardi suggest not only an upright posture and long legs and feet that enabled Ardi to walk, but the likelihood that male and female paired off to raise their family. It was another early step in evolution toward the socialized human being. A million years later, the next earliest complete skeleton is called "Lucy" and Lucy also shows evidence of such pairing, undoubtedly more advanced than Ardi's. As anthropologists plumb deeper into these and other discoveries, we may learn more of the early stages of the expanding self.

Perhaps the most important learning of human history thus far is that which now presses upon us: there is no need for us to be arrogant. The ancients, as a matter of legend and historical documentation as well, inveighed against pride. Perhaps the lessons of the recent past can teach us what, previously, we have refused to incorporate into our culture: humility. One might think that the low image of humans typical through the Middle Ages would surely have inculcated humility in Europeans, but, it seems that those lessons were largely canceled out by the euphoria of the Enlightenment and the Industrial Age.

Nonetheless, our capacity for sensitive relations not only to our own kind, but to the whole world, and our ability to think about it and act responsibly in relation to it, do make us different from all the rest of creation. We have proudly exploited the world, as a sign of our prowess. Now it is time to love the whole world, and again to become part of the natural healing processes of it, aided by our particularly and peculiarly human intelligence.

Richard Dawkins, respected biologist, and other outspoken materialists have exercised their highly developed capacity to make choices to reject the longstanding human belief in a realm beyond our physical world. He reminds us that we are definitely part of the perceptible world, not spirits, but also, we are not super-intelligences capable of plumbing the depths of creation.[47] We are nonetheless capable of transcending our physical reality in scores of ways.

The materialists' interpretation of humanness stretches credulity. They insist that we are capable of seeing all of reality and reducing it to our rational limits. What they miss is that humans have been exceeding their rational limits for a very long time. Even science begins with assumptions, faith statements, which reach beyond present knowledge. We can see our transcendent capability even in the small time frame of centuries to which we ourselves have access as "history." Again and again in the twentieth century efforts to prove the materialist position have failed or proven faulty -- so it was for Whitehead and Russell within a few years after publishing *Principia Mathematica* in 1910. In less than thirty years Kurt Godel proved conclusively that any formal mathematical system must contain statements that are apparently true but not provable.[48] Are these not faith statements? (Discussion of faith will have to wait for another volume!) And has not the persistent growth in our human mathematical capability proved adequately the evolution of the human mind so that we should recognize transcendence as a blessing?

We know a great deal, then, beyond the material world: history itself is the record of our predecessors. Such as it is, multifarious and uneven, limited and disturbing, the historic record is full of the evidence of our ability to exceed previous physical and instinctual limits. We know a great deal of ancient history and pre-history by inference from archaeological work and speculation. And as we have grown increasingly self-critical, our speculation has become less bizarre and more often correct.

We know that religion has been part of our social fabric from long before written records. We know that we ourselves have grown more capable, one may suggest, constantly through time. In fact the characteristic of *time* most significant to us is *change* -- just as it was to the earliest Greek philosophers. Heraclitus is credited with pointing out that one cannot step into the same river twice. He believed that everything was made of fire – distinct from Thales (100 years earlier) who believed the base element was water based in part on the fact that it was the element which one could easily see had three distinct phases – ice, water, vapor depending on temperature.

In spite of the brilliance of many individuals over many thousands of years, we must admit that, in generality, our "selfs" are significantly different from those of our early ancestors. The bright minds of a few do not represent the great mass of humanity. Evolution is uneven. It follows no known pattern. In every population there will always be some bright people and some whose minds languish in the past. How those minds are used will also vary from place to place and time to time, perhaps linked to different populations. And evolution continues, unpredictably. Professor Bruce Lahn reported out of the University of Chicago in 2005 the identity of two genes that have physically evolved in the brain since the advent of *Homo sapiens*, one 37,000 years ago and one 6,000 years ago, very recent in evolutionary time. However, their functions are by no means clear.[49]

B. Human Self Development

We are separated from an earlier species by perhaps five and a half million years of evolution. After the development of our unique esophageal conformation we found ourselves able to make a fantastic range of vocal sounds. The development of language and means of recording those sounds for transmission and audible reproduction by others, has produced something in human beings which has captured our imagination. We know too little about early Stone Age culture to say very much about the early human self-image. The nature and development of the primitive self is open to speculation. But beginning with the emergence of the city, the New Stone Age produced a variety of evidences of the self to cause us to wonder at the explosion of human capacity, perhaps somewhat spasmodically, as our world developed.

Some critics have tried to deal with the character of human life which we call "culture" under the German notion of *Zeitgeist* (spirit of the times). Culture experts will have to assess the appropriateness of that borrowing of language. The problem with Richard Dawkins' argument is that he seems to reduce the complex social reality called "culture" to a simple mechanism focused on the sort of cultural changes we find within twentieth century America: From straight-laced Victorian culture to loose Twenties flapper culture to the consumer culture of post World War II America with its sexual revolution and "drug culture." But all such decade-bound changes are short of the mark we speak of, and from our perspective they appear largely as fads and indulgences.[50] Culture as we are using the term is far more complex, carrying over in some form each generation's complex adaptations, sexual preferences, and innumerable learnings and dispositions.

The importance of each generation in the development of culture is evident. But that contribution is not the ephemeral excitement of a populace. Gradually people absorb some aspects of current life around them as their own and, apparently, what they buy of it gets incorporated in their genes. The development of culture is the working out of continuously changing life in the concrete arena of living people. Some such changes instigate familiar memories. Some are more subtle. Often these more subtle aspects of our lives become incorporated in our culture quite unconsciously. Some day, scholars will help us to identify how such change takes place in society. For now, we must be content with recognizing the inevitability of change. Very recent DNA work suggests to some scientists that there is evidence of evolutionary changes in animals over amazingly short periods – less than 6000 years. Like Lewis Mumford's concept of civilization, culture is a continuous and inevitable product of human life in community. One is tempted to say that culture evolves, like life itself. And some changes seem to us to be evident within our own century.

How cultural change occurs seems to be coming clear in the fast-growing fields of neural science. First, let us recognize the complexity of the human "self." We begin the formation of our selves in the womb, appropriating from our parents the DNA which shapes our whole physical self. It also transmits into us, in the "old brain," certain learnings of our human progenitors. After birth our eyes and ears first spring into action, followed quickly by the other senses. Babies immediately begin to take into the brain the light and the dark, and, particularly, the faces of those who first gaze at them. It is not long before the baby learns to focus on the eyes of these other creatures. That alerts us to the animal capacity to transmit important information to others by sight or to see it in their eyes. This is the beginning of one's self. Life-long patterns of thought begin forming immediately. The child learns very quickly to expect loving nurture from parents and other care-givers – or it may begin growing into a withdrawn, frightened human being afraid of others. This child thus begins to identify his/her self as a dependent and aid-receiving being among others who either help or hinder its development. Perhaps this first lesson of *Homo sapiens* is the root of our interlocking interdependence. The difference between people who trust one another and those who don't ranges from love to cynicism. The vast middle seems to be made up of those who struggle throughout life to achieve a satisfactory balance.

The child begins its formation of the self by observing the faces of these necessary others. We begin seeing ourselves in others' eyes. If a child is deprived of loving parents, perhaps raised by persons whom we might continue to call "others," meaning those with whom we are not familiar, this child will not respond easily to its earliest sight of smiling faces since it has not so early been acquainted with them, and he will have to learn belatedly the pleasure of returning the smile, the giggle, and the laugh.[51] In the first three months of life, the child's disposition is already shaped importantly. Unfortunately, there are people who never find the happy gifts comfortable. But even these may find happy opportunities, they may recover a deeper human self-understanding bit by bit, day by day, as their world grows larger because humans are immensely adaptable.

By nature we rejoice in pleasure, and very soon begin to learn that happiness depends on reciprocation. This shaping of self is a natural business of the brain. It will express itself except under the most severe repression. Beginning with dependence, the individual self must learn how to express his or her underlying selfhood. The most detrimental parenting is repressive and can severely damage a child's emerging self. But when we grow beyond three years we have begun the long trek toward becoming part of our society. A small vocabulary will already have been learned. We also become increasingly aware of our selves, individually. It is a difficult path our children must traverse to develop a sense of self that begins to prepare them for the exercise of objectivity and abstraction and life in society. It is the "terrible" part of growing up for many children. Dunbar says:

> Although the appearance of ToM (theory of mind) strikes us as a very sudden process in children, in fact it is the outcome of a long process of intellectual experimentation.... At first they apparently believe that dolls share with humans all the qualities of volition they see in humans. But ... by about age three children can recognize that other individuals have wants and desires that are similar to those they experience. Over the following year, they use this knowledge to build up a picture of how other individuals tick. It's a very complex task ... more difficult than understanding the physical world.[52]

In our self-awareness we become self-assertive almost immediately. "I want" is a common childhood plea. Parents and others help us from the beginning to understand that the world must accommodate the wants and needs of others as well as our own, beginning with the parents. Perhaps reluctantly, but with growing understanding of ourselves as well as our world, we become our socialized selves.

The shape of this self is determined only partly by what we absorb from our parents and peers. It is also shaped by the incessant choices we make as individuals which determine how we focus our attention. These choices, constantly shaping our selves, make us different from any other human being, even if we are genetically identical twins or if we are experiencing the same events.

If we are guided to *think* early in life, we will choose bit by bit to focus on things which interest us, things that give us pleasure, and on things which will contribute to our maturing. What we choose helps to shape us into *our own selves*. In an almost invisible way, every day will see in us a new self in a new, unfolding world.[53] It should be the constant joy of childhood that one is constantly uncovering one's self. Over our years we trust that we will become selves which are freed from the instinctual pressures of fear, escape, "fight or flight," from immediate gratification, from the urgency of sexual gratification and many other basic "wants and needs," and also from the ingrained animal habit of copying our fellow human beings.[54] Mimicry is a behavior so natural that it easily becomes a habit to escape thinking. Control is decisively learned in adolescence.

Mimicry has traditionally been thought of as "learning." For a very long time teachers thought we "learned" everything this way, and that everything could be learned from teachers and books. All students had to do was absorb, soak up! Guidance of parents and teachers during our growing up was heavily dependent on learning what they thought we should know and on how these persons thought we should behave. They expected us to act accordingly, as if "learning" meant shaping our volition, our very capacity to choose. But such learning is only another input to the shaping of our selves, not the whole game; our individual selves will be shaped not by such learning but by choosing how shall live.

Another term which has been mixed with the self is the idea of "will." No dobt the term comes from our ambiguous use of the word. "I will do something" can mean that the something fits me or that I accept a task whether or not it is consistent with who I am. At one time will was thought to be shaped permanently; changing our minds after a decision was simply not done. But I myself in each instance determine an action to be consistent with who I am. In a deterministic period, when it was presumed that people behaved by instinct or by habit, this was not a matter of choice but of how one has been raised or taught. As we came to understand better how we ourselves can be responsible, we gradually came to use "will" more often to indicate our choice to do something. To will came to mean "I decide."

The focus on "will" became a way of dealing with the problem of human choice, of making decisions.[55] The Scholastic definition is close to ours. Though we do not talk as they did of "faculties of the soul," we understand that in the act of volition we decide how we act. We are and we do what we choose, not what instincts direct. None of us in most cases of common life can consider ourselves helpless before forces of instinct, "nature," or "learning." Our attention to the human self commends self-conscious attention to who we are and to deciding how to behave in accord with that self-image, giving integrity new meaning.

To "will" is to decide -- most often the word "will" has been used in connection with actions. As John Dryden said, "The most difficult thing I have to do is to decide." Like "volition" (which is an abstraction for the power to decide), "will" serves no ordinary purpose as a concept. We use the word frequently as a verbal: "I am willing," a noun with a sense of a verb, or in partnership with a verb. Neither our "knowledge" nor our "will" is who we are, ourselves. Few of us have not chosen an act lacking integrity by determining that "we will do it!" We are not more or less willing, except in relation to a particular action, though we sometimes admit to being "willing to help anytime," a rather commendable condition of our being in community – when we mean it. And it usually means that we are willing to help within our capabilities, and who we ourselves "are." Sometimes in such decisions we ourselves become aware of what we have become – in the way we have become participants in "being," the "Being" philosophers have spent their lives trying to understand and explicate.

We shape ourselves daily by paying attention to what we can learn. In this sense, learning takes on the full meaning of knowing with understanding. When students pay attention to teaching, whether it is a mathematical manipulation of figures, or a scientific theory, whatever, it becomes part of their minds. If they have paid attention to what they have learned, their decisions will reflect this knowledge – if they choose to make it their own. But if they fail to "pay attention," they miss an opportunity to make it a part of themselves.

If we understand, we *know*, and we can make that knowledge a powerful part of our intellects, that is, of our minds. This is not just knowing about a thing. Our lifetime choices shaping our selves guide our discrimination between alternate interpretations of facts, critically affecting what we "know" and, consequently, who we are. Thus, as we mature, knowledge increasingly shapes our selves and, if we are not discriminating in our use of it, it can isolate us from others and from optional choices we might make. Having made particular knowledge part of ourselves, we are informed by it as we make choices, pursue our careers, live our lives. We are not determined by any knowledge. We ourselves choose our paths moment by moment, picking what knowledge we choose to apply.

As we grow older, our growing store of knowledge can easily make us opinionated. We have already weighed many facts and alternative interpretations, and our "knowledge" can easily become fixed and inflexible. But we all know that at any age such fixations can pervert our judgment and our participation in the perpetually changing culture. Science is at root knowledge. But modern "science" builds on immense sets of very clear and precise methods to assure that we look carefully at our subject matter. We have become aware that the scientific method itself can become fixed and inflexible. This malady had developed into a new scholasticism by the mid-twentieth century when Thomas Kuhn uncovered a powerful and revealing sense of changing paradigms in science.[56] Even science undergoes revolutions and sometimes it seems to take a generation of new professionals to fully adopt such revelations. But we maintain that the new mind of humanity becoming evident today has the capacity to incorporate such critical thinking into itself, not as specific methodologies, but as a predisposition. Persistent attention to our thinking can help us maintain alert minds as years pass. Here again, "attention" is a keyword. It is a pre-disposition we can embrace.

In her recent *Absence of Mind*, Marilynne Robinson applies her considerable talents to articulating the significant way in which we become what we are disposed to be.

By "self-awareness" I do not mean merely consciousness of one's identity, or of the complex flow of thought, perception, memory, and desire, important as these are. I mean primarily the self that stands apart from itself, that questions, reconsiders, appraises. I have read that microorganisms can equip themselves with genes useful to their survival – that is, genes conferring resistance to antibiotics – by choosing them out of the ambient flux of organic material.... If a supposedly simple entity can by any means negotiate its own enhancement, then an extremely complex entity, largely composed of these lesser entities – that is, a human being – should be assumed to have analogous capabilities. For the purposes of the mind, these might be called conscience or aspiration. We receive their specific forms culturally and historically, as the microorganism does also when it absorbs the consequences of other germ's encounters with the human pharmacopoeia.[57]

To remain open to this constantly changing world, our humanity calls on us to develop open minds, utilizing our primitive human capacity for adaptation. Adaptability is always a matter of choice. If it were instinctual, we might find it to be an instinct we cherish. But, no, it apparently developed fairly late in the evolutionary scheme long after "instincts" were embedded in our old brain. Thus it is necessary for us to choose to be flexible, to compromise, to cooperate. Having chosen to be flexible, we probably find inflexible people onerous. It then becomes incumbent on us to take care in our construction of "self" to include a component to help others as we have opportunity and to encourage them to grow themselves.

With the consolidation of our knowledge base through disciplined listening, study, reiteration, sharing, and practice, we will increasingly act in terms of the character of the self we have formed in our minds. Our confidence is a product of our thoughtful attention to ourselves. Therefore we own ourselves. We are who we are by choice. That may require repentance and shame, but we understand as we achieve the new mind of humanity, that we are responsible for being who we are. It will include our adaptation to such unfortunate maladies as Lou Gehrig's disease or a natural disaster that overtakes us. Our world, however, continues to change and we must avoid the smug pride which often accompanies knowledge. It poisons our relations with others. We must continue to change through all of life. We must discipline our self to inform our thinking, and not block our way to new understanding. As we grow up we must be careful to avoid learnings which get in the way of seeing alternatives.

To choose is to act in accord with our self, its shape and its intellectual knowledge. But the self does not dictate our choices. It is ourselves making choices. It is not a "thing." It is our whole being in action, doing what we are capable of doing. Unless we have appropriated a rigidity into our selves, we will be able to act freely in any instance. If we fail to so act, we lack integrity, that is, then our behavior has been inconsistent with who we are. It is possible to choose to act differently. It is the act of choosing (that is, volition, the end result of thinking) that is the issue. The good word "deliberate" applies to this turning over in our minds of how we choose to behave. If we behave with integrity, our choices will reflect what we have made of ourselves quite literally, what fits us, what fits our self understanding. Our word is "responsibility."

What parents and teachers must do in their singular roles in the momentary development of a young person's self, is help the child, the adolescent, the young man or woman see clearly, and think carefully. When a man or woman then makes a choice -- and as a child makes his or her choices on the basis of whom he or she has become so far -- the "will," the desire to make choices, will issue in the best choice of which we are capable. The probability that we will make choices that we regret is the problem of "sin," not as the indwelling of "evil" in us, but as the simple problem of being human.

It is at this point that we must come to trust our own judgment. The professional must arrive at this confidence in order to practice his/her profession. Volition will operate; we must make choices or be washed to and fro in the waves of social or professional pressures. Best of all, I know that the choices I make are mine. I own them. I am responsible for them.

C. Developing the Social Self

At another level, responsibility as integrity is not enough when we violate community standards in regard to the sanctity of person or property.[58] Responsibility requires us to compare ourselves (and others) against the community standard. The criminal whom we say suffers a character defect may act with integrity in robbing others, but in doing this he is not a responsible member of the community. Responsibility adds another dimension about how we respond to our community. Learning to incorporate responsibility in our culture has taken us thousands of years, a critical dimension of our socialization.

It is not strange, then, to find that only now have scholars discovered what we will consider the basis for a sense of responsibility in evolution. In their book *Evolution, Games and God: The Principle of Cooperation*, Harvard evolutionary biologist Martin A. Nowak and theologian Sarah Coakley lay out their research related to the mathematical understanding of evolutionary theory. Coakley tells us that

> cooperation must be counted a third evolutionary principle alongside of ... mutation and selection. Cooperation, Nowak's analysis shows, can be a kind of contrapuntal accompaniment, without which selection itself would not go on operating as it does.[59]

We will leave to others how evolutionary theorists understand "cooperation." Coakley reminds us that in the technical, evolutionary sense, cooperation does not have the same volitional sense we usually think of. But "it does show us that the whole evolutionary struggle has a sacrificial accompaniment." Above the level of bacteria or cancer cells, we find widespread sacrificial activities among social insects and the practice of dolphins, for example, to surround a dying companion at risk to themselves. Coakley concludes:

> Evolution delivers to us humans, made in the (image of God), the greatest possible inheritance of responsibility: to crown those regular intimations of evolutionary cooperation ... with acts of intentional sacrificial altruism that now alone can save the planet.

When we make choices, we are being responsible if our choices contribute to our common good.[60] This does not mean "conform to everyone else's choice." If we vote in a civic election contrary to the majority but express ourselves with integrity, we are responsible members of the community.

This understanding has been a major contribution to civilization of the American culture. Now we look at the sort of gridlock that our congress constantly faces, however, and we realize that our system needs tweaking. Too many members of Congress have too narrow a sense of who they are. The role of legislator fixed in many of their minds was shaped when now antique notions rode high – Enlightenment, Rationality and Orthodoxy were all defined before the current revolution became evident. And the American religious sickness, Fundamentalism, has infiltrated many of their religious commitments.

Our nation was formed on the cutting edge of the Enlightenment, but that movement has been severely critiqued. Our culture has not yet caught up with these newer insights. Rationality has undergone important challenges in the past century. Orthodoxy has undergone radical reassessment throughout the whole history of Christianity and most radically in the twentieth century. Yet in each age, some people become so attached to old sets of ideas as to turn off their critical faculties. They tend to fasten onto old ideas as a radar system "locks" onto a target. Failure to understand the changes taking place demonstrates the staying power of antiquated human culture though this has a fiduciary[61] value. It assures that established cultural patterns are not dismissed lightly.

The American story demonstrates an alternative way to commit ourselves to important ideas. From our point of view, it is one of adherence to certain assurances while argument about infinite detail proceeds. Our legal system is perpetually changing, but also thoughtful, it is constantly tested.

This, too, is part of the change occurring in the human self. It is time to revise many ideas of longstanding, and the process is already well under way. The nature of responsibility has changed. Even on the international level, there is an increasing sense of this change in suggestions for a new definition of national sovereignty.[62]

Responsibility is a matter of responding to whom we really are, our selves, the person we have become, in the context of our society. We are not independent beings. We are social beings. We must live in response to our environments. And we have the ability to do this with intelligence and self-control. Many do not yet realize the extent of changes that have taken place, the emergence of the global village and the flat world,[63] and that our responsibility as human beings now includes almost seven billion people! But we exercise different kinds of responsibility at different distances.

Our capability for "responsibility" has often been identified as accountability, as making the "right" decision. It is closely related to "integrity." This was the outstanding advance in the human self image in the transition from the ancient through the Medieval periods, and into the Modern world.

In any case, if one has committed to be a craftsperson or a professional or some other standard of conduct or practice, it is incumbent upon us to incorporate related responsibilities into our selfness. It is not enough to practice the techniques of a skill. We no longer simply conform to certain social standards. We choose in such roles to be responsible. By this choice we exhibit our confidence that we have become trustworthy, persons who carry responsibility in regard to this profession or position in the social order, a responsibility to behave in a manner that exceeds the social standard, contributing to the current redefinition in the new culture. It is who I am -- and who I pledge myself to be in accepting a position of responsibility. If I fail so to act, I am irresponsible.

Though this sense of responsibility seems to us very old, it was quite embryonic among human beings of the early city even in the New Stone Age. It had already existed as an attribute of elders, fathers, chiefs, healers and prophets. But some of these many leaders and many kings lived in an irresponsible world corrupted by a long history of the exploitation of power; in which only a few powerful people, it appears, chose to be responsible.

For most of our existence on earth, examination of "self" was limited by our mental evolution and by cultures which inhibited open exploration. Now and then since the emergence of our attention to self-consciousness, we have nibbled around the edges of self-understanding that might lead us to recognize every person's responsibility in life. I suspect that ancient sensitivity to the possibility of spirits who seemed to control rain, sunshine, stars, seasons and everything else helped in the gradual emergence of sensitivity to the self. Such spirits were, after all, not so different from others as persons like ourselves, except for being amorphous. Probably after the great agricultural revolution (10,000 BCE) self-reflection became a possibility. Perhaps shamans were among the first reflective people recognized in communities. They were persons whose self-image was unusually acute among many who lacked much self-consciousness at all.

Restricted though life was, the creative forces which blossomed in the ancient city exhibited the evolving self. There, the greatly increased human interaction stimulated our self-consciousness so that, continuing this path, after another four thousand years in the fourteenth and fifteenth centuries (CE), the time of the Renaissance, creative expression of selfhood broke out in many forms among diverse people.

Since then the persistent effort of humans to understand themselves has continued unabated through the centuries. Perhaps we can credit the greatest advances to the penitent spirit encouraged by the Medieval Church – to an awareness of shortcomings. The mystics shared in the journey. Though the church was paternalistic, it helped develop individual capacity for personalizing the self-discipline first developed as a social necessity in the ancient city. This discipline was required by the expanding sense of vocation -- every Christian's role in the world. In the words of John Calvin, "the priesthood of all believers," was instituted explicitly in the family of Reformed Churches in the sixteenth century. The subservient, quiescent individualism of the early city had gradually transformed into obedience and then into self-discipline.

But we did not really begin to explore ourselves (as the science of psychology would do) until the twentieth century. We had named the virtues -- they were basic to significant discussion for several centuries.[64] We talked a lot about exercising volition as a human thing to do, but we continued the age-old posture of acting as if one learned to make the right choices. That meant learning all the rules, all the options, all the errors and mistakes humans make, and always choosing the right way. No wonder repentance for dumb acts became a central Christian ritual! The problem of human error was misunderstood as a failure to know what was right, and one could hardly know all the rules. No wonder modern teen-agers rebelled at authority! They got filled up with rules and guides and corrections and all the things that were supposed to enable them to choose correctly. They knew in themselves their capacity to choose how they would act and it would not be by straight-laced obedience.

The human mind was evolving and it persistently showed itself in what we have miscalled "teen-age rebellion." Unfortunately, at the middle of this century, our substitution of *training* for education (not grasping the difference) did not provide the young much help in grasping the self-discipline necessary to implement their pregnant freedom. Though the young have regularly presumed that they are ready to take on the world, most young adults, research tells us, are still forming their adult minds. The end of teen years does not spell the end of adolescence. Evidence since the 1960s demonstrates the resilience of the human mind in a culture in a major transition. It is evident in the maturity achieved by many post-war children in spite of an antiquated educational system.

We had presumed that everything we needed to know could be taught the same way. Learning meant memorization, memorization required repeating. People in ancient times taught by singing their stories and poems. It is very human to love to sing songs, and the words somehow stick well in the mind, as does poetry, implementing a very ancient learning about human beings. Unfortunately, long after the Greeks learned to teach through dialogue, we gradually dropped from our teaching the practices of listening and responding, and ended up with indoctrination. The Medieval catechism was the preferred device for generations, until in the modern period we gradually rediscovered the necessity of participation and the art of dialogue.[65]

And we also learned that each child (not to omit adults as well) learns differently. In a sense the best education is one in which each of us learns how we can best learn -- and at the same time gains an enthusiasm for using our minds. Everything we learn, on the one hand, should help us to make better choices. Volition -- that is, how to make decisions, how to choose -- volition can be taught, but it is not about learning all the options. That is both impossible and counterproductive. Learning all the textbooks have to teach cannot substitute for an education which helps us understand how to deal intelligently with a subject. The one may be sufficient knowledge for a person who is an ordinary, even an exacting worker. The other might allow the knowledgeable person to design, to discover new methods and relationships, as well as to perform helpfully -- and grow throughout his or her lifetime in understanding and breadth and depth of the self.

Meaning, on the other hand, is not private. It is gained through social interaction, if George Herbert Mead (1863-1931) was right at the beginning of the twentieth century.

Words enable others to react to our thinking. If we must define a word for our listener to understand it, he or she listening has the opportunity to ask whether the word means this or that, whether it is always blue, how large it may grow, and whether there isn't another word for this that people already know. When the word enters our vocabulary, (unless it is a private symbol for example, something used in a private journal) it is a social word. "Vocabulary" means our common language. It might, of course, be a vocabulary used in a special group -- among chemists, and it is, then, social in a restricted community.

John Dewey, about the same time as Mead, took a similar position and both he and Mead anticipate the work of a key figure in twentieth century philosophy, Ludwig Wittgenstein. In his *Philosophical Investigations*, Wittgenstein argued that words do not point to objects or events in the sense of giving them meaning. Meaning comes only from our human interaction: the way we use words, the inflection we use, our posture, and our facial expression, and how our listeners respond – all these contribute to communication.

Misusing a word can cause someone to challenge our meaning. In our discussion of that challenge, we may change our wording and rearrange our mental picture of what we are trying to say. The meaning that emerges among us may be helpful among others, or it may be confusing until we explain how we arrived at it; the new responses may clarify further or throw a monkey wrench into the whole idea -- in other words, challenge our idea. Together, over time, we arrive at a consensus as to the meanings we employ in conversation. Thus it is that language has a crucial role in shaping our culture.

Vocabulary is one of the bugaboos of education. School children often are expected to learn a certain basic list of words fit for them. To do so expands their capacity to understand. If they are alert, they will sometimes question whether a word is used correctly. Often it will have second, third, or fourth meanings. Each may represent the current vocabulary of a certain generation, and their use may be out of date, but understanding them in their earlier context can help us broaden our minds. An adroit author of historical fiction makes good use of such obsolete words by making them clear in his or her context.

Human communication is a perpetual challenge. It should be enough to keep us alert and growing all through life. By the time we have reached our latter years, we should not only have an immense vocabulary, but our sense of self should have grown to encompass a vast history and to help us prepare our children for a productive and happy future. When our vocabularies cease to grow, it is a choice of death, not life.

No matter how complex life becomes, the human aspect will be huge. Any notion that we can encompass all our communication within one dictionary is bound to prove wrong. We may gain more than one advanced university degree, but, hopefully all together still will not circumscribe our breadth, but rather enlarge our sense of self to embrace more people who themselves represent even more diversity and knowledge.

All this bears on the development of our religious sense. If God represents in our minds all that is beyond our understanding, both the world and all that transcends it, to say nothing of being master of all that we do know, then our expanding selves will represent in our lives an expansion of our appreciation of God. Presuming that God is the eternal constant, what changes with the passage of time is our human understanding -- really with our changing culture, and our changing selves.

This is the process of growth that most concerns teachers and preachers, all who try to contribute to the welfare and happiness of others. We are concerned that each person grasps his or her own "self" and makes of it what one chooses. Experience teaches that often we are given new options. Circumstances can dictate change. And we must confront a human problem: It is true that all minds do not evolve at the same rate in the same way.

Evolution seems to follow an ancient course toward complexity, but the stimuli have always varied so much from place to place, even person to person, that the capacity for self-understanding is one of the things that vary greatly among us. It is not necessary or considerate to assume that everyone follows the same path to understand. We always must allow for others' individuality as well as to be alert to our differences. And we need to be concerned that everyone has the chance to choose to become a self who contributes to our society, who helps to make community meaningful, who gives others pleasure and finds pleasure in relationships – a person who is responsible.

There is, of course, a place for simple "learning." We can and need to learn how to add figures, to keep simple books of account, to know the nature of Jesus' orientation to life. The mechanic needs to know something about wrenches and how to size bolts and nuts. The writer better know adjective and adverb, syntax, and grammar. There seems to be no end of the subjects which at the college level must be taught in our complex society. Someone must know how to tweak technology and the bureaucracy, and how to celebrate the great events of growing up, raising a family, and aging. The contributions of such specialties began to grow as the city came into existence, Their number continues to grow with a vengeance!

At each point of contact between two or more human beings, something else is really more important. It is care and concern for the *other*. Each other person is a unique self, and every one of us requires love and attention. We have no right to ride roughshod (to use a really obsolete vernacular phrase), we have no right to act in ways which violate others' selves. In all ordinary life situations we are called upon to correct, guide, help, teach, encourage, support, assist others. To viciously attack another person, physically or in any other way is *verboten!* (the German to make absolutely sure I communicate) "forbidden."[66]

Perhaps the most significant difference between high school and college instructors is their assumption of the average student's readiness to stretch his mind. Nothing is a greater challenge for any teacher than to help an indifferent student to wake up, to become alert, to his or her potential, in any fashion. The college student presumably is in class with an interest in learning, in shaping his or her self. The latter may not be true, however. This is particularly a problem for religion, though it may apply to obsolete understanding of retailing or any other field of study.[67] If mentors to date have misconstrued their role in relation to the student as simply informing her or him about how one operates in the field at hand, the younger person may not ever have perceived that changes are inevitably taking place in this his or her field of interest, in his community, and in herself. It never hurts for any parent, teacher, or preacher to remind people of the basic, changing nature of the real world. Every reminder should be cause for joy!

It is fitting in our leisure culture to remind ourselves of one of the instincts we all fight. It is the tendency to relax, to enjoy the ease and privilege available to us. It has been so from the time life began. Every living thing seeks the salutary food, location, and comfort which are part of its nature. Animals seek good food and shelter. When the village folk moved into the early cities, those who sought the comfort and security of life inside the citadel also quickly sought the amenities that come with power to adjust the environment: gardens, open space, tiled drains, running water "piped" in. If we ourselves worked on the moats, aqueduct, the reservoirs, canals, and irrigation ditches that served the citadel, why would we not also seek the fruits of such amenities?

Ease has always been a human temptation. It is true of each one of us; it is the unusual, and the admirable person who persistently seeks active participation in life. Out of the plenty we have enjoyed we have learned to respect everyone's leisure. Comfortable relaxation may contribute to extension of knowledge or understanding. One of the reasons aristocracy contributed so much to early cultural advances, was the availability to privileged people of the leisure denied to most of their peers. All the same, there is no guarantee of responsible use of leisure as is evident in historic time.

All of us can contribute to society through our own skills – by expressing the true person, by being ourselves. Just as there are still people in our midst who rejoice in tracking and killing animals, as did our early ancestors, there are others who must have the strenuous exercise of vigorous, competitive activity. We see it as no different from those who enjoy reading or mathematics. Any such activity is better for the human being than neglect of that part of the self which governs its activity, making the choices that shape us. The better it encourages our pursuit of self-understanding in our social context, the better off is our own self and also the common mind, our culture.

But it is never, never acceptable human behavior to violate another person's selfhood out of our laziness. The emergent human mind has arrived at the point at which every human being can learn to respect others, and never, never take advantage of another's weakness or vulnerability. When we let our selves cease to grow, we begin to die. Our instinct for leisure must be disciplined just as our other appetites if we are to become responsible.

III. EVOLUTION OF OUR SELF: FROM EARLY MAN TO PYTHAGORAS

A. THE VICTORY OVER INSTINCT

Human beings have not always had highly self-conscious selves as we do today. Sometimes we say that it is "providential" that we arrive on the scene of human life at a time when we might have a fairly complete, whole view of ourselves as well as of the world, of the universe, history, and almost everything else one can imagine. But this is not to say that we now know everything; nothing could be further from the truth. The wise sophisticated scholar will quickly admit limits to his knowledge and understanding. It is, rather, to say that the self-image available to us is larger, more complete, more wholistic than has ever before been possible for human beings. How we view this development of the truly human being is important to broadening our grasp of who we are today.

It is inconceivable to think of the earliest humans as self-conscious much beyond the sense of the bonobos and chimpanzees. Chimps have been thought of as close ancestors much longer than have bonobo apes, and some of us adopted a view of all apes which is vicious. But these primates have a cooperative, sympathetic side to them although they can be brutal, as can humans and all other animals. Recent research (since the 1960s) has painted a more endearing picture of these near-relatives -- after Jane Goodall began her work and came to realize that chimpanzees were not simply savage. Our knowledge of bonobos is much more recent although the bonobo was recognized as a distinct animal in the ape family in 1929.

Only since about 1980 have we begun to understand this other, possibly closer relative, the bonobo. Noted primatologist Frans de Waal says, "In 1978, I first saw bonobos up close at a Dutch zoo. The label on the cage identified them as pygmy chimpanzees," implying they were just a smaller version of their better known cousins. Bonobos are not much smaller than chimps. His description of this late comer to our pantheon of familiar animals is helpful:

A bonobo is physically as different from a chimpanzee as a Concorde is from a Boeing 747. Even a chimp would have to admit that the bonobo has more style. A bonobo's body is graceful and elegant, with piano-player hands and a relatively small head. The bonobo has a flatter, more open face with a higher forehead than a chimpanzee. A bonobo's face is black, its lips are pink, its ears small, and its nostrils wide. Females have breasts; they are not as prominent as in our species, but definitely A-cup compared to the flat-chested other apes. Topping it all off is the bonobo's trademark hairstyle, long black hair neatly parted in the middle.[68]

It is helpful to repeat also a 1990s anecdote about our reactions to the bonobo. It illustrates the role of our choices in shaping our culture. Professional pride long inhibited our acquaintance with this remarkable animal. Perhaps the most recent incident found crews filming bonobos for a documentary turning off their cameras whenever the bonobos' behavior embarrassed them. Asked why, they replied that their audience wouldn't be interested in that (sex, copulation, display of intimate affection). So public acquaintance with the bonobo was trounced again.[69]

The reason for this is that bonobos are almost constantly involved in sex. Whereas chimp females display genital swelling perhaps five percent of the time, bonobo females are in this state almost fifty percent of the time. But sex and swellings are largely disconnected from fertility.[70] After all, recognizing the link between copulation and birth of young is a fairly modern, human achievement.

The point here is this: The bonobo has appropriated the instinctual sex drive to facilitate a peaceful social order. Approval and agreement among them are represented by engaging in sex. In most species the alpha-male enforces his right to copulate as he chooses simply out of superior strength. Bonobos depart from this pattern

All bonobos after puberty (which comes late as with humans) copulate often. Both sexes copulate in every possible combination of each and every method of copulation according to whim. Genital rubbing may or may not end in copulation. Sexual stimuli are consciously used to caress, cajole, mediate, and reconcile. Male and female. Intercourse precedes eating. Females control distribution of food and provide males the privilege of copulation as part of the bargain.

If apes use sex effectively as a tool to control antagonism between group members, how is it that we humans have developed an ethic in which sex is supposed to be used only for reproduction? Everyone knows the pleasurable experience of sexual copulation. It is clearly part of the self-awareness of bonobos, and so it is also among us. A painting by Pieter Bruegel (1525-1569) in Belgium, influenced by the humanism which broke out in the Renaissance,[71] has long titillated young men who observe the obviously sex-aware costumes of the men. Their "cod-pieces" cover their enlarged penises while they engage in jubilant village dancing. This does not imply anything the word "libertine" suggests[72]. It is only intended to illustrate the basic, pleasurable exercise of our human nature, expressed in dancing.

Naturally, dancing probably gained a sexual component very early; yet it has many values unrelated to sex. The very common dancing of men with men is not an indication of homosexuality. It is a natural expression of joy in life, the exuberance of youth, and pleasure in active fellowship. This is the same understanding of self which undergirded the development of larger and larger settlements 4000 years ago. It is the joy of human association.

The recurring notion that men are aggressively (often implying uncontrollably) promiscuous is simply an excuse for our failure to teach young men from early ages to exercise self control. Finally, in the twenty-first century, we will be driven to take seriously this primal educational task. If the bonobo apes learned to control their sexual instinct for the good of the community, surely we should not think it beyond ourselves. The Medieval denigration of sexuality is a rather stunning surprise in the evolution of the human being. Authorities succeeded in inculcating the idea that copulation was only for procreation, a wild and clearly mistaken idea. This could only be done in a population which was cowed by power and submissive to authority. But it also attests to the growing self-awareness of the people whose sexual maturity exceeded the mentality of the ancient fertility cult.

The Church added to this influential mix its magical, ethereal power. We must not underestimate the depth of religion in the psyches of ancient and Medieval people. We remember that religion was probably a very early social activity, however distant from our religious practices. It was reinforced in every generation by our native awe of natural phenomena and also by the perennial reinforcement of the earliest myths about supernatural forces by telling and retelling the familiar stories. It was part of the complex social structure that emerged from antiquity and held the growing social understanding of the people in tension with their native egotism. The autocratic Church exercised its paternalistic control over the people just as had the kings and emperors who preceded it. And it decided that sex must be kept under control. Perhaps it was right to demonstrate a new style of life in contrast to the excesses of the fertility cults. Church Father, Augustine, surely thought so about 400 CE.

Repression of sexuality was only mildly effective. The population continued to grow (at the encouragement of the Church). The idea of repressed sexuality, nonetheless, persisted through the post-Reformation period. Whatever its success, the repression of sexuality demonstrates both the ingrained authoritarianism of the aristocracy of the church and the depth of the self-discipline of the long-depressed population. This self-discipline is one of the tenacious blessings learned in ancient times. It has for a long time put the power to control instinct in our own hands.

The long human journey from the forest to modern Europe has required many human explorations of self-discipline. The dangers of life outside the forest, among new predators, with new foods, and, over the centuries, with changes in habitat, climate, and society, persistently prodded humans to think. Their unusually capable brains enabled them to survive, thrive and to grow increasingly aware of themselves and the circumstances of their lives. At first, their social awareness (as with every child) was of themselves among others/. Soon they learn that others, like themselves, have personal identity as somehow different from that of other people. Animals share the ability to distinguish others but apparently not the self-awareness that children soon achieve. And animals never extend their consciousness very far past this innate boundary. This difference of self from others is hardly "self-consciousness" as we understand that phrase today, but it is a necessary step children take toward their full adult selves.

Human selfness for thousands of years was probably quite like the self-identity of animals, so that people knew themselves as members of a family or tribe. If we measure self-consciousness as a sense of responsibility, these primitive people were already blessed with a parental sense, to protect, and enjoy their children. Perhaps from the beginning they appreciated their elders with whom they had bonded as children. And even animals have been observed showing deference to older members of their groups. After departing from our evolutionary stem five and a half million years ago, over five million of those years were given to early hominids before the emergence of *Homo sapiens* and the early appearance of human self-consciousness.

Leslie Brothers suggests that we are able to connect ourselves to our experience and to others because our minds begin to form with our first experience.[73] We are social animals (not unlike apes, ants and others up to a point) but we are able to choose our way among impressions because of our mind-making brains. Like our adoption of our "mother tongue," our brains pick up the forms of culture within our social field and give us a place in it. This is the formation of our "selves." Our world, then, contains others from the beginning. We speak English. We are part of a particular community, school, church, etc. We form our selfhood in our own particular social context.

Strangely, there seem to be no graves of *Homo sapiens* in early Europe for a long time after they arrived there perhaps 40,000 years ago. Although we have found graves and evidence of ritual among the Neanderthals whom they replaced, we have no such evidence in our own species until the Old Stone Age. It seems impossible to know whether our early European ancestors may have cremated such remains or exposed them to natural disintegration in the weather. There is little help here in understanding our early human selfness. But the Neanderthal graves do confirm our belief in emergence of the self-understanding that enables us to identify with these early people.[74]

Recently, a skull found in the 1950s in South Africa has been dated (by means not available then) to 36,000 years ago. It matched measurements of early European *Homo sapiens'* skulls elegantly. The claim is made that this links all of today's human beings with Africa. We are left to speculate backward from late pre-historical evidence of nomadic settlement of Asia and Europe, of early villages, using some documents like proud monuments of early kings engraved on stone. Remnants of early settlements, such as those in prehistoric Scotland, have been dated back to 6,000 BC.

> The inhabitants were hunters and fishermen. About two thousand years later, a
> second group arrived -- the Neolithic people. Some of their stone houses remain in
> Orkney; the well-preserved stone-built village, Skara Brae, attests to the wealth
> and stability of its builders.[75]

Residual humans such as the cannibalistic Korowai of New Guinea[76] give us a few clues about early people, though we recognize their own evolution. With the help of recent scholars our speculations should always be tempered by our own careful examinations. For all we have learned about ourselves, hopefully our thoughtfulness will not be as biased as speculators of the past.

A recent scholars, Lewis Mumford, mid-twentieth century historian[77] examined an amazing array of ancient documents and archaeological findings and with great care speculated on the thousands of years of human evolution. It seems that little progress had been made in what we call "civilization" during the greater part of the long span of years before the Agricultural Revolution. Yet, by the time the city emerges, there was sophisticated stone knapping, and people had been solving problems of their environments for a long time. They had long been singing and dancing together in simple expression of their humanity, and there must have been substantial progress in the development of languages in families, tribes, and villages, already spreading some

elements of common vocabulary and ability to speak more than one language. They had begun a lengthy period of experimentation with what we call "socialization." I find this emergence well symbolized by the familiar life cycle of the butterfly; the larva forms the chrysalis where the miracle transformation occurs. But the analogy breaks down immediately since it is usually only a matter of weeks before it escapes from its cocoon, transformed. Nonetheless, in those few weeks, the metamorphosis is complete; a different creature emerges from the cocoon. Mumford's picture is of the painfully slow metamorphosis of socialization, taking literally thousands of years. And so in this study, we find that a rather new human being has emerged in the cultural transformation we call civilization.

In primitive times we must have been like the butterfly governed by instinct. But the gift which sets us apart also requires that mature humanity would only be reached by learning from trial and error. By using our active, imaginative brains we have the grace to consciously choose our path of development, however innocently that was once done. There are many, lacking perspective on this lengthy process of human learning, who cannot free themselves from the fact that humans have often been as cruel to one another as any animal. These speculators insist that it was warfare that shaped the social human being, ignoring the earlier honored history of primate and human cooperation.[78] The advent of oligarchs in the larger settlements and early cities seems irrelevant to them, apparently. But the binding qualities of song and dance in any size gathering of humans has long evoked the pleasures of people innately sensitive and increasingly social and thoughtful, producing what we call celebrations.

These were celebrations of life, not of blood lust. That they were turned from free giving of self to others in joyful play was an accident of human choice. Even the generosity exemplified in the Pacific Northwest native American potlatch got out of hand.

Returning gifts of greater value could drive people into poverty. It could easily follow the path of others and become a giving of gifts to leaders of whom one wished favors. It was not suited to very large groups.

No doubt the practice of placating spirits with gifts empowered people to live with greater confidence. Hand crafted gifts gave way to animal sacrifice. Only sophisticated religious organizations could put large bulls to death for religious rites. And it has been speculated that human sacrifice still practiced in biblical times was the ultimate perversion of what began as simple generosity. That this bizarre development was instigated by proud and powerful leaders cannot be doubted, and civilization suffered as a result. This perversion of human community came to require slaughter and became a grotesque sickness.[79] What began as a practice of thankfulness, generosity, became sacrifice.

One of the long-lasting products of ancient socialization was the refinement of the art of persuasion. While its origin may have been in common, ordinary community, skill became an important contribution we call "rhetoric." Likely, it was also perverted by self-serving dissimulation within growing aristocracies and the unscrupulous could use tricks of rhetoric to their own ends.

By the one word, "city," we quite literally refer to the abode of "citizens" and their culture in the various "civil" units of "civilization.". Here the polyglot, multi-cultural villagers came together into new, creative relationships. However else we may evaluate the city, it is the civil unit which evolved since about 5000 BCE into a stable and flexible social form to govern large numbers of people. In my view it was in its origins a happy and felicitous coming together. There must have been joy in these people to make the city so attractive to them that cities grew quite naturally for a while. In them the people shared their previous village dances, songs and rituals; they shared the cultural elements already part of their lives. They could show off. And they were stimulated by association.

During the long prior span of time after the emergence of *Homo sapiens* (which some estimate occurred only 200,000 years ago), human beings had developed a substantial culture of multiple families living near one another in extremely primitive hovels, as Mumford says, "little better than a beaver's lodge." The space each claimed for private living was tiny. Clearly, though their self-consciousness had been developing, society was still extraordinarily local and parochial. The wider world had only an "out there" identity. People were self-protective and a little proud of themselves and their families. Throughout our existence, the instincts inherited from our past served to help us survive the rugged uncivilized world "out there." As civilization began, the chrysalis of socialization began to shape a new culture for humans. As urban civilization emerged, unlike the order Lepidoptera, people had to learn to put the instincts of early survival behind them. Those inborn behaviors became impediments as people gradually took control of their lives, shaping first our physical environment and adapting to it. And then, over immense stretches of time, our predecessors realized that their capabilities stretched far beyond their immediate environs and they reached out. In their developing intelligence humans have persistently chosen to control their animal instincts and adopt more humane behaviors to realize their full humanity.[80]

B. PREPARATION FOR CIVILIZATION

The city appears to have been the cocoon of civilization. Our primitive ancestors had come a long way to create human beings capable of being citizens. In the previous tens of thousands of years their advance in social skills was substantial. And then the movement to cities began. The challenge of living side by side with a bewildering variety of others in the magical new city challenged their adaptive ability further. The "magic" in the minds of early citizens was in a massive extension of their intellectual capabilities. It was a scintillating variety of people, stimulating their imaginations. In this magic, they had begun forming their new urban culture, the basic form of civilization. With this background ancient people would gradually define the city, the culture, and our civilization.

Earlier folk, after the Agricultural Revolution, still spent little time indoors. Outdoors they foraged for food and hunted, and spent much time observing and figuring out the world about them. Apparently, their brains were ready for developments they initiated. It appears that very early in evolution the brain structure called the amygdala had become the center of the sense of smell. In our animal predecessors, the insect eaters (insectivores) were nocturnal. At night they had little need for sight, but a keen sense of smell was of great value. Before primates emerged from the evolutionary tree, the amygdala also had absorbed the functions of sight and hearing.[81] It was on its way to becoming the motor center of the brain. These enabled the human mind to develop into a socializing human being. The hundreds of thousands of years that passed as the various predecessors to humanity developed were vividly illustrated in the recent discovery of a complete skeleton of a three-year-old child dated about 3.3 million years ago. This child probably died in a flash flood and the body was deposited in sand which covered and preserved it in northeast Ethiopia. This three-year-old was only 18 inches tall. The ancient woman named "Lucy" (of the same species, *Australopithecus afarensis*) was also very small. She lived 150,000 years later.

The remains of this ancient child reveal that about 2 million years after departure from the primate stem of evolution, our ancestors still retained some ape-like characteristics. The throat structure of the three year old child, scientists said, would have produced sounds more like chimpanzees than like humans.[82] It would seem that language was yet to develop. Some now estimate that human language might date back 500,000 years. Geneticists have found that most of the genes involved in language have some sort of close counterpart in other species.

That does not mean that people were talking to one another, as we do, anytime early in humanoid evolution. After the brain's earlier allocation of neurons to acute scent gradually migrated to serve the human eye and ear, evolution had other changes to make before the human mind was ready to explore the sounds of voices. In that interval, people carried on communication. We are quite aware of our use of gestures, "looks," and facial expressions. The brain's allocation of much of it to deciphering visual awareness of lips and eyes reminds us of the persistence of nonlinguistic communication. Early people surely used these and vocal sounds now totally lost. We have sometimes called pre-lingual communication "telepathy." Arnold Toynbee suggests that this "is still an indispensable means of communication for human beings, and if the use of language were ever to cause this 'sixth sense' to atrophy, we might find that language, unaided by telepathy, is an inadequate instrument."[83] In fact we have little evidence of the use of language until the emergence of use of abstract symbols we have found on the recording sticks of shamans (perhaps 5000 BCE). Recently, human scratches on rocks as early as 77,000 years ago have been found.[84] And pictures of human forms possibly drawn 600,000 years ago have been found in England. These suggest that symbol-making had a very long history before the shamans began using them to aid recollection of events, the movement of the sun, and passage of seasons. Possibly there were marks in the sand, and also some broadly understood postures, as well as the possible "sixth sense," which preceded even these. Or maybe the scratchings were part of the human search for expression beyond these.

One might suppose that by the time such symbols had been created, the human mind had been constructing words to designate specific locations, animals and other things for a long time, shall we guess, 100,000 years? We will also guess that these things were beginning to take shape, bit by bit, in the thousands of years before that and the development of language probably accelerated after this late date, so that by the critical date of 10,000 BCE, a vocabulary sufficient to deal with all aspects of life -- and the explosion of agriculture at that time -- was practiced at least here and there, particularly in the developing aristocracies. The people who lived in this culture were stimulated to develop a view of self much larger than the view of self held by their predecessors and, thus, their need for language to communicate about it expanded.

Surely by this time, perhaps as language itself developed, they would repeat what others had said and begin to compare views of others with their own. Naming provided for comparison. And the mind developed further. Some would remember a favored idea and the brighter of them might well have insisted on everyone repeating it. Like a chorus responding to a narrator, people spontaneously responded to their story-tellers. Perhaps that was the earliest – and natural – rote learning. The sound of one's voice is pleasant and awareness of self was enhanced by voice games which led eventually to speech.

Eventually certain such sounds might have been routinized during their occasional celebrations.[85] Again, those who were more fluent likely would lead the people in speaking their common knowledge. Speech must have become a universal fun activity, perhaps second to listening to the human voice. Early religious leaders undoubtedly evolved fairly naturally from their fluency. They surely began to develop leadership skills at the same time. Ritual would evolve from community celebrations, from singing and dancing. Leaders would gain skills which later could easily be exploited for personal gain. Insistence on repetition of events would naturally follow a proud leader's success. No doubt the people loved such leaders for their prowess, and for their provision of opportunities to gather, to speak, to sing.

Some of their events eventually became "sacred." Some leaders would insist on their own recollections of previous patterns of group behavior. Over scores of years these would gradually become set and difficult to change. Some of them became attached to certain language, and even to special meanings created about their origins, about the gods whom they believed to be in charge of nature, the stars, the winds, the rain. Those who became adept at leading such sacred rituals we have come to call "priests."

We easily speak of earlier beliefs as myths, but for some people these remain powerful symbols of their past.[86] In the myths we may well find embedded evidence of our evolution. Some people in each generation had chosen to develop skills of perception and thought and became shamans who often were able to reiterate large parts of the mythic history of their people.

Eventually some people became medical experts fitting the accumulated knowledge of illness to the body of knowledge of their own time. They came to be called "doctors." They may have been the first empiricists who literally felt the body for indications of swelling and brokenness. In late ancient times, an immense sensitivity had developed to the salutary effects of herbs and spices -- perhaps the first store of human knowledge. It is evidence of the evolution of the mind first tuned to survival – a long, slow exploration of environment.

Weaving, pot making, even stone cutting probably became common skills. Some people became engineers, constructing dams, canals, moats and irrigation systems. With the late development of cities, some people became architects and began a long tradition of extensive use of stone in buildings and monuments. Such building projects, entirely dependent on subservient labor, nonetheless stimulated untold minds to think beyond their plight. Though totally intimidated, the human mind struggled against the current realities of life.

The list is endless, incorporating every trade and skill of the ancient world. These people created every possible option for storing and carrying grain. They wove nets for fishing and capturing birds. They created garments of skin and of woven cloth. They invented sewing, perhaps first with sinew, until they learned to spin yarn, string, thread and rope. They made needles from bones. They drilled holes long before hand cranks and gears. They were ingenious at shaping and construction of wood. Long after invention of the sled someone made a wheel with an axle and constructed the first wagon, eventually fitted with hard-metal rims to add to the clatter of civilized life. Civilization had begun to shape the nature of human life and of peoples' perceptions of themselves as capable of modifying environments and living as self-conscious beings.

C. THE EMERGENT CITY

After adroit leaders persuaded the people to build secure storage for excess food, the city began its ascent in function and complexity. Religious leaders no doubt insisted that such an auspicious place would be fit for a shrine, a focus of developing rituals, setting in place patterns of respect for the secure center of their emergency food supply. Eventually, this powerful place became the natural location for the residence of the city leader and his growing retinue. It has been labeled "citadel."

Such a move of the chief away from the residences of the people into a protected location probably occurred after early civil chiefs allied themselves with religious leaders (we would call priests) to consolidate their power. With the priests' help (shamans had long been keeping track of things), the civil leaders could better anticipate seasons, droughts and floods, When chiefs joined priests in the secure center of the city, the power of the citadel was enhanced with an important exception.

The people had always been vulnerable to attacks of predators. Wild animals – large ones – were common in their day. The lion remained a symbol of this threat long into the ancient period. In the villages the best hunters would naturally kill the predator. The Chief of a tribe also would enlist the best hunters to kill them. Was it not a natural step from this function to house these strong men in the citadel? There they could be quickly mobilized. And now our image of the citadel is complete. The citadel was impregnable. The leaders were secure within its walls. Soon the Chief would become King.

The people were uncovering the mist of animal ignorance and instinct, discovering and remembering, as they expanded their thinking repertoire. Before the city emerged, they had begun to talk of things, places, people, and that people were all different. My self was different from your self. As the millennia passed, slowly, ever so slowly, older children saw life a little differently from their parents. The age-old pattern of teenage rebellion became more pronounced. Little human beings were not only dependent on their parents; when they grew old enough to hunt and forage with their fathers and mothers, they had also to observe different things, better strategies, improved methods, and how they felt close to their peers and increasingly distant from their parents. "Different" took on a new coloration. The basic human self was beginning to show itself.

Generation after generation, the growing ability to discriminate shaped an increasing sense of "otherness" among human beings in their many villages. Stray travelers from far away places seemed really strange, sometimes to the point of aversion. Although there was already a strong sense of the very ancient habit of showing kindness to strangers, a growing sense of self gave people sharper questions, more inquiring minds and perhaps more suspicions. All of these were important new sensibilities. The people had a new sense of their own distinctiveness of which they would have been, like ourselves, just a bit proud.

It is important to note that early strangers were probably isolated adventurers or persons who had been chastised by ostracism in their previous communities.[87] Ostracism, was of course, a nearly universal sentence of death in those many, many years when people could not easily survive apart from a community. (Robinson Crusoe's foundling Friday is modern myth.) On the one hand, everyone knew that ostracism might have resulted from someone more powerful in a community taking spite out on this unfortunate person now found wandering into a different group of humans.

On the other hand, adventurers and traders would bring stories with them. Humans developed the skills of hosts to gain as much from strangers as possible, to learn of "others," to learn of their inventions, to understand better the strangeness -- differences

-- among people and to have new stories to tell neighbors. It was an advance in the sense of self, a reaching out of myself toward the contributions of others to my knowledge and to me, my self.

All of these things (and no doubt others) were stimuli to development of *Homo sapiens'* self-image. The human mind, we know now, is always growing, always changing. But this knowledge has for many, many thousands of years not been understood as an enlargement of the human capacity for self-understanding. We incorporated knowledge into our culture as "learning." It was something added to our understanding. From the earliest times, when adults grasped that their progeny understood more today than they had yesterday, they sensed that children could be taught things. They began to see people as animals who store knowledge in their memories. That knowledge was understood to be the learnings of those who have preceded us, first our parents, then our peers, then all others. We humans were, definitely, part of the world and the world seemed to be largely a stable, unchanging place. Yes, storms, floods and earthquakes occurred. But they were aberrations, exceptions, attributed, as religious explanations developed, to the will or caprice of inexplicable forces.

Learning was not just "factual." In fact, people probably had no sense of truth as we know it. Everything seemed to be as it was. They did not differentiate imagination from dream from physical or factual, literal, or analogous. The shaman or leader of ritual might try to induce participation of those listening in his realistic portrayal of a dream. We still treasure the story-teller's skill but we do so in a very different culture. All human beings have been involved in this misunderstanding; it is part of the maturing of the human mind, a recognition of our growing awareness of our amazing human mental capabilities. Memory, piecing together the bits of experience, comparing views of what happened, realizing that others have different recollections, accommodating leaders' views while holding one's own views in abeyance. As understanding of our learning capability has grown, we came to idolize the agreed version of knowledge as the font of all good. Culture ruled.

D. THE ANCIENT CITY SHAPED OUR CULTURE

As small cities gave way to larger cities, some human beings began to see themselves as organizers and rulers. Leaders had begun to understand that they could command their fellows to build canals and walls. Someone decided to raise the area where their granary rested above the level which flooded regularly and enlisted enough manpower to move the dirt and construct walls. Thus the citadel higher than the plain on which all others lived began its ubiquitous existence.[88]

And, no doubt, as protector of the sacred and of the religious leaders themselves, and of the warriors who protected the city from wild animals, the leader of the city moved his domicile onto the mound and into the protection of the citadel. The setting was prepared for the emergence of the large city ruled by the oligarch, eventually a king. All this was capped, often, by the claim of the king to divinity, as interpreter of their gods' commands if not himself the giver.

Long before, tribal leaders had learned to designate loyal followers to manage certain of the affairs charged to them. Such small-scale bureaucracy worked rather well until, perhaps by example of the "king," selfishness prevailed over stewardship, and corruption became commonplace. Greedy self-images were rationalized easily as the social scene was regularly defined in terms of the ignorance of average people. As civilization burgeoned, leaders could find bright people to tutor their children and those of others (should they see the value). But probably for a long time before that the pied piper of English legend was a person who especially enjoyed teaching children stories, songs and dances and was supported by willing sharing of resources by their parents. Kings could host visitors from distant and nearby cities, and learn of their inventions and their solutions to problems. Neighbor cities' plans for aggressiveness was brought by wandering dissidents. Leaders became managers not only of projects to benefit the community but of information affecting the defense of the city.

Leaders' self-image grew with the growing civilization of the city. Unfortunately, the greedy part of the self seems to have prevailed. If it had not been so attractive to leaders as seems to have been the case, it is possible that peaceable relations could have become the rulers' dominant pattern, but this did not happen. The social Darwinists have often identified altruistically inclined groups negatively. From that point of view they were futile and unrealistic. Without defense they would inevitably be easily defeated and not survive. No doubt leaders did feel forced to meet force with force, perhaps to resist raiding of their stores of food by a city where crops failed for two or three years and the people were faced with starvation. The granary was a critical innovation of the city, allowing secure storage of grain for years if necessary. Joseph in Egypt has long been the Western symbol of this much earlier learning. So the belief that force must be met by force would generally prevail. The spiral into a violent culture was bound to prevail long after the cost of warfare exceeded the wealth of rulers and their capacity to rule huge numers of people. The ordinary people would be driven into poverty as community wealth was usurped by militarism.

In many cases the motive for aggression was probably no more complicated than simple greed like that of the king of Pythagoras' home city of Samos who used his vast navy for piracy. There were, after all, trading conventions already in place very early in the history of the city which could have been used to purchase neighbor's excess food stores; records of trading are numerous. But instead, mobilizing residents to resist impending attacks, sending out spies, counseling warrior leaders, and commanding citizen armies became the leader's calling. The culture of war had been established for any motive.

The average farmer (as the vast majority of people were) was probably not fully aware of the vortex into which city life had moved. As kings became more powerful, they extracted "tribute" from weaker cities around them, and eventually established empires, exacting tribute with which they built monuments to themselves, adorned themselves with rich and elaborate costumes, and bullied and coerced all kinds of people into obedience. Of course, this didn't always work, and there were rivalries, coups and defections -- even from Alexander's highly disciplined Greek forces after his death -- the second last Western empire. Rome followed directly on this debacle, having perfected its sophisticated military in the Adriatic basin.

In the ancient cities the average human being had been emerging from the primitive with increasing rapidity. The economy was very small, mostly a matter of food-gathering and hunting. That world was almost completely individualistic. But those with close associations in family and tribe could be counted on to assist in moments of injury or illness. All the while, the human self was evolving, becoming increasingly self-conscious, and social. The people thoroughly enjoyed associations with nearby families and celebrations when they gathered naturally from time to time. It is probable that they developed patterns of social activity which we might identify as religious very early in this context. When they assembled, the drum beating, shouting and singing gathered others. "Singing" may have been in weird tones unfamiliar to our sophisticated ears. There was no form, no scale, no conscious harmony. And yet, musical pipes 35,000 years old have been discovered and tuned pan-pipes from 2,000 years BCE. In assembly they expressed joy in life and shared stories of visitors, if any, or stories of encounters with beasts. They eagerly shared the invention of the potter's wheel, and the plow, well before 3500 BCE. By then, all the chief forms of containers (clay jugs, woven pots, stone bowls) were also known.

People were increasingly attracted to the common, safe life of the walled city. It seems to us that they gave up much of their individuality, and their freedom for it. But we must remember that at the early stages of city development the peoples' sense of self was not highly developed. Apparently the tradeoff was felt as a pleasure and an advantage, or perhaps as a necessary move. The countryside was getting more crowded, and belligerent attitudes were more frequently expressed. "A tooth for a tooth" was a substantial improvement over lawless, ruleless, ruthless behavior of which all animals are capable. That primitive code is engraved on a stone carved to commemorate the humanitarian rule of Hammurabi over Babylonia at perhaps 2100 BCE. His code was a genuine improvement.

By this time all the animals that we know today as "domesticated" had already been tamed, and their flocks and herds invited predators. In the villages before the cities we might identify the first marks of civilization: the ditch, the canal. The reservoir, the moat, the aqueduct, the drain, the sewer are all essential to the development of the city. The image of common power, "look what we can do," motivated more control by the king and further exploitation and control of the people.

About 3500 BCE the smelting of bronze was invented, the first hard metal of the modern world. As usual, it was the kings who had the resources to commission bronze work and in that practice the production of armaments was most important. It made the city with bronze weapons much superior to the neighbor with none. But it was not long before other kings managed to accumulate sufficient wealth to obtain bronze weapons also and the battle widened.

As cities became empires, it seems that they had no trouble raising armies to undertake their plunder. No doubt there were many immigrant hunters in these cities, chiefly men whose skills lay in stalking and killing. Power exhibited in successful battles made them more feared. Clearly less powerful kings would agree to pay tribute without battle, increasingly concentrating wealth. Babylon, Assyria, Egypt, and many others gained total sovereignty over hundreds of thousands of people before Greece and then Rome achieved supremacy.

The people apparently were wholly intimidated to comply with the call to arms and to face death with a sort of ferocious animal-like resolve, slaughtering other humans as if they were savage beasts. Their experiences of predators and enemies was renewed by skillful oratory. The pride they may have had in happy village life was replaced by identity in an invincible city. They had been deprived of individuality and were made part of a great and mighty empire made up mostly of the ignorant and the slave. These people had recourse only to the king, or his minister, who replaced the wise village elder or chief who had tried to help resolve ordinary interpersonal problems in earlier communities.

Except for a residual self hidden behind subservience, people became obedient animals. Still, their creative minds continued the taming of nature. About 1500 BCE humans learned to smelt iron and a cycle like that of bronze application to farming tools and to weaponry was repeated. And war became more costly. Outside the eastern Mediterranean orbit, populations had also grown. Cities were also centers of community life, and oligarchy was also taking form. But for the most part they escaped the tens of centuries of subservience which had shaped the dominant eastern culture. The Greek people escaped that repression and created a rather different culture.

Karl Popper, in exploring the pre-Socratic philosophers of ancient Greece,[89] supposes that it was Thales, who broke the pattern of rote learning. It seems that Thales (636-546 BCE), who had been singing his lessons to listening students for years, was questioned by an innocent nephew; teachers simply were not questioned! In this encounter, however, Thales recognized that other teaching techniques -- specifically questioning -- might be preferable to rote mimicry. It was such an obvious improvement in their teaching technique that most Greek philosophers adopted it. Thus the whole panoply of Greek philosophers demonstrates early emerging signs of modern self-consciousness. We have habitually credited the method of questioning to Socrates -- the "socratic method" -- for within the century he had become a master of it, recorded by Plato.

It is evidence of the power of human culture that the Greeks' focus on learning, on the sharing of knowledge, especially through Socrates' embodiment in Plato's writings, should have raised human consciousness of the nature of knowing so high as to dominate all Western culture, and, in the modern period, most of the world. It may be that Socrates' voluntary acceptance of the deadly judgment of the city fathers was the ultimate demonstration to date of the capacity of the human being to overturn animal instinct as well as a demonstration of his commitment to knowledge.

But it is not knowledge as such which makes us human. It is an even more primitive capacity to discriminate, that is, to think about almost anything, to make sense of almost everything and to choose between alternatives. We have been working at this skill for a long, long time. The earliest human being also had to make sense of his or her life. It made sense to find good sources of familiar foods. It made sense to find some sort of shelter from storms and predators. It made sense, when cities were formed, to find the security they offered as well as the beauty of human fellowship. Everything in human life can make sense if we use our heads -- think. In thinking lies the possibility of wisdom, and of being truly human -- and the capability of overcoming residual instincts.

E. THE EMERGENT SELF

Knowing everything is not what makes us wise. This is a truth of life which is not new. It was familiar to ancient people. The wisdom literature of the Bible was not secular understanding by less spiritual members of the community. In wisdom literature our progenitors recognized all kinds of learnings which may lead to wisdom. Each may be helpful in the right circumstances.[90] But knowledge is not the ultimate question. As we learn in the greatest wisdom book of all time, the biblical book of Job, wisdom is better described by humbled joy than by pride in human knowledge.

The human bias toward knowledge has impeded our self-understanding. This is not because knowledge as such is not good, but because we humans have not been alert to how easily we make things into idols; knowledge was gradually established as the end-all of human society. It seems that early in our evolution knowledge served us well, providing for passing insights on to others, first to family members, and very quickly to others living close by. We learned automatically, we moderns say; earlier people would have said, "naturally," perhaps, with an almost instinctual recognition that humans are learning animals. In "lower" animals, the capacity for learning is very restricted. In human beings it seems to be limitless, especially since we have developed the capacity to abstract, to think in categories, to formulate ideas, and to project into the future. There have been stumbling blocks, such as the long-time barrier in science and mathematics named "non-linearity." But conquering these piece by piece began during the ancient period. (Where would mathematics be without the Eastern discovery of "zero"!) Viewed from an evolutionary point of view, it is well to understand that such capabilities began forming in ancient people.[91] Modern achievements build on a long evolutionary past. And their essence is to be found in learning to think, a skill shown in the extraordinary modern development of methods..

For example, take the capacity to abstract. Surely, the shaman's carved symbols demonstrate his early abstraction. At the time of the earliest city-state, language probably still lacked most of the needed organizational and abstract words needed in the emerging world. But we had become facile at constructing language by then, and the vocabulary grew so that by the beginning of the iron age (the biblical period) it was capable of the immense range of discussion evident in the Old Testament. At the same time the Greek philosophers developed abstraction and progressed to the point of an extensive and elaborate vocabulary fit to describe nature and ideas. And the Greeks enjoyed a flexible language made manageable by early introduction of the alphabet about 800 BCE. Vocabulary, a knowledge of words, became the measure of intelligence, of who we are intellectually.

Though it was only elites who learned to read and write until modern times, even in the iron age (1400 BCE - 300 BCE)[92] literary skills had developed to a very high polish, demonstrating the ancient beginnings of this skill. The writings of Isaiah (perhaps 700 BCE) are among the world's great poetry, and the sophistication of much other ancient literature is quite amazing. It demonstrates the establishment of human intelligence. It was unequally distributed in the population as are all human traits today. There is no way to discount the "smarts' of ancient humanity. But neither is it strange that so much of this writing is in poetic form. Each person was part of the culture in which he was born and matured. The teachers of those centuries learned long before that putting their wisdom into verse made it much more amenable to learning. But it would take literally thousands of years for the numerous literary forms we enjoy to evolve. Advertisers today from time to time hit on jingles that get repeated as icons of specific products, too.

This sophistication demonstrates the persistent growth (even in an oppressive world) in the capacity of the mind to handle complexity. The self-image of primitive people was severely limited by the simplicity of their minds, but as the millennia passed their capacity increased. Humans invented plows and irrigation. They created doodles and ornaments. They made images out of clay and carved symbols into sticks that they carried from place to place. They recorded trade on clay tablets and papyrus to report to kings' ministers. They learned and repeated stories and sang songs. They danced and participated in rituals. They loved one another and ministered to each other in sickness, trouble, and sorrow. The human being grew in capacity steadily through the oppression of the city-state and continued to grow when authority became a right of government, and obedience a requirement of citizens.

From the beginnings of development of society, leaders have functioned as intermediaries, natural aides to communication. Some communication we think of as daily business. It has proved beneficial for leaders to manage relations between cities or states. People have always marveled at those who were fluent in their language and those who could comprehend strange tongues. Perhaps naively, they gladly assented to support decisions made for all of them, knowing the leaders and trusting in their judgment.

Human pleasure at hearing their tongue used well seems to have continued. So demagoguery has always blossomed. Speaking is basic humanity closely allied with human sociability. But gradually the ascendency of people in exercising authority became a burden. With emergence of the power-usurping kings of the city-states the age of natural community was long since over; rulers replaced leaders in increasingly demanding social hierarchies. Condescension replaced friendly assumption of leadership. These were the forerunners of those who maintained the oligarchic character of Medieval society. We call them aristocracies., Since more people shared elements of power and authority in such a society, more people became supporters of the status quo. Even among the Israelites the sheep-like character of human beings in the iron age encouraged the excesses of oligarchy. Whether popular support of Samuel's reminder of the kingly exercise of power might have changed Israel's future one can only guess;[93] again, social evolutionists would probably tell us that it would have spelled the end of Israel in ignominious defeat. Their insistence on kingly rule did not save them that ignominy. One presumes that assent of prophets brought many kings to power. The power of individuals to shape human community requires our attention.

Egyptian cities did not have the same conflicted history as those in Mesopotamia; they are not characterized by citadels. Nonetheless, the whole Nile valley was for much of the ancient period under autocratic rule of an absolute monarch who often claimed divinity. And the people were enslaved as in the east.

In 500 BCE the Persian empire included all of western Asia as well as Egypt. It included some Greek cities which revolted and incited Darius I to seek revenge and add Greece to his empire. His army encamped only twenty miles from Athens, but was attacked and routed by a smaller force of fierce Greeks. Darius died while planning another attack. His successor, Xerxes, approached Athens with a huge force through the pass at Thermopylae defended by Sparta. He took Athens only to be defeated by its navy near Salamis. Xerxes left a large force in Greece only to be defeated again, ending the Persian threat. By this time, larger numbers of intelligent people had begun to find themselves as thinking, discriminating people.

F. THE ANCIENT MIND OF PYTHAGORAS

The Greek history was different from Mesopotamia and Egypt.. Tribal independence was sustained longer in the mountainous topography of the Balkan Peninsula. Greece (now the south end of the peninsula) has always included many islands. Its numerous city-states were assorted monarchies and democracies dating back to the New Stone Age, the period of Mesopotamian city development.

The end of the early Iron Age corresponds roughly with the end of the golden age of the Greek philosophers. The Greek city-states disintegrated in internal warfare, and war against Persia, following the same path as the rest of the Mediterranean basin. During the life of Aristotle, Philip of Macedonia in the north achieved victories sufficient to dominate the Greeks, and his son, Alexander, then conquered the greatest extent of the known world before Rome. He used the well-trained generals of his father effectively. The spread of Greek culture and language is marked by the establishment of cities named "Alexandria" throughout the east. It was a mark also of the emergence of a new mentality in *Homo sapiens*.

The defeat of Persia in 449 BCE spurred a surge in Greek civilization. In the previous century Thales was perhaps first of the "pre-socratic" philosophers. Thales is dated by his prediction of an eclipse which astronomers tell us occurred in 585 BCE. Thales may have traveled to Egypt where he appropriated their knowledge of geometry, a very simple geometry which enabled him to calculate the distance of a ship at sea from observations taken at two points on land, and to estimate the height of a pyramid from its shadow. Thales' science and his philosophy were by our standards crude, but out of them grew the first school of philosophers called Milesian.

Miletus was a thriving commercial city, Bertrand Russell tells us, in which there was a large slave population and a bitter class struggle between the rich and the poor. We are familiar with the warring history of modern Europe; so also the "golden age" of Greece was not a "time of peace." Russell quotes to us, to set the record straight:

> At Miletus, the people were at first victorious and murdered the wives and children of the aristocrats. Then the aristocrats prevailed and burned their opponents in the open spaces in the city as live torches.[94]

If one wishes to emphasize it, the evidence is that the militaristic heritage of the early cities bequeathed to the culture of Europe a severe cruelty -- even as a new world was in the birthing. The ancient class structure had become increasingly entrenched, a necessity in governing growing thousands of people, but breeding internal social conflict. What sort of image of self could humans have developed? They were dependent on civil order but only gradually came to realize that they were in themselves more than slaves. In fact they began to understand that those who were socially their superiors were often less intelligent than they themselves.

Of all the Mediterranean peoples, those in the Aegean peninsula seem to have enjoyed a longer period of freedom from the hyperbolic war culture of Mesopotamia. Perhaps this is what enabled individuals to realize more of their own potential than was usually true of their Eastern counterparts. By the eighth century BCE Homer arose among the aristocrats and he shared their viewpoint. Within a century Zoroaster in Persia and Josiah in Israel had also established names for themselves, and soon after the early Greek philosophers emerged. Pythagoras (582-507 BCE) was born when Thales was about 54 years old. Bertrand Russell says, "(Pythagoras) was intellectually one of the most important men that ever lived, both when he was wise and when he was unwise."[95] (It is a reminder that all wisdom does not flow from any one great thinker!) Pythagorus also visited Egypt. He settled in Croton, one of the Greek cities in southern Italy (like Miletus) that fought each other fiercely. Obviously, brutality and violence were not unknown among human beings. The people eventually turned against Pythagorus, and he moved to another of the Greek cities where he died, a man of his own time but more acutely aware of himself than most.

Pythagoras founded a religion in which many of the precepts were primitive nonsense. Cornford considers Pythagoreanism a reform of Orphism and through it of Dionysus.[96] Pythagorus' mysticism was peculiarly intellectual. It was an opposition between the Olympic gods and other gods. Pythagoras had a marked influence on Parmenides and on Plato who found him a source of inspiration. After another century and a half, Plato, like Pythagoras, was strongly dualistic and was committed to life after death, which was an escape from the very harsh character of life everywhere in ancient times. "All the systems he inspired tend to be otherworldly ... condemning the visible world as false and illusive."[97] The opposition of the rational and the mystical first appears among the Greeks, and Pythagoras was definitely a mystic; however it was a contemplative mysticism, a frame of mind in which he produced a new mathematical knowledge.

Pythagoras lived in the sixth century BCE. It was the middle of the golden age of Grecian culture. The primitive antagonism to strangers had long been put aside. Greeks knew and respected one another, except when they didn't – aggression was part of the ancient culture. Greek city-states were independent and remained so (until Phillip) while

Babylon had already passed through a series of empires.

Pythagoras' self-image had evolved to support his independent mind in a free-ranging exploration of his world and construction of his own views of it. Mathematics became his strong suit and, with typical human hubris, he found it all-encompassing. He is the source of our meaning of "theory." He thought mathematics the supreme knowledge. Mathematician *par excellance*, Russell, reminds us that to those who have experienced the intoxicating delight of sudden understanding that mathematics has often given, the Pythagorean view will seem completely natural, even if untrue. Pythagoras, in any case, in the contemplative mood, is the father of pure mathematics. "Number" was as basic to existence for Pythagoras as water was to Thales. The exhilaration of mathematical discoveries undoubtedly had something to do with this. It speaks of a fertile mind and an unrestrained imagination.

Like all human beings, Pythagoras was a child of his time. His religious sensitivities were like those of his time and place. It was the zeal of his followers which established his considerable reputation in Croton. They embodied aspects of secrecy, and apocryphal stories of intimidation of his followers to maintain secrecy are not hard to find. Like the contemplative mind which he brought to mathematics, his religion was an intellectual mysticism, a pattern which reappears throughout history, especially among bright people. It is a view which exudes self-confidence and extensive intellectual constructions. Within such a mind things fit together perfectly without examination of every "unnecessary" detail. But such minds often overlook things that are not so easily dismissed by others -- exactly why we take pride to task and seek humble consultation and conversation. The distance between Pythagoras' self-understanding and our emerging sense of self is the subject of another chapter.

The value to human beings of the contemplative ideal was thus enhanced and became important to both theology and philosophy. Later, the monastic urge developed with a vengeance, one might say, and contributed to the success of gnosticism which severely challenged early Christianity. We might see the growing emphasis on this withdrawal into secluded quarters as the beginning of the age of asceticism, an almost frantic effort to deny the degradation of the time and find paths to contemplative unity with God.

IV. THE SURVIVAL OF THE SELF: FROM REPRESSION TO ERASMUS

Beaten down and brutalized, the citizens of the ancient world suffered severe repression. In spite of this, at all levels the burgeoning civilization had continued to invent itself, earlier in regard to control of water supplies and physical protection of crops, and later in organizing vast gangs to build monuments and empires. These huge crews of slaves have been characterized in Enlightenment thinking as the first machines.

The negative effect of this oppression on the self-development of people was to have consequences for tens of centuries. But gradually the evolution of the human self worked its magic. Here and there bright people found themselves in circumstances in which they might make significant contributions to the mind of human beings. Here we look at emergence of the West from what we call the "ancient" period, from the founding of the cities in the Mid-east to the emergence of Europe and its blossoming in the Renaissance. It is a period of four or five thousand years, the starting point being rather ambiguous. It encompasses the end of the ancient world and the early Middle Ages.

A. TWO LESSONS OF REPRESSION

Our civilization emerged from the primitive foundations of largely independent, small-group learnings from tribal and village cultures. We had much to learn about getting along together in growing cities. This was fraught with perils. Not the least of these perils was the misuse of language. Sometime after we began speaking, people learned to use their talk to influence others. They could teach and they could persuade others -- and they could deceive and coerce. People learned to influence others for good or ill.

As it developed, the city and especially the citadel became the source and symbol of the power of an aristocracy which one person usually dominated. This person probably became chief because he (or she) was the most adept in the community in the use of language. And before long such leaders discovered that they also could use force to control unruly neighbors, as well as wild animals and intrusive marauders. Chances are good that leaders quickly learned two sets of skills: First, the use of persuasion and second, the use of force. The end result was the rule of wealth based on slavery and a culture of violence.

Something else occurred which may be the root of one of our most difficult social problems today.   Leaders soon discovered that any valuable thing they had was safe in the citadel. In fact they were masters of the food stuffs stored in the granary and of a growing store of lethal weapons needed by their warriors. As belligerence boiled over into opportunistic warfare the flow of spoils and of tribute could amount to more wealth than anyone had laid eyes on before. Leaders could quite covertly assemble wealth far beyond the ordinary accumulation of extra goods in any home. It eventually infected leaders with the sin we call avarice. Of course their language skills provided easy explanations.

In spite of the destructive effects of oligarchy on the self-understanding of people, the positive products of that horrendous past must not be forgotten. Out of four millennia of autocratic repression, human beings learned and packed away in the old brain, not only humble self-denigration, but also a priceless capacity for self-discipline. The human self is not just the free spirit who emerged from Africa a hundred thousand years ago to carry his DNA into every habitable place on earth. During those early years *Homo sapiens* were learning about the world and himself. By 10,000 BCE people had learned to till the earth, scatter seed, and nurse the ill. His pleasure in associating with other people brought him into larger and larger settlements, tribes and villages and eventually into cities. That is where we find the first signs of what we call "civilization." Humans had already begun to incorporate discipline into the primitive self.

The ordinary tasks of the village joining with others to hunt down a marauding beast stalking them or watching for enemy hunters infringing on their favored watering holes contributed to developing self-discipline . As people moved to the larger and larger settlements which became the early cities, they necessarily had to learn new ways to relate to others, new ways to cooperate. Though their self-understanding was limited, they learned the self-discipline needed for socialization. They learned to restrain themselves. As the cities grew, the demands on them increased. Innovative attackers made old fortifications inadequate. The walls built to protect their food supplies became gargantuan. At every stage of development there were new challenges and the people adapted to them. Without notice, the people were learning new social skills while being forced ever more fully into the condition of slavery. Today we consider this vicious oppression, but then it gradually became the condition of most people world-wide.

We are free spirits embodied in the physical world, pummeled by life-enabling and life-constraining forces. Before cities, people had already learned to respond to the drums calling them together. They might know from the drums whether it was a call to celebration and perhaps feasting, or to a village project, perhaps to build a new irrigation ditch, or address a serious problem, a move to a more fertile or better watered location – or signs of belligerence from a neighboring or "enemy" village. We had begun to learn to control our preference for roaming free without any constraint. People were learning more and more who they were. But oligarchy repressed the evolutionary trajectory developing the minds of people toward increasing responsibility. Oligarchy forced human beings to think of themselves with exaggerated humility. The habit became so deeply engrained in them that we have labeled their demeanor to be sheeplike – following without question. The late modern "humble self-denigration" identifies this attitude carried over from Medieval culture.

In the emergence of Europe, huge numbers of people carried this culture to extremes. But Europe also produced the phenomenon of institutions of selfless service in the many groups, small and large, involved in caring for the sick and poor, and in monasteries copying manuscripts. The self-image of such people was self-effacing, compared with early human life when people had been able to live and move pretty much as they pleased, subject only to constraints of survival and primary relations. The role of monks in collecting and burying dead bodies in the desperate times of plague is an illustration of the amazing growth of this social consciousness in the development of Europe. Building on the humility of the repressed self, the Church contributed a rising awareness of humans' individual value by its focus on forgiveness and eternal reward. Sin, remember, was quite universally acknowledged. Accepting the burdens of monastic service gave evidence of both humility and self-discipline. Both of these are important capabilities of human beings.

B. EARLY SOCIALIZATION

We live among other persons to whom we must in large measure adjust. We call it society. Only recently have we learned the amazing intricacy of human social relations. Nonverbal interpersonal communication began among the animals and has found new heights of subtlety in *Homo sapiens*. Signs found in postures, hand signals, facial grimaces and smiles, and hundreds of other unconscious acts are an important part of our communication still today. We take most of these signs for granted, learning how to be members of our society beginning as babies.

The stages of human life have become the subjects of intense study for at least fifty years. We know now how to read and influence others even better than people did before us. They had only their experience and a limited insight into the childhood, youth, and young adult development on which to build their relationships. These and other stages occur before children are ready to assume adulthood. Unfortunately, as civilization grew in the early cities under repressive rulers, children and young people Inevitably learned when they were very young how to sublimate their native curiosity. Their growing minds became subservient, and generation after generation lived as quiescent "sheep." Consequently, their contributions to their cultures were severely restricted. Nonetheless, evolution of the human self continued. The challenges of living were severe and real and provided creative outlets. The search for food, the raising of crops, domestication of animals absorbed skills as they emerged. Even in whole life experiences of repression the elders of forty or more years embodied increasing stores of learnings and skills. Life was short and by the Roman period it had become cynical, but there is increasing evidence of the evolution of the human self.

It seems to us strange that kings very early assumed so much power and even claimed to mediate divine power to their people. Some think their access to shamans gave the early kings privileged access to their memory sticks to predict some natural phenomena. In addition to assembling power in their own person this gave these leaders a mythological power, Mumford suggests, expanding their ability to achieve public works (in modern terminology) of immense magnitude. Dams, aqueducts, and irrigation projects were public goods. The huge walls of citadels and cities became major signs of power. A leader acting as a natural aid to communication, as between ordinary people and rulers of other cities, could also become a mediator between people and a fearsome god. After all, humans had only begun learning to express their own thinking, and this contributed to the humbling of the people.

In the warmer lands, we know that many kings exploited their positions of power to the extent of assuming divinity themselves. This assumption of spiritual power appeared sporadically over the centuries. Undoubtedly, some monarchs and sincere religious elites may well have been a little fearful of such appropriation. But it does appear in all civilizations from China to the Mediterranean world to America.

From our point of view, this seems to have postponed the development of self-confidence and thus of the development of modernity. The art of persuasion was polished as leaders exercised almost magical control over hoards of people. In ancient Greece this skill became articulate, and the Sophists, like Gorgias (485-380 BCE) were polished experts in the art of persuasion. Their golden tongues established the art of rhetoric classically demonstrated in the Roman Cicero (first century BCE) whose text on rhetoric was taught for 1500 years. We note that leaders' use of rhetoric contributed to the persistent evolution of the Western mind as people were challenged to follow speaker's arguments and, increasingly, to evaluate their intent.

The flexible, and intelligent human being was an ideal slave. Like automation today, once instructions were loaded, they ran according to programs under the control of elites. Some have likened these masses to the first "machines" fit to serve their masters. Slavery, still a world-wide phenomena today, became more unbearable as the millennia passed until by the nineteenth century voices throughout Europe and America renounced slavery categorically. This is one of the signs of the evolution of the human mind. Nonetheless, the persistence of slavery is one of the pieces of unfinished human business that begs decisive attention in our day.

The long period of oppression in the early cities was instrumental in increasing the capacity of people for self-control. The irritation of people no doubt flared often. In it there was a natural learning about living together. But over hundreds of years of repression, gradually, the independent spirit was crushed by rulers who feared unruly crowds and mobilized the aid of aggressive hunters to control the people. In the city, self-control came to mean obedience to the rulers. Like their domestication of animals, ordinary people became like sheep. Their self-development was stymied. Their society was autocratic. But nonetheless they learned to live together in growing and diverse communities.

The capacity for self-discipline which emerged from this repression is a blessing which will be felt increasingly as we continue to evolve as people in mass society. Even our lengthy experience with aristocracy has had its salutary values, Out of the pangs of simple oligarchy we learned how to use hierarchy and bureaucracy This is not to say such capacities might not have developed without repression. That this was our path, however, is a fact of world history. We rejoice in the survival of humanity from that audacious period of leadership development. In the disastrous lessons of thorough egotism, we humans learned important social lessons for successful civilization.

C. CONSOLIDATION OF AUTHORITY

The repression worked so effectively that oligarchic control of large populations became an unquestioned cultural necessity. Well into the modern period the assumption that people required centralized, autocratic control to live together peaceably governed most of Europe and the rest of the world as well. Hobbes immortalized the view in

Leviathon in the seventeenth century. Unfortunately, no one expected this view to bring peace; war was an accepted solution to human aggressiveness..

The repressive condition of populations in Europe persisted for another thousand years after the fall of the Roman Empire. From 500 to 1500 CE authority was understood as "authorities," that is, as those who exercise authority over the people. We remember that authority was originally authorization by people to lead them in a task or to guide them as a people. Authority was originally *given* by people to one another, to family members, to clan leaders, with a willingness to participate. Among the "uncivilized" of the Western world this natural democratic practice seems to have hung on much longer than in the Mediterranean basin and Middle East. Gradually, the social pressure of accepted life patterns we call "culture" was shaped by leaders into an authority to which the increasingly sheep-like people gave *obedience*.

Somewhat later than in Mesopotamia, the provision of kingship to govern some of the cities of Greece also took root. They were not entirely free of the effects of restrictive oligarchy. History records government by "tyrants." Greece, too, had a repressive, slave-based economy. It was a condition of life throughout the world, found also in the great civilizations of the Americas. The difference seems to be that in Greece the cities were separated by mountains and fast streams. They had different experiences and learned the value of an aristocracy of a more democratic sort along with lessons of oligarchy.

In North America and, especially, in northern Europe many people seem to have persisted into the Iron Age in relatively "primitive" modes of direct human conduct of relationships. Perhaps harsher conditions of life kept the population more sparse until later in history. America, like northern Europe, contains many regions, that is, areas largely separated from one another by natural barriers. There the residual spirit of individual independence apparently contributed to development of democratic flickerings such as the Iroquois Confederacy of Five Nations,[98] and to the Reformation challenge to the established order. We know too little about the ancient Picts and Celts to say much more. But they once populated both the northern islands we know as Ireland and Britain and a strip of the central European continent as far east as the Black Sea.

In the first century CE and then another 1500 years, the repressed mentality of the ancient world characterized the culture of our immature civilization. John Dominic Crossan describes the "Mediterranean culture" of New Testament times as one in which everything reflected the patron-client relationship. Brokers, Crossan tells us, "were clients to those above them and patrons to those below. The system, at its best, gave some hope for recognition to lower class individuals but, at its worst, confirmed their dependency and oppression."[99] When Roman authority self-destructed in the middle of the first millennium CE, the evolved conception of authority was well-developed. At least three thousand years of experience gave authority a universal venue.

There was no other trusted method of governing than strong exercise of power. But there was for some time a power vacuum after Rome disintegrated. The northern tribes in Europe had been making incursions into the Roman empire for many years when Kublai Khan swept down out of the far east mountains into the Middle East. Alaric took

Rome in 410 and Gaiseric in 455. Pope Leo I somehow kept Atilla from sacking Rome. The Franks and the Normans were gradually converted to Christianity and became leaders in the southern European remnants of the Empire. In the process the Roman infrastructure deteriorated and there was no effective central power. In 476 the last Roman emperor was deposed by Adoacer.

The Church was building its image in the religious sphere, trying to fill the vacuum left by the end of Roman power. It was not long before the paternalism of past authoritarian regimes was institutionalized in its assumptions. The church's old network of "bishops" (overseers), located in population centers throughout the Roman empire, had grown up among those perceptive church leaders who demonstrated their faithfulness and their insight. They were accorded authority by the institutional church to exercise a degree of power over the believers in their area of jurisdiction. Devoted monks persistently launched out into the wilderness among the pagans, eventually converting many, including the northern tribes.

Originally, conceived in the model of a shepherd who cared for the sheep, the role of bishop reflects the best of the ancient paternalistic, caring attitude toward the people. But as the fourth century broke, the Church had literally become the church of the empire at the behest of Constantine. The cultural role of moral authority increasingly fell to it. It was closely related to the people themselves. The Church did what religion has always done. It knit people together. And people together form a unique force in evolution, the creation of culture.

D. EXPANSION OF THE NEW CULTURE

The new culture of Europe was beginning to take shape. Augustus who died in 14 CE left the Roman Empire one great nation. The names of Caligula and Nero stand out as tyrants in the next few years. Claudius extended the empire to Britain, a conquest extended by Agricola after Titus destroyed Jerusalem (70 CE). Emperor Hadrian built a wall eight feet thick across the narrow part of Britain about 125 CE to ward off the barbarians from the north. Throughout the Empire Christianity expanded constantly. It was a time of sifting and of exploring through encounters with people who lived beyond the Mediterranean basin. All the time these encounters were expanding the mind, finding more people receptive to the religious orientation of the invaders.

Early Christianity was preached by Jews to Jews as the central authority at Jerusalem recognized by Paul attests. But Paul was a Roman citizen who grew up as a Jew at the far northeast corner of the Mediterranean Sea. Tarsus was on the Grand Roman Road from France across Europe to Palestine. He was well acquainted with Greek thought and sensitivity and pressed the view that Gentiles should be baptized although they were not circumcised, leaving the ancient rituals of Judaism behind. Peter, our story goes, fortuitously had a vision supporting Paul, and he had an opportunity to baptize an uncircumcised Roman. This spelled the end of domination of the young Christian community by the Jewish rituals and opened the emerging church to expand into the Gentile world. It also attests the depth of baptism, a more ancient religious rite.

A variety of forces were driving a wedge between Jews we would call orthodox and Jews whom we might call liberal, who were less tied to the historic rituals of Judaism. The ritual of sacrifice was left in the Temple when Jews started meeting in synagogs., But the view that Jews were chosen by God who had saved them from the degradation of the ancient world was not lost in the process. The Jews held firmly to this belief though it was rejected by the Gnostics. Uniquely, legendary Jewish beliefs always contained that element of history to which they attested. Elaborate rituals of cleansing and righteousness ("purity") multiplied, unfortunately, distracting people from the central focus – but being chosen was always there, never forgotten.

The end of ritual-based religion was already evident by the time monotheism developed. Perhaps it was a necessary evolutionary step in focusing attention and understanding responsibility. Like all ancient people, the Jews had been trapped by the effectiveness of ritual in uniting the people. Jewish ritual was focused on the Temple. When the Temple was finally destroyed, they were set adrift, except for those who had already divorced themselves from the Temple component. But giving up the ritual practices around Temple life, including sacrifice, these Jews retained their commitment to being the people of God and used the Hebrew ritual language to sustain it. They found in the innovative activity of the synagogue, the reading of the Torah and the Prophets, and the conversational debating of meaning, the new path toward fulfillment of their faith. Faithfulness and duty were being effectively transmuted (not replaced) by fellowship. The people knew better than any in the past who they were as individual persons and their social context in Judaism.

Ritual had become an instrument of class distinction. This was held in tension with its religious significance. There was a succession of temples over the Jew's long history, a consequence of Jerusalem's location at the crossroads between Egypt, the East, and the North.[100] In the process, the Ark had been lost. But the Holy of Holies which once contained it remained, stark empty. It might have been taken as a final sign of the end of all efforts to represent the presence of God, and of the outspoken denial of objects of veneration. The logic of the Jewish history was that God needs no stand-in, not an idol, not a sacred object of any kind, not even a sacred place. During the siege of Jerusalem by the Romans in 70 CE the last Temple was leveled. The Jews dispersed and the central focus of Jewish ritual on the Temple became a thing of the past, speeding the evolution of the Jewish mind.

The major voices shaping Europe in the first millennium were those of Plato and Aristotle on the one hand and Paul and the four gospels on the other hand. Both voices were accompanied by great choruses of interpreters and teachers and there was no cause in either for them to be antagonistic. The one focused on secular knowledge, the other on knowledge of God. Though Plato dabbled in philosophy of religion, he was far from being a religious leader. And Paul urged a way of life which was hard to fault until the first century Christians followed the ancient Jewish practice of refusing to give obeisance in pagan rites. The division was a circumstance of culture, of nationality, and of location in the Mediterranean world. But most of all it is a signal of a major cultural change: the untangling of religion from politics and philosophy. Plato and Paul represent the keenest minds yet involved in this sphere of confusion.

Plato was in no small part responsible for the exaggerated emphasis in the Medieval Church on the spiritual dimension. To him the body was a distraction from the pursuit of knowledge and the vision of truth. On both counts the Medieval monastery was a relief from the burdensome body. But there was never a time when the Church embraced Plato's extreme elevation of the spirit over the body. The age old position of Judaism emphasizes their unity, and this was always understood among Christians, except for those who sought Gnostic views or escape from reality.

Plato developed Socrates' thought and his sagacious questions about the meaning of words such as justice and goodness. In the first millennium his influence on the development of European culture was immense. His eternal Forms fit nicely into a Christian view of heaven. His *Timaeus* – an imaginative account of creation of the world – was easily interpreted to fit Genesis.

Plato's philosophy of a permanent and eternal realm was popular. The Church found itself struggling often to justify its doctrines of the unity of mind and body and of bodily resurrection, though it found Plato's notion of immortality attractive. In that atmosphere, Aquinas suffered for his Aristotelianism though it might be said that his appreciation for Aristotle's empiricism contributed importantly to the Renaissance and the Enlightenment. This was a world-shaking departure from the ingrained tendency to focus on the spiritual, but Aquinas is still fundamentally Platonic; he is said to have been nearer to Plotinus than to Aristotle.

Plotinus was known largely through the work of Porphyry who, on the one hand adopted Aristotle's logic and on the other was anti-Christian. This provoked a reaction by Justinian who closed the schools at Athens in 529 CE. The writers of the New Testament were not much influenced by philosophy, but by the second century (well after the end of New Testament writing) the Greek way of thinking had matured, and Plato became the leading non-church thinker. Clement and Origen added an intellectual spirituality in which Christians sought control of the body and its passions through the cultivation of the mind. This meant study of philosophy and the Bible. Eusebius collected texts which supported meditation on Christian doctrine and Gregory of Nyssa developed allegorical or "mystical" interpretations of scripture.

Plotinus, 204-270, is considered the last of the great philosophers of antiquity. His life spanned a desperate, decline in Roman fortunes. Russell tells us that about 200 CE the Roman army had begun exercising its power, choosing emperors in return for monetary rewards and then assassinating them to obtain another round of rewards. This military sickness opened the empire to the incursions of the Germans from the north who decided to seek their own ends rather than hire themselves to the Emperor. The Persians threatened from the east. Increased taxation and a population reduced by disease spelled the end of a disastrous century. Emperors Diocletian and Constantine saved it temporarily after Plotinus' death. That world, Russell reminds us, seemed hopeless to nearly everyone.

Perhaps the dour Christian image is a reflection of Plotinus in this misfortune. But the Platonic spiritual world of goodness and beauty, the eternal world of Forms attracted all of them, "pagans" and Christians alike. Russell tells us that "The theory of ideas, the mystical doctrines of the *Phaedo* and of Book VI of the *Republic*, and the discussion of love in the *Symposium*, make up almost the whole of Plato as he appears in the *Enneads* (the books of Plotinus)."

Yet it has been said that in Plotinus Plato lived again. In Plotinus a "trinity" is made up of unequals – no doubt a source of much of the persistent debate about the Christian Trinity. His trinity is, first, One (which has no need of others), the second person as *Nous* (difficult to translate, but usually "spirit" with an intellectual dimension), and the third person as Soul (which, contrary to the Stoics, lives after death). "The Stoics had identified Nature with God, but Plotinus regards Nature as the lowest sphere, emanating from the soul.... This might suggest the Gnostic view that the visible world is evil, but Plotinus does not take this view. The visible world is beautiful; it is the abode of blessed spirits."[101] Some passages of Plotinus are beautiful enough to be compared with Dante's *Paradiso*.

Russell considers Plotinus the end of Greek philosophy and a beginning for Christianity:

To the ancient world, weary with centuries of disappointment, exhausted by despair, his doctrine might be acceptable, but could not be stimulating. To the cruder barbarian world, where superabundant energy needed to be restrained and regulated,... [Plotinus helped] since the evil to be combated was not languor but brutality.[102]

Christian philosophers would carry Plotinus' views forward as neo-platonism. It was Plato with a twist. All in all, nonetheless, mental capacity was growing and with it the confidence of an astounding number of people to express themselves at the end of the ancient period.

Christendom gradually took charge of constructing a viable world view in the embers of antiquity. It was a conscious construction of a new culture. It was pursued with immense energy and care, and no small learning. The long, slow development of knowledge and of effective means of passing it on through generations prevailed over the mean mentality of primitive human beings impatient for immediate gratification. These patterns eventually produced the educational breakthrough of academia. In the twelfth century cathedral schools gave way to universities which, at least in England, have had an unbroken history. With that development, the West settled on a basic societal structure of three institutions: Government, Church, and School.

The main sources of books of Greek learning were translations made in Spain from the Arabic. The East was Arabic, Greek and Persian, not Latin, and when the Arabs invaded Spain, they provided a pathway for the Greek heritage to reenter Europe, albeit in Arabic. Averroes Arabic Aristotle was made available to the West in Latin early in the thirteenth century. His writing had been lost in the Germanic invasions in the fifth and sixth centuries when Belisarius added southern Spain temporarily to the Byzantine empire.

After another invasion by Arian Germans, a common legal code was instituted and clergy encouraged learning. Byzantine culture remained strong, but it was the Jews who had immigrated in large numbers who shaped Spanish culture. Early in the eighth century the Muslim Tarik crossed the Straits of Gibraltar to open a period of Moorish dominance until 1174. As Christians began a slow reconquest, they expelled thousands of skilled farmers, craftsmen, and scholars. The process ended with total expulsion of unconverted Jews in 1492 under Ferdinand and Isabella. Unseen, in the prism of contemporary bias, Spain had been an amazing melting-pot of exchange among Islamic, Jewish and Christian scholars and Europe was the beneficiary.

Before this debacle, Archbishop Raymond of Toledo instituted a college of Muslim, Jewish and Christian scholars skilled in Arabic, Greek, and Latin who translated Aristotle and others from the Greek and Arabic into Latin. This stimulated awareness among Western scholars of a rich trove of unknown Greek work. Russell tells us that the yoke of orthodoxy was not so severe in Europe as to squelch writers. A man could write, and then if necessary, after public discussion, withdraw parts considered heretical. [103]

Strange as it may seem, since Plato was so generally embraced in the young Christian Europe, Plato says that God created only what is good. That was welcome news in the unhappy conditions of life of the time. But it leads to a divine pluralism, though the human capacity for rationalization produced intellectual solutions to this conundrum. Nonetheless, some Gnostics were incredibly consistent leading to views in which God was the creator only of evil -- an illusion which fit that depressed world differently.

Gnosticism is said to be more ancient than the Church. The Greek *gnosis* applies to an oriental secret knowledge which must be learned. It establishes a religious aristocracy of secret knowledge. It attempted to explain all cults. It had done battle with the Greeks and the Jews. Such popular philosophies threatened much like pundits of radio and television do today. Alexander's proud march east had brought to Greece the influence of Eastern religions. Their speculative thinking fascinated Greek and Western intellectuals and tended quickly, if temporarily, to dominate. In its residue Christian mysticism recurred.

How Christianity escaped being one of the many forgotten creeds of the early Roman Empire and emerged in a viable form is a study in itself But we remember that the Jews had already experienced the Eastern influence in the Babylonian exile, and returned to Palestine under the Persian Cyrus with Ezra and Nehemiah to reestablish a modified orthodoxy. Its singularly practical and unspeculative cultus did adopt Eastern mystical doctrines of angels and spirits, and hierarchies of heavenly beings. But these did not dominate Judaism and have been increasingly ignored.

The unrestrained allegory of Eastern religion shows contempt for reality. It seems to be another approach to the problem of evil which preoccupied the Gnostics – denying evil by preoccupation with fanciful tales . The imagination of human beings had made immense progress out of oppression! Yet the possibility of twisting stories into negatives remains a human capacity. The particular patterns of long and active central ritual of story telling among the Jews may be the reason for their successful negotiation of early

Gnosticism. For them, ritual was not "rites" as we know religious practices, but an active rehearsal of historic events albeit often in the mode of legend. The Jews retained a lively sense of history.

The *Zendavesta*, said to be written as early as 1200 BCE, is the scripture of Persian Zoroastrianism. It tells of conflict between Ormuzd and Ahriman. Ahriman in jealousy at the creations of Ormuzd created evil spirits who destroyed the good. The shattered pieces were reformed into man and woman. Ahriman seduced the woman and filled the world with noxious things. In the third century CE the Persian Mani developed his own version of Zoroastrianism. Ostracized in Persia, he wandered far and wide preaching his religion.

The influence of this story is evident in the fourth century Manichaeism that seduced Augustine during his school days. It is seen in the Kabbalistic literature of the Jews and in the Gnostic heresies. The Essenes it has been said gave the Kabbalistic theory practical form. Their practice was to withdraw from the world into asceticism in seclusion. Mystics have often drawn from such Eastern traditions. Noteworthy, perhaps, is the Essenes' unwillingness to offer sacrifices in the Temple and a shrinking from taking animal life which is characteristic of Oriental philosophy. Though Buddhism never established itself in Europe, it made its presence felt through Gnosticism, especially in Alexandria. All these influences contributed to the emerging shape of Europe and witnessed to the world-wide evolution of the human self seeking fulfillment.

Alexandria had long been the seedbed of Gnosticism, true to its ancient role in polytheism, materialism, and superstition. The essence of Gnosticism is an aristocracy of enlightenment explaining a popular creed. The Gnostics claimed that the plain sense of Homer and of the Old and New Testaments concealed a hidden meaning of spiritual truths veiled in allegory. Philo (20 BCE - 50 CE) produced a Gnosticism in the days of the Apostles. Philo was a Platonist influenced by the Stoics. After the fall of Jerusalem, Christians found Philo helpful in reconciling Greek philosophy with Jewish Scripture. The letter of Paul to the Colossians seems to have been occasioned by a Gnostic Christian Essene orientation as contrasted to Pharisaism.

Marcion was eminently practical and at the beginning of the second century reflected the rationalism of the Greek world rather than the romantic mind of the East. For him the Old Testament opposed the New. His arguments sound very modern. He did not say that the God of the Jews was evil; God was just, but limited in intelligence. He believed that redemption is from ignorance and is the imparting of higher knowledge, a prime Gnostic belief. Marcion was not troubled by the mystery that preoccupied many Gnostics. Like other Gnostics, Marcion divided people into spiritual, psychical, and carnal, but unlike many others, insisted on a rigid purity of life. He is the first rationalistic critic of Christianity and shared the error of pronouncing all passages not squaring with his view to be spurious or corrupt. It was a hubris anticipating the emerging self-confidence that later consumed nineteenth century Rationalists.

It was Origen (185-254) who provided the bridge between the Jewish scripture and Christianity. His writings are more compatible with Plotinus than with what orthodoxy would ultimately allow. Well versed in Greek literature, Origen studied under a great Neo-platonist; he also studied Hebrew and compiled a six-column Old Testament, the first column being Hebrew, the others various Greek versions. His intent was to correct some errors and to show the superiority of the Septuagint. It was a step toward the biblical criticism that emerged with force in the nineteenth century.

The fallout from Gnosticism is worth noting. One is tempted to wonder that the first commentator on a canonical Gospel, the first harmonist of the Evangelical narrative, and the first scholar to pronounce an opinion on the Canon were not orthodox Christians but Gnostics. The drive to explain, define, and understand the writings of the New Testament was due to Gnosticism, and to the opposition it aroused.[104]

It appears that this evaluation by a reputed church historian commends our view that growing self-confidence demonstrated the advanced mentality that would dominate the future a few years ahead. After the end of the first millennium Europe was finding its way in a new world. Europe had emerged from ancient obscurity in our history. And Tamerlane's audacious fourteenth century in the East was near the end of rapacious oligarchy.

Confusion followed Plotinus' formulation of Neo-platonism in which the Aristotelian conception of God as "self thinking thought" became fused with the Platonic world of eternal Forms, the world of changeless perfection. Aristotle's logic was extensively used for centuries. But generally he was considered an atheist and he denied the immortality of the soul. Aristotle was forty-one years younger than Plato who was his mentor for many years. He left Plato's academy and formed his own school which gave us Aristotelianism.

E. END OF THE OLD ORDER

For centuries it was expected that the name under which writing was presented was intended to provide it an appropriate reception. Three of the Christian Gospels were given the names of men who everyone knew were part of Jesus' original band, Matthew, Mark (associated with both Peter and Paul), and John. Luke accompanied Paul. As Europe opened a new era, the importance of authorship became of first importance. The martyrdom of Polycarp (bishop of Smyrna) in 156 suddenly thrust this issue of written records into the foreground. He was the last person alive who had spoken with a person who actually knew Jesus, the disciple John. The time when face-to-face acquaintance could demonstrate authority was over.

Faced with multiplying forgeries by those who enjoyed the convention of applying famous names to their works, the Church found it necessary to identify acceptable writings. The "Muratorian Fragment" represents a midway position between limiting the accepted records to the four Gospels (Matthew, Mark, Luke and John) and the Gnostic addition of other memoirs and denial of a place for John.[105] This quandary disturbed the second century Fathers and was not settled until 325 at the Council of Nicea. By then Arius was busily preaching his view that Jesus was only a creature like ourselves, not divine.

The content of additions was the problem, of course, and the "Church Fathers," those conscientious bishops who felt the weight of perpetuating the Gospel, considered themselves obligated to speak forthrightly about those who propagated views which they felt were heretical. In the culture of the day, opinions were forcefully presented and argued. To our ears, the controversies which raged may seem biased and vituperative. But it is worth remembering that participants were part of a culture in which for thousands of years the eloquent person had achieved leadership with skill in persuasion. That demonstrated the practicality of training bright potential leaders in rhetoric, the art of persuasion, which continued to the sixteenth century. The development of rhetoric showed the growing ability of bright people to analyze speech and politics. The long cultural emphasis on the art of rhetoric paid off in developing many articulate spokespersons. This was the end of the old order in which writing was still subordinate to speaking.

In my opinion the patterns of Aristotelian logic and ancient rhetoric laid the groundwork for development of a gentile art of discussion, but that would take even more time. Like the vitriolic verbiage often heard today in legislatures, people who argue a point often exaggerate descriptions and extend illustrations past all likeness.[106]   Our brains are entirely capable of deceiving us, misremembering, revising, and neglecting aspects we dislike. The art of persuasion (rhetoric) was now becoming the art of controversy (politics). Until very recently, debate (dispute) was the common word for intellectual dialogue.

Unfortunately the failure of the Roman state early in the fourth century could not be stopped by a few new minds in key positions like Diocletian and Constantine. Allying with Christianity could not save it. Effective and sagacious innovations failed. Soon the chaos of private bailiwicks (power centers) extended the pattern of overlordship. Eventually, feudal enslavement grew throughout Europe. Feudalism was brutal and it was exploitative, no matter what acts of kindness and generosity might have occurred in the spreading sensitivity to others, and to the masses of people. It was still a culture based on strength, power. The underclass was still expected to know its place.

In the period from 600 to 1000 CE the popes achieved independence from the Greek emperors in Constantinople while the Greek church remained subservient to the emperor and refused to submit to papal power. In the last flickers of the empire, the Western pope allied with the Lombards and later with the Franks under Charlemagne who ruled for 72 years through the end of the eighth century. The title of emperor was passed on for over one hundred years as Europe fell into chaos. After Charlemagne Europe shifted to the feudal system, essentially a chaotic array of tiny bailiwicks each governed according to the dictates of its lord.   In 962 Otto I claimed the title of emperor of the Holy Roman Empire. He was to be temporal ruler while the pope ruled in spiritual matters. It was a period of experimentation with a form of government fit for a culture yet to be.

Feudalism, to be overly simple, was just another form of economic slavery. The increasingly independent landowners utilized the same organizational principles that the culture inherited. But changes were taking place. In 1356 the Golden Bull tried to regularize the election of the emperor but the ancient practice of hereditary succession prevailed as common practice. After 1438 the Hapsburgs were always elected, but after the 1530 coronation of Charles V the practice of obtaining the blessing of the pope ceased. It was a fairly ignominious ending to the imperial period. Nonetheless, the tenacity of outdated cultural patterns is demonstrated by the nature of feudalism and by the continuation into the eighteenth century of the coronation of emperors by the pope.

More centuries would pass before another lesson would be learned from the story of the ancient world. The end of papal coronation of the dying institution of emperor signaled the eventual end of the ancient subservience of religion to the oligarchs. While the earldy ancient liaison of religion with the rulers of cities may have been both amicable and appropriate, religious leaders ("priests"?) soon found themselves of necessity following the direction of the ruler. It was henceforth into the medieval period an unequal partnership in which the power and authority devolved to the ruler. We must remember that people had only just begun the long journey to appropriate human self-awareness and thus to social consciousness. We cannot expect that they would have realized what was going on.

Sometime in the middle of the ancient period some religious leaders must have begun to exercise their rising self-consciousness to examine the subservient effects of oligarchy. Obviously the people were treated like sheep. Thoughtful religious leaders began to ponder the thinking in their many cultures about the nature of gods who would make people subservient. They themselves were used to reinforcing leaders' needs for authority over the people. Some memories of ancient legends of pre-oligarchic religion, ceremonies and rituals remained embedded in their stories. There were among these priests some thoughtful persons who had been rationalizing their customs and exploring the place of God in their ritual. No doubt some of their people, as bright as the leaders themselves, were irritated at the meaninglessness of much of it and pressed them for better stories. The authority assumed by the oligarchs was increasingly resisted.

No doubt the clamoring of the people effectively started the process of separating the sacred from the secular. The marvelous unevenness of the evolution of the mind produced bright people to carry on this inquiry in all classes, in the aristocracy, the priesthood, and among the people themselves.

In the early Roman Empire, it seems that Augustus already made evident that the secular government had only a utilitarian interest in religious authority. It was not that leaders disbelieved in God or God's Providence, but only that for the most part they had to rely for all practical purposes on themselves. Their minds were mightily preoccupied by the development of organization and politics. Perhaps it was ultimately this evidence of the evolution of the human mind that shaped their gradual loss of secular power in and of itself. Secular authority, after all, had been using its power over religious authority less and less successfully for a long time.

The conflict between duty to God and duty to state sustained by Christianity became conflict between king and Church. The unity of the Church focused on Rome created a formidable power without arms. The Church represented the emergent culture – "continuity with the past and what was most civilized in the present." From our point of view the church embodied, beneath all superficialities, the humanity represented in Jesus. The heritage into which Christianity was introduced was increasingly individualistic. "From Alexander onward, individualism developed and was represented by the Cynics and the Stoics." At the beginning of the Enlightenment, Descartes captured it in his "fundamental certainty, 'I think therefore I am.' ... Most philosophy since has had this intellectually individualistic aspect in a greater or lesser degree."[107]

The secular rulers had become increasingly cynical, illustrated by Marcus Aurelius (121-180).[108] It was a frequent consequence of skepticism. The end of the Empire was not only written in the signs of an unmanageably extended geography, but also it was evident in the increasing self-confidence of its burgeoning population. Now, there were not only the power and wealth of emperors' and their related aristocracies. There was a growing class of professionals. And there were blocks of entrepreneurs making a good living and accruing wealth in trade. Marco Polo (1254-1324) and his family did not undertake the perilous journey into the hostile East lightly. They were well prepared to encounter selfish bargainers and highway robbers (who also made a nice living). They were shrewd in the very senses so valued today. By the end of the ancient period, which we set arbitrarily at the beginning of the Middle Ages, trade had long been a major factor in urban economy everywhere. The amount of travel across all lines is astounding. The accumulation of foodstuffs in the vast plains of the Roman empire was wealth ready to leverage the accumulation of gems and gold. Aristocrats the world over wanted their share of such wealth. And the cycle of avarice was set in motion for all time.

A consequence of the ancient regime was the effective separation of the people from their religious leaders who had obtained privileges of aristocracy. Religion had tasted the privilege of the citadel and the favor of the oligarchs. As it claimed its place in the emerging European society, it demonstrated the same repetitive instinct we have observed. The Church hierarchy, after institutionalization of the Church, came to emulate the secular authority in both arrogance and opulence. But most unhappily, the Church continued the practice of treating people as ignorant sheep. It was a significant error made evident as the Middle Ages moved toward the Renaissance.

Until the twelfth century the available Latin translations of Aristotle were incomplete and inadequate as demonstrated by Aquinas (1227-1274).[109] He modified his Neoplatonism with a serious use of Aristotle's empiricism. He saw our individual perception of material objects as the first source of knowledge. From this he inferred the existence of spiritual reality. His proofs for the existence of God at the beginning of his *Summa Theologiae* owe much to Aristotle. Nonetheless, the universities of Europe resisted him though no earlier Catholic philosopher understood Aristotle so thoroughly. Thomism was condemned at Paris in 1277 and then at Oxford.

I suspect that the expanding intellectual rigors of mathematics set in motion by Pythagoras contributed to the development of Scholasticism. By the time of Aquinas, Scholastic philosophy had developed into a very clear and rigid form which this doctor of the Church epitomized. Aquinas' long path of influence in European culture began in the thirteenth century. Unfortunately, it tended toward a very narrow acceptance of different views. The art of persuasion was still paramount, moving the culture ever more toward the art of controversy. The common element was the embedded sense of the adversarial – that is to say, my correct perceptions over against others' mistakes.

That narrow sense of self lacked the sort of self-confidence that we take for granted today. The Medieval society was still dependent on the labor of the large majority of people whose sense of self as inferior had been ingrained for thousands of years. Gradually that was changing. Authoritarian leadership was abundantly evident in the monasteries. As a member of the new Dominican Order, Aquinas enjoyed the aristocratic freedom of studying in Paris, teaching there and in the Papal Court, and eventually founding his own school. He also is an example of the value of lessons from the ancient past. His rigorous logic and exacting, simple Latin demonstrate the priceless heritage of self-discipline. For our argument here, we want to note that his brilliance foreshadowed the increasing numbers of scholars sufficiently self-confident to break out of dependence on the cultural authority of the time.

The Franciscans were not inclined to accept the views of Aquinas. Three important Franciscan philosophers were Roger Bacon, Duns Scotus, and William of Occam, all destined to be significant in the fourteenth century. Bacon was a mathematician with broad learning. He broke out of the authoritarian past in a confident and outspoken style. Among other vitriolic opinions, he maintained that the current translations of the philosophers from Greek and Arabic were incompetent. It was just one of his many offensive opinions, however true. He valued experiment highly (at a time when alchemy was popular) and identified four causes of ignorance: (1) Frail and unsuited authority. (2) Custom. (3) Popular opinion. (4) Obscurantism (concealing ignorance). These produce all human evils. He justified these by quoting authorities from Seneca and Cicero to Jerome and Chrysostom. He respected Aristotle. Porphyry he thought childish. He provides good evidence of the evolution of the critical faculties of the mind.

Duns Scotus was an Augustinian. A moderate realist, he believed in free will and leaned toward Pelagianism. William of Occam did not go as far toward democracy as Marsiglio of Padua, but he worked out a completely democratic method of electing the Church General Council. Within the church Marsiglio aimed at preserving it by democratic means. It is one more instance of the growing consciousness of the power of people and the need for major changes in the Church in what Tuchman calls "the calamitous fourteeth century."

After Charlemagne, the names associated with outstanding contributions to the formation of Europe began a doubling. In three centuries Avicenna, Anselm, Averroes, Mimonides, and Francis of Assisi arise. Then in just the thirteenth century we find Roger Bacon, Kublai Khan, Aquinas, Dante, Scotus. In the next century, in spite of the Inquisition, creativity then broke out in philosophy (Occam, Petrarch), in poetry and literature (Boccaccio, Chaucer), in science and engineering (Da Vinci, Copernicus). They included Wycliffe, Tamerlane, Huss, and Gutenberg. By then a reaction to Scholasticism had matured. Gutenberg had no sooner introduced moveable type when Erasmus and Machiavelli made their stunning contributions to the burgeoning understanding of self. But all were still supported by the feudal economy. The magnificent art of Michelangelo was financed by the sweat of the same subservient population as well as by a rapidly growing number of entrepreneurs. Evolution was evident, but working in its natural, uneven, but persistent way, change was occurring.

It is important to note that the creativity of the Renaissance occurred as the distribution of wealth spread. In the wings was Mercantilism, soon to replace anarchic feudalism, as more and more people engaged in creating wealth for themselves. That probably will prove to have been the natural burgeoning of one the most ancient means of sharing the earth's wealth, as prehistoric finders of gold and gems, and those who recognized the value of fields of stone suited to tool-making, traded them for goods they needed long before cities. In the growing lucrative trade the world grew larger. It spawned immense urban growth and supportive businesses. The human interaction spawned creativity and it has not abated.

John Wycliffe and Johan Huss exercised their considerable intelligences intending to reform the Church. Wycliffe was a highly respected don of Oxford, and his followers were expected to be scholars. Among them there were no "orders," meaning they were not placed in a hierarchy of church authority. Their task was to use their minds carefully and to preach constantly – persuade, persuade, persuade! He followed an English pattern sensitive to the vastly growing variety of people in every population. It exercised caution to avoid the impression that all good ideas could be put into practice quickly, and Wycliffe's early followers were equally careful. But after his death there were those who stretched the limits. There was a popular mind beginning to recognize the flexible human capacity to do much and to think expansively. It was oriented to explicit action and literal application of sophisticated doctrines (which tends to ignore subtlety). "Dominion by grace" was soon interpreted to bring ecclesiastical anarchy. This and two other points best identify Wycliffe's teaching: Acceptance of the Bible as the sole rule of faith, and his teaching on the sacraments. It soon became evident that the opulence of both Avignon and Rome in 1400 ignored the condition of multitudes of "meek and poor, and the charitable living of Christ." But the larger point of centralization of church power was contradicted also by the two papal residences, one under the heel of the French king.

Neither Wycliffe nor his followers had much sense of history or appreciation of the development of Church organization from the first to the fourteenth centuries. A bit like some reformers today, they wanted to recover the early church without regard to the necessary development of culture. In 1378 Wycliffe's enemies attack his "Lollard" theology of the sacraments and forced him to retreat from Oxford.[110] He died some months later. He signals the immense cultural change taking place. Wycliffe escaped the fate of other reformers but the tide of popular vigilante justice was rising. Theirs was a new self-consciousness still under the control of a vicious, outmoded culture. In some cases crowd behavior was not a lot different from the retributive ways in Miletus in the time of Pythagoras (cf. III. F.). The fourteenth century cultural self-image was still dominated by the sense of sheepishness – follow the one ahead.

Adequate government for this new world was still in the future. Its time was coming. It was not until the twelfth century that punishment of *heretics* by death, especially burning, occurred. The emperor Justinian's codification of Roman law in the sixth century had been promulgated far and wide and taught to barbarians by the church. Much was borrowed from it by the church, and in the twelfth century "sacred canons" were harmonized on the model of Justinian's *Code*. In 527 Justinian had issued severe laws for the punishment of heretics. "The stake had been sanctioned by Roman law for killing of parents, for arson, for sorcery and for a few other crimes; the burning of witches and sorcerers was still practiced." Heresy was not a civil offense but such burnings, so much a part of ancient times, had full popular approval. Savage times were not yet left behind.[111] Many clergy protested, but many apparently felt that it was a way to keep heretical teaching in check. Still, the French Waldensians[112] from 1200 and the English Lollards from 1400 succeeded in maintaining their existence until the Reformation.

Wycliffe's new translation of the Bible into English was not unique. In most countries vernacular versions had been prepared. Previously only nobles had been able to afford books, but soon rich townsmen could also buy them. There were many printers laboriously turning out wood-carved pages of individual books of the Bible in quantities never before available. Gutenberg's invention of moveable type was timely just a few years later (1454).

It was the time of the emergence of sensitivity to human capability, generally labeled "humanism." Petrarch (1304-1374) is often considered its first spokesperson. Chaucer was an early translator of Petrarch from Latin to English. Noteworthy among a growing number of humanists were Lorenzo Valla (who showed that the "Donation of Constantine" was a forgery), John Colet, and Erasmus. Colet followed the typical pattern of such people, studying in France and Italy. After founding the new St. Paul's school in London, Colet collaborated with Erasmus and William Lilly in a new Latin grammar used for generations. He died just when the Reformation began, but, like many of his peers, he was critical of abuses in the Church. Erasmus considered Colet his spiritual father.

Erasmus (1466-1536), a Dutchman, was, like Colet and many others of the time, a lifelong Catholic who was critical of the Church. His association with Colet, More and others stimulated him to learn Greek in order to translate the newly available Greek texts. He aimed his work at print publication. He urged his friend, Colet to write and publish also, but Colet preferred to lecture, a skill in which he was proficient. Erasmus was widely acquainted with a broad range of elites, especially in England. He was esteemed the model man of culture and was undoubtedly the broadest of all the humanists.

As the Renaissance faded into the Reformation, Martin Luther, John Mair, Ulrich Zwingli, Cranmer, Ignatius Loyola, John Knox, George Buchanan, and John Calvin appeared vocally on the scene with many others. They all demonstrated the emergent modern sense of self. All were northern Europeans except Loyola, a Spaniard. The economic system of the time has been labeled "Mercantilism." All of it was evidence of an expanding confidence in the human self.

The influence of Plato continued unabated, refreshed by Erasmus' definitive translations from new Greek manuscripts flowing in from the East. His translation of the newly recovered Greek version of Aristotle became a standard part of intellectual discourse, while Aristotelian Augustine proved a mainstay in formal debate. The evidence of human intellectual growth was everywhere in Europe.

V. RECOVERING THE SELF: FROM CONFUSION TO ARROGANCE

A. The Stimulus to Recovery

It seems evident that evolution is part of the order of creation, just as is the stability of mathematics, and the apparent regularity of physical phenomena, of birth and of death. We find at the beginning of the Common Era the conjunction or convergence of two significant strains of ancient eastern Mediterranean cultures, the Jewish and the Greek. The greatness of both of these will become evident in the twenty-first century. The end of the classical empires spelled confusion for that world. The collapse of Rome opened the door to the resurgence of familiar Greek culture and opportunity for the Judeo-Christian heritage to fill a critical vacuum in the culture of the Mediterranean. It was, in retrospect, the first clear occasion of evident evolution in Western culture.

Greece represents an intellectual culture, not an empire-in-waiting. Judaism represents in essence the recovery of a primitive religious impulse by the evolving human mind. The death of Rome signaled the end of several thousand years of the domination by the power of wealthy states infecting the Mediterranean basin and the Mid-east. At the end of the ancient period and in our struggle through modernity, we see the confusion such major cultural change wrecks on human beings. And we see the persistent twisting and tortuous reshaping of the nature and role of religion in human life – often in despair, but increasingly in hope, as we grasp the immense capability of the human brain.

Just as the vitality of the city was generated by the convergence of people from hundreds of separate and independent villages facing the necessity of adaptation to one another and to a new culture, so this spectacular macro-junction of Greek culture and Jewish culture produced a dynamic new Europe. The Roman habit of allowing popular local practices (granted the people's allegiance to Rome) set the stage. In both Greek and Jewish cultures the people had already been thinking beyond their neighbors for some time. This is the capacity at work at the difficulties in life of many minds, the ability to adapt to new conditions, and it shines forth throughout the history of Western culture. The Jews and Greeks had been learning the skills of adaptation with an unusual self-consciousness long before most others. The Greeks were stimulated by their varied tribes outside the Mesopotamian origins of empire. The difficulty of Greek terrain saved them from centuries of oligarchic domination that produced the sheep mentality of the Mediterranean basin. The Jews lived at a crossroads and had been incorporating others from their beginnings when they claimed to have been freed from slavery in Egypt in the middle of the ancient period. This gave them a significant sense of independence from the slave culture. The independence of both cultures was only relative, but its roots freed the intelligence still trapped in the slave culture to enjoy an enhanced new European sense of self.

This conjunction brought together two vibrant human strains.[113] Whenever human beings have faced the difficulties of adapting to one another and to accommodating one another, there has been a cultural explosion. Perhaps it was not always huge as in ancient Mesopotamia or nascent Europe, but small explosions can also do creditable work!

The presuppositions of the Jewish culture revolve around belief in a God who in the Jewish experience was a super-natural sentient being who is concerned for human welfare. I believe that the "children of Israel" shared their basic heritage more intimately than people of any other culture of record. It was not simply a ritual. It had not been reduced to abstruse symbols. The reason, of course, is that they claimed the story as their own past. Their story was not of abstracted gods; it was their own story. The people – still familiar with slavery -- shared in hearing the story of how their own flesh had been freed by God, as God's "chosen" people. The Jews always felt very special.[114] They had their own identity. Their identity was that of a community (like most people of the time) but also as individuals loved by God. While other people had rituals to point them to their religious beliefs, the Jews' rituals pointed to their own past which included selection as God's people. They understood this to mean that they were expected to be responsible by God and by their fellow Jews.

Before Moses, the children of an early, prescient man named "Israel" practiced the universal memory device of their world, repeated telling of significant stories. The progeny of Abraham constantly re-told the story of Abraham, Isaac, and Jacob, so that these people knew the legends about their "fathers" and appropriated them early in life. The story was a typical ancient amalgamation of fact and legend, but the Israelites were confident that the early encounters of these fathers with their personal God had occurred in the distant past and that this passionate God cared for their welfare too.

Their religious sense was unique. All ancient people had to face the bewildering passage of time. What was within their own memories was supplemented by strange legends constructed by their predecessors about an even longer period before that. Some of these constructions were pure imaginative fancy, we believe. Others were attributions of superior intelligence to extraordinary men (we think of the Buddha) who saw themselves clearly and were articulate about their world in the light of its burgeoning wisdom. Such people knew the stories of their cultures and created growing literary constructs out of their understandings. Some ancient religions grew as agglomerations of tribal gods (we think of early Hinduism) creating the view we call polytheism. Those stories tended to be descriptions of their gods behaving much like human beings.

All of the many known "religious" understandings of humanity and the world give us windows into the varied experiences of human beings evolving from animal to the twenty-first century. Vestiges of the earliest known religions tend to be focused on ritual and retelling of often fanciful stories. Especially in the East people focused on total commitment and absorbed excess energy in constant ritual. Both ritual and story demonstrate the active imaginations of evolving human beings. They, like all of us, tried to express together their origins, the purpose of their life, and the future of their progeny. It is native to the human being to seek to understand the present and past, and to anticipate the future.

In all these things, the bias in our culture is a preference for Judeo-Christian realism. We have as our heritage a long list of explorations of ways of explaining and relating to reality. In spite of conflict and dissimulation -- all the familiar foibles of human beings -- the Jews never lost their sense of history. This is a people who learned to listen and to respond out of their own experience; God was as real to them as to their forebears. The early hearing of the stories helped to fix in their minds a predisposition to identify themselves with those before them. They were a people who, persistently reminded, believed that they enjoyed that same attention of God. The word "personal" is modern. But this ancient people already had grown accustomed to a personal God. And that is the God we have inherited.

It is true that the Jewish people regularly neglected the core idea of their religion, and had to be called back to it. The prophets performed the duty faithfully over several centuries. The prophets were in a real way agents of the best in their culture, fully committed to its lessons, and open to its leadings. One of the most significant occasions was Ezekiel's call to return to Jerusalem, saving the Jews from absorption into Babylon. Those elites who had been deported could probably have stayed there (as some did) and disappeared into that culture. That is exactly what Moses saw happening to his people as he reflected during his exile with Jethro. The people had become inattentive to their faith. The comforts of Egypt left them half-hearted in their own identity.

Still Jewish faithfulness remained fairly stable throughout the historic period. The words of the prophets outlasted their short lives many, many times. Their messages were told, read and reread generation after generation for the hearing of the people. This depth of commitment to the basic message stands in wry contrast to the ritual-based religious commitments of most other ancient peoples, and to the reactionary involvements of the Greek people in fertility and mystical religion.

In the historic period we can trace Greek origins back about as far as those of the Middle East. Helenes were probably among those mentioned in Numbers as raiders from the North. They colonized communities in various islands and in southern Italy. In the New Stone age, when the city emerged in Mesopotamia, the ground was laid for the Bronze Age civilizations named Minoan and Mycenaean which disappeared before the Dorian invasion in about 1000 BCE when Greek city-states appeared. Though they never rivaled the Phoenicians (Canaanites), trade and expansion were open to the Greeks from both east and west coasts. Their city-states developed quite independently being separated by seas, mountains and fast-flowing streams. Monarchies gave way to aristocracies and then, we are told, to tyrants "who usually gained power by espousing the cause of the underprivileged and the merchants and by the use of force."[115] Defeat of Persia in 449 BCE began the Greek golden age. Actually, the first philosophers had already emerged: Thales and Pythagoras, Euripides, Socrates, Democritus, Euclid and many others followed.

As a people, the Greeks practiced various versions of fertility and mystical religious rituals. Their myths were fanciful imaginings of sovereign gods who indulged themselves much as did the rulers of the ancient cities. (Is this not an early covert admission that gods were made in human images?) Often these gods were given specific, different characteristics, not unlike the eastern Hindu gods who embodied specific stories.[116] The growing rationality of the elite Greek thinkers often accommodated such myths, the passionate other side of Greek culture. Homer is sometimes understood to have been an aristocratic observer of plebeian superstitions. Bertrand Russell tells us that these and other much darker popular beliefs were held in check by the Greek intellect, though such myths would lie in wait to reassert their primitive power in times of misery. But among the elites, at least, awareness of Eastern preoccupation with negativity did not undermine their focus on their present environment, on reason and facts. The Greek culture rejected anti-rationalism. The Eastern intellect seems to have been predisposed to imaginative constructions. Youthful vigor may have played a part in withstanding thorough mysticism. The role of youth has been variously understood. Russell quotes Beloch:

> The Greek nation was too full of youthful vigour for the general acceptance of (the Orphic definition of the world as trouble, pain, and weariness) which transfers real life to the Beyond.... [117]

This may explain the late turning of Greek life to oligarchy, conflict, and war, not unlike the rest of the world.

Youth generally are so full of life that they presume to understand beyond their capabilities. When children soon after puberty are already capable of doing adult tasks, they soon gain a self-confidence that belies their actual understanding. This presumption has caused many belligerent conflicts among people. The elderly have often recognized this danger (as among Native Americans who also demonstrated some remarkable achievements in peaceful relationships) but often they were too feeble or had not accrued the respect of younger people to be able to constrain the youths. This surely operated in Greece and everywhere else, varying in its consequences. Today it is a particularly severe problem in countries with swelling youth populations. Oliver Roy points out that alienated youths are attracted to versions of Islam that refuse to acknowledge reasonable limits on their authority. These interpretations of Islam also emphasize "hatred of oneself and one's desires," a negative view of humanity and of life itself which found no traction in ancient Greece.[118]

The effect of this youthful vigor may have been ameliorated in the East by their pervasive religion. Vedas, it is supposed, emerged some time after the Aryan invasion of the Indian subcontinent, a very long time ago, long before the era of war emerged in the cities. In the Orient this early religious ethos may have allowed for development of greater thoughtfulness among young people than in the West, or it might be simply that the eastern ethos constrained youth more effectively. On the other hand, it is possible that a delay in Greek development due to its position outside the Near East together with its rough terrain[119] provided the time needed for the human mind to mature further without such extensive repression and religious diversions. The late-ancient Greek thinkers seem to have been able to set the old myths aside and think intellectually without interference of antique emotions.

The presuppositions of the elite portion of the Greek culture have to do with the capacity of the human mind to think clearly. While abstraction emerged in Greek thought, they still focused their attention on the ancient world. About the same time (580 BCE) Gautama was born in India. Like most of the people of the Mediterranean basin, Indians also suffered a bitter life. After centuries of enduring every year the devastation by monsoons (and flooding in all deltas) in addition to the repression of oligarchy, the people had grown desperate for relief. The solution for the Buddha was, like the Greek, intellectual, demonstrating the worldwide evolution of the human mind. But it seems also to have reflected Eastern dualism, degraded physical versus enlightened mental.

The last thousand years of the Ancient Period were a time in human development when resignation to the conditions of life was embracing cynicism, a solution to human suffering which too often yields to sarcasm, back-biting, sneering, and fault-finding. The Buddha, and other bright leaders refused to distance themselves from the human condition in that way, and, like Jews and Christians, produced a substantial (and evangelistic) concern for the conditions of life.[120] The Greeks apparently had developed a unique escape from cynicism in total absorption in the intellectual life. But it was a temporary fix and misery and frustration reasserted themselves. Christianity was timely, filling the dark void of cynicism and useless, antiquated religions.

The Greek and Jewish sets of presuppositions are not contradictory; the brilliant Apostle Paul understood that. Nonetheless, from time to time, someone appears among us to argue that view. The Jews had learned to use their minds as well as did the Greeks, but with a substantially different set of presuppositions. Seventeen hundred years after Paul, the same insight powered the introduction of the liberal transition in Scotland under the overarching influence of Francis Hutcheson.

B. THE REDEVELOPMENT OF SUBMISSIVENESS

God was not dead in Greece, but Greek religion had not matured. Russell suggests that the culture did not follow the logic of Orphism into the paths taken in the East, but was constrained by its overpowering concern with reason. While the Jews saw beyond human appetites to the reality of divinity, the Greeks had taken the path of the intellect. The refocusing of Western cultural development from the mid-east to the emerging Europe forced the Mediterranean sheepish culture to confront their human capacity to think. Perhaps for the first time in generations, the anti-intellectual tendencies of the ancient world crumbled beneath the overpowering evolution of the human mind.

Nonetheless, ancient religious patterns hung on among the Greeks. Such religion as flourished in mystery religions and the last strains of fertility cults was degrading. It included ritual human sacrifice, sexual orgies, and vastly expanded myths of "divine" but subhuman beings. It supported and continued the ancient underestimation of humanity as largely ignorant. It was familiar to Homer though he was critical of it. He was a story-teller, perhaps one should say an early historian, but not a philosopher. In another 200 years, the philosophers emerged but still could not deal effectively with religion from their rationalistic base. For the most-part they did not seriously challenge the prevailing god-concepts except to call attention to the juvenile nature of their gods. The philosophers were preoccupied with their exploration of the mind's perception of the world. They were, after all, men of the ancient world, not self-conscious modern men. The path they were on tended toward skepticism and this engendered the cynicism which failed in its test with the Judaic cult that became Christianity.

Apart from the philosophic questions, the works of Plato and others encouraged various inherited religious concepts in Europe, notably, dualism and belief in a life after death. This is not to enter the argument as to whether the first century Jews had arrived at a concept of life after death (though it seems to have taken root after Alexander's invasion of the Middle East). These concepts were so attractive that both dualism and life after death, with the auspicious support of the revered Plato, substantially shaped Western intellectual history. In the third century, Plotinus founded Neoplatonism embodying these concepts. Plotinus sublimated his revulsion at the awful realities of his lifetime, "the spectacle of ruin and misery, to contemplate an eternal world of goodness and beauty," in harmony with serious men of his time. Only the "other world" seemed worthy of attention. "To the Platonist, it was the eternal world of ideas."[121] It was a view easily embraced by Christian leaders.

The Greek myths of gods behaving like juvenile humans were obviously doomed in a culture with the intellectual depth of Greece. Gods need more than submissiveness to survive in an intelligent culture. This sort of conceptual confusion was endemic. Philosophy had uncovered some of the holes in men's thinking, problems of misinformation and misconstruction. The give and take of thinkers in the forums and schools of Greece provided the sort of dialogue out of which people come to critical appraisal of their own minds. In time, the confusion would be resolved – by human conversation. But another aspect of that world was also virulent. Russell says, "The ancient world was obsessed with sin and had bequeathed this as an oppression to the Middle Ages"[122] Thinking people did not know what to do with the dilemmas this thrust upon them. Sin was the catch-all word for all that was wrong and evil. Even in the Medieval world there was as yet no distinction between personal and social "sin."

The great philosophers of Greece did not wrestle with a distinctive experience with the nature of God as the Jews did. Like the Jews they were inclined to the realism of practical reality. But the Jews, untrammeled by the intellectualism of developing Grecian thought -- or by the proud exploitation and denigration of peonage by ancient religion -- the Jews grasped and updated their inherited God concept and gave us the wholly intelligent, compassionate God we know in Jesus. But the Jews also had appropriated the nearly universal concept of sin to deal with the problem of evil in human behavior. And "sin" lent itself easily to undergirding submissiveness. So it was inherited by the early Church.

The Jews were still trapped by the inherited repressive attitude toward people, reinforced by their attention to "sin." Everyone knew of truculence, anger, violence. They feared rebellion, but no one thought of solutions which might involve, for example, reform of social institutions. "Organization," "socialization" and "reform" were still very young concepts in the human experience. The concepts did not exist then. Yet, we can see from our perspective, they had been evident, without a name, for a very long time.

The Jewish God embodied expectations of the people which urged them to mature. Their God was not juvenile, not childish. The concept of responsibility shows through the ancient liturgy. Their God is viewed through the inherited worldview, embodying the primitive awe of the stupendous hugeness of the world, its immensity and complexity beyond human grasp, and the childlike joy this God inspires in God's "children." The family image remained paramount and was not lost in the long centuries of oligarchic authoritarian rule.

The most ancient of all social images by thousands of years,, was the family. It was familiar throughout the ancient period, a primitive, basic, human reality, however perverted. It eventually found expression and redemption in Jesus' parables and in himself in the common acclamation of Jesus as son. While "Son of God" could mean different things, the second century Church Fathers, among them Irenaeus, adopted the relational image of Jesus as God's son. The Gospel of John exudes confidence in this perception named "incarnation" (God in flesh). It was not an unknown concept. Almost every religion had ascribed divinity to a key figure. Could Christians (with the mind of human beings 2000 years ago) claim less? Their perceptions of Jesus' continued presence with them after his crucifixion were entirely normal human reactions to a major relational loss.[123]. The roles of memory and recollection had not come to mind. There was no concept of the unconscious nor of such a thing as culture. Divinity was the way Jesus' living presence was spoken.

It is well to remember that the trinitarian definition of God came. much later, not a description, but a self-conscious formula, fitting the emerging mind of the church. All of these conceptions require articulation in a community of speaking human beings. Language must be found to express them. All languages allow for some sort of metaphorical expression to describe new things which have not previously been named. Whatever their roots, they tend to stick.

Metaphorical language is powerful and respected. God's joy in the people is like the great satisfaction that parents have in the happiness of their children. The inherited worldview includes the wisdom of progenitors whose vision penetrated beyond the view of ordinary people. Called "seers" (read "see-ers") these prophets spoke the wisdom that is based on their disciplined view of humans and human antics in a world that is fundamentally good and contains enough for everyone. Of course there are adults who quickly forget their unmatched pleasure in a child's responses to them. As the long centuries wore on in the repressive atmosphere of our recent past, it is not strange that degrading views of human destiny would emerge and come to dominate large populations. They often led to skepticism and cynicism as well. But others, like the seers, would hold potentially promising insights high and not neglect them when the cards seemed to be stacked against them. The prophets would remind the people persuasively of their obligation to be faithful to this God who, in the prophets' eyes, in spite of the evidence, never abandoned them. But the prophets, like everyone else at the time, could not see past the reality of sin.

Our inherited worldview is extraordinarily different but has left us with equally intractable problems. The twentieth century began with a dominant civic religion vaguely mimicking Christianity, but poisoned by three hundred years of a rampant rationalism. The intellectual progress during the twentieth century essentially put extreme rationalism out of commission. But we had only begun to apply this rationality to the notion of "sin." The Social Gospel had recalled the church to caring for the destitute, the poor, and the sick.

But the social nature of exploitation of children, for example, had only been tweeked. Orphan Trains continued taking children from their homes in eastern cities to a "healthier" life on western farms. Women's suffrage had only made a small dent in the social fabric. Poverty was still treated as an object for charity. Reason was not extended to caring for human beings. The fruits of those misguided years will be with us for a long time and require us to work hard to correct the related errors. The chief among errors were currently hubris and certainty.

Michael L. Lindvall (Pastor, Brick Church, New York City) recently displayed the mid-century hubris in recalling to mind the two General Motors *Futurama* exhibits in 1939-40 World's Fair and, 25 years later, in the 1964-65 World's Fair. He called them "emblems of an older, blissfully positive secular 'eschatology' that trusted in science, technology, and human ingenuity to create an infinitely better future." This super-human hubris began with the Enlightenment. It was not the view of Rene Descartes, who lived in Hobbes' generation, nor of Isaac Newton, both modestly religious men reflecting the dominant religious view of the time. Newton was of the generation following Hobbes. It was the generation of Baruch Spinoza and John Locke. What they set in motion has had unfortunate consequences as well as the beneficial ones we know so well. Hobbes usually gets credit and blame in about equal measure as one of he most articulate of the elites.

Russell tells us that the rejection of ecclesiastical authority began earlier than the acceptance of science. The opening of minds associated with the Reformation spread like wildfire through Europe. There were dozens of voices speaking, speaking and being heard, and soon their constructions were producing a flood of views of how to understand the emerging world. The most primitive of human skills took command of the newfound rationality, reordering our world. Russell notes the variety of views of power reacting to the past. The views inspired by Decartes and then Newton were technique philosophies; the ends are unimportant compared with the expression of power. "Only the the skillfulness of process is valued. This also is a madness, (one which should call forth an antidote)" He goes on:

> The ancient world found an end to anarchy in the Roman Empire, but the Roman Empire was a brute fact, not an idea. The Catholic world sought an end to anarchy in the Church, which was an idea but was never adequately embodied in fact. Neither the ancient nor the Medieval solution was satisfactory.[124]

Hobbes (1588-1679), in particular, demonstrated the confusion in that world, confident in his personal logic. Unfortunately, his sight was severely limited, judging by our view, because his century knew so little about history and anthropology. But with all of the bright progenitors of the Enlightenment he shared the euphoria of the emergence into daylight of the human capacity for rationality. All were able thinkers, increasingly free of aristocratic restraints, but still, unfortunately, limited in vision by the knowledge and the biases of their time. Nonetheless, Russell tells us, "although most men of science were models of piety ... their work was disturbing to orthodoxy, and the theologians were quite justified in feeling uneasy."[125] It is always difficult to distinguish seers from "false prophets."

The short-sightedness of Hobbes is of particular note, because his view of man was extremely influential for three hundred years. His vision was limited to the historical period in which violence and war have been major expressions of power. His conclusion that people can only live together peaceably under an autocratic authority has influenced much political life since. Even in the twentieth century many intellectuals have been known to justify their view of humanity on Hobbes' basis. We must see the end of that! We may be grateful that Hutcheson and others could not stomach it.

Typical of his time, Hobbes appreciated the heritage from Greece. He knew and referred to the Greek myths, and, like many others for many centuries, thought Plato the greatest of the classical philosophers. The liberal spirit, which praised liberty at the end of the ancient period, in Hobbes' eye favored sedition and conflict, the product of man's selfishness and self-interest. He thought man so depraved that he had to be corralled by autocratic authority. The only exception in Hobbes' political philosophy was that a man has a right to refuse to serve in armed forces since he regarded even subjects as having the right of self-defense. This is in itself an important break with the authoritarian past. For Hobbes, self-preservation is the whole basis for people to institute government, that each may live his own life without fear of his neighbor (who, like all humans, was to Hobbes a beast).[126] He apparently could not see the evolution of submissive human beings moving toward self-conscious self-governance. The concept of sin ruled the world. It was a perverse and cynical individualism.

The beginnings of autocracy have emerged very differently than Hobbes and similar thinkers guessed. In the ancient freedom of human beings before the advent of cities, anarchy reigned, but the "freedom" was little more than life prior to development of submission to autocratic authority. Population was so sparse that few concerns for social order emerged. Anyone they followed, as in a hunting party, or in defense of robbers, was one of their own. However, we can surmise that "society" was beginning to develop. Humans already had learned to enjoy their interactions in dance and song. When the city began, it held not only a degree of safety but provided a much-enhanced community in which people enjoyed one another. Under the thumb of city leaders these independent and not very self-conscious people gave up much of their presumed freedom and learned to submit to authority imposed on them. They became "obedient." At the end of the ancient period, this submissiveness was confused with willing obedience, delaying recognition of the capability of the human mind. Autocrats persisted for centuries as the modern world unfolded. Humans were learning to creatively combine their primal independence with the necessities of social order, but most able and intelligent people did not yet have a mind to see what was going on.

Over many centuries things changed little. While the submissive attitude of the vast majority of the people had been reinforced persistently so as to become almost instinctual, their servitude was relieved by their meager self-expression in dance, song and religious activities. But with the gradual evolution of the self, humans began to want something we call "self-determination" (a very modern term). This "willfulness" was feared by rulers. Force had so long been the means of controlling anything that did not fit the worldview of leaders ("sin"), that Hobbes and monarchists of all stripes did not grasp the possibility of overcoming human "beastiality" through the development of self-conscious intelligence. It only gradually dawned on leaders that submissiveness might morph (unnoticed, like a caterpillar to a butterfly) into intelligent obedience and reveal human freedom. The habit of seeing people as sheep had settled deep in human consciousness and was still the driving force in Europe. But a new consciousness was dawning.

C. THE INTELLIGENT BASIS OF HUBRIS

Some leaders did begin to recognize the emerging new mind. More and more of the people demonstrated intelligence. They could not only hear and accept the guidance of prophets, they could think about such things, and argue about them. By the time of the Enlightenment the emergent intelligence of human beings was generally recognized. Increasing numbers of people demonstrated intelligence and found ways to express their own humanity. Almost always the brightest ones required the support of those with accumulated wealth. But in a rare exhibition of egalitarianism, the University of Glasgow maintained student fees far below other advanced schools attracting students from a wide swath of Scot society. The fruits of this new culture of the mind began to change the Scot ethos.

Some of those whom we have already named stand out. Inevitably, many of these privileged persons, enjoyed the fruits of the intellect, the thrill of discovery, and developing views of the world which combined, recombined, and innovated ideas beyond their heritage. Many of these, like ancient kings, became consumed with their privileged views. Driven by the basic human tendency to make sense of their context, their thoughts led them on and on, to elaborate and to write fairly coherent systems. In their own views these explained the constraints under which humans must live and how humans and nature were related. These were often exciting views and their authors were justly proud of their care in conceptualization.

The new philosophic systems were the products of minds of men who were bright and well-disciplined. They had grasped the methods of thinking developed over centuries, not the least of these rhetoric and Aristotelian logic. But the late Medieval mind had yet to generally reflect the maturity we have come to expect of intellectual giants. In the mode of the oligarchic past, most of them wrote with a sense of finality, constructing systems with a sense that they had plumbed the true and eternal. They exuded confidence in human reason (their own) and introduced the philosophic school we call "Rationalism."[127] Its core belief was that the minds of humans can reflect the actual reality of the world. The laws discovered were set in the stars and our reading of them had to be correct. Over and over, the magic of mathematics seduced scholars into a sense of security in their rationality.

They promoted and defended their views with determination. And many of them were deterministic, meaning they saw human freedom to be very minimal; reality was written in the laws of the universe. They understood the human mind as a logical machine, capable of perceiving a world based on the logic of nature. Each of them thought his self-important view was a reflection of true reality. They were no longer in the habit of their predecessors of expressing their views allegorically; their language and mind-set were literal and correct. Words had become sacred.

This Greek sense of coincidence between the human mind and the real world had attracted the Church Fathers. But as the Medieval world emerged it adopted the slave mentality of its inheritance and operated as if human beings were incapable of most anything significant but to work hard, worship God and prepare for the life after death. Scholasticism was rationalistic and argued that God would not implant in humans a rationality that would mislead them. Such rationality paired with the negative view of people reinforced the ancient dualism of body and mind.

The separateness of mind and body made attention to the physical world natural. The aspect of mind called "soul" was the province of the Church which developed meditation and memorization to a high degree in search of paths of salvation to another world. It was as unfortunate as it was misleading, neglecting the immense human capacity to think. The capability to turn things over in the mind and ask ourselves questions, to contemplate the ineffable, the artistic, the aesthetic, the idea and even the concept were not really included in the emerging empirical views. The management of physical understanding seems to have absorbed all attention as if the mind were simply the master of reality. The exploration of the empirical world simply ignored the long-standing Jewish sense of the unity of the human being embodied in the word for flesh, nephish. The West moved closer to the thoroughly mechanistic view which produced the Industrial Age. Paul the Jew had distinguished flesh from spirit, and this was soon confused with body and soul to fit the orthodox Christian interpretation of life after death. Both paths of the dualism failed to explore or account for the growing sense of self in the European population which included the growing realization of individuals' responsibility.

With the church's tenacious hold on dualism, the emerging empiricists seemed forced to assume that human perception of truth was limited by the senses. Only what could be grasped by human senses was "real." The dualism fomented separation of sacred and secular. This might have been salutary, but for the antagonism that developed in Modernity between science and the Church.[128] For a long time the distinction of spiritual insight given as revelation from God was exempted from the sort of increasingly critical examination given "secular" matters. In the Middle Ages huge effort was expended to find personal paths to spiritual insight. It encouraged mysticism and a move toward Eastern religious views. Perhaps this was also a rekindling of the antiquated religious practice of entering a trance to make contact with another world.

The long-standing belief that moral judgment is embedded in nature and its laws was regarded as obsolete by some thinkers. In the Enlightenment, the thought we call "rationalism'" began to claim that morality is simply the work of human reason. For Hobbes this was vested in his animal conception of humanity which creates the state and morality to protect us against the avarice of our beast-like neighbors.

The tendency was to assume that human knowledge is limited to perception of concrete physical things. Strangely, it was as if the human mind had surmounted the immense mystery of life and no longer needed to "imagine" what was not yet evident to us.

This was never universally believed; the religious sense is so ancient that it seems like an instinct. Most men of science were pious individuals who granted to the theologians their sphere of inquiry. But in the period we call the Enlightenment, there were some very influential thinkers who grew quite arrogant in their rationality.

A similar arrogance might be attributed to the Greek skeptics. As philosophy developed, a number of cynical thinkers gathered many followers. The Greek Sophists, Protagoras and later Gorgias cannot be charged with shading the truth. But they tended to undermine the authority of moral standards even though their conduct and their teaching of morality were beyond reproach. Protagoras' religious agnosticism led to denial of the existence of any absolute and universal truth. To such thinkers truth was purely relative and subjective. Each man was his own measure of truth. In his *On Nature or the Non-existent* Gorgias (485-380; a severe sophist) challenged the power of reason to discover any reality beyond the flux of sensible experience.[129] This point of view keeps reappearing in the modern period. Russell goes on to point out that if individual men are their own arbiter of what is good and true, there is no way to argue. Each person is then his own measure of truth.

The sense of eventual intellectual victory over everything came slowly to dominate the thinking of some skeptics. It was carried right into the twentieth century in spite of serious challenges and rejection by the majority of scientists. In the twenty-first century there will continue to be those who insist that because human capacity to measure everything constantly improves, all things will one day be within our comprehension. The logic of rationalism hardly justifies pride in this position. We presume that the gradual undermining of its presuppositions will eventually reduce rationalism to being a minor if persistent irritant. This is not to say humans are not rational; *it* is to dethrone *rationalism*.

At the beginning of the eighteenth century, Francis Hutcheson, the Glasgow humanist, found Hobbes as mistaken as his own Presbyterian predecessors. He spent his life refuting Hobbes, evidence of the confusion which reigned a long time in the West. This was the maturing of along brewing humanism.[130] Strange, he thought, that Hobbes ended up with a coercive state, and the old Presbyterians ended up from a similar view of a depraved humanity with a coercive church to invoke its godly discipline. Both points of view, typical of the contentious mind of the time, squared off for public battle, more evidence of the emergence of a broader and more thoughtful human mind. Finally the time had come when thinkers would engage in debate.

Initially, modern liberalism emerged in the British Isles and in Holland, where there was a long-standing liberal orientation. Freed from Spanish control, Holland had attracted intellectuals from all over the continent as the hard-bitten Scholastic world ground to its end. Humanism, an evident expression of the liberal mind in Holland, had engaged the thinking of others elsewhere as well, and beginning with George Buchanan (1506-1582) it led the Scots toward a vibrant movement kicking the British Enlightenment into orbit. Buchanan was a contemporary of John Knox, Ignatius Loyola, and John Calvin. Arthur Herman puts the pieces together for us in his popular *How the Scots Invented the Modern World:*

The Scottish enlightenment ... was robust and original.... In a list of the books that dominated the thinking of Europeans in the last quarter of the eighteenth century, the Scottish names stand out. Adam Smith's *A Theory of Moral Sentiments and Wealth of Nations*. David Hume's *Treatise of Human Nature* and *Essays Political, Literary, and Moral*. William Robertson's *History of Scotland and History of the Reign of Charles V*. Adam Ferguson's *Essay on the History of Civil Society*. John Millar's *The Origin of The Distinction of Ranks*. Reid's *Inquiry into the Human Mind*. And at the top of the page, Francis Hutcheson's *System of Moral Philosophy* and Lord Kames's *Sketches of the History of Man*.[131]

Practically all of these intellectual lights of the time studied moral philosophy under Francis Hutcheson. Hutcheson (1694-1746) grew up in Ulster where Scots had been imported by the British to counter the strong Roman Catholic influence in Ireland. These Scots were followers of John Knox. They suffered persecution and returned the favor in kind. They were known for their fierce warring in Scotland. That world was still under the influence of the ancient regime. But by the eighteenth century a "new light" among the clergy in England and Holland found support in Ulster. Hutcheson fell under the influence of those who had begun questioning the harsh dogmas of Knoxian Calvinism and they pleaded for an image of man made in the image of their loving God. Hutcheson, himself a clergyman, was son and grandson of Knox Presbyterian ministers. He began his education at Dublin, founded in 1581 on the foundation of a twelfth century monastery. There he absorbed this new light and took it to Glasgow, a university founded in 1451.

William III (1650-1702) who had been raised a Calvinist gave the Kirk of Scotland its independence. He threw out the bishops and established the Kirk. He also insisted that the old "fire-breathing, anti-monarchical Covenant Theology had to go." He appointed the liberal William Carstares (1649-1715) to accomplish these changes in Glasgow. Carstares' reforms laid the groundwork for the scientific side of the Scot Enlightenment.

It seems that the opening up of the liberal mind burst forth with a growing array of towering figures, mostly Scots, among whom, however, were sprinkled some Germans, French and English (including Isaac Newton). Many of them sat at the feet of Hutcheson in moral philosophy. Carstares appointed John Simson, a liberal voice, to the chair of Sacred Theology at Glasgow. Though he was detested by the conservatives, he was attractive to Hutcheson and others. It is an early instance of the modern reactionary to developing thought which recently claimed the name "conservative."

Thus the liberal orientation began to shape the Scot mind. A brilliant Scot, Dugald Stewart (1753-1828)came to Glasgow and began a program to make science the core description of intellectual effort. The front rank of the Scottish Enlightenment was gone by 1800, but its legacy prevailed: inquisitive, penetrating, unsentimental thinking, impatient at pious dogmas or cant, relentlessly thorough, sometimes to the point of pedantry. The Scots were rational, but buoyed by a tough-minded sense of humor and grasp of the practical.[132]

Stewart merged Adam Smith's moral realism with the common sense philosophy of Reid. In Stewart's hands, the "common" aspect of common sense philosophy should really be read as "that prudence and discretion which are the foundation of successful conduct." "Science" became the preferred operation of the human mind at its highest pitch. Herman tells us, "Science defined progress. Stewart wanted every student of human nature to strive for the same level of exactitude and precision as the chemist, the physicist, or the biologist." Science, then, was recognized as a method of applying the mind in order to facilitate human happiness. The liberal spirit spelled the end of the old Scotland.

D. SELF-CONFIDENCE REPLACES CONFUSION

Beginning in Glasgow, the Scots began to reorder human knowledge. The continuing publication of the *Encyclopaedia Britannica* beginning in 1768 (in Edinburgh) bears witness to their success.[133] But there was an overarching pride that this self-confidence bred into the Western culture. The long list of Enlightenment intellectuals perpetrated upon us a confidence in human capability that encouraged perpetuation of the Greek sense of understanding as the accumulation of knowledge. It also engendered a self-sufficient, anti-religious bias. The culture encouraged both pride and a sense of certainty that grew into a rampant individualism in the twentieth century when sociologist Robert Bellah called this individualism "the default mode" of American culture.

David Hume (1711-1776), for example, exemplified the long-standing adulation of the classical Greek-Roman culture. He chose to think in terms of Greek mythology, rather than Christian, even on his deathbed, which was desperately hard for his fellows to swallow in the face of the religiosity of the day. Samuel Johnson told James Boswell, who was particularly upset with Hume's disinclination, to calm himself because in spite of his erudition, Hume had never read the New Testament with attention.[134] Thus the ever insightful Johnson named the key personal discipline that governs the use of our minds: The focusing of our attention.

A cursory look at the New Testament could not help Hume appreciate it. We choose to pay attention. In the military attention is commanded and for the troops it is an act. But in real life we choose to pay attention until it becomes our habit. Paying attention is hard work that is easier when it becomes habitual. In the Enlightenment period increasing numbers of people neglected a heritage which increasing scientism considered old fashioned. They focused their attention with increasing self-confidence on the details of a growing number of disciplines. Their preoccupations with the marvelous worlds these uncovered made many disciplined people loquacious. They often failed to recognize the narrowness of their focus and neglected attention to the roots of faith.

Hume was hardly a religious man. He inherited not only hard-won self-discipline, but the satisfaction derived from freedom to focus his attention where he chose. The independence of the person to choose a path not endorsed by the culture occurred many times in history, but never so openly until now. In the next two centuries his choice would be interpreted as precedent for a growing resentment of Christian orthodoxy. In the judgment of ordinary people Hume's views were understood either as detestable or laudable. But his contributions to philosophy and political thought were highly regarded. Like others since the beginning of Christianity, the people were feeling increasingly empowered to speak their own views.

Outspokenness was never a problem among those in power in the ancient world. The religion practiced in the ancient city was appropriated and used by the ruling power, and departure from it was not permissible. After all, leaders were self-confident and the people were like sheep. When Christianity became the religion of the Roman Empire, first the bishops and then the Church itself took on the role of chief of human thought previously ascribed to kings and emperors. Under the anthropology inherited from Judaism, the many bright theologians of the Church struggled to shape the doctrines of the church. They began the theological conversation that has extended for most of the past 2000 years, intermittently. We have noted the expansive role of Scholasticism through the Middle Ages, culminating in the outspoken views of Aquinas, and pushed to philosophic extremities by brilliant philosophers Duns Scotus and William of Occam in the thirteenth and fourteenth centuries. Among those who had the authority to speak about such things, speech tended to be outspoken.

Like the scholars, the bishops of the church tended to speak "with authority." This was a new self-consciousness born of knowledge and awareness of human inter-dependence. But it was an authority which was no longer punishable by brute force. The old social regulators of coercion, ostracism, shunning, had increasingly been replaced by social pressure – the displeasure of peers. It was evidence of the evolving human self. It would take longer to grow out of the authoritarian nature of social conventions and to take on the character of life we call freedom. Nonetheless, as the Middle Ages wound down, that sense of freedom grew. It was no longer a simple matter of not being slaves. It would not be named and sought after consciously for a long time, but it was in the air, a sense of relief from coercion and acknowledgment of the role of authority in maintaining civil order.

It proves the point. As human beings recovered their natural independence, their increasing freedom allowed more independent thought. Increasingly, each person exercised his or her gift of speech. This refinement of the emerging new individual consciousness spelled the beginning of the end of the prolonged period of the mass of sheep obediently following singular shepherds subject to control of hierarchical authority. This by no means ended the useful pattern of hierarchical control of masses of people to which they had grown accustomed, nor of teaching by lecturing, by speaking to others, by repetition, by hearing and mimicking. All these were now deeply embedded. But it does point toward the end of using such time-honored techniques coercively. Listening, repeating and learning became a new thing with the emergence of the new self-consciousness, signaled by the Renaissance, implemented in the Reformation, and developed in the Enlightenment and modernity.

Scholasticism had fit the tenor of the ancient world to which it was heir. But in the Middle Ages it brought forth increasing tension between those who had begun thinking for themselves and those in authority. For thousands of years hundreds of thousands of people had been cowed into submission to the current view of those in power, be that religious or civil. As the Middle Ages faded, generation after generation extended its capacity to think critically through use of many words This expansion of language continued through the modern period at an increasing rate. *Homo loquens* was coming into his own!

E. EMERGENCE OF THE NEW SELF

New words and phrases, the very changing nature of language itself, added to the confusion of conflicting ideas and loyalties. The turmoil of the transition from ancient oligarchy, authority and hierarchy ran headlong into the re-emergence of the individual human being. Inevitably many people would pine for the old certainties and the easy absolutes of handed-down truth. And the Church worked mightily to meet their needs. The early Church Fathers and the several Councils used the early conciliar method of reaching common ground. It was a step toward consciousness of the wisdom that emerges in dialogue from the many views of multiple human beings' minds. This was clearly an ancient indication of the evolution of a new self-confidence; people were learning to speak their minds.

By the time we call the Enlightenment, new wealth had provided more and more individuals a measure of freedom from the constant harassment of oligarchy. Their awakening to mental capacity was a natural development. Descartes and others had put their minds to work in the construction of new views of the world. A prime objective was to free themselves from the growing confusion of an increasing cacophony of ideas. The sixteenth and seventeenth centuries were another renaissance, a pregnant time of increasing numbers of astute, relatively free minds interacting through print. Evidence is focused on the intellectual elites. It was too easy for these privileged of the new economy to neglect the multitudes of poor and needy people. A thousand years of legal development had polished the aristocracy of the wealthy to operate quite effectively. As all aristocracies do, they had assured themselves the privileges of the elite.

The Scots had come through a social revolution which transformed their world. We are all familiar with the Magna Charta of 1215, forced on King John at Runnymede. The ordinary person had begun to see the world differently and to struggle for a part in new prosperity. Over the next five hundred years people achieved a better balance than life held for folk in the ancient world. There were more satisfactions and fewer embarrassments and the human mind fashioned a way to enjoy the past as well as to forge ahead. By a combination of reading and a humanistic Christianity the Scots got a head start on the rest of Europe. Robert Burns and Sir Walter Scott made their unique contributions.

> Raised as a farmhand, virtually self-taught, Robert Burns arrived in Edinburgh with a reputation as a boy genius.... Burns could write verse in the standard highbrow classical vein perfectly well, But he sensed that his true talent lay in turning the everyday speech, songs, and stories of the people he had grown up with into poetry, and communicating to readers the latent power, eloquence and nobility of the ordinary man and woman. It made Burns Scotland's most beloved poet, even today.[135]

Burns died at 37. Sir Walter Scott lived to 61. He managed in his writing to generate another Scotland parallel to the one being thrust into the nineteenth century. It was a Scotland of the imagination, a place where honor, courage, and integrity could still survive, and even thrive within the individual. Scott created an imaginary national identity, based on the myth of the strong and noble Highlander. The "inclosures" or "clearings" of the late eighteenth and early nineteenth centuries in the transition from feudalism sent huge numbers of Scots to America and Australia. The rest of Britain could take comfort and pride in the notion that in the north the old, premodern virtues were still being kept alive. Later, of course, people of Scottish descent outside Britain would gloat on the image. St. Andrew's Society dinners were celebrated everywhere.[136] After all, Andrew was their patron saint and Romanticism revived the adulation of heroes.

Adam Smith (1723-1790) had shown that imagination was the basis of modern society itself. This world was hopeful about the future, even as the old ways were fading away. The lesson Scott taught the modern world was that the past does not have to die or vanish: it can live on, in a nation's memory, and help to nourish its posterity. Our personal recollections may serve many purposes. With Scot's encouragement, his readers took renewed confidence in themselves. Contempt for the past infuriated Scott. It was what he most disliked about Presbyterianism after John Knox and his followers had destroyed ancient churches and monasteries, and blotted out ageless popular customs and reverence for the monarchy.

Scott's legacy includes the shape of the modern historical novel, caring about details, and respectful of the time past. The ancient world's institution of warfare is reflected in Scott's novels. We find there history revealed as a series of "culture wars": Frank versus Saracen (in *The Talisman*), Jew versus Christian (in *Ivanhoe*), Norman versus Saxon, Scotsman versus Englishman, Lowlander versus Highlander, Presbyterian versus Episcopalian. And which side is superior, and which deserved to lose, is never fully resolved. Scott hated old-style Scottish Calvinism -- but in a novel such as *Old Mortality* he treated it sympathetically and left no trace of his own feelings. Herman tells us

> Scott the novelist introduced a key ingredient of the modern consciousness, a sense of historical detachment -- something that Macaulay (who was a great admirer of Scott) and other historians of the early Victorian age still lacked.

> Part of his detachment arose from an insight that the modern world generates opposing tensions.... "The Scottish mind was made up of poetry and strong common sense," he wrote to a friend, "and the very strength of the latter gave perpetuity and luxuriance to the former." The credit for defining the artist as a person who can hold two inconsistent ideas at once goes to F. Scott Fitzgerald. The credit for realizing that is precisely what all modern men can do -- indeed must be able to do -- belongs to Sir Walter Scott.[137]

Scott preceded Fitzgerald by over half a century. Virginia Woolf once called Scott "the last of the minstrels." His preservation of Scottish Border Minstrelsy inspired Washington Irving's love of folklore. Scott's love for the past and the monarchy remind us that he had not forgotten the ancient world. As a minstrel he sang of them, but was well aware that he was mourning their passing.[138]

Again, we find evidence that our human mind was changing. At one and the same time, we were bending the world to our desire, and living in a world which largely held an orthodox Christian worldview. Our culture seemed to be increasingly independent both of the tyranny of the present government and the hierarchy of religion. This was more evident in Britain than anywhere else. No ancient man could foresee the end of the autocratic city that had been the cause of much desperate resignation. But Hobbes, Descartes, Locke, Newton, Hutcheson, Reid, Hume, Rousseau, Kant, and many others demonstrated in under two hundred years that humanity was winning the battle for the human spirit. While it retained some of the arrogance of the past, the new aristocracy of the mind was both kinder and gentler.

Inevitably, some who constructed great closed systems of thought did so with a determination that appears to us as arrogance. Self-righteous pride was far from finished in misleading the people; after all, the new philosophers believed they had brought (their own) order into the chaotic world of conflicting words and ideologies. Such self-confidence was not new, but had become a social reality infecting many. Western people have suffered much from this self-righteousness as their predecessors did under former regimes.

VI. A NEW AUTHORITY FITTING THE NEW SELF: FROM MONARCHY TO DEMOCRACY

A. RESIDUAL ARISTOCRACIES

The western world has faced a major psychological restructuring of itself. Having inherited several thousand years of repressive and instructive oligarchy, the amazing Roman version of empire had, nonetheless, fallen apart without leaving clear successors. The independent tribes of the north had continued their intrusions. But at that time understanding what we call psychology was insufficient to establish control of instinctual responses to power. For the vast majority of people, the inherited means of social control remained obedience to authority. Though oligarchy was fading the established aristocracies of privileged people continued in the authoritative ethos of the past. The changing cultural paradigm was not grasped by the established institutions. The Church, too, followed this pattern, especially in maintaining morality in the emerging chaos of the destruction of the last great ancient empire.

From the fifth through the tenth centuries, there were a number of outstanding leaders, particularly Gregory I (590-604) and Charlemagne (742-814), but the path into the future was unclear. Gregory established the temporal independence of the Pope and also the important principle of divided powers, as we say, the separation of church and state. This was an important step into the future, but no one yet questioned the autocratic exercise of power.

Strong and able, Charlemagne, fought wars with kings of the Lombards, lent his support to various popes, and eventually was put down by Danes and Norse. He supported local laws, codifying them when possible, and established a pattern of personal representatives in far-flung lands who regularly inspected their assigned turf and kept the emperor informed; a happy contribution to the development of bureaucracy. He was concerned with the welfare of the poor and prevention of abuse. But the pattern of oligarchy had not been broken. Singular authority was still the only established way to govern large populations.

Charlemagne showed himself a representative of the emerging modern mind in his attention to education. He called on Alcuin of York (in British Northumbria) whose school in his court became famous by educating the Emperor, his sons, and many others, and introducing the liberal arts. Alcuin (735-804) wrote a dialogue text of rhetoric, *Compendia*. But his greatest contribution to history probably lies in establishment of schools throughout the empire for children of all classes. His were among the significant efforts during the Middle Ages to maintain the place of classical literature and to encourage the evolution of the human mind.

Alcuin's legacy helps us to keep our perspective on the Middle Ages. He carried on much correspondence from the court, including a letter to Aethelheard, Archbishop of Canterbury concerning the Viking attack on Lindisfarne (an island off the coast of

Northumberland) which had been an early locale of Christianity in Britain.[139] In spite of the destructive attacks of the "barbarians," individuals like Alcuin with the support of powerful and wealthy people kept alive the achievements of previous generations. His progressive orientation led him to persuade Charlemagne to abolish the death penalty for paganism.

Such gifts bless humanity, often without leaving the names of the givers. Before individualistic modernity, recording the true author of copied material was often neglected. In ancient times the work of followers was often labeled with the leaders' names, but not their own. The biblical "Book of Isaiah" is a good example.[140] Names, we see, belong to us by social convention. Often the time comes when outstanding names are fixed in our minds with associated events or ideas, or whole writings. In exploring the past we try to remember the real lives they represented, and the nurture, sweat, and tears these people experienced. But our human minds hold only limited views of others; what we see, what has come into our field of vision is what we ourselves know as witnesses, often second-hand. The real people of the past were, nonetheless, like ourselves. And we revere them though they always reflected the residual aristocracies under which they existed.

We might call Peter Damian (1007-1072), legate of the pope in Milan, a sign of the future. He found that every cleric in the city had been guilty of a convenient exercise of illicit power among upper clergy. The error he uncovered was simony,[141] receiving payment for ecclesiastical office. It is interesting that Damian certified his observation with a comprehensive survey of the clergy of Milan – a rather advanced intellectual step – and as legate of the pope received in return exactly what one would expect in a still sheep-like culture, total obedience.

Again we are reminded that the sense of self that undergirds responsibility has appeared here and there all through human history, even before most people had outgrown their sheep-like self-image. Damian, on the one hand, inherited sufficient self-consciousness to strike out in critique of upper clergy under the authority of the pope. The clergy, on the other hand, exhibited the developing sense of responsibility to cooperate with Damian; of course, obedience was operational. This should remind us how complex selfness is. Even though we might see a flicker of a fuller human being in Damian, he was still operating in an autocratic authority structure.

Our modern individuality was freshly crystallized in the Enlightenment it is true. Building on the sense of selfness as that had evolved through the Middle Ages, the bright lights of the Enlightenment often succumbed to the same ancient pride that had perverted human history, at least as far back as the first cities. Selfishness, thinking primarily of one's own satisfaction, remains deep in our culture and remains a drag on evolution. It was part of primal humanity, constantly whittled away as human beings gradually were socialized.

It was surely not the case that the wisdom of humility went unnoticed in ancient times. Ancient wisdom literature contains its share of admonitions against pride. Nonetheless, among those who gained power, the strong instinct to exercise it prevailed, only modestly constrained by accumulated human wisdom. The belief that humanity needed autocracy to restrain native aggressiveness prevailed in their short-term view of humanity and was sustained far into modern history.

The Scots who helped to shape America were certainly not immune to this sickness. They, too, suffered the residue of aristocratic leadership. The late eighteenth century "inclosures" began shifting agriculture so as to dispossess thousands of Highlanders. Many of them fled to North America. Why did people continue their sheep-act far into the emergence of the new selfness we now find engulfing the Western world? In Herman's analysis of the role of the poor Scots in shaping our modern world lies his unsuspecting contribution to our theme: And what was different about the Scots?

The Scots never learned as well as their southern cousins to be sheep. Many Scots, like the Irish, never lived under the Romans' extension of ancient oligarchy. These were fiercely independent people, who exercised a native human individuality among themselves. In the second century the Roman Emperor Hadrian built a wall across northern England to reduce the threat from Northumberland. That is where the unruly Picts were concentrated. "In perhaps typical Celtic fashion, the Picts and Scots had spent more time fighting against each other than against their common enemies..... By the end of the fourth century, the remaining Roman outposts in Scotland were abandoned. Any civilized benefits of Roman rule enjoyed by southern Britain were thus denied to their northern neighbors."[142]   The Celts, who lived south of the Picts suffered Roman pacification intermittently in the first millennium. The Picts shared much of the Celt culture. The Celts eventually absorbed them and carried their shared, primitive individuality directly into the British culture.

So the Scots were not subjected to the extended, repressive heritage of Mediterranean-basin oligarchy as was most of southern Europe by the end of the first millennium CE. This is not to say that the oligarchic mind set did not touch the Scots. By the middle of the second millennium the clan chiefs had absorbed the exploitative feudal mentality of Europe and like them exercised aristocratic power. Nevertheless, the perseverance of Celt independence is evident even today in the existence of the Celtic roots of the Gaelic languages of Ireland, Wales and Scotland.

This analysis rests on this more self-assured, less subdued culture of the Scots. Their British brothers and sisters to the south were occupied by Romans until the fifth century. Then it is said that St. Patrick was carried off by the Irish in a raid. Soon the Germans (who had defeated Rome under Odoacer in 476) began two centuries of occupation. The demeaning Mediterranean slave culture was carried throughout Europe by the Romans and some of them stayed permanently in Britain. But British affinity with the Scots grew out of their common Celtic heritage and eventually won out.

This same power and persistence of character from the ancient world shows itself in many ways in the modern world. It is evident in Hobbes (1588-1679). He was born a few years before Descartes. He thought that the people only needed to accede to a monarch and then they could live in peace.   Hobbes was thought to be extraordinarily bright and entered Oxford at 15. As early as 1638 he published a piece intended to show the evils of democracy. He was clearly a Royalist and fled to Paris out of fear of local developments in England; when the Civil War broke out it confirmed his fears with its usual excesses. He was a rigid determinist. That was an influential philosophy, which fit the lingering self-image of dependence in the people. It was operative in the eighteenth century when philosophers were building systems of thought based on the rational capability of human beings. A school we call Rationalism had begun its march to dominance, especially in Germany where scholars embraced it with a didactic vengeance. It was already evident in Hobbes' *Leviathon* (1651). It was immensely attractive.

Hobbes' book begins with his thorough materialism. Leviathon is the commonwealth, and the covenants and pacts which created it take the place of God's fiat when he said "Let us make man." A nominalist, Hobbes says only names are universal "and without words we could not conceive any general idea. Without language, there would be no truth or falsehood, for 'true' and 'false' are attributes of speech." It is clear that Hobbes and others of his generation exhibited a refreshing freedom to think that was overcoming some of the worst aspects of antiquity.

Though rationalism and determinism were to become immensely influential among intellectuals, most Scots sided with Francis Hutcheson's lifelong resistance to Hobbes. Humanist philosophy maintained a respect for humanity as *Homo sapiens*, thinking persons, which determinism persistently undercut. Hobbes and others reduced everything to mechanics, and mechanical things are attractively predictable and repetitive.

Acknowledging the brilliance of the people of the Enlightenment, Bertrand Russell credits David Hume with a critique of rationalism "that paralyzes every effort to prove one line of action better than another" (though he thought Hume was "inconsistently skeptical"). Russell tells us that Kant and Hegel (c.1800) had not assimilated Hume's argument and therefore represent a pre-humian type of rationalism. He says they are easily refuted by Hume.[143] The philosophers who cannot be refuted in this way are those who do not pretend to be rational, such as Rousseau, Schopenhauer and Nietzsche. The growth of unreason throughout the nineteenth and twentieth centuries is a natural sequel to Hume's critique of empiricism.[144]

We agree. The modern period has been tumultuous intellectually. Intellectuals had broken free of the oligarchic heritage from ancient history; they were free and independent spirits. But they had yet to provide a thoughtful, linear whole view of humanity to control their hubris. That would take another hundred or more years. It was a time when intellectuals indulged their rationality and neglected the honored principle of balance. Arguments and discussions were full of accusation, vituperation and self-righteousness. The culture had not yet fully emerged from an era of antagonism.

Again the British Isles played a significant part in our story. There scholars ameliorated the proud assertions of Rationalists in the nineteenth century. German scholars had been applying their newly-emerging sense of history to the Bible. One in particular wrote a "Life of Jesus" in the new historical mode which seriously challenged popular concepts of Jesus' life.[145] On the continent it caused a furor. By the time it was translated into English, however, it had already stimulated a reaction among the still-clergy-dominated universities in Britain.

British scholars had begun publishing new "lives of Jesus" which were far less hyper-critical than the German rationalistic versions. The British scholars were, simply, tuned to listening to the people in a way that had not yet been felt among academics on the continent.[146] This must be understood as a product of the Hutcheson-Reid humanism that grew out of the liberal critique of Knox Presbyterianism and Hobbesian determinism. Toward the end of the nineteenth century, the newer, rationalistic histories were accepted in Britain without public outcry. This, too, shows us the rapidly emerging new mind in Britain. It was more open, more generous of difference, kinder to those with whom people differed than previous attitudes had allowed, and particularly more generous than the practice in French and German elite cultures.[147] It was, in a word, more self-confident if also, perhaps, less self-righteous.

The most destructive political upheaval of the eighteenth century was, of course, the French revolution. After generations of oligarchic control of church and of state, its dominance and the forces of intellectual leadership boiling under the surface erupted in the sort of vicious play that Hobbes had feared. It was the sort of popular rebellion long suppressed that was inevitable under the old regime.

We have seen before (in Pythagoras, Galileo, Descartes), how mathematics has stimulated many intellectuals by the sense of certainty that accompanied achievements in the field. Russell's challenge to Hume's skepticism rests on what we call probability theory. If a sufficient number of instances of association are gathered, then we can conclude that the association will usually (if not always) be true. Without noticing, Russell and many others who found probability helpful began to turn attention to this statistical theory.[148] In doing so they were heralding the emergence of a new sophisticated sense of the human self. We have matured, as we say, to a new way of thinking. We are able to put aside the sort of "I am right, otherwise nothing makes sense" thinking that had grown particularly obnoxious in the nineteenth century and early twentieth century.

It seems anachronous that the brilliant Hobbes should have been among the persistent supporters of royalty but the growing unrest (really a reaction to millennia of oligarchy) seemed to justify him. In reading his work one is impressed with the thoughtful rationality of his mind. But evidently his self-image had not embraced the native drive toward self-determination of humanity necessarily growing into a post-oligarchic mind. Hobbes seems never to consider the balancing influence a self-conscious electorate might have on political power. Self-consciousness was too new. The independent Celtic spirit demonstrated in the Scottish Presbyterian Church provided an example destined to influence the birth of American democracy.

The Act of Union of 1707 had ended generations of conflict between the English and the Scots. It was the beginning of the end of the residual power of the old aristocracies. As a formally united, new, proudly British people, they chose to forge ahead. In both peoples, the sense of self had outgrown both the rough, individualistic selves of the Celtic Scots and the sheepishness of the English. They began to recognize themselves as a new people, able to participate in the common effort to forge ahead. We must note this as an important example of a major cultural change in a large population.

B. REALIZATION OF PATHS TO DEMOCRACY

"To forge ahead" seems to me a useful concept in place, perhaps, of "being progressive." The idea is that with thought, human beings are always capable of forging, welding together, of "cobbling," of creating, a more humane social order. Crafting is another interesting word in this context. Having come through the amazing Industrial Revolution, we might find industrial metaphors, like forging, related to this cultural change helpful. Forging from earliest bronze age to present suggests individual sweat, hard work and application to the task. These are skills we learned in the New Stone Age. They have long been applicable to human creativity. In applying them we have learned many lessons painfully.

In our twenty-first century privileged view of the past, we realize that there have been many occasions when humanity took steps forging democracy. It is significant in retrospect to understand that people have forged democracy out of their basic socialized being. It has been necessary to learn who we are, our minds as well as our bodies, our spirits, our selves. We have learned not to fear one another when we utilize our gifts of mind and speech to find amicable solutions to our problems. We have learned to transcend the limits of all environments (with the exception of the deepest space and oceans, perhaps). We know that the work of "governing" involves more than control; control is necessary to solve the most tenacious of human problems (hunger, disease, social pathology). We have learned to think beyond today, into tomorrow to an amazing degree, assuring food for huge populations against short term droughts. We are prepared to respond to human needs produced by unforeseen natural disasters (witness response to the spate of catastrophic events in 2010 and 2011). In short, we can see what no people before us have foreseen, not completely, not eternally, but to a degree fitting our humanity -- a remarkable humanity forged by millions before us.

Our present understanding of our humanity is the product of history. Forging suggests an individuality and a personal drive characteristic of the entrepreneurs who led the way in nineteenth century America. We might even recognize an association with our "frontier." [149] That image is one of brute individuality, but keep in mind that every cowboy was part of a community in which he lived and, perhaps, too often fought. It was tamed a bit in the phrase "self-reliance." In the nineteenth century particularly, forging suggests huge, steam-powered equipment, symbolic of the Enlightenment devotion to mechanization -- and the World's Columbian Exposition of 1893 in Chicago. Let us not fail to note that all of these forgings were common, corporate, group endeavors. None of them make sense outside a common effort and cultural progress. [150] Learning to labor together was a long, slow process, achieved over thousands of years. Its twists and turns gradually hammered out democracy.

We have remembered the probable origins of authority among leaders of primitive human groupings when populations were very sparse. It is unlikely that leaders at the beginning seized power without regard to the consent of the people. Nor is it likely that "consent" was ever obtained in a formal sense. We recall the gradual evolution of villages and the earliest cities over thousands of years. In this period it is probable that some leaders began to treat power as their own, as the right to exercise authority over people.

But it was during the development of cities into empires that oligarchy assumed the comprehensive right to govern, to exercise authority, and to demand obedience. The people gave up the right to be themselves (however that might have been perceived in those primitive times) and followed their oligarchs. Whatever the leaders may have been called, they had learned to treat people like animals. A major contribution to civilization was the domestication in the Stone Age of all the animals we consider "domesticated." Was that a model for the leaders?[151] Breaking a horse requires teaching it that you are its master.

After sublimation beneath the overarching power of the oligarchs, the role of religion in freeing people from social constraints began slowly. The emergence of Buddhism, Zoroastrian religion and monotheism about the sixth century BCE demonstrates this gradual development. They saw the mental capacity of people to exceed the derogatory image of "dumb" animals. Crafting these new religions may have been the first step in recovery of personal independence from the regimentation of city life in the empires of antiquity. It was a long way from our self-consciousness, but in evolution, small steps can be significant. The word "folk" in a devotional poem of the ninth century was not intended derogatorily, I think, but, over a thousand years later it still carried the sense of being common, the ordinary people, not an elite, an image of a people expected to know their place.[152] Even this minimal respect for "folk" indicates the gradual formation of a new image of people, particularly in the religious context.

The reawakening of the sense of self as the empires disappeared raised people's awareness of their deprivation. Their culture inherited the experience of thousands of years of avaricious leadership in towns and cities following the discovery that things could be hoarded in the citadel -- that wealth could accumulate. By the Middle Ages many people had gathered sufficient wealth to join the aristocracies of privilege. It may very well be that our major preoccupation today with material well-being grows directly out of the Middle Ages aided and abetted by modernity. Barbara Tuchman described Medieval materialism in the Church as an "insistent principle" dominating the culture. The Platonic idea of eternal ideas fit the popular ancient notion of a life after death and made it superior to anything the world could offer. But humanism had begun to challenge that with a new appreciation for the person himself. This was not always focused on a religious orientation. The emergence of the individual out of thousands of years submergence under oligarchy challenged the primacy of life after death and it is "what created the modern world and ended the Middle Ages." Tuchman points out that this transition was compounded by the disjuncture between belief in renouncing material life and practice.

There never was a time when more attention was given to money and possessions than in the 14th century, and its concern with the flesh was the same as at any other time. Economic man and sensual man are not suppressible.[153]

It seems evident that accumulation of wealth contributed to the evolution of our culture. As this occurred with its accompanying leisure, some of the people recovered a bit of the creativity that very ancient people demonstrated in the caves of France late in the Paleolithic era 25,000 years before submitting to the driven character of oligarchic life.

Ancient people had not noticed the distinction we make in work and leisure activities. They expressed their creative side when and how they wished. By the fourteenth century wealth again had begun to provide resources as well as some personal control over time, both of them essential to the development of freedom and self-determination. We had to relearn how to use the resources within our reach. The gradual reintroduction of a degree of freedom had begun to create situations in which we could recover our humanity. The accumulation of wealth, or perhaps more important, the broader distribution of wealth, had begun to make a contribution to Western culture.

Other steps transforming common life were forged along the way. The British forged a parliamentary system which has shown some staying power. Its long history began with the famous Magna Charta of 1215 in which barons cemented their gains in governance with the monarch. The monarchy's checkered history proceeded (with only limited external interference and the Puritan civil war) until the remarkable peace of the Act of Union of 1707 uniting Scotland and England in the new British people. The Church has often been on the reactionary side of progress. But the Scottish Kirk demonstrated the flexibility and appropriateness of democratic governance. That was John Knox's legacy of the sixteenth century. It became the outstanding example of democracy in the world until the American Revolution.

Still, today, the British monarchy is honored in title and pomp, thus knitting the past and future together (as Scott pictured). The French Revolution (1789) produced a rather different system. It, too, has lasted over two hundred years. These are not long spans of time by which to measure stability among nations. But they do represent in our world important new forms of authority in large populations and democratic refinement of the hard won lesson that distributed power is less apt to be misused than oligarchy.

C. MODERN IMPLICATIONS OF ARISTOCRACY

In the seventeenth century, enjoying the fruits of over ten thousand years of growing civilization (since the agricultural revolution), Europeans were found debating the merits of oligarchy versus newly shaping forms of government reflecting their emerging humanity. They knew that they were capable of choosing their leaders and behaving responsibly. In their eyes, they had been doing that for a very long time in their crafts guilds, professional societies, fire-fighting brigades, etc. (with the persistent restraint of residual aristocracy). Since feudalism still prevailed in the sixteenth century, the advent of the Enlightenment began to flicker before the end of the dominant oligarchy. While the new self of the Enlightenment was ready to bloom, it perpetuated much of the past we can lump under the label "aristocracy."

The emergence of the Enlightenment self required two transitions: First, a substantially growing populace of self-conscious people. Only a very self-conscious people could produce the electricity of this period. People had been growing in this direction for literally tens of thousands of years. Within history people had developed among themselves the vocabulary necessary to the habit of thinking and debating the fruits of their thought. And they were aware of the remnants of the feudal past. Though servitude would not end soon, there was a growing middle class of merchants, crafts people and professionals – people who were learning who they were, at least partially free of suppression. And their wealth allowed them some privileges. The nobility had for some time been establishing small libraries; learning broke the bounds of the monasteries.

Second, the emergence of a new culture also required a social revelation. The United States demonstrated the beginning of the end of the illusion that people had to be controlled autocratically. We have tried to detail the gradual emergence of a self-consciousness of sufficient proportions to require the end of oligarchy. It grew slowly through hundreds of generations. The evidence of it is quite plain now, looking back over those centuries of its evolution. The second transition is young. The needed social revelation appeared and gained a place among the emerging nations in a very short period. The United States is only two hundred years old. One might say, with little exaggeration, that these two transitions took, perhaps 1500 years.

This is a very short period in the timetable of human habitation. As it progressed, difficulty in developing the emergent society was complicated by human impatience. Over and over, advanced intellects assumed the clarity and finality of their visions. Erasmus marks a turning point in that he self-consciously understood himself to be participating in the revolution; he did not assume an aristocratic pose as many of his intellectual equals did. The normal failure of a regime was often its entrapment in antiquated thinking so that ideas which might have contributed to success of a regime were dismissed -- perhaps by a tribunal or court of some kind which detected its loss of privilege in the novelty presented. Was this not a major cause of the end of Roman sovereignty? While the long-developing aristocracies of history have helped to create a new human self-consciousness, they have, like the oligarchies out of which they grew, too often assumed a right to protect their own privileges.

While the empires and monarchies had been the turf of aristocracies, the American experiment in democracy was led by the proletarian product of that vast history. Historian Bernard Bailyn calls Americans "provincials." These people were not part of the makers and shakers of that period – increasingly the elites rather than the old aristocrats – who resided chiefly in major cities of England and France. But these "provincials" possessed the self-understanding to accumulate enough wealth to climb to a largely forgotten kind of natural leadership we might consider a unique American aristocracy.

Benjamin Franklin "shrewdly overcame (the provincial) stigma in France by flaunting it." "As a gifted backwoods innocent he (became) the very embodiment of the fashionable ideas of the *philosophes*." And so he secured much needed help for the emergent nation. Within a very short time, the United States demonstrated itself to be a part of their new world. Bailyn gives us perspective on the emergent self in the Revolutionary period in describing the flagrantly inconsistent Jefferson. Like Hume, Jefferson behaved at various times out of pure self-interest, even in areas which he publicly declared "an abominable crime" (i.e. slavery).[154] These prodigious intellects fueled the breaking out of immense human intelligence among these provincial people who under oligarchy might never have been more than overseers of slaves. The provincials, with their modern consciousness of the individuality of human beings within community, brought into reality the new culture of America.

Whereas ancient aristocracy developed as a reflection of the power of oligarchs, this word "aristocracy" now means something more like "prestige" as it accrues to persons of demonstrated capabilities, not only elites, but the intelligence among ordinary people which often gets called simply "common sense." The arrogance that has often infected our language has mellowed in this word. Whereas power deteriorates into violence, populism persistently produces anarchy. Rather than power, leadership (better than aristocracy) reflects a very primitive, natural, and at once a very new concept of authority.[155] It appears that one of the learnings of humanity over these years we have surveyed is the value of leaders in achieving a stable and free social order. We learned the hard way to discredit a variety of styles of leadership. Authority had never accrued to the provincial or the proletariat until the "provincials" in America produced a nation the equal of those in Europe. Society finally had proof that leadership does not derive from social position but from native humanity. Perhaps it was popular reaction to the excesses of aristocracies that taught us how to govern ourselves democratically. But this, too, was "teaching" in the old/new sense of learning through experience.[156] The early American "provincials" were well aware of the shortfall of aristocracies of their time.

D. THE TWENTIETH CENTURY CHALLENGE

The transition is still under way; cultural change has no beginning and no ending. Few would still endorse pure monarchy, though some in our world still exploit oligarchic forms of governance. One of the interesting ongoing experiments is in China today with its new combination of the oligarchy of the party and democratization. Is it likely to be any less bloody than the European transition from monarchy to various democratic regimes? It might be argued whether the path to this combination in China allowed for the development of the productive modern bureaucracy found in the modern West. In the face of 2011 mid-East popular uprisings, again in typical oligarchic fashion, China has chosen to repress popular expressions. All freedom movements are to some extent populist.

We would favor the opinion of J. B. Priestley who suggests that "all politicians who know their business (practice a generous altruism and a sound ethical basis) ... that Machiaveli himself strongly advocates."[157] What seems to be missing from the development of democracy in much of the world is the European experience with morality. Respect for bureaucracy in the West derives from a cultural expectation of honesty and decency . On that basis, we can to an important extent trust one another. While such morality is not uniform nor always practiced, it informs Western culture. Alarms of its disintegration are overdrawn, but always deserve concern. Alarmists have usually overlooked something that should be given more attention. Such is true of the last gasps of old style demagoguery we have witnessed recently.

The quest for individual freedom is dangerous. Villages and cities provided solutions to its tendency to anarchy. Still, the clear individuality of every human being tends to call forth in each person different solutions to every problem of living together.

Even where there is a deep familial history as in China neglect of rural elders by urban families is becoming a problem. It reveals the difference between democracy and freedom. David Harsanyi of the *Denver Post* recently wrote a column on this subject. He reminds us that "both left and right regularly accuse each other of surrendering to the temptation of choosing safety over freedom." The ultra-conservative contradiction of the moment is evident in easy spending for military safety and easy denial of government participation in relief of social ills and in participation in the costs of government. This shows a deeper problem than safety and freedom; it is the denigration of caring. Care for the conditions of the lives of others is a serious moral issue in democracy.

"Decency" has developed a wide range of associations in the West. Many of these seem to be cares of Eastern peoples also, but one Western word describes the cultural difference: "corruption" stands out as a public exception – the deceit and graft that characterize much Eastern dealing. This is not to say that these are not found in the West, but the normal vehicles for dealing with them are extraordinarily different. In our new world, everyone needs to learn how to work at these human differences.

Harsanyi notes that "when liberals crusade ... they fight for a more direct centralized democracy in which liberty becomes susceptible to the temporary whims, ideological currents and fears (rational and sometimes not) of the majority."[158] Liberals tend to expect the operation of Western ethics, while conservatives are yet more selective. As conservatives stimulate the voice of the Center, so the liberal does the same. All dialogue contributes to the humanization of society when people feel sufficient self-confidence to disagree. Then all can learn from their experience. Democracy is the growing agreement not with a particular economic or commercial theory, but of the readiness of the people to live together in constant conversation – bearing the costs of sociality. It is not only a big improvement over all autocracies, it is an implementation of the maturing mind of people

No one can any longer neglect the evolution of the human self toward alert, self-conscious, responsible selfhood. Nonetheless, as residual cultural forms have always confused the transitions of humanity, there are two or three aspects of the past which particularly demand our attention in the twenty-first century.

One of these is the outbreak of reactionary conservatism evident in the term Fundamentalist. It is one of the achievements of the twentieth century that we largely outgrew this popular Protestant orientation, but it hangs on. Even before its resurgence in the 1980s it was a negative influence in America for much of the century. Fundamentalism fostered Jingoism In wartime and reactionary social pressures in peacetime while contributing little to the advancement of uman culture. In the turmoil of the beginning of the twentieth century some mainline churchmen had fixed their attention on an antiquated notion of ationality and were so driven by their preoccupation with certainty -- an outgrowth of the Enlightenment and ationalism -- that they misappropriated obsolete notions of science and used this scientism to build a reactionary religious ethos. Those who found the certainty it espoused irresistible have objected to every mainline church step forward that incorporated current thought about biblical interpretation.

The attitude of certainty is always contagious. It is a component of "charisma." Having found a level of comfort in present conditions, people fear losing anything. They love to be affirmed in their most entertaining whimsies and in their worst fear of others. Fundamentalists do both of these well, witness the popular apocalyptic press. People who have not yet tasted the new mind still depend on being told what to think by antiquated authority structures. They lack the intellectual experience to be critical of their emotional reactions.

Many psychologists have been reminding us that people always tend to interpret anything they come upon to support their beliefs; it happens even if it means twisting reality to fit. This irrational functioning of the brain is demonstrated in a recent study of how police officers who fired their guns remembered the event. We are reminded that a peace officer who fires his or her gun must believe that life is threatened:

> Over a period of five years, the researcher gave hundreds of police officers a written survey to fill out about their shooting experiences. Her findings said that virtually all the officers reported experiencing at least one major perceptual distortion. Most experienced several. For some, time moved in slow motion. For others, it sped up. Sounds intensified or disappeared altogether. Actions seemed to happen without conscious control. The mind played tricks.[159]

Sophisticated skills of human social life include ignoring contradictions and rationalizing other difficulties. Fundamentalists have stretched these practices to absurdity. The mind evolved first, like those of all animals, to assure survival and to reproduce. It was tuned to finding food and to mating. It secured the sleep necessary to the life of higher animals catch as catch can. Rationality has been imposed on it by its innate enjoyment of beauty and the reflection which this encouraged as the brain developed. The Enlightenment illusion of a human achievement of cosmic rationality capable of embracing all of reality does not add up. To be curt about it, we are sinners – that is fundamentally flawed by our self-interest – all of us.

The elite reaction to rationalism is usually called "romanticism."[160] It tended to be reactionary: cult of the hero, revulsion of the ugliness and cruelties brought by industrialism, nostalgia for the idealized Middle Ages. Byron was the poet. Fichte, Carlyle, and Nietzsche were its philosophers. Whatever in these movements helped to free us from residues of oligarchy and subservience was genuinely embraced by many people. But they were in themselves still typified by the either-or, black-and-white sort of thinking of the mind we are learning to leave behind. In the nineteenth century we in the West were still shaking off a residue of the Middle Ages and its rigid Scholastic philosophy.

In the United States, rationalism and romanticism had important effects. The controversy of Charles Briggs in New York, which brought about the separation of Union Theological Seminary from the Presbyterian Church, was fallout from rationalism. Briggs withdrew from his fellow editors of the *Presbyterian Review* (a revered line of Princeton journals) after they insisted on publishing a landmark fundamentalist work. Benjamin Warfield and Archibald A. Hodge published an article that came to be regarded as the classic exposition of the "certainty" sought by popular realism to counter perceived threats of historicist relativity. It joined its view of certainty closely to the idea of an inerrant Bible.[161] In these terms it largely defined the public debate for the next generation. Briggs and Warfield continued the series through growing controversy, a sign of the end of the age of antagonistic scholarship. In 1882 A. A. Hodge resigned as co-editor of the *Review*. In 1883 Briggs challenged the Princeton theology as a corruption of true orthodoxy.[162]

The assumptions of Common Sense Realism included the now obsolescent idea of scientific investigation as value-free and "objective." It also included the ahistorical nature of truth. These contributed to a distinctly Princetonian militant joining of older evangelical views with a magical mathematical specificity and concreteness which was foreign to those views. It was a static way of interpreting the conservative Princeton theology. Hodge and Warfield thus provided an anti-modernist base for religious conservatives of the next generation. Named "Fundamentalism,"[163] its popularity was awesome. It fit the remnant culture of the early nineteenth century and confirmed early American anti-intellectualism following the long preoccupation with the frontier.

For a century we had been preoccupied with building up a whole new continent. For a great part of that time the "West" meant unlimited land and natural resources, not unlike the early spread of *Homo sapiens* across the Eurasian continents. Though we persisted in establishing churches and schools everywhere, the schools largely engaged in the ancient practices of rote learning. "Rote" basically means habit or practice and was applied to mechanical performance or mere routine without particular understanding. The sophisticated debates of Rationalism and Romanticism were esoteric, simply below the radar of that population, though not of the intellectual elites. Americans in the early twentieth century were largely literate, but hardly an educated population.

The two astute Princeton theologians presented themselves as "resolutely rational and scientific" but their claims could not be sustained.[164] Both in relation to Baconian principles[165] and the actual wording of the Westminster Confession[166] their case fell apart. Though it was Briggs who won the following debate, the antiquated scientific orientation of Hodge and Warfield was popular, and this popularity confirmed them in their bias. It perpetuated their views among millions of Americans as fundamentalism swept over the land. "Baconianism" had been adopted as the view of a moderate Enlightenment and moderate Calvinist position so that in 1856 the *American Journal of Science* could assert that "almost all works on science in our language endeavor to uphold the Sacred Word." "The combination of Newtonian science and Protestant religion formed a distinctively American ethos during the first half of the nineteenth century."[167] Dugald Stewart's fluent version of Reid's Common Sense Philosophy was popular among American intellectuals.

This was not unlike the phenomenal Great Awakening of the eighteenth century. Both illustrate the persistence of an antiquated self-consciousness re-enliving the past in the very midst of a major change in human self-awareness. But while the Great Awakening occurred within a culture dominated by a boring and quietly fading Christendom, Fundamentalism occurred during the outspokenly *public* transition from the Rationalism and Romanticism of the nineteenth century to twentieth century modernity. The non-intellectual character of nineteenth century America had not prepared people for this controversy. The Industrial Revolution had thrust change forward to a pace never before experienced. We have labeled the twentieth century movement the Third Reformation. It occurred because American culture did not enjoy the sort of gradual, incremental development of its mind enjoyed in Britain in the Second Reformation. In fact, the sea-change in America was more subtle and more pervasive, as well as more public.

The popularity of the Fundamentalist misconstruction undercut the transition of Christianity in the United States for most of a century. This does not mean that there was no development, but that church people, lay and professional, spent much time worrying about the obsolescent issues of Fundamentalism when they should have been growing under the tutelage of twentieth century scholars like Richard and Reinhold Niebuhr, Karl Barth, Martin Heidegger, Paul Tillich, Karl Rahner, Douglas John Hall, Alfred North Whitehead, George Herbert Mead, Rudolph Otto, Martin Buber, Hans Frei, George Lindbeck, Hans Kung and many others. The twentieth century has seen a huge number of thinkers who have been largely ignored by a public preoccupied with anachronisms like apocalypse. It has been a particularly magnificent intellectual journey from Industrialism. But the new twentieth century mass media have contributed to this ignorance of the public by their preoccupation with what we can only call pandering to the market.

The crystallization of Fundamentalism was, for the Church, then, the defining moment of the twentieth century. It was so pervasive that a secular version of it came to be called American civil religion. Presbyterians especially would be trapped in the ensuing controversy by the residual popular dependence on authority disguised in the rhetoric of religious freedom and orthodoxy. The familiar name of these errors is "Fundamentalism," and their popularity clearly indicates that many Americans were still living in the confusion of mind of the nineteenth century. What we have called arrogance among the elites in the nineteenth century was reflected in the opinionated certainty of the public in the twentieth.[168]

This brand of conservatism has also perpetuated the science-religion debate in the United States. It is part of the background of the Intelligent Design advocates who have been a serious diversion from the business of educating our children. More important, it diverted many intelligent people to focus their religious understanding on the most reactionary forms of Christianity.

While Americans were preoccupied with this nonsense, two world-shaking events were taking shape among the downtrodden of the world. Mahatma Ghandhi forged the nonviolent freeing of India from Britain in the mid-century. And in its last decade, South Africa, where Christians had invoked antiquated moral standards, Desmond Tutu and Nelson Mandela brilliantly and nonviolently forged the end of Apartheid. With only a noting of other liberation movements, particularly in Central America, these two events reset true north on the compass of the twentieth century. These new democratic governments continued a world-wide movement toward democracy.

Our long experience with governing ourselves has suffered for our lack of vision as our minds developed. While tribes and villages had already experienced more natural forms of governing themselves, the growth in populations complicated this problem with numbers of independent people which defied every scheme for control. Over-controlling proved futile, though some in our present world persist in it. Splitting responsibilities for military and taxing functions complemented the existing specialties of shaman and priest. Still there was more complexity, and education and trade required their own governance. While many special areas of social responsibility could be consolidated in "government," religion defied boundaries and won freedom from others at a high cost. We have a long way to go, still, to iron out the bumps and impediments to governance of free people.

While our culture forged its technological character in the caldrons of science, people found new means of expressing their expectations of society. Most recently, they forged thousands of not-for-profit groups which transformed the self-centered nineteenth century into a magnificent philanthropic enterprise. Never before have so many people outspokenly attacked the decadent residues of past cultures with such amazing vigor and for the most part, intelligence. The emergent authority in human life has demonstrated itself in self-disciplined social consciousness. It has gradually dawned on us that it is this refined self-discipline that is the true gift of the Enlightenment. Science is one result, the culmination of centuries of learning to understand our environment. Another result is the refinement of our capacity to care beyond our personal worlds (which are circumscribed by our own kind of humanity) by organizing ourselves and our wealth and applying them to specific human problems. These sophisticated organizations with pointed purposes are so numerous at the beginning of the twenty-first century as to suggest a new institution of civilization.

There are those who will complain about the tyranny of "special interests" in government. Non-Government Organizations (NGOs) in the international scene and non-profit groups in the United States are evidence of the rising sense of selfhood of the population of the world. The contrast to the many people of the world still live in tribal cultures is startling. The misadventure of the United States in Afghanistan is making clear that tribal people have been evolving along with the rest of us. The "aboriginal" folk of New Guinea are not still living, as is often said, in the Stone Age. Evolution, uneven as it is, particularly in the social scene, operates as do the laws of mathematics and physics. Far more complicated, however, the evolution of the science of biology into the specialties of psychology and neurology have been slower in coming to the early points of discovery of life beyond physiology. Why this lag? Probably because we are prone to oversimplify. We love our ability to solve riddles. This points to the special interest most dangerous in the twenty-first century. That is the persistent dominance of science in the Western world.

Science, we are slowly realizing, is another major human discipline, not the supreme human achievement. In fact, like art, music, medicine, and religion before it, science is an indeterminate number of disciplines. The transitions of philosophy and history into varieties of specialization has not come until the past hundred years. But these are finding existence with each other compatible. And religions, too, are coming to terms with the complexity of human expression of awe and wonder, and their many syntheses into worship patterns fitting for the variety of human cultures.

But perhaps most important, our awareness of our unfinished business is increasingly public. As people of conscience world-wide grasp the potentials in our new electronic communication, we will anticipate broadening and deepening of attention to human need – and continued democratization. A song from *Les Miserables* has become the song of rebellion in the public learning of its new identity:

Do you hear the people sing
Singing the song of angry men
It is the music of a people
Who will not be slaves again[169]

But anger itself is a very different thing from the past. Once it was ferocious survival anger. Later it was a protective response to familial identity. It became a rebellion against authority to be feared by cities and eventually nations. And anger can still take any of these patterns. But today we have learned to recognize in anger the need for social change as well as personal adaptation. Over time, people have forged the social mechanisms to enable changes to take place. Our task in the twenty-first century is to refine these and add to them the depth of perception that can allow for all people to live together in peace.

VII. SEARCHING FOR A NEW LANGUAGE FITTING FOR THE NEW SELF

A. THE MODERN FUNCTIONS OF SOCIALITY

Through this long period of the infancy of Western civilization, humans have developed a world-wide culture in which, if they have nothing else in common, they all use language. Early in the development of this new culture, people used unrelated tongues as well as those closely related; the variety when they associated in villages and cities stimulated their brain development. The urge to communicate vocally is apparently part of being human. After long centuries finding no peace under the thumbs of oligarchs, the imaginative ideas of democracy began seeping into the picture. They began to respond to ideas reflecting the original, natural rising to leadership which all knew intuitively. Their minds had been encouraged and stimulated by the rising level of literacy. Then printing and moveable type vastly increased the available supply of reading material. In the late Middle Ages people craved to learn and to create. The period is marked by the pregnant Renaissance. In another five centuries the world would have an example of democratic government working and proving itself flexible and dependable. The United States was to become the world's most powerful nation. But it was not oligarchic. In it the language of democracy would be worked out. Social humanity had evolved dramatically.

The United States reflects its past in many ways. First, it respects individuals, strives to educate them, and provides as it can for justice, peace, prosperity, freedom of thought and religion. We have learned how to express both ourselves and our social nature in all of these areas. The goal is to persistently seek a creative life for all people in constant reconstruction and regular and strictly regulated, yet free, changes in leadership. Second, it bows to the ancient past in acknowledging the contributions of those who have lived before it, and particularly the critical value of centralized government.[170] As doubters of monarchy feared, any centralized power can be dangerous. Fortunately, the Founding Fathers were not governed by fear. They introduced the unitary yet balanced form of governance we call "executive."

The human problem is to resolve problems to the benefit of the people in order to provide order, justice, and necessary services -- the peace which eluded all forms of oligarchy. As persistently adjusted through democratic means, this form has proved it possible to centralize enough power to regulate relations within its parts and reduce conflict to manageable dimensions through the balance of power. Democracy seems to be more successful than any of its predecessors -- with the possible exception of a few exceptionally benevolent individual oligarchs. The monarchists of the seventeenth century feared that democracy would be no better than the uneven and too often despotic monarchies. In a sense they were right; monarchs can be benevolent. But monarchs at that time could not grasp a humanity capable of responsible participation. The prevalent notion of sin was universality, not a social distinction. When the social implications of sin were recognized, constitutional monarchy became a reality and the faith of those who believed that democracies might overcome the ignorance and susceptibility of crowds to demagoguery was vindicated -- even if both still lack perfection.

Our language reflects this learning, but we still use monarchical concepts and persistently seek to shape aristocratic needs to fit our new culture. With self-consciousness, adherence to the democratic process is not dangerous, if we stay mindful of our human nature and of the suffering endured by our predecessors. Within our memories, the industrial age continued the ancient denigration of common workers; the riots and strikes of the twentieth century are familiar reminders of our fathers' and grandfathers' pasts. This can be a healthy social memory if we do not (as so many of our predecessors did of their remembered pasts) idealize it, ignore its suffering, and call it by such names as "golden age" thinking only of the various blessings it did bring. The past is full of its own problems. We don't need to import any of them unnecessarily but neither shall we neglect them. We must learn from them.

Today the major social functions required by human beings are order, justice, education, finance, military, food distribution, waste disposal and religion. Most of all, government provides for peaceful association. These reflect the successful learnings of the variety of human needs which require social control. Military (or "defense" in prescient minds of the mid-twentieth century) has remained a function to be controlled by government, but not without significant restrictions in governmental power. In the United States the military is effectively controlled by non-military people. This civilian control over the military has proved helpful. The classic case of its effectiveness in recent history was General MacArthur's discipline by President Truman in 1951. With the threat of nuclear power it is even more significant that the danger of returning to ancient oligarchic control of the military be restrained. While it is obvious that a military cabal could occur here, it has not happened, and apparently human beings have, in our culture, learned to respect the wisdom in the body politic sufficiently to avoid any sort of coup. In 2010 the President exercised his authority over the military with finese; we see the evolution of the new mind. In fact the function of maintaining the peace has become a self-conscious part of the military domain, and we may hope an indicator of the direction of continued change and greater accountability of the military control apparatus (the Pentagon, especially).

We have dealt here very little with the separation of "an independent judiciary," partly because in the United States the courts are a separate function plainly within the public view. A few conditions are within the power of government to effect: open court records, open court behavior, free and protected counsel for accused persons and for witnesses. Government control of social order can effectively specify a great variety of justice concerns such as limits on punishments, limits on guardianship, etc. It can be watched to provide timely correction of abusive tendencies. Those who have functioned as judges have come under social control. No longer are our judges simply wise men sitting in the judgment seat at the city gate.

The outstanding contrast of the success of democratic mixing and matching of people at the beginning of the twenty-first century over against the long-time failure of oligarchy leaves us with a vocabulary only beginning to adjust to this new world. With the emergence of a newly human mind in humanity we must pay attention to our language. I suggest that we need to weed out and leave behind many of our allusions to warfare and its practice. Sports language today often uses it, and that may be fair venue for much of it, since contact sports in particular are in part a way for people to exercise the modern residue of primitive physical behavior. The tournaments of chivalric knighthood exercised the skills of horsemanship and use of weapons in highly refined ways that became the grist for courts of love and romantic literature. It was a melding of Middle Ages early technological militarism and crystallizing Scholastic theology. Chivalric love (Platonic: only a virgin or another man's wife could be the object) induced the code of conduct. The tournament was the scene of proof.

Chivalry became an effort to exalt women, reversing a long period of denigration. Its ideals instituted piety, bravery, loyalty, and honor in our cultural language; they had been practiced for hundreds of years before the words we use for them emerged. Romanticism at least gave us that; it is no small thing. Modern sports also move us toward a world-wide culture in the universal acceptance of rules, adherence to standards of sportsmanship, and attraction to unfamiliar sports by observation of others dedicated to them. Sports give occasion for much human interaction we would miss without them, with the remarkable capacity to bring magnificent cross-sections of populations together in massive audiences contributing to cultural enrichment. It is evident that sports – not the entertainment industry – command the road to cultural cross-fertilization.

The lack of a neuter form in English produced a language crisis in twentieth century America when the rising feminist movement took umbrage at the persistent use of "man" to mean "humanity." The problem remains without an agreed solution. But eventually, Americans will solve this problem comfortably.

The problem of gender, the problem of physical aggression, the problem of disrespect -- especially of disabled persons and minorities -- all such problems represent challenges to twenty-first century language and culture. Individually, we can contribute to the development of our new culture by controlling our use of obsolescent language and by engaging in extensive and caring use of language in conversation. We have observed the perverse tendency to drive wedges between people (as in the favoritism of aristocrats) and to exploit prevalent idiosyncrasies (as in all demagoguery). Yet the basic human love of personal interaction has produced increasingly effective government, cooperative solutions to human problems (increasing food production), conversion of degenerate practices to creative correction of cultural nonsense (chivalry), and awakening to the quality of life prescient people have pointed to for thousands of years (the end of slavery).

B. THE NEW MIND'S AWARENESS OF CHANGE

We have noted throughout the text anticipations of progressive development of the human mind. It seems there have always been among us some human beings whose minds were far more perceptive than others, some without a clue, and many who followed their more voluble and sometimes charismatic leaders. It often turned out that these latter leaders were not newly evolving persons but reactionary blind leaders of the blind. Fluency has often enabled pedants to beguile many. This pattern is more evident in society as the society is more transparent. Human response to fluency was probably responsible for the emergence of aristocracy from the beginning. As organization began to percolate through human communities, the need for leaders expanded beyond the oligarchs' abilities, and the more articulate members of the community would naturally be chosen to fill these needs. Each one contributed to the emergent culture. Even those who blindly followed the ubiquitous blind leaders have contributed, even if only by restraining progress. Their slower perception of their critical capacities has unfortunately made progress difficult.

The universal tendency of crowd psychology, sheep following sheep, has always been reactionary. We have used this word often because it is such a succinct way to say "going backwards." Partly because language, for all its flexibility, tends to develop after people have begun to perceive changes in their world, those fluent at any given moment tend to use language which may already be obsolete or at least obsolescent. The current conservative drum beating against government "interference" is an excellent example. Since any regulation of behavior is perceived negatively by some people, these will perceive any effort to improve the conditions of life negatively. Modern road-planners, try as they may to improve the flow of traffic, will change the way traffic flows, and also they will often find it necessary for the public good to use some land that has been used "as long as anyone can remember" for a private use, for example, the old little corner grocery. During the twentieth century the "mom and pop" shop was an entrepreneurial bonanza which has practically disappeared. While there is seldom a single cause for such changes, they are easy fodder for demagogues.

So, along with natural evolution of the mind evident in almost concurrent worldwide social changes, long before written history, we see that human beings themselves have contributed significantly to the evolution of culture. We have tried to highlight a few of the individuals who have made noteworthy contributions. Evidence of the emergent mind seems to multiply as years pass. Record-keeping, for example, has expanded incrementally; it seems that this expansion is itself evidence of the evolution of the human mind. Of course it also reflects the persistent growth in commerce. The expansion goes hand in hand with changes in the cultures of each of the people involved. It seems doubtful that many of those people were at all aware of evolution. But no doubt many did sense that these changes were of value to others.

Transference of learnings was aided by the curiosity we sometimes call wander-lust. Human beings have carried news hither and yon since the first adventurers out of their nests made friendly contact with other humans elsewhere. The skills of "adventurers" undoubtedly included the same friendly demeanor we associate with certain people today. The ancient Phoenicians must have developed such skills to become the dominant traders of the Mediterranean world, doing business with many different people. Thus, when they discovered the earliest known use of the alphabet in a Sinai gem mine, they were in a position to spread the technique far and wide. Based on sound rather than sight, it simplified their own record-keeping in dealing with many languages in different ports. The alphabet reshaped not only Greek and Hebrew, but many other languages. They must have recognized the value of such changes. But it is entirely unlikely that anyone thought of anything evolving ! Change was simply something one noticed.

129

When we turn to the important changes in the twentieth century, we understand that these started long before in changes such as we have noted. But in the nineteenth and early twentieth centuries (we can see now better than we could then) a few laid the groundwork for changes that we can now document. There are many noteworthy names in this period. We purposely avoid exploring the momentous progress of science, particularly psychology which has grown from infancy to maturity in this period. But three names among them most relevant to our concern in this paper were born in the last half of the nineteenth century: Alfred North Whitehead, Martin Heidegger and Ludwig Wittgenstein. These three (with many others) leaped into the future on the backs of the innumerable others to whom we allude. We will note again that they are all philosophers.

Whitehead was born in 1861 a few years before his co-author of the landmark *Principia Mathematica*, Bertrand Russell (1872). It was Russell who brought the third member of this group into academia by writing the forward to his *Tractatus*, published a few years after Russell and Whitehead's *magnum opus* in the second decade of the twentieth century. Those were the heady days ending the overconfidence of the Enlightenment, and Wittgenstein (1889-1951) has long been credited with early critique of that decisive period.

Whitehead, at the end of the twentieth century, has become the doyen of post-modern theology known generally as "process theology."[171] In 1973 Floyd Matson and Harold Shilling built on Whitehead's position to advocate a "postmodern science." David Ray Griffin tells us that "Charles Altieri argued that it is Whitehead's philosophy, even more than Heidegger's, that best explains the connection between fact and value suggested by a number of American poets considered by Altieri to be distinctively postmodern.... Frederick Ferre shortly suggested that process theology presents a postmodern version of Christianity."[172]

Altieri's link with poetry holds two lessons: (1) Art, even more importantly than mathematics, throughout human existence was prolegomena to cultural development. So we find the ancient art in French caves as sophisticated in some respects as modern art. And (2) he reminds us of the great variety of forms human beings have made with words. As an undefinable spectrum, the range from poetry to philosophy, to criticism, to science, to literature, to news, to commentary, to talk radio might be described as detail, precision, elaboration or exotica. Words, words, words! It is no longer necessary for us to insist on our words with our definitions. Communication is more than words, even before them, humans found ways to communicate and still depend on these more than we admit. In our ingenuity, we surely can find ways to explore the height and depth of our understanding and include art and music. The day has arrived when we are at ease with a variety of words to express ourselves. But a very few years ago, that was not the case.

Martin Heidegger, born in 1889, of course had his direct predecessors in the nineteenth century panoply of too many names to rehearse. In the age of Existentialism,[173] he was mistakenly identified with Jean Paul Sartre. But Heidegger argued that he was concerned not with man but with being. Man was integral to his thinking though his concern was with existence and the finitude of being.

Heidegger's influence on the twentieth century is profound. He spent his career asking big questions, "rethinking the entire history of Western philosophy" according to Edward B. Fiske. His keystone *Being and Time* was published in German in 1927 and in English in 1949. The delay reminds us how different the world was before 1950! The long delay in translation contributed to the persistence of the German terms in the work, for example, *Dasein* ("human being","being there," "living"). Like *Dasein* (capitalized as a German noun) even those words which are translated often appear abstruse, such as "readiness-at-hand" and "presence-at-hand." One must think about their meanings. "His wide influence is due to the fact that Heidegger does not ground his thinking in concepts, but in average, everyday practice; in what people do, not in what they say." That is to emphasize our finitude, being as part of the physical world in a world still carrying forward the culture of the Middle Ages when transcendence of the physical world was the almost universal reaction to the degradation of human life produced by the exploitative ancient culture.

Because he looks for what makes our practices hang together, Heidegger also discovers and thinks about marginal practices that do not fit in with the dominant ones. History proceeds by the re-gestalting of the relationship between marginal and central practices. This understanding in turn requires an account of the cultural role of rituals, sagas, and gods -- territory that (also) fascinated Wittgenstein, but which he thought was beyond philosophy.[174]

These authors could as well have said, "Culture proceeds by re-gestalting..." since the process of cultural change is the persistent rethinking that goes on in human concourse; the result is history. But our concerns were not theirs. Heidegger prepared the ground for post-modernism in his unique application of empiricism, overcoming the long-standing temptation to explore concepts.

It was a gratifying surprise to find in this same volume an article by John Haugeland (University of Pittsburgh), "Dasein's Disclosedness." The title demonstrates its relevance. It is in Haugeland's revealing discussion that we find a clear conjunction with the thinking in this paper. He quotes Heidegger:

Self and world belong together in one entity, Dasein. Self and world are not two entities, like subject and object, or like I and thou; rather, self and world are the basic determination of Dasein itself, in the unity of the structure of being-in-the-world.[175]

For Haugeland, Heidegger's Dasein is not equivalent to person or individual subject both because (like the individual's awareness of the integrity of other people called "ToM,"[176]) it comprises more than one person and because it comprises more than just people. Yet, unquestionably, "Dasein" is Heidegger's technical term for whatever it is that is essentially distinctive of people; and, in each case, we *are it*. How can this be? Haugeland then proposes to "sketch an interpretation according to which Dasein is a 'living' (currently being lived) *way of life*." We remember that "culture" is the way we live!

In this sketch, Haugeland discusses this typical philosophical problem. With a variety of special words, Heideger explains his thinking with notions of "foundness" and "telling." By "foundness" he means the sense in which we discover ourselves already situated. Regardless of our choices, the fact is that we are where we are. We cannot be somewhere else except by another choice. In our Christian vocabulary we have spoken of Providential location for a purpose. Heidegger does not discuss purpose. But where I am is where the world and I are in conjunction at this moment and where I must act.

"Telling" approaches the discussion of purpose obliquely. It is the articulation of the significance or intelligibility of what we know, says Haugeland, both in the sense of separating or carving up, and in the reductive sense of expressing in words. "Carving up" is not intended as dissection (as in biology) but is the essential public expression of distinguishing characteristics. This use of words always misses the wholeness of its subject but it suggests, it indicates. It is essential to the public formation of our culture.

In regard to "telling," Haugeland hypothesizes that we are, in fact, saying whether we believe that what we have heard in communication "does or does not accord with the norms we share -- in effect, telling right from wrong."[177] In conversation it is the nature of human communication to reveal and influence the stance of the current culture. Telling is balanced by listening. It is worth pondering how this coincides with the discussion of truth in chapter VIII, section A.

Understanding, Heidegger says, is projecting in terms of possibilities. But projecting is not predicting the future direction of things, nor is it planning a project. Possibilities are not things or states of affairs. *Possibilities* for Heidegger are *new options* and alternatives opened up: roles that might be played and ways they can be played. Such possibilities are opened up in democratic discussion. Of course we need planners and planning. But it is always worth our attention to explore possibilities in the planning process, especially options and alternatives.

Heidegger avoids determinism by insisting that it is in the nature of Dasein that roles emerge, in which we deal with things and take care of business. It is not outside forces that determine our paths, but because we deal with things as having roles and proper uses, they do have them. It seems to me that he is saying that it is we ourselves who have them in our heads (minds). We choose to accept roles and to perform duties. We have a habit of ascribing them to things and to our dealings. But, like our habitual ascription of reality to constructions of abstractions (like emotion), we construct paths which enable us to escape from responsibility. Determinism is an unhappy construction.

> When Heidegger Introduces his account of understanding as projecting in terms of possibilities, he speaks first and foremost of self-understanding. On the present reading, self-understanding would be casting oneself into roles; part of my self-understanding, might be my casting myself as schoolteacher or a chess-player.... To cast oneself into such a role is to take on the relevant norms -- both in the sense of undertaking to abide by them and in the sense of accepting responsibility for failings.[178]

Thus we find in contemporary thought considerable support for the notion of self we have been discussing just as we find repeated support for Whitehead's notion of creativity. The passage of the past hundred years has brought corroboration of the prescience of a wide variety of late nineteenth century intellectuals. The special language Heidegger fathered into American philosophic debate may or may not need extension, but the extended discussion of his ideas may help us to understand the nature of our new *selfs*. Outside of psychological literature, it may be the most pregnant new language available. Whitehead also helps on this score. Such language and the events of our past century give us grist for our efforts as we move on.

As Heidegger struggled to surmount Romanticism, he found English and American thinkers at the beginning of the twentieth century exploring linguistics as a way to keep philosophy an "armchair discipline" with territory safe from the intrusion of science, art and history. Richard Rorty suggests that this was an attempt "to find a substitute for Kant's 'transcendental standpoint.' Replacement of 'mind' or 'experience' by 'meaning' was supposed to insure the purity and autonomy of philosophy by providing it with nonempirical subject matter."[179] Or, possibly, Rorty's suggestion is an obsolescent evaluation. Might it be that no effort to maintain a place for philosophy was involved. What was happening was release from the overpowering pursuit of knowledge (whether about reason or substance) to grasp the fundamental human capacity for more disciplined thinking. That, after all, is what science is. Richard Feynman put it graphically: scientific creativity is a straitjacket, as unyielding as liberating. Science in the modern world is an extraordinarily sophisticated set of disciplines. Knowledge has become simply our best accumulated common sense, no longer a holy grail.[180]

Science is not a new religion. It is many highly disciplined methods of searching for a grasp of various aspects of reality. And application of our intelligence to solving human problems (as we are doing increasingly through NGOs and reformation of government) is another demonstration of our growing human capacity for a thoroughly socialized self-discipline. The common denominator is the culmination of five millennia of human development out of an embryonic agreement to cooperate. The journey has taken us through three thousand years of obedient servitude into growing self-discipline. Heidegger's contribution is that of an early post-modern thinker detailing the evolution of the human mind.

It seems to me that there is great correspondence between the thinking in this paper and Haugeland's interpretation of Heidegger. To proceed into the twenty-first century we might want to acknowledge the leading of Heidegger along with many other prescient thinkers. In many ways they uncovered for us the new sense of self we can only now see burgeoning around us. Evolution seems to creep along. I should expect philosophers to grasp their relevance to the situation in which we now find ourselves. People like Heidegger opened the way. There is a new awareness of the wholeness of the human being, a concept basic to the Bible, quite beyond the reductive tendency in the Enlightenment. Whitehead and Wittgenstein too began to see through that error. It suggests to me the physical evolution of the brain, but at least, perhaps, the persistent development of human consciousness seeing beyond the obvious. Two additional names in different venues bear attention here, Margaret Mead and George Steiner. Both had much larger views.

In 1970 anthropologist Margaret Mead published *Culture and Commitment* detailing her plea to see beyond the obvious in viewing the new world bursting forth in the hands of the young. She was well qualified to consider the "youth revolution" in the context of cultural change The first of the generation of young which she described have now become senior citizens, the complex years of their lives now concluding. A larger percentage of them than any previous generation survive. We move ahead together. Together with them, we who are really old have an unparalleled opportunity, for we are heirs of the most progressive century in all history.

By World War II a residual pride in nuclear families induced the burgeoning parental generation which followed to treat their children much as they had been treated, with confident adjustments to the new freedoms of the suburban culture. But there were no farm chores to teach discipline and responsibility, no town ethos with its knowledge and trust in which to communicate to parents the obstreperous behavior of their young. The rush of the rural population to the city accelerated this disjuncture. The continued enlargement of the size of urban settlements exacerbated all the existing problems. Suddenly, it seemed, a majority of us became urbanized. Though we had been experiencing this same growth phenomenon for a very long time, we had not learned to anticipate its implications. As always, we found ourselves confused. Times of confusion have always produced cultural change.

The immediate effect was to loose the tongues of the young. In the West youth were considered to be countercultural naturally. But they had seldom before been so large a portion of a very large population. As the market responded to this huge group, the airwaves suffered persistent language problems. Sloppy language, disrespect for conventions, and the use of terms that were private or even technical became commonplace. "Blip" and "Beep" became bywords. By the 1970s the more avaunt guard adults were trying to learn to use the new, rather loose language. "Sex" was in. Churches adopted gender-free rules for speech. The confusion was evident in the allowance by the mainline churches of both grape juice and wine in communion without regard to the effect of this on the symbolism of the "common" cup. The Roman Catholic Church (and others) found restrictions on contraceptives blatantly disregarded. Parents joined the young people in their rebellion.

As the proverbial teen rebellion exploded in the sixties, it shaped up in the 1970s as resistance to hard-won intelligent compliance with authority. Enlisted elders encouraged explosive language, innocent shall we say, or unaware at least, of the danger of anarchism that had long Impeded the conversion of exploitative authority to democracy. Perhaps this was one of the last remnants of our oligarchic beginnings; it was part and parcel with the ending of patriarchal authority. As we encouraged the movement of women toward whole equality with men, we faced changes in the way we had raised our children. In our national origins, remember, we had perpetuated a paternalistic culture while fearing authority. That had contributed to forming a very weak -- too weak -- democratic government. The Articles of Confederation proved within months of origin that our central government had to be strengthened. In six years it was replaced by what is called a "rigid" Constitution; it is hard to change. We had already learned something else

134

about authority in a few months of freedom in our new country. Social controls over large
populations are necessary even in a democracy.

Strangely, the ordering of life in all its parts followed a course of its own. It was an
apparent "ying and yang." In the loosening of restraints in the 1960s and 1970s, the
conservative right wing began agitating with increasing effectiveness for "family values." It
was a dangerous "ying"! As the English enjoyed the maintenance of old values in their
Scottish branch with Walter Scott's stirring novels, the residual hunger for former ways is
apt to overshadow the troubles associated with them. However, modern communications
vastly complicated their tendency to reaction. The trouble with their antiquated approach,
of course, was that they essentially made the rest of the world their adversaries – the
yang set in motion -- even though many people throughout America agreed with some or
all of their positions. It was the beginning of the end of adversarial partisanship. Politicos
followed the money flowing through the expansive right wing television pundits' hands.
But far from representing most Americans, the conservative movement was a vocal
minority endowed with familiar language persuading many others to join them.

The young, and many adult conservatives also, had grown up and taken on their
adult minds in the comfort of the materialistic post-war culture. The Me Culture failed to
recognize a progressive opportunity in its antagonism to the rapidly changing dominant
culture. The immaturity of the "ying" was showing in the persistence of antiquated views,
reactionary tendencies, and foot-dragging familiar among the recalcitrant in every decade.
They called themselves the Moral Majority. As they gathered confidence, people of
common sense were gradually getting their act together without capitulating. The "yang"
kept growing quite invisibly.

Some of this settled down by the 1980s when reactionary conservatives were
feeling their muscle, but this "majority" movement would soon disband. We have
previously reviewed some of the results of that movement. But the new mind was
gestating in all that had happened. It would be another twenty years before it could
demonstrate an alternate unity that began to excite the younger generation. Even many
congressional leaders gave up their sense of the whole nation to assume a narrow,
evangelistic religious agenda. All in all, the interplay generated a broad-based public
reaction to a Congress sorely tempted by populist readings. It was fertile ground for a new
group of vitriolic pundits (read "false prophets"). Again, as in the development of the city
four thousand years ago, people's self-understanding suffered appropriation by power.
This time is was the persuasive power of antiquated religious sentiments. What then was
simple ignorance, today is the unfortunate fruit of anti-intellectualism.

Social change is instigated by any important change in the social context.[181] In the
democratic context of the United States, changes like those of the post World War II period
are instigated first by a powerful segment of the population to which the media and all
institutions must respond. So, immediately, authorities began to clamp down on the
surprisingly large and growing number of young people in the 1960s and outright rebellion
took place. Government use of power to control people (such as armed national guard
troops at Kent State University) was reactionary. But this was not solely a youth rebellion;
the Civil Rights Movement and the Open Housing efforts, to say nothing of the Women's

Movement were largely led by adults. The change taking place in America was something dramatically new. Language began changing immediately.

After the seriousness of the cultural change became apparent, various institutions, certain churches among them, began to change language and the nature of ministry among the young. Strangely, in this period we are reminded that evolution does not favor any part of the population (certainly not academics among whom were Tim Leary types who smoked pot with the kids). People in all walks of life sought to understand the evident transition. People of slums and suburbs, in science, religion, government, and elsewhere sought to participate responsibly according to their own insights. At the same time, of course, the technological juggernaut loosed after World War II continued to expand the world available to everyone, especially through electronic communication, affecting practically everybody in every walk of life. Eventually it produced the "flat world."

Our approach in this book suggests that all of us seeking a new path consider the origins of our culture and how we ourselves affect the culture. As we talk we are shaping the culture of our children and our neighbors as well as ourselves. By grasping this view of ourselves, each person unique among the billions we have become, we can learn to prepare all children for wider fields of vision, for greater accommodation of differences among human beings, for friendly competitive patterns that do not destroy adversaries. If, as some think, men played little part in nurture of young children until late in the twentieth century, it is time for men as well as women to pay attention to the critical early years of life. We can help adolescents, also, in their difficult transition to adult mentality. We can establish patterns of communication in which we are seen by our peers to listen when we hear them speak. We can choose community leaders whose sense of self is not driven by unfortunate residues of antiquated cultures. We must choose leaders who are tuned to this new world already emerging.

George Steiner was one of the great minds of the late twentieth century. In 1971 he caught the sweep of the cultural change we have been discussing, and in a salubrious short passage identified the very serious problem now facing us in the twenty-first century. In his *In Bluebeard's Castle*, he analyzed the tumult of the 1960s. His summary holds wisdom for us as we proceed.

> An explicit grammar is an acceptance of order: it is a hierarchization, the more penetrating for being enforced so early in the individual life-span, of the forces and valuations prevailing in the body politic. The tonalities of "class," "classification," and "classic" are naturally cognate. The sinews of Western speech closely enacted and, in turn, stabilized, carried forward, the power relations of the Western social order.

Steiner dissected the use of language against the establishment in the Sixties, pointing out the ways in which language differentiates the sexes as well as plebian and aristocracy. He points out the explorations of Heidegger and Ricoeur and how our language is action based ("performative") and has substantially affected our ideas of knowledge and of art. In the "fabric of life ... language holds a sovereign, almost magically validated role." The countercultures of the Sixties used this to "demolish the hierarchies and transcendence-values of a classic civilization.... The insurgent and the freak-out (broke) off discourse with a cultural system which they despise as a cruel, antiquated fraud." He saw this as a threat to the ties between us produced by a common language.

Steiner suggests (in the middle of the mid-century turmoil) that care of our cultural values might be necessary to avoid a total cultural collapse. But he is not referring to the "family values" captured a decade later in the attacks of the ultra-right wing. Attention to values, like peace, justice, self-confidence, openness and honest communication on the other hand, may be required to build a healthy and sustainable culture for the twenty-first century. The events of the next twenty years vindicate him. And fifty years later we still suffer the open conflict that marked the Sixties. It was taken as an opportunity by the reactionary element in the population which then exercised the humiliating crying of bold voices to energize the latent conservatives of many stripes against American institutions. Any doubt about the depth of such reaction was dispelled by the gross events of the Sixties and the moving novel by Harper Lee, *To Kill a Mockingbird* (1962).

The self-serving battle lines of the present stalemate in American government is a direct result. Not only does it reflect the same misunderstandings of cultural change as did the progenitors of American Fundamentalism, it adds the sophistication of an advancing culture which has come to terms with the same massive evolution of Western life. Thus the emergence of probability theory, Einstein's general theory of relativity, the rejection of the Newtonian clockwork worldview, and the emergence of a balanced socialized individual view in psychology have given the reactionary arguments new fuel for argument. Their enslavement to the neat absolutism of the old world view remains diametrically opposed to the contextual sensitivity of the new mind. As the twentieth century progressed, they attacked every development in its infancy before it had time to mature. And their persistent enemy-psychology continues still to foment dissension among elites no longer facile at parrying with such attacks. Unfortunately, they are only recently beginning to wake up to the folly of their early Enlightenment attachments.

But day by day, there are signs visible to perceptive people that the unreality of the Conservative orientation must be put behind us. The prominence of the "Tea Party" signals its own bankruptcy. The apogee of that movement has been passed and the evolution of the new mind promises a new future.

C. OPENING OF A NEW FIELD: THE EXPANDING SELF

The twentieth century has been marked by this surprising expansion of our understanding of ourselves and of our world marked so well by Steiner. The array of "micro" prefixes on old disciplines is lengthy. But we have most recently been excited by the emergence in our own time of the successful probing of fields which have seemed beyond our reach like the "fathomless" deeps of the oceans, the heavens, and intellect (e.g. chaos theory).

Chaos is the fathomless sinkhole of ordinary things which so far we have been satisfied to force into intelligible shape rather than understand. Understanding chaos was probably totally beyond the capability of pre-modern minds. The Greek root of "chaos" means "gape," as "yawn"! But striving at the edges of our understanding has played an important part in the emergence of the new mentality among us. The advent of chaos studies should shock us into realizing the momentous advance we are now witnessing.

Our best illustration of chaos may be the shape of the British Isles (to use a familiar territory); Euclid's idealized shapes cannot fit the shape of sea shore borders anywhere. For thousands of years we have thought of the ocean deeps and most natural shapes as chaotic. It is a case of naming something to make it manageable. But, more important, this meant making it easy to avoid. Whenever natural science has run into "chaos" we have largely ignored it as impenetrable and called it – "noise." (The static that interferes with electronic communication has long been called noise!) Our science and its models were limited to 'linear" statistics – Euclidean shapes as it were – forcing "non-linear" problems into noisy obscurity.

James Gleick tells us, "In 1977 chaos offered no mentors. There were no classes in chaos, no centers for nonlinear studies and complex systems research, no chaos textbooks, not even a chaos journal."[182] There was no vocabulary for it. Yet, true to the pattern of innovation throughout history in the whole world, elements of discovery were made at first by a very few people, and only with their brilliance and hard work did their number multiply in many fields of inquiry. In the beginning there was no language to explore the ins and outs of chaos.

One of these early explorers was Mitchell Feigenbaum, an extraordinarily bright man who never seemed to produce anything of his own, but solved others' difficult problems as with a snap of his fingers. Yet in 1974 he was working on aspects of science that had always been elusive, "the disorder of the atmosphere, the turbulent sea, the fluctuations of wildlife populations and the oscillations of the heart and the brain. The irregular side of nature, the discontinuous and erratic side" has always been full of imponderable puzzles to science, or as Gleick adds, or worse, full of "monstrosities."[183] Until the very end of the twentieth century the long-standing human tendency to ignore or mystify the imponderable and the unknown had controlled and limited thinking that otherwise might have been done. Language to deal with it never emerged. Then, suddenly it seems, chaos theory could finally be explored with impunity, and the new mind we have been noting expanded to growing numbers of scientists, theologians, and philosophers (to say nothing of others).

Feigenbaum was one of a very small number of thinkers who were unknown to one another. They were scattered in the United States, England, France, Russia and elsewhere working on everything from weather to movement of animal populations. They began to search for language to carry on the work. It was a French scientist who introduced the term "strange attractors" in his search for words to describe strange and elusive discoveries in his work. A mathematician at Berkeley created a small group to study "dynamical systems." Benoit Mandelbrot at IBM (who began to ponder the subject vaguely as early as 1960) concocted the name "fractals" in 1975 for the uneven, irregular shapes his geometry had generated.

Mandelbrot was acutely aware that Euclidean geometry did not do justice to many natural shapes. Clouds are not spheres, mountains are not cones, and lightning does not travel in straight lines. Euclid reduced such shapes into overly simple spheres, triangles, and cones and gave us a new form of Pythagorean geometry which had lasted 2500 years.[184] Fractals are shapes as hard to identify as the British Isles. Mandelbrot had uncovered an article from the 1920s about the problems posed by coastline definitions. Some such problems seem obvious or tedious. But measurement is the grist of science and fractals began to open up the measurement of the innumerable phenomenon which are not Euclidean in nature.

The growing array of people pushing open this new frontier we call chaos included seasoned professionals and younger people as well, a sign of the growing number of people who seem to embody the emergent mind of the twenty-first century. As a rule, however, as we age, we become more and more enslaved to our familiar language, so we find an Einstein having difficulty adjusting to later twentieth century innovations like quantum mechanics.[185] We note again that one of the problems in education has been the misdirection of students away from innovation by older mentors who fail to see the potential for grants and new jobs in their strange new orientations.[186] The key to our new mental receptiveness to the new world ahead of us is most generally labeled "openness." It is an old idea of human mentality that increasingly characterizes us. We are no longer afraid of new ideas – and we are aware of our tendency to hold on to old ones. We will, then, inevitably find more "new minds" among those who are younger, but not necessarily.

The number of contributors to chaos theory has multiplied over the past 25 years, beginning with a conference in 1980. In these few years language to pursue chaos has evolved. It is an example of how self-conscious we must be in using the basic tool that makes us human -- words. George Steiner noted the tie between classic values and the premier role of language. Now we recognize that language is in itself cheap. As the source of our culture, it is the way we use it in our culture which enhances or cheapens its role. The very uniqueness of chaos language has helped to sustain its short, developing life.

Robert Stetson Shaw, bearded Boston native and Harvard graduate, was just a few months away from completing his doctoral thesis on superconductivity. Shaw gradually weaned himself from superconductivity to embrace the exploration of chaos theory with three other students in what they called "The Dynamical Systems Collective" -- others sometimes called it the "Chaos Cabal." The three students were Doyne Farmer, Norman Packard and James Crutchfield. Originally supported in the physics department at Santa Cruz, their project eventually was set loose and they survived by hook and crook on their own. Farmer's explanation:

The same thing really drew all of us: the notion that you could have determinism, but not really. The idea that all these classical deterministic systems we'd learned about could generate randomness was intriguing. We were driven to understand what made that tick. You can't appreciate the kind of revelation that is unless you've been brainwashed by six or seven years of a typical physics curriculum....

Nonlinear was a word you only encountered in the back of the book.... You would usually skip the last chapter on nonlinear equations (which simply reduced) them to linear equations, so you just get approximate solutions anyway.... (Nonlinearity) seemed like something for nothing, or something out of nothing.... Why wasn't it part of what we were taught?[187]

Their leaps to determinism, the nature of intelligence, and the direction of biological evolution dismayed their professors. Such language was not really acceptable in the field of physics which pointed in another direction. The students' language reflected the philosophic topic of free will to reconcile it with determinism, recognizing the impossibility of predicting what any case of chaos will do next. Farmer continued, expressing the universal Whitehead identified, creativity: "At the same time I'd always felt that the important problems out there in the world had to do with the creation of organization, in life or intelligence...."

D. EMERGENT WORLD ORDER

The chaos pioneers were forging a new understanding of order, with randomness emerging in our scientific world with means of talking about it and observing it in meticulous detail. Their growing experience led them to anticipate that they could find an underlying order in chaos. Their individual intuition led them on against a variety of social forces, and they had the help of an increasing variety of people.

Albert Libchaber, born in Paris son of Polish Jews, had obtained a rare copy of Goethe's monograph *On the Transformation of Plants*. In it Goethe expressed his concern that critical thinkers were focusing on static things. But, with Plato, we are aware that change is constant; vital forces fill life. These are the forces which give us constantly changing shapes on the computer screens of chaos researchers. Libchaber was an experimenter. Feigenbaum, the theorist, had by 1979 discovered *universality*. It was Pierre Hohenberg, of AT&T Bell Laboratories in New Jersey, who brought the two men together. This illustrates the growing acceptance of contributions from a variety of people during the twentieth century.

Feigenbaum's "universality" emerged from a rigorous schedule of continuous work required by the primitive computer facilities available. Universality made the difference between beautiful and useful. Universality offered the hope that by solving an easy problem physicists could solve much harder problems. Feigenbaum believed that his theory expressed a natural law about systems at the point of transition between orderly and turbulent. With the theory, one could see the frequencies building toward turbulence. Though its general applicability seemed clear to Feigenbaum, it was difficult for others to grasp.

The experimenters' discoveries helped set in motion the era of computer experimentation. Computers could produce the same qualitative pictures as real experiments and do so millions of times faster and more reliably. The word "flows" had become current, such as the flow of currents in the Gulf Stream in which a warm flow "builds its own banks out of the cold water through which it flows." "In the age of computer simulation, when flows in everything from jet turbines to heart valves are modeled in supercomputers, it is hard to remember how easily nature can confound an experimenter."[188]

But we are told that "no computer can completely simulate even so simple a system as Libchaber's liquid helium cell." It was the experimenter's creed that Libchaber liked to say that he would not want to fly in a simulated airplane for wondering what had been omitted from the computer model. The old tension between physics and mathematics reared its head. But Libchaber would first agree that he was doing mathematics, and then insist that his patterns, though abstract, reflected real life. They were *experiments* in which the universal Feigenbaum constants turned into a physical reality, measurable and reproducible.[189]

We humans seem to be disposed to find order: From hunters watching the habits of their prey to discover the best method of killing them, or chaos scientists insisting on the existence of an underlying order in random events. In our avoidance of error we try to find the optimum ordering of our lives. Over and over people have stretched credulity by extending their core concepts of order to absurdity. But, in the process of searching, we are often at a loss to know when we have gone too far. Like the snowflake building itself larger and larger as it falls and wafts to and fro in the air's turbulence, we are inclined to pursue an idea, a direction, an organizing principle as far as we have time and energy.

Perhaps death is the only exit from our determination. Or is it? By opening our minds to the thoughts of others we can provide ourselves and our cultures the immense advantage of including the contributions of multiple minds. The result of some five million years of evolution after leaving our nearest animal ancestors, combined with the learnings of untold generations, especially in historic time, we find ourselves personally in need of the connectivity provided humans by speech. We are not driven by base drives beyond our control. We have powerful minds and we can choose to listen to one another. We can choose to be productive, participating, joyful members of our many communities, constantly listening for clues to correct our paths.

E. LIMITS TO GROWTH

Is our long-standing hunger for knowledge at a place now where we can corral our appetite? Or are we doomed to pursue our knowledge-hunger regarding the physical world to infinity? I think not. The time has come when we can establish cultural goals which are more profound than expansion of knowledge. There still is much to learn, much to know about what we already have uncovered. But it becomes increasingly clear that our pursuit of knowledge has been one-sided. It has issued in a plethora of material goods and made us all materialists. That was the easier part of using our minds after the Enlightenment. In the Middle Ages, before the development of what we call "method" and the emergence of science, it was easier for people to focus attention on spiritual development and the pursuit of abstractions. Yet even then the culture was perverted by the appetites of wealth and sexual satision as eloquently described by Barbara Tuchman.

We forgot the ancient wisdom of balance as we realized our fantastically diverse capabilities. It seemed that nothing was beyond our grasp. We have a bad habit of satisfying our appetites to the point of satiation.

True enough, we rediscovered our fantastic evolutionary roots in the past five centuries, and we applied those capacities to careful examination of the imaginary realities fomented upon our civilization through the natural exaggerations of story-telling cultures. At the same time we neglected the continued development of understanding the whole of which we are part, and only recently have we recognized our gross error of exploiting the earth. We also have forgotten our long, arduous trek toward spiritual maturity, and this book is an effort to remedy that error. Materialism has not served us as well as we like to think. It is inimical to thoughtfulness as it encourages being lazy.

Today, as in the early Middle Ages people face an extraordinary lethargy. Then it was the hopeless failure of oligarchy to sustain peace and opportunity. Today these are again under the degrading lethargy of a culture still mired in predispostions of one hundred years ago. To continue to pour public wealth into an absurd race to exceed the military buildup of a potential adversary is as debilitating as was the anarchy of the end of empire. Today archaic minds are pressing to turn back the clock on the will to remedy social injustice and inequality world-wide. People are hungry for intelligent balance. We have no lack of talent and energy. Power rests with those whose wants and needs have been satiated. Of the seven billion of us who are not among them, the basic needs of human beings must be addressed.

The twentieth century saw us blessed with the turning point in this perception. We sought and found ways to control a number of serious health plagues. Small pox is all but gone from the face of the earth. Diphtheria, tuberculosis, and pneumonia have been controlled (though not destroyed) as enemies of human physical health. Immunology is making strides against HIV, gonorrhea, and many other diseases. To emphasize the connection with military spending, Jimmy Carter's fight against the guinea worm in Sudan begun in 1994 has only made significant progress since peace came in 2005.[190] On another front, DNA research is uncovering new approaches to controlling a broad variety of human maladies, including Altzheimers disease. *The objective is not longevity but arresting the most debilitating of problems in order that people might live creatively as human beings.* At the same time that we applied ourselves to such maladies, we have continued to probe the far reaches of space and the inner forces of atoms as if human resources were without limit. But there are limits. We may live to one hundred but our objective should be to enable all people to contribute more productive, imaginative years to development of our culture.

It is as if we could go on extending the boundaries we broke with the invention of a bewildering variety of types and styles of boat and ship construction to conquer the second great barrier to human expansion. The first parochial wall was breeched naturally for living space as families expanded on the endless continents. The second barrier was the sea. Homer's *Odyssey* is an account of an early voyage. By the eighteenth century the Chinese developed an awesome armada of ships three times the size of Columbus's tiny ships and then retreated again into isolation. Alfred the Great recovered English boat-building skills and only then could the English repel the inroads of the sea-wise Vikings. Breaching boundaries has contributed to development of culture.

Alfred (849-899? CE) is the father of the British navy. Breaking the grip of the Viking incursions was important. But our propensity to persist in doing what we have learned to do eventually became the tail that wagged the dog at the end of Britain's empire days. Its navy was the envy of Germany's Bismark. We need no more such tails! Was the English loss and redevelopment of sea-going skills the result of conscious choice? Probably not. The decline of those skills was rather the reaction of people to other needs and a feeling of relative safety from distant people. We have been driven by one crisis after another for a very long time. When the Vikings expanded after the seventh century[191] it drove the Britons to rebuild their navigational capabilities. It was another signal to humanity that established authority to govern was preferable to ad hoc solutions to external threats. Once again, a community forced to defend itself followed the vicissitudes of occasion, only to begin a centuries-long process of growing pride in naval power which ended in World War I. We can avoid this pitfall by expanding our perceptions of reality to include others' views.

It will require us to change our cultural priorities. We conquered land and sea and thought we should go on to air and then space. Today the cost of this path in a suffering world must be contested. The vast numbers of human beings in the twenty-first century will have talent, intelligence, and time to accomplish more substantive miracles if we expand our cultural attention to less ostentatious pursuits than military power, space travel and atomic physics. Biology and psychology have long been in the doldrums and need attention in new directions, with less single-mindedness and broader innovation. These are only two of the more obvious areas awaiting fresh thinking among minds which are newly capable of attention to multiple foci.[192] Perhaps more important in the West is expanding of our knowledge to languages and cultures of peoples we have been satisfied to call "backward" or "undeveloped," taking initiative to share with them in their quests for health and hope. Reaching out to others and overcoming our proud knowledge, we may be enriched by their wisdom and trajectories of self-development.

More often than in the past, young people are choosing to prepare for work at occupations, trades, professions that they knew nothing about through family or friends, or in response to advertising (armed services, for example) which added an aura of romance, power, or authority to the work. Popular occupations are those which promise personal gain and/or make contact with a young person's self-consciousness. Young people have always had their moments of idealism and today's youth are no different. Our definitions of self-interest in these matters will effect our choices, and these are expanding rapidly. Adult encouragement to learn new languages will contribute to successful negotiation of the difficult entry into the culture of the twenty-first century.

It is difficult to say what will be socially helpful occupations as we move deeper into the twenty-first century. It appears, nonetheless, that how we talk about our life together will make a substantial difference in what youth choose to do. Our language is consequential not only in shaping the individual's self-understanding and identity, but in how each of us chooses to spend her/his life. If one is familiar with language of care and assistance or only with the mechanics of trades and professions, choices will reflect that. If one talks of others in terms love and concern for welfare rather than of mechanical behaviors, it will affect how he or she will nourish children and participate in family.

It will also effect how each one participates in society. Youthful leaders in Tahrir Square in Egypt recently demonstrated that they are figuring out what works as they go along in their rebellion. An Israeli-born Arab says, "We want to get past all the old identitites – Fatah, Hamas, religious, secular, Israeli and Palestinian Arab – and create a mass non-violent movement." It is a newly energetic orientation, no longer sheep-like in any respect, intelligently speaking out and listening, consciously contributing to our culture.

Our language limits our options. Expanding our vocabularies is more important than creating new abbreviations for common words. "Texting" looks like reversion to picture language subverting alphabetic (sound-mimicing) vocabulary development. It remains to be seen if the mechanical translation of languages into oral and written form in other languages will dumb down or enhance interpersonal communication. But it has already begun to break down the barriers between us worldwide.

Our speech utilizes our brains extensively. It requires listening as well as speaking. And, the Middle American has begun to figure out, listening cannot be neglected. We have begun to see that leaders who encourage dissension are not the leaders for a democracy to follow. With a bit of attention we can discern the difference between criticism and distortion. This discovery was confirmed with a divisive, two term Federal administration. By the time it ended, with all the rotten fruit it produced spread around for the world to see, it seemed that the silent middle had recovered its voice and begun again to speak. Unfortunately, we have not yet broadly developed the capacity for discernment that is required to choose leaders wisely. So the reactionary right was able easily to reinvigorate the old, destructive patterns of thought. Fear was brought to the fore. The lethargic instinct to simply enjoy what we have been holding dear still prevails. The self-disciplined mind has not yet arrived among us in cultural strength.

This is the way of the future, nonetheless. It requires vigilance which we have not recently been inclined to sustain. That is kin to discernment and discernment is kin to predisposition. The disposition is a wholistic grasp of our humanity: individuals related to others. In biblical terms, we must "gird up our loins" – take ourselves to task, stay on message. The message is to refine and enhance our interrelationships. We are faced squarely today with the necessity of relearning self-discipline freshly. We must not become complacent once more when we regain our optimism as Americans. We must assume a new self-hood in which we accept the personal disciplines learned over literally thousands of years to listen carefully, respond intelligently, act thoughtfully, and seek to maintain the balance and progressive orientation in which we focus our energies to solve present human problems. Doing as well as possible on that score, we need to accept the failures of past actions with equanimity, but not approval. Trying again is a tried and true procedure.

Christianity has for many years provided a religious vehicle for this social necessity in the function of repentance before peers and the forgiveness of God. If God forgives, why should we not recognize the past as over and move on? Such proven religious rituals will continue to be helpful to people quite apart from the volumes of theology interpreting them. But rituals are religious devices, and like abstractions, are not reality, but only aids to expression of our deepest convictions. Ritual will grow past all resemblance to "aids" if we are not discerning. Unfortunately, they tend to be limits to growth. Past encouragement to give ourselves with abandon to ritual is dangerous. Our self-discipline requires us to engage in ritual very thoughtfully. Our deepest convictions are not set in stone anymore. We are privileged as human beings to grow daily in our deepest selves.

Key to our new role is our language. America's recent wars laid bare our self-centered Western myopia. We scrambled to find interpreters of languages and cultures we presumed to address. We assume that our national pride is justified, but the pride of other peoples in their countries has often been seen just an impediment to progress. It is good to be reminded by one such as Nelson Mandela that democracy has roots unrelated to our own. In his African home town as a young boy, he watched democracy in action:

> Everyone who wanted to speak did so. It was democracy in its
> purest form. There may have been a hierarchy of importance among the
> speakers, but everyone was heard, chief and subject, warrior and medicine man,
> shopkeeper and farmer, landowner and laborer.[193]

But our own daily tongue is also in need of attention. We must cease to use the archaic adversarial language we are so accustomed to without trying to find better expressions. Most obvious is use of war-talk. We have long assumed that war is the inevitable ultimate solution to intractable international problems and that we must change those foreign modes of government we disapprove. Our language is full of unnecessary adversarial, enemy, competitor ideas.

We must learn to be patient. We have been impatient long enough. Our new view of humankind is of an ancient animal still evolving to live its inevitably social life after populating the entire earth. Fortunately, human beings have been blessed with minds which have been able to learn century by century to think. It was this mind which early among its social skills learned to rejoice in the beauty of the sunset and the rainbow and of human association. Such subtlety did not escape us from the very beginning. But our sensitivity to it did grow and we have now even established sophisticated institutions which are learning to help us in all our differences to be sensitive human beings. Far from all-comprehending, we have only begun to tap our human potential which has no known limits. As Jacques Maritain has said:

> Such a renovation has internal dimensions of incomparably greater height and
> breadth and depth than any other revolution; it is linked to the vast historical
> process of integration and reintegration.[194]

VIII. THE SECOND CHRISTIAN REFORMATION

Rationalism had been developing for decades on the Continent and among scholars produced a reaction to orthodox Christianity. Insights into the historical nature of cultural development had begun to raise difficult questions about the contemporary rather literal interpretation of scripture – and to sow doubt of a typically modern sort. All the churches had been taking the Bible at face value although the gross discrepancies in the Gospels that bothered these scholars had been recognized for a thousand years. They were largely dealt with by the old techniques of story and allegorical interpretation.

Daniel L. Pals' *Victorian Lives of Jesus* details a "second reformation" in Christian thinking in nineteenth century Britain. The first Reformation had put the Bible in the hands of the people. This "second reformation" smoothed the way for British people to move through a major cultural change in an exemplary way. For us this second reformation in Britain stands in contrast to a third Christian reformation to follow in the United States. Both relate to the Rationalism which dominated the Continent. But the British were more influenced by the Romantic reaction and in absorption of their momentous humanist awakening in the eighteenth century than Americans who were busy with continental expansion. The British, in contrast, were led to grasp the new rationality

While they were guided to reinterpret the life of Jesus in thoughtful ways, Americans were so preoccupied with their frontier and industrial success that their intellectual development suffered severely. Americans were filled with the same sort of hubris that perverted Continental philosophy but in an entirely non-intellectual, even anti-intellectual way. They inherited the earlier "city set on a hill" vision and interpreted it self-righteously (common-sensically in a popularized version of Christianity) without grasping the growing recognition of the rational capacity of human beings. The American stance might be compared to the light-minded, ephemeral focus on enthusiasm on the Continent. With a sort of smug, self-satisfied grasp of the present, Americans neglected their intellectual heritage..

Pals tells us that along side German efforts in historical research[195] British scholars published a large number of "lives of Jesus" in a steady stream after 1860. Few of these were significant contributions to academic literature, but together they substantially affected the British culture. The Gospels themselves had been written when the eye-witnesses to Jesus' life were dying, and devoted followers realized that they had to preserve in writing what they knew about him and his work. Some scholars consider these accounts to be a new literary form in the first century CE. Those writings consolidated the base for the first Christian reformation shared in the sixteenth century by all Western Christians, Catholic and Protestant. The new sense of history gave it all a new twist – and lifted consciousness. Earlier spiritualization of Jesus fell into place beside reality as Western Christians adapted to the new views.

A. The British Bridge Over Another Gap

In Britain, in the last half of the nineteenth century, critical scholarship and the urge to make the Christian story freshly available to the public came together. In a collaborative spirit, scholars addressed a certain boredom that had settled on the people. The issues involved a new awareness of discrepancies between the Gospels which Tatian had first noted in his *Diatessaron* in the second century, followed by Origen in the fourth century and Augustine early in the fifth century. For hundreds of years thereafter, the few scholarly efforts in biblical interpretation were almost entirely devoted to public interpretation and private devotion.

By the end of the fifteenth century there was a resurgence of critical work. The Renaissance made ancient texts newly available, especially fresh Greek editions soon translated into more familiar Latin and the vernacular. Erasmus had spearheaded the resurgence with his extraordinary output. In the Reformation, many parallel columns of texts opened the doors of dialogue.

The nineteenth century revolution in historical studies was an engine to explore scripture with renewed vigor and consciousness of human critical capacity. It initiated the Second Christian Reformation. Albert Schweitzer has told the story of the emergence in Germany of this "critical spirit." But Schweitzer had little to say about what was going on in Britain at this time when scholars and public in Britain "all were captivated by the search for the historical Jesus." Pals' account fills this gap in our recollections:

> British Lives were quite different from the continental literature examined by Schweitzer.... The Germans came nearer achieving a tradition of pure scholarship. In contrast, the typical British Life of Christ, even when unorthodox, sought to turn scholarship into public literature. It endeavored to bridge the inevitable gap between cloistered scholar and common reader. Many of the authors were active churchmen writing for interested churchgoers, and they frequently opted for literary indulgences....
>
> At the same time, the pressures to popularize never shook the Victorians from the strong conviction that they were composing sound, accurate, and scientifically credible Lives of Jesus.... This should be recognized as an extraordinarily ambitious enterprise. Even before the rise of the modern critical style in Germany, it must be remembered, the analytical style ... and the popular approach ... had traveled largely separate paths....
>
> British authors now set about the even more difficult task of blending popular concerns not with the ways of the harmonist but with the foreboding new techniques of the modern historian. Despite the risks, it must be counted at least a partial success....[196]

Success, indeed! The British authors identified not only an extremely demanding application of scholarly behavior, but a concern for the mind of the people who were their public. With another hundred years perspective, we can see this as an application of the emerging mind which carried forward the biblical anthropology focused on individual persons. It is a humanistic rationality. And it helped to shape our culture. The British posture put aside the continental aristocratic hubris in which scholarship had long been trapped. It implemented in another way the human capabilities already substantially displayed in the American Revolution, that is, attention to ordinary people – a legacy of eighteenth century liberal humanism in Britain

The new mind reshapes rhetoric firmly in the service of truth. Instead of a focus on persuasion, the rhetorical thrust of this effort trusted in the capacity of the people to grasp the significance of critical insight. It sought to display what enlightenment scholars discovered in critical reading of Scripture: How we understand things in the present situation using our best minds. Every listener, every reader is expected to bring the microscope of his or her own mind to consider what is said. This method supersedes the way for endless centuries that people were treated like sheep, dumb, blind. That culture expected the people to accept (as they always had in the past) the ideas of rulers reinforced by their control of the civil religion. The projection of that method through the Middle Ages was endorsed by the aristocratic Church. The amazing reality of the Enlightenment era is that the liberal spirit provided the context in which the British orientation could thrive. The people were expected to consider the insight scholars unearthed, not simply accept it. They were expected to think and they did. The British scholars who to the German purists looked like foot-dragers were blazing an intellectual path required for the future. No longer captive, a new freedom was in the air.

The British Second Reformation pioneered a new style of scholarly behavior perfectly adapted to the needs of the United States. The emerging British paradigm of religion overlay seventeenth century British humanism and in 1800 permitted a comfortable coexistence with science. The new educational institutions of America fell in step with it. Literally dozens of small colleges established throughout the country embodied the humanist idea while holding tightly to orthodox Christianity. Americans generally were preoccupied with expansion of the frontier, and they failed to pay attention to the revolution in understanding of history that was reshaping their religious paradigm. But, the new mind expanded, and the ground for the twentieth century American Third Reformation was prepared. American theologians began grappling with the unfolding new paradigm in anticipation of the approaching controversy.

Before we examine the Third Reformation, let us examine John Dewey's distinctive contribution to understanding truth. In 1900 Dewey was already forty years old. He had grown up during the maturing of the nineteenth century and the unfolding of the new mind which introduced modernity. The New Mind, as we are calling the emergent capacity of humanity, was flowering, with the early challenges to presuppositions of the Enlightenment. One of the most insidious of these was its antiquated orientation to truth. Bertrand Russell says, "the chief importance of Dewey's work lies in his criticism of the traditional notion of 'truth'." The Truth had suffered the conceptual baggage of "eternal", "reality", "absolute" language which made a lie of so many things. This confusion developed largely out of Plato over many centuries. Mathematicians who sought the true relationship of numbers and applied their findings to real world applications fell into the same confused state of mind. Ideas rode high; an accepted idea became a rule for thinking people – their "truth." In spite of Locke's contrary orientation, the platonic view reigned in the first half of the twentieth century.

Dewey was the most popular philosopher in America, and Russell agreed with him most of the time. Dewey carried on the tradition of New England (British) liberalism along with William James. He had a major influence on American education embodied in his *The School and Society* (1899).

Dewey conceived of a process he called 'inquiry' which is a form of mental adjustment between an organism and the environment. "Inquiry is the controlled or directed transformation of an indeterminate situation into one that is so determinate in its constituent distinctions and relations as to convert the elements of the original situation into a unified whole," Dewey said. That sounds like philosophical mumbo-jumbo! But the clue is in the last two words. A unified whole is the objective, i.e. truth. Dewey was saying that in the ongoing dialogue of human efforts to understand their world, the truth may well emerge. Inquiry is a form of dialogue.[197] And it is from dialogue that truth emerges.

If this interpretation holds, we are on a track which seems to be consistent with the very recent history of the Scot-British-American hybrid liberalism. Truth has to do with how we interact with our lives. It is our culture which defines truth for the present, truth as we live it together. When we ask "Is it true?" we are inquiring of ourselves and those about us how they understand the world.

This was the stance also of William James (1842-1910). His voice was one that fulfilled democratic kindness as Wittgenstein acknowledged. James' Puritan roots gave him "a deep-seated belief that what is of most importance is good conduct, and he could not acquiesce in the notion of one truth for philosophers and another for the vulgar."[198] He rejected the subject-object relationship which governed almost everything in philosophy and the use of "consciousness" as a thing (reified). This tendency to turn concepts into things was particularly evident in 1900 and James began to unpack that.

His was a practical orientation kin to Scot humanism, another indication of the new mind emergent in America. But it has taken the twentieth century to substantiate the wisdom in this practical new mind. It had to butt heads with idealism still carrying on the Platonic tradition. John Caputo reminds us that Heidegger connected the call of conscience to the call of care. But, Heidegger scholar Caputo says, "The middle term between the 'call' and 'care' is the phenomenon of 'uncanniness,' an uneasiness which tears us away from the tranquilizing comfort of everydayness...."---[199] Psychologist William James was especially helpful at the turn of the century in recovering "canny-ness."[200]

One of the best and most famous examples of how our culture has been affected by this fresh orientation is in the knee-jerk reaction shunning Galileo because he advocated Copernicus' system. He acknowledged the sun to be the center of the solar system and the earth to move around it like the other planets. Much has been made of resistance to Galileo as an illustration of Medieval rigidity. Reviewing his work now in our emerging mind we understand his critical contribution to introducing the Enlightenment to be his understanding of what Harvard's Owen Gingerich describes as the establishment of scientific method as a matter of coherence rather than as singular proof.[201] The liberal mind explored meaning in dialogue, engaging others in finding conceptions which fit their world. Those who failed to grasp this new mind and make it their own are found to have been locked into obsolete ideas of truth. They held onto notions of scientific method which installed misconceptions in the mind's driver's seat.[202]

Closely linked with the kind of perfection familiar in mathematics, truth had been entangled with religion with very different connotations. With mathematics, truth suggested static, final, perfect, and eternal. Ever since the Middle Ages, our culture has tended to take on similar Platonic notions. Dewey viewed things, rather, from a biological point of view. He conceived of thought as evolutionary, but not, as for Hegel, the unfolding of an eternal idea.

B. America Emerges From Early Modernism

The Protestant religion of 1900 was substantially different from that of 1800. The difference reflects the shift of power everywhere in the West from church to community. It was a fulfillment of Calvin's doctrine of the priesthood of all believers. Every occupation is a vocation in which each person is called to serve God piously.

Especially in the United States with our abundant resources the Industrial Revolution dominated the life of the nation. People went through tension and struggle to break loose from residual feudal notions. The stable churches gave an immense workforce substantial security. The workers and their families were more free of pressures to conform than ever before. No feudal lord, no local chieftain, no government official could drag them out of bed to face military service or surprise judicial charges. There was a new sense of order and it attributed value and worth to individual people.

Another change had taken place in the way people thought in their freedom. They still adhered largely to their inherited religions, but the intellectual world to which their religions connected them through education of their clergy was undergoing the ravaging controversies of both Rationalism and Romanticism. And they felt the onslaught of a rationalistic scientism. The early scientistic certainties of the Enlightenment attracted Scholastically oriented theologians in the two centuries after the Reformers. This old science gave them an unfortunately mistaken handle on certainty. And the culture did not yet possess the open dialogical character which would soon permit almost instantaneous critique of such overbearing notions.

As always there were many religious leaders whose comfort with early "scientific" views interfered with their appropriation of intellectual developments. As Whitehead notes, the notion that there was only one true view of the world, had ruled Western culture for over two thousand years.[203] But the late Enlightenment period was opening the minds of thoughtful people to new views of history, philosophy, and religion.

Other church leaders worked at more thoughtful accommodation of emerging science. The distance between these two different groups gradually grew. And by 1900 there had been ruptures ("Old School" vs."New School"[204]) and attempts at reconciliation. That experience reflected the increasingly antiquated adversarial culture which still plagues reactionary American politics today. It is the residue of the dying culture.

Today these differences are increasingly recognized as part of the past. Another hundred years have seen immense strides in intellectual responsibility and in the maturity of American democracy. So to the evolution of the large corporation, the conglomerate, and the emerging global business organization, we must add the stumbling religious organizations which had been trapped in the past. In the twentieth century two attempts to provide an umbrella for the Christian denominations are now joined by the early shape of a third, larger, more inclusive, more intelligent body. And we can hope that denominational identities forged during four centuries since the first Reformation will mellow, coalesce and reform into new, more appropriate organizations. The twenty-first century mind requires change in the face of almost universal entrapment in misconstructions of the past.

Intellectually, all of this signals a dramatic increase in our awareness of our mental capacity. But experience should tell us that we should expect to find imbalances in society which we have not yet noticed. It is a new willingness on the part of increasing numbers of Christians to grasp the sort of thinking voiced by Gary Dorrien. He tells us that Evangelicals like himself must learn again to listen, to hear without responding, to seek understanding without explaining. Dorrien, now filling the Reinhold Niebuhr Chair of Theology at Union Seminary (NYC), is a Unitarian.[205]

And the drum will keep drumming. A stalwart voice in the evangelical wing of the Presbyterian Church (USA) for many years has recently demonstrated this reality. Through deep experience over a number of years, P. Mark Achtemeier changed his mind after many years of resistance to support of the ordination of lesbian and gay elders. An able and articulate theologian, Achtemeier has publicly explained himself. Others, like him respected theologians, led the way.[206] These, once lonely Evangelicals, can expect the vituperative reaction of many who languish in the mind of the past.

In the United States a late nineteenth century decline in focus on the church accompanied the rise of science to its recent prominence. Few people at that time could handle this intellectual challenge along with the immense social changes taking place simultaneously. The power of the large corporation became overpowering, and in the two decades at the beginning of the twentieth century we saw the first efforts to control financial power. Regulatory resolve varied over the new century and some see in this only a cyclical repeat of social engineering. We have documented economic crashes and depressions for well over one hundred years. To some it all looks like repetition. But among the many of us for whom Calvin's viewpoint has become a part of our culture, this was not persuasive, and we forged on, continuing the slow building of a viable human community which we have long understood must include economic regulation – that is to say, common control over the antique path of avarice.

The euphoric nineteenth century expansion in territory and industry blinded Americans to a dangerous hubris and opened them as a people to an unnoticed self-righteousness. This hubris had already played out in Britain but had not been noticed in the United States, as pride driving accomplishment of common sense objectives drove America west. It was soon evident in large oil, large steel, large electric, large industry and the great railroads. The Great Exposition of 1893 displayed the huge machines that steam power brought to American factories to turn out an increasing barrage of consumer goods. Secularization as we know it was well under way. Materialism crowed. Our American free enterprise system was obviously the best economic system in the world – a concept lending itself well to proud slogans! Such slogans have dominated American politics.

But everything is different today, most particularly, we ourselves. It is exactly the first error of the ultra-conservative mentality, neglectful of the most basic Christian affirmation, to assume persistence of conditions which gave rise to guiding principles of one's fathers. Though it held true for thousands of years, it was clear even to many ancients that change was occurring faster than that. Every day is a new day. This highlights the difference between religion and science in the nineteenth century. The flood of immigrants to America from Europe early in the twentieth century reinforced old, dependable cultural elements in the midst of their fast-changing world.

At the turn of the century, an increasing flood of immigrants from rural America contributed to stuffing the housing in American cities. The cities had entered a new era of growth and it would not stop. In 1900 there were 27 cities in the US over 100,000 population. In 1950 the number had grown to 53 cities over 100,000, and by 2000 the number approached 100. We had become urban. These are now only medium-size cities.

While the West had been won, thousands of small towns in America were populated by masses of people who exuded a proud parochialism and frontier independence associated with the popular 1950's musical "Oklahoma." This mentality was vaguely reflective of the primitive social orientation of the Celts of Britain, Wales and Ireland, and of the German and Eastern European tribes, and the more ancient move from the earliest villages into the first cities. This independence had only been submerged beneath the surface by the constant repression of oligarchic power to evolve into the earnest and focused populations which characterized America early in the twentieth century. It was fertile ground for demagoguery highlighting individualism. And the remnant of determined anti-monarchialism was exploited by demagogues as a virulent anti-institutionalism in the latter half of the twentieth century.

The American transition from agricultural to industrial economy was comparable to the Agricultural Revolution which provided the base for the building of cities six thousand years earlier. Here the cultural change from largely isolated farms and tiny villages emulated that move from tribe and village. In both cases, the city was the attraction. By the middle of the twentieth century our country was half urban. The transition from "overalls"[207] to blue collar and white collar occurred quickly. Small farms disappeared at an alarming rate; cities and mega-farmers were gobbling up the countryside. At the end of the 20th century the Metropolitan Areas covering 12 percent of the land held 65 percent of the people. Half of the American domestic food supply was produced by just two percent of the farms while one hundred years earlier this half of our food had required 17 percent of all farms.[208] Many small, private entrepreneurs who served Americans' needs for everything were replaced by large conglomerates capable of contracting for salable products wherever they could most cheaply be obtained. Post-war productivity turned increasing numbers of people into participating capitalists. The standard of living continued to rise until the end of the century.

In the first half of the twentieth century art and music anticipated the cultural reformation we faced: Jazz and Tin-Pan Alley shattered the hold of classical music on concert halls and introduced popular music widely through the radio, the phonograph and a succession of other recording devices[209]. Pablo Picasso emerged in 1900 and in 1920 introduced cubism. Expressing our complete domination of nature begun by pre-stone age human beings, Picasso has been quoted: "Through art we express our conception of what nature is not."[210] And thus the reaction to scientism found sophisticated roots in fresh waves of graphic artistry and music. In spite of such brilliant bridges as Gershwin's *Rhapsody in Blue* (1927), such iconoclasm could not be absorbed by conservative religious thinkers leading them to vociferously reject anything they could label "liberal." Intellectual turmoil covered their retreat from growing mental sophistication and laid the ground for the abortive twentieth century phenomenon Fundamentalism, an anti-intellectual scientism.

By mid-century such countercultural phenomena as Woodstock and the Chicago Seven remind us of the extremity of behavior which broke loose. We had not yet put behind us the antiquated educational culture which in the freeing of human beings from restriction had lost control of teenage hubris.[211] The baby-boomers were making their tween-age fury their own. What teens understood of adult culture was absorbed from the war culture in which they grew up. While modern warfare, as well as frontier vigilantism, were no longer options for expression of their misled exuberance, they fell into the historic pattern of urban disruptions to effect change no one understood and could not predict. It would be some years before we entered the age of brain research which has recently reminded us that the self-assertive self-image of youth is not the completion of their self-image but another step along the way in becoming responsible adults.

The real change already in motion had begun transforming the universities into megaliths of complex specialties.[212] General Motors success was evident in its imposing headquarters on Grand Boulevard in Detroit a symbol of the aristocratic way we organized industry. At the same time schools of social work emerged out of fresh understanding of human beings and organization. They were defined (like the new schools of Business Administration) largely by competitive capitalism. The workplace was redefining the urban worker from blue collar to white collar. The computer had emerged in a *tour de force* as International Business Machines (IBM) staked its future on electronics replacing complex mechanical accounting machines. It was not the only firm in the field, but few competed in the upper reaches of computer innovation. Incredibly complex electronics replaced the leading innovative power of marvelous mechanics of the industrial revolution. Without the growing capacity and miniaturization of electronic components, the rest of the century would have been very different.[213]

Gradually, this sophistication, long evident in the great universities,[214] made strides in literary criticism, history, and anthropology. It drove a wedge between thinking Christians and those who chose to hang their hats on certainties.[215] These were insistent about exactly those things which drew the most severe rebuttals by critics of religion: the virgin birth of Jesus, inerrancy of Scripture and verbal inspiration. All of these were being critically analyzed within the church. The gestation of Unitarianism in the nineteenth century demonstrates the difficulty some religious people had to adapt to the rapid changes in culture.[216] Higher education has also struggled to adjust to this deluge. The latest in a long line of books critical of education is "a critical assault" which advocates Cardinal Newman's classic nineteenth century *The Idea of a University*. This view sees colleges as a "cultural expedition ... to make students more interesting people"[217] not as facilities to produce highly technically-trained workers.

Within the Christian church liberal voices like that of Walter Rauschenbusch (1861-1918) were busily restructuring theology to accommodate advances in thinking. His orientation was shaped by his eleven year ministry in Hell's Kitchen in NYC, a notorious slum. The locale was evidence of the failure of nineteenth century capitalism to address the social needs of people in a highly industrialized society. During his life, the American church was struggling to recover its long-neglected role of care for unfortunate people. As a young person, Rauschenbusch observed that the church "had no social expression in it." Harry Emerson Fosdick later observed that "The field was pretty much divided between unsocial Christians and unchristian Socialists."[218]

The battle line was drawn between freedom and definitive truth. American freedom facilitated the ability of Christians to choose to ignore the needs of other people. Unfortunately, through much of the twentieth century many Christians were still blinded from the wholeness of the pregnant "liberal" theology by the popular but archaic focus on certainty. These were not only religious people, but many "scientists" as well. It would be almost a century before this error could be conclusively terminated in American intellectual life. In the meantime, a variety of related errors persisted among us, the most persistent ones rekindled by right-wing pundits. Douglas John Hall poses the problem:

> The problems (of contemporary evangelicalism) are visible in two extremes particularly.... It is not accidental that the most avowedly "evangelical" churches in North America today are aligned with the politics of the Right and the morality of the "moral majority." What this type of evangelism does for people, apparently, is to confirm in them their most deeply seated fears of any and every alternative to "the American way" and to stifle whatever critical consciousness may be native to their humanity.[219]

"Deeply seated fears" rekindle the old brain instincts of self-protection. Like oligarchy, forces that stifle our critical consciousness interfere with the basic freedom of human beings to express their own perceptions and to form their own concepts. Repressive fear has always made it difficult for thoughtful people to explore implications of their insights about everyday things. It reduces conversation to expression of fear.

Within a century after Descartes, the brilliance of Isaac Newton laid the ground for two centuries of unparalleled human invention. But in the euphoria of that unparalleled achievement, we did not, of course, avoid all possible missteps. And there seems always to be another demagogue who will rekindle old fears.

Robert Lypsyte tells us that such fear makes us passive, drives us to lose heart, to quit making informed decisions, to quit voting or caring.[220] But his plea for proof is mistaken. We have only evidence, not "proof" as if there were some final argument that would end all debate. Fear is fed by our *disposition* to fear, by lack of trust, by a disposition to avoid admitting that we just might be wrong in our judgment. It assumes that we must judge, and that life is over if we are not right, and thus we must fight about it. But, as Calvin pointed out some 500 years ago, in the Western transition from the Ancient-Medieval world of fear to a thoughtful society, we are called, rather, to adopt a disposition, as he said, "to live piously." As Serene Jones puts it, this piety is knowledge in which we apprehend God. For such knowledge demagogues have never been known. In now antique language, they can only try to induce a "fear of God."

Our cultural problem with fear, leaving us open to the perpetual temptations of demagoguery, is to distrust other people. If others are distrusted, we must trust in ourselves – or the persuasive voices always ready to enlist us. But when we grasp our capabilities as human beings to understand and stand firmly, faithfully, as self-confident persons, we need not fear. "We shall not be moved" by the nonsense of demagogues. We do not fear others, but embrace them as brothers and sisters. When they speak, we listen, and we trust them also to listen to us. We are always able to choose.

I think the "editor," as Leslie Brothers calls the brain's selective function, must be governed by some such intentionality as Hall names "critical consciousness." Is it this that Ed Farley identifies as the Presbyterian mind?[221] Michael Gazzaniga talks about an "interpreter" in his review of current psychology. Some psychologists are inclined to concretize this function in "cognitive modules."[222] This seems to me an expression of a residual mechanistic thinking. The mind's critical function has been in evidence for many years. For Augustine it was embodied in the human self. It was understood as "rationality" in the Enlightenment. Calvin, assuming rationality, talks about disposition – to be disposed to use the mind to see "higher things" (piety). The question is about how we are disposed to use our minds. Sixteenth century Calvin accepts the orthodox world as God's creation in which we are free to choose to be pious participants. The human "disposition" or propensity is itself subject to our choice. Today we reach toward appropriate twenty-first century language for this deep concept of piety and how we can better use it. It unifies the whole, bringing with it the coherence for which we crave in the sense of order which we humans have so arduously sought.

Beyond a simple functioning of the brain, we have come to understand that we can *choose* to exercise the critical function. We can make specific constructions as well as observations accessible to consciousness by *paying attention*. We can *initiate* both memories and constructions and *exercise* our minds by choice.

IX. THE THIRD CHRISTIAN REFORMATION

The "conservative" impulse in our culture is the modern version of the ancient instinct for self-preservation. Every primitive person who achieved adulthood had created a store of habits and goods, food, clothing and tools which would be conserved at some cost. In the twentieth century the word "conservative" has been loaded with both innuendo and approbation so as to become unrecognizable. It is the watchword of the right wing of Americans and at the moment has captured public attention in demagogic reaction to election of a liberal administration. But "conservative" is better associated with the conservation movement seeking a healthy ecology, a balance and harmony of nature, and the judicious preservation of what is worthwhile in the present culture. Sensitive to these problems of American English, we proceed to discuss the hugely important Third Christian Reformation now becoming evident.

The Church has served a legitimate conservative purpose. Initially, before institutionalization, the people whom we now call the early church sought to conserve the information they had about Jesus and his message. The Roman Catholic Church and its nemesis, Protestantism, conserved the orthodox "Christendom" which the early church defined, though they interpreted it very differently. The first Reformation conserved the fruits of criticism of over a thousand years' evolution of the Church. In each case, bright and conscientious people constructed the institution they felt best conserved the truth of the Christian Gospel. In each case, they were limited by their humanity to see only part of the truth. Our understanding of their contributions to our culture is clouded by their assumption that conflict was a necessary characteristic of human community, and that the present relations of people were inevitably contentious. That was the expression of a reactionary conservatism.

A. The Origins of the Conservative Shape of the Popular Mind

From 1978 to 2006 the Presbyterian Church (U.S.A.) was embroiled in a transitional controversy. While the problem appeared to be a narrow issue, it was symptomatic of the current transitions in our culture. The subject was typical twentieth century thinking focused on sexuality. The ultra-conservative prudery and hypocrisy of the popular Victorian Era provided the backdrop for advocacy of social control of sexuality. People were still trapped in the ideology-saturated mind of the Enlightenment in which we gravitated to the idea that we could know everything. It was a long time before psychology emerged and matured to reveal absurdities we now commonly recognize – racial prejudice, masculine superiority, "normality."

The current fear of sexuality remains because people have never before considered personal control of the sex instinct either desirable or possible. This error has been conserved in cultures throughout the history of humanity. Today we know that, beginning with abstinence and castration, we have successfully controlled sex in many only partially successful ways. Having begun to free ourselves from paternalism by recognizing women as the equal of men, today we know that we can uncouple ourselves from all kinds of mistakes of past cultures. Conservatives have usually recognized that such self-discipline must begin in the first years of life. This self-discipline is not austere denial of self (learning rules), not the intent of emasculation (denying existence of the offending organ), but adopting self-control as a way of life. Anyone who has learned such pervasive patterns of self-identity (as in mastering a musical instrument) knows that persistently reinforced (like avoiding adolescent "back-sliding" when the hormones kick in), self-discipline makes life much easier. Perhaps most important, we know others can trust us. And the real reward is growing sensitivity to the wholeness of persons about us. The truly conservative mind is a genuinely always-thinking mind.

The American conservative mindset inherited its mistaken rigid-by-rule orientation from Medieval Scholasticism. It was another implementation of autocratic governance. One hundred years after the Reformation, many people reinvented that frame of mind with a typical mistaken confidence in their own thinking. Francoi Turetine (early eighteenth century) was one of the most influential in the formation of American Fundamentalism having influenced revision of the Westminster Standards. We will rehearse that battle. But the stand-off can easily be traced back to Augustine (about 400 CE). Augustine got trapped in the ancient paternalistic practice of sex when copulation was a male privilege. Early in life he satisfied his sexual instincts grossly. But he also had a highly developed mind which escaped that trap though he fell into others that have also, like sex, plagued the West.[223] In spite of what seems to us an egregious error he was one of the brilliant intellectuals at the end of the ancient period. His brilliance still fuels thinking today. Every intellectual leader of the intervening years has had to deal with Augustine, though in the Modern Period we have lost track of our past in the hubris which has consumed us.

Among Augustine's progressive behaviors was his habit of writing voluminously, and one of his works (the most remarkable in light of the present discussion) was his *Confessions*. In it he bitterly repents of his life in Carthage where he went to school. His mother (Monica) had raised him as a Christian, but he became a Manichaean. As young men are prone to impulsive action, he thought Mani to be enlightening. He was, after all, a youth of the fourth century.

Mani (who considered himself a successor to Zoroaster, Buddha, and Jesus) was a third century (CE) Persian prophet banished at the behest of Zoroastrian priests. After twenty years he returned to Persia where he was flayed to death. But he had traveled widely and his attractive sect grew. He conserved Zoroastrian dualism but refined it introducing a sophisticated mystical understanding of the battle between light and darkness. That was an Eastern rationalism that fathered Gnosticism in the West but could not stand up to the Greek-fueled early rationalism of the Christian Fathers.

Augustine, having studied Plato and skepticism while teaching rhetoric in Rome, renounced Manichaeism and became the hub of its rejection in the West. He was baptized a Christian in 387. His excessive life before his conversion led to a period of ascetic withdrawal. The *Confessions* express remorse at that waste of his life. His articulate rejection of dualism and sexual license helped to shape the Christianity we have inherited. Though he learned to use his mind, to think, he could not shake off the reactionary influence of his culture. Like most men of that time, Augustine's view of women was generally negative. His skill in the chief educational field of the time, rhetoric, served him well in finding teaching positions, and led to his position as Bishop of Hippo before 400 CE.

We recall that this was the period in which the Church was just getting formed. Ambrose is the father of the Church's conception of its independence within the state. Augustine's role in the formation of the church is thought by many theologians to be second only to the Apostle Paul. Aquinas was still 800 years in the future, but both shared a mindset already well-established: oligarchic and paternalistic, strong conservative biases. All of these, nonetheless, were brilliant men. The conservative impetus is not a matter of intellectual brilliance, but often just an inability to grasp and critique all that needs attention. From this perspective it is a fear of chaos. This fear has very deep roots in early human being's exercise of our capacity for organizing our environment. Having tasted the fruits of knowing the shape of the world taking form in their minds, our early ancestors established a fear of disorganization we call chaos. Ancient thought is full of this fear.

Just how Augustine's puritanical views of sexual relations influenced the church for centuries is a study in itself, undertaken by enough others to make it unnecessary to rehearse it here. His voluminous writings, in good style, touched on almost everything. Unfortunately, his retention of views we now consider archaic have fueled church life in the West. It is not surprising, then, that our institutions in the twentieth century bear his fingerprints. We have finally adopted an egalitarian stance that, in spite of his dualism and Plato's, were already part of Plato's utopia. We read, "Women are to have complete equality with men in all respects.... Their original nature is the same. No doubt there are differences between men and women, but they have nothing to do with politics."[224] Such observations reveal the unsettled ancient intellectual world that was not ready to challenge directly the yet unnoticed absurdities of the time. There have always been pregnant insights floating in the minds of people.

Negative attitudes toward sexual intercourse did not begin with Augustine, of course. As most thinkers habitually did, he conserved the paternalism of his time. Long before, Epicurus had considered that the "dynamic pleasure" of sexual expression had "never done a man good." But Lucretius saw no harm in intercourse if it was divorced from passion! The early church adopted a negativity toward sexual pleasure quite naturally, fitting its opposition to the sexual license rampant in the ancient world, like a virus in the air. Sex was never associated with the idea of exploitation we call paternalism. The dominance of the male human being was deeply ingrained, never questioned. It was conserved as a matter of course. The paternalistic culture had never seen a need to discipline this animal appetite, so we must recognize the stance of the early church to be revolutionary.

The restrictive stance of the church was actually one of the attractions of Christianity among thinking people according to the testimony of Justin Martyr. It is evidence of the basic tendency of human beings toward morality. At that moment sexual excess was so widespread that it became abhorrent. It was a view that fit well with the popular dualism of body-mind. But it was the association of "soul" with "mind" on which the church focused its attention. The three Doctors of the church, Ambrose ("In Praise of Virginity"), Jerome (translated the Greek Bible into Latin, the Vulgate), and Augustine (a theologian) all influenced the negative treatment of sex throughout the Middle Ages and after.[225] It was the moral issue of the time. We remember that at that time when much of what people thought and how they thought about it was governed by a culture largely imposed by authorities calculated to conserve their paternalistic power. All authorities reinforced the domination of males. But the early church also identified itself with self-control, decency, and a new degree of respect for women.

Augustine's insights can be traced through Calvin and the Scots to the emergence of the United States. We often note the conservative nature of their influence, but we must recognize how their innovations were focused on institutionalizing the humanist appreciation of human beings, a decidedly moral point of view. In the Act of Union of 1707 England and Scotland became Great Britain; King William III some years earlier had established the Scottish Presbyterian church. In what seems to us reactionary, he insisted the Scots leave behind their anti-monarchical past. But the bulk of the culture of the Knoxian Scots went unchallenged, and this contradiction fit the dominant old pattern well. The Scot church, nonetheless, thus broke an iron-clad cultural commitment to oligarchic control and represented the only example of democratic governance in an otherwise totally monarchical Europe. Francis Hutcheson was bringing humanism to the forefront of British culture. The pattern they pioneered influenced the development of the United States.

From 1710 to 1750 unrest in Scotland brought three to six thousand Scots to the United States annually. Naturally, these Scots brought with them the basic humanity of the Celtic Scots together with an increasingly intellectual humanism embodying the Christian-Judeo unity of mind and body. These were embedded in a rigid conservatism, an integral part of Orthodox Christianity. It is clear that the Scots had drunk deeply of the humanistic changes rapidly moving Scotland forward. Arthur Herman tells us:

A new mental world was taking shape in Scotland's cities and universities, very different from that of Medieval Scotland or the [austerity] of the Reformation kirk. At its center lay not God any longer, but human beings. Human beings considered as individuals but also as the products, even the playthings, of historical and social change....[226]

Again this apparent inconsistency demonstrates the unevenness of evolution.

The Ulster Scots (Scots living in northern Ireland) represented the residue of the work of sixteenth century Calvinist John Knox. Positively speaking, they were aggressively egalitarian, and they had a great love of education that is characteristic of Presbyterians. -- relatively new values in large populations There was a Bible accessible in every home and it was read. Readiness of the Scots to move forward, to leave "Scotland's cramped, crabbed, and violent past" behind, provided the disposition for their emergence as leaders in America. While they broke aspects of the contemporary conservative mold, theirs was still a conservative zealousness that became associated with Fundamentalism in the twentieth century.

In the United States, the influence of the Ulster Scots was religiously orthodox. It was comfortable with Jonathan Edwards in New England. The austerity of the sixteenth century Scot reformation remained, selectively, and it reinforced the pattern emerging of American Puritanical civil religion.[227] Edwards, pastor of the Congregational Church in Northampton, Massachusetts, was the light of New England in the eighteenth century. He was a Puritan who influenced Congregational and Presbyterian theology. And his preaching was influential in the series of movements in the mid-1700s we call the Great Awakening.

Edwards' brand of Christianity, from our point of view, was conservative,[228] but that was the cultural mindset in the eighteenth century. Unfortunately, the development of the critical dimension of thought, not yet filtered through the culture, set the stage for the nineteenth century proliferation of Christian denominations. As freedom matured in a conservative culture, however, that freedom of critical thought also benefited the heritage of liberal humanism. There were, of course, liberal religious movements afoot also, which brought forth Universalist and Unitarian fellowships, for example, and the Christian Social Gospel. But in the nineteenth century the conservative American public was largely untouched by the British Second Reformation. We were preoccupied with building the new nation. Americans were not prepared for the new views of history seeping in through the small and still elite group of educated people. Historical criticism of the Bible came as a shock. While some Americans (many clergy) began absorbing the new historical understandings of the British and the Germans, the tensions around them began to rise and the New School-Old School controversy split the Presbyterian Church.

Through the eighteenth century Presbyterians straddled the fence between the orthodox church and the formative effects of the Scottish Enlightenment in the United States. Perhaps most importantly we inherited the Scot insistence on education, on schooling, and on democratic -- not to say individualistic -- governance. Immigrants from Great Britain dominated America from the beginning.[229] The Episcopalians started William and Mary College in 1693. The fourth colonial college, Princeton University (so renamed beginning in 1896 after several moves) was started by Presbyterian William Tennet in 1746. Jonathan Edwards was its first president, followed by John Witherspoon (1723-1794) in 1768, the only clergy person signing the Declaration of Independence.[230] Their emphasis on education was not unlike the British at the beginning of the nineteenth century as rationalist historicism began to work its slow way toward the Second and Third Reformations.

This progression is symbolic. James Madison was educated at Princeton and thought highly of Witherspoon as well as of David Hume, who was Witherspoon's nemesis back in Scotland's conservative wing. Nonetheless, the new mind emerging in Scotland influenced Witherspoon, who instituted a regimen at the pre-Princeton "College of New Jersey" which reflected Scot humanism. Reid, the Scottish father of Common Sense Philosophy, also personally played an important part in the young country. This humanism combined with the individualism of the Ulster Scots, and their concurrence with Jonathan Edwards' Puritanism contributed to the imposition of limits on government to balance Madison's centralized federal bias.[231] The result was a weak Federal system. This serious problem was soon remedied by the provisions of the Land Act of 1787, predecessor of the Constitution written later that year. Americans had learned how to handle the social needs of a democracy through discussion, debate, and legislation. All of this was still within the very conservative mentality of Scottish Common Sense Philosophy. Modernism was only beginning to shape up.

In this experience and many others, Americans engaged in the kind of intense, honest, probing conversation necessary in a democratic government, and it demonstrates again the emergence of the new mind of humanity. It follows on the self-assurance emerging among the people, the recovery of a primitive independence of mind including a much-evolved sense of self and a healthy social awareness. When such people found themselves opposed to one another in some basic religious concerns, their voluntary ties in the various churches frayed, producing new churches. It was evidence of the residue of the past. But nationally, we moved beyond the dominance of adversarial behavior and extended the art of compromise. The Presbyterian Old school-New school split was healed sufficiently to reunite these two branches, and at the beginning of the twentieth century the mainline Protestant churches formed the Federal Council of Churches and formalized "ecumenism."

In this respect, the United States freshly demonstrated itself to be a new culture created by those who framed our Constitution and the panoply of people who influenced them. And it is a culture in which people will adopt different orientations and find themselves at loggerheads. But the body politic can embody both conservative and liberal inclinations in the democratic process. Conservatives and liberals are learning to live together. The "new mental world" of the Scots was not to be limited to the British Isles.

B. The Scientific Base of the New Mind

The effort of Dugald Stewart at Glasgow (see chapter V) to shape even the humanities into scientific enterprises had its effect on the humanism of our Founding Fathers. Though at that time psychology hardly resembled a science, the Scot bias we call practicality undergirded the basic empiricism of science which was a legacy of Aristotle. The American educational system has embodied this orientation from its beginnings. One of the resulting developments of the late twentieth century that opens up our minds to us is the application of radiation scanning to brain research. Psychiatrists have been exploring with increasing sophistication the way in which the brain behaves, the flow of blood and the various other mechanisms which reveal aspects of its operation. Stewart's program has had far more extensive application than he could envision.

One of those who has eloquently articulated the scientific progress made in our self-understanding before the turn of the century is Leslie Brothers, a psychiatrist at the University of California in Los Angeles, who wrote a provocative book published in 1997 called *Friday's Footprints*. She references Daniel Defoe's famous eighteenth century *Robinson Crusoe* which popularized John Locke's *tabula rosa* concept of the blank mind. Defoe assigned such a mind to the refugee "Friday." Brothers shows us how our minds are shaped by our culture and how we in turn individually influence our cultures.

I digress here to attempt to draw a coherent picture of the emergence of the "new mind" of the twenty-first century. An increasing number of references have piled up recognizing the nature of *culture* as the product of human living. Leslie Brothers says culture "arises from the joint activity of human brains." In other words, the product of human minds. Thus culture is "communal," not the product of some unseen force. Her scientist's description links culture with DNA:

> Just as chromatin [name given in the nineteenth century to nucleic material in which DNA has recently been isolated and described] proved to hold the key to the mystery of [physiological] inheritance, human conversation holds the key to the mind.[232]

The practical mind might have dictated routinely cleaning the messy "chromatin" from cells before exploration since it seemed to be largely without significance, like the fat which forms in the voids between muscles. Perhaps a better example is the "spandrels" which architects find when designing a necessary structure; the *waste* space beneath a staircase. But because chromatin was not discarded in the research discipline -- a conservative scientific rule is to preserve the whole in all its parts -- deoxyribonucleic acid (DNA) was there to be uncovered as techniques that emerged in the 1980s made this possible. Brothers gives us a new handle on culture by her observations, neither dualistic nor mechanistic. A good word to describe culture is "whole," the wholeness of living encompassed in conversation.

As we converse we share in the shaping of our culture. Talking allows us to hear our own formulations of responses to others' stimuli. Often we are surprised in conversations at how we formulate our own ideas. In other words, we ourselves learn as we converse, both from what others contribute, and from opportunities in conversation to speak what our minds are thinking. It is a truism that this learning, by all parties to a conversation, can alter everyone's self-perception, that is, our minds. It is more mysterious how it contributes to the cultures we share with others.[233]

Because we can individually control what we consciously tuck away in our memories, it is impossible to know how changes in perception take place. Culture has always been hard to define. Now we understand why. Only when we look back over time (as the past half-century within the memories of many of us) do we see how substantially culture can and does change.

A related concept which fits this discussion is the word "person." This word is critical to our understanding of mind. Some have suggested that each person has a sense of self. Each of us "owns" our conscious subjective experience. We seek to understand "I." Descartes pinned his entire philosophy on this, finding in it a beginning assumption which could be made with certainty: "I think therefore I am." It represents a complete dualism, mind separate from body.[234] Others have also found *cogito ergo sum* a convenient basis for thinking, among them, much earlier, Augustine.[235] Each person's awareness of other persons and our awareness that each other person harbors his or her own self like ourselves, enlarges the world we share. I am enlarged by others' selves. Our culture is changed by each person and all persons.

The importance of the constant activity of our brains ruminating over our inheritance and our experience, directed by our "editors" and expressing ourselves as we speak is hard to overstate. I define the person I am by myself in my mind's grasp of my brain's connections. I can think of myself as involved in mental activity, thinking, or physical activity, exercise. I can be political, religious, scientific, artistic, and/or practical.[236] In all cases I remain myself, though I am constantly receiving data from my world and my senses and, associating this with prior knowledge, thus giving me the opportunity to redefine who I am. If I recognize this same sort of change in others, I stand ready to find life constantly a new thing. This is the business of *personhood*.

This contemporary view confirms our personal independence and common dependence all at once. The American Revolutionary period was the same phenomenon expanded to the political level. It occurred in the subconsciousness of the proletarians who engineered the republic. It was largely unconscious, a social advance of momentous proportions. Its roots were in the long gestation of humanism flowing out of the Jewish perception of anthropology. Then the long development of that germinal self-awareness of personhood. All the time we were experiencing enlargement of the sense of responsibility which produced awareness of our complete control over our instincts, our emotions, our minds, and behavior. And out of this we persistently increase our sociability. The beginning is indeterminate. Every step of evolution has precedents.

The thoughtful men who assembled to constitute this country brought their presuppositions, their own self-understandings with them. This included a disciplined capacity to listen to one another, critique each idea, engage in argument, and draft the relatively timeless documents that have for two hundred years withstood the onslaughts of every critic. These people were thinking. They inherited centuries of European struggle to reshape repressive oligarchy and the British had been nearly free of political repression for decades. They were exercising their new freedom. Enlightenment thinking had stimulated a new mental discipline in their culture.

It is miraculous that the forces of change worked together to win the participation of such diverse colonies as North Carolina and Massachusetts. But such seminal events as the formation of the United States do not end the human search for the best means to live together.[237] We ought not to be lulled into complacence as we realize the beauty of growing together into a new sense of self. The ancient wisdom still holds: "The price of liberty is eternal vigilance." The new self we embody in the twenty-first century provides us with the intellectual capacity to bring many tens of centuries of political experience to bear on continuous refinement of our means of self-government. The scientific method has given us readiness to include it all in our consideration. Dugald Stewart could be proud of the incorporation of the method into our culture. Our refinement of the sense of self of the Enlightenment has proven valid: our human rationality is great enough to enable us to build the way we live with participation of every human being.

C. Awareness of New Mind

As the Presbyterians wrestled at the end of the twentieth century with the issues raised by the conservative mind, the so-called evangelicals built and dismantled a superb public relations effort.[238] Conservative spokespersons had been saying since the 1960s that they felt shut-out of the church, discounted, and without voice. It was a reflection of their low level of self-esteem. They were still under the shadow of oligarchy, seeking comfort in authority. The shadow persisted throughout the twentieth century.

There was a lack of significant conversation among Americans throughout the twentieth century which was the residue of the centuries-long pattern of *being told* -- by teachers, preachers and priests and an endless array of demagogues. Long after governments ceased to issue commands, "authorities" spoke to the people (one might say speaking *at* the people) as if they were still sheep. The Socratic method was not forgotten, but was practically ignored or reduced to catechisms throughout the West, even in the twentieth century. People learned to speak little but trivia to one another. It is taking a long time to restore dialogue to a central role in our society. But conversation is a natural sharing and people have long understood that sociality requires us to avoid unnecessarily antagonizing one another. Unfortunately, the Victorian Era so enhanced the authority of a culture of nicety that common language degenerated into anger at authority on the one hand or trivia on the other. Americans lost the capacity to talk about significant aspects of their lives with hope and imagination. This is an important part of our story today, of the awakening among a growing segment of Americans to the importance of each one participating in persistent conversation.

Some of the best educated of Americans have been Presbyterians. That does not make them better than anyone else; it simply emphasizes the importance of the human intellect in the achievement of human life. They have played a disproportionately large role in American history because they persistently required clergy to be educated. In the nineteenth century Presbyterians went through the struggle to bring old ideas into line with emerging ideas of history. The Old School – New School controversy split them for a short time, and when they reunited the irritations still rankled. There were those who grasped the new views and embraced the "social gospel' instigated by Rauschenbusch. But after the turn of the century the conservative mind boiled over and was systematically encouraged by some educated people who had not absorbed the new historicism. They gained an immense public following and persuaded Presbyterians and other democratically organized churches to adopt what came to be known as Fundamentalism.

After a very few years under the regimen of the Five Essentials, centrist voices put an end to that Fundamentalist tangent by rekindling their dialogue. Those years under the Five Essentials are an instance in which thoughtful people were unprepared to think together about the reactionary inclinations of some charismatic leaders. The 1924 Auburn Affirmation signed by over a thousand Presbyterian clergy stands as a breakthrough. The demagogues had won, but only temporarily. Insisting on the correctness of one's views when facing other opinions increasingly was left behind.

Today, sophisticated study has demonstrated the anti-intellectual error of resisting dialogue. Open conversation is our most basic human activity, essential to becoming our own best socialized selves. By mid-century attention to process had provided the first tools to analyze speech and group behavior. "Group process" became the rage. In the 1980s the new urge to talk became more than a rediscovery of John Dewey's "inquiry," or of Socrates' questioning. More than that by the turn of the century, increasing numbers of people were recognizing that everyday conversation should include questioning one another and the common search for understanding.

The maturing of Kuhn's understanding of the philosophy of science clarified a variety of misunderstandings of science and certainty.[239] It is easy enough for people to engage in scientific activities without exercising the shakedown processes which change scientific paradigms. We had adopted cultural patterns that restricted the use of our minds to paths of the past and the disciplines of established methods of inquiry. We were not yet ready to challenge ordinary people to use their heads adroitly. The quiescent ideal of classical education created people who were in the habit of thinking, but technique gradually replaced those disciplines. Socratic questioning (as we call the technique generally) had revealed that being open to one another vastly improves the functioning of the human mind. By questioning one another we learn not only what people have to say, but how our own minds work in regard to the words at their disposal – how we react. In speaking we discover what is rankling in our heads as we reflect on what we hear, see, read, and think. The process of listening and speaking together is conversation, the way we interact as intelligent (brain exercising) people!

Gradually, the centrists found voice and stimulated a "silent majority" of thinking people to act. Among Presbyterians the Auburn Affirmation was largely accepted, but as the century waned so did vigilance; it was another case of human lethargy.[240] We failed to grasp the need for conversation; that is to say, we did not understand its power in society nor the reactionary tendency of the conservative mind. The old tricks of fundamentalist certainty reappeared and were found attractive by large numbers of uncritical people. Among these the habits of the past prevailed plunging the nation into reaction at the same time of unprecedented scientific progress. The new mind was not yet evident.

Fundamentalism was actually formulated by professors at Princeton Seminary who carried early nineteenth century rationalism too far. The Scottish realism instituted there by John Witherspoon seemed always to confirm the harmony of science and religion, but it proved to be incapable also of accommodating changes emerging out of science itself. The Princeton Theology was based on an obsession with the certainty of scientific knowledge. Considering itself to be scientific, its advocates insisted that the "Fundamentals" were absolute certainties, even in the face of disagreement about them within the church.[241]

The Auburn Affirmation was the centrists' reaction to the thinking that had instigated Fundamentalism. The separation of Union Theological Seminary in New York City from the Presbyterian Church was based on Charles Briggs bringing to Union Seminary original documents of the Westminster Confession composed by Puritans in the seventeenth century English upheaval (1643-1647). This confession had been adopted by the Scot Presbyterians and was treated as sacred by those behind Fundamentalism. Briggs showed, however, that Warfield and Hodge used a corrupted version of the confession with roots in eighteenth century Scholastic interpretation of Calvin.[242]

The Fundamentalists were caught in their rationalism, but it took a common action, the Auburn Affirmation, to stop them. Some thousand clergy signed the Affirmation and soon brought the official status of Fundamentalism in Presbyterianism to an end. This demonstrates the firm establishment in our culture of the value of democratic self-government, and a reawakening to our interdependence. It did not end the age of individualism, but signaled its denouement in a course correction.

Still, more than one of the elements of Fundamentalist thinking persisted, conserved, if you will, by the culture. These included the hyper-individualism reminiscent of the Ulster Scots, and the certainty the old orthodoxy achieved long before by a natural, rational human capability operating in the medieval context. This latter can be traced to the Scholasticism of the Middle Ages. Unfortunately, it also reflects a growing anti-intellectualism which has especially dogged conservatives throughout the twentieth century. It was an antiquated notion of reason. William Placher reminds us that before the late nineteenth century "Hume, Rousseau, Lessing, and Kant had led a challenge to some of the assumptions of the age of reason.... The great edifice of modern science rested on the inductive method."[243] Hume had been satisfied with human inclinations and assumptions since we cannot prove some matters of common sense; they simply are the way things are. "He would admit that science and his own philosophy rested on unprovable assumptions." Rousseau doubted the value of civilization which corrupts and enslaves people. Lessing published the manuscript of Hermann Reimarus posthumously which set the stage for moving the study of history into a more scientific posture. And Kant reset the nature of rationality. The movement was clearly toward a new rationality which was not anti-intellectual. But advocates of Fundamentalism were unwilling to bend their minds to such modernisms.

The ideas behind the unreconstructed thinking of conservative people led to a growing disrespect for the role of the Federal Government. It emanated from the residue of distrust of authority and monarchy of the American Revolution and produced the doctrine of "American exceptionalism." In spite of their entrapment in the residue of ancient authority, this Enlightenment development of distaste of monarchy remains a strong part of our heritage. The Great Depression and Franklin Delano Roosevelt's redemption of the American experiment through expansive Federal works -- like the Work Projects Administration (WPA) – kindled renewed fear of centralized authority and produced a growing popular ethos of distrust. World War II enlistment of enthusiastic national support empowered a rising self-righteousness among Americans. And the sin of hubris reasserted itself over against thoughtful participation in forging a grand social reality.

At the same time a generally rampant materialism supported the emergence of the "me" culture. Conservative leaders, gaining confidence by demonstrating the power of demagoguery to capture the people (as if they were sheep), became increasingly outspoken in opposition to progressive social patterns. This exploitation of the re-emergence of ancient individualism brought with it a resurgence of rebellion against authority and all institutions. An inordinate fear of Communism after World War II had been simmering for years reflecting an earlier fear of socialism

Those who were trapped in this variety of obsolescent points of view are at the core of our early twenty-first century explosion of the "far right" and the "far left." Evolution of the mind occurs very unevenly. It does not much favor survival. It occurs randomly by the very nature of the control by DNA of the genetic heritage of each person. Adding to that complexity are the innumerable responses of genes and self to environment. The combination of two sets of DNA in mating assures significant passage to offspring of traits of the parents. In addition, some cultures are always inclined to be specially concerned with preserving the cultural gains they have inherited. These inclinations are naturally absorbed in the process of growing up, and when the culture is concerned primarily about preservation (or "conservation" today) the children absorb a reticence to change. Add all this to the natural persistence of elements of the past in every culture, and we have the makings for reactionary development. The natural conservative phenomenon is expanded by conservative choices.

The great rise in our American standard of living, riding on the back of religious fatalism for a hundred years, has produced generations fearful of losing their gains. The comfort found in the conservative mind increasingly suffered in the past two centuries with the increasing pace of change. The threat of evolutionary theory became too much for religious conservatives to handle. Historian Martin Marty says, "Grief over their loss, resentment over the seizures of their bastions, and fear of threats to faith" led to the invention of hardline and reactive evangelicalism.[244] This took on institutional form in the Christian development of a new view of history which produced the Fundamentalist movement of the early 1900s. Subsequently, evangelicals appeared to be rigid, defensive, and belligerent, especially within the Presbyterian and Baptist denominations. They became, in the telling of historian Mark Noll, "mindless." In our schema their behavior is understood as reactionary, a throwback to earlier mind sets. Human history is full of occasions in which fear of loss exceeded confidence in our capability as human beings. The strangest piece of that fear is how it contradicts faith in the "all-powerful," "omnipotent," "wise," and "benevolent" God professed as a rule by Christian conservatives.

As twentieth century anti-institutionalism built steam, it capitalized on the early American revulsion at our monarchical past. It seemed to conservative people that the church had been captured by their liberal antagonists. They greedily mined the popularity of ultra-conservative pundits who had large radio and television audiences, mimicked their methods, and built an antagonistic following in the church and community. By the 1980s they had corralled what these leaders called a "moral majority." It embraced a huge number of people always available in transitional periods to demagogues who knowingly or carelessly exploit language and ideas to satisfy their audiences. "Half-truths" are the grist of such leaders. Again the Presbyterians were plagued by an oil-funded millionaire[245] and an editor who produced a "newspaper" which centrists considered a perpetrator of lies. It was published for fifty years, a thorn in the flesh to the institutional church. But, like many such reactionary efforts, it contributed to breaking loose the voices of other humans.

This stand-off repeated a pattern of contentiousness which years ago produced a reticence to converse. The early American redneck tendency to resort quickly to fists and knives continued in the "frontier mentality" which reflected the same knee-jerk tendency, though seldom with knives.[246] This fed the European image of a "provincial" America. There, the lengthy cultural adherence to orthodox "virtues" produced a polite society (labeled "Victorian") which, nonetheless, in its sophisticated language was as acidic as any. In America's self-preoccupied and multi-farious constituency the inability to handle differences of opinion produced a quietude that settled on the dominant culture of nice, upstanding Americans. One didn't want to alienate neighbors so, unfamiliar with open dialogue, people put religion and politics out of bounds. We can see that this would interfere with the normal human clarification of thinking which happens in conversation. It was a somewhat counterproductive way to reduce conflict. It impeded natural conversation about important civil and religious matters that needed the thrashing out that occurs in dialogue. And in the late twentieth-century, when the antagonistic orientation of the "Right" provoked the quiet majority to enter into public life defensively, the vituperative explosion of public discourse produced what someone named "culture wars." "The Right" came to mean not just conservatives, but "war" with the equally self-righteous ultra-progressives, the far Left. The contentiousness encouraged self-righteousness.

The name "culture wars" was closer to reality than most supposed. The culture at issue, however, was not as defined by the issues of the demagogues, homosexuality and abortion. It was, rather, self-righteousness which produced an impatience with disagreement among the "Right" and irritation at implied judgment on their grasp of the always rather satisfactory status quo. This produced resistance to the growing capacity of human beings to think carefully, thoroughly, sensitively through the difficulties the world presents to us. It was produced by a cultural anti-intellectualism fomented by the same hankering felt earlier for the certainty embodied in Fundamentalism. The American dream had encouraged two propensities we are still seeking to reconcile: individual freedom and social responsibility. But golden-age dreams encouraged by Romanticism contributed only dissension.

This nation was founded on recognition of the need for government while its purpose is to preserve the independence of the person. The issue, however, was not acceptance of governance, but accommodation of the diversity of human beings in one society. We call it freedom. It is the historic modern achievement that a workable synthesis of social controls and personal freedom has been achieved to a large degree. These antithetical goals have produced a culture in which freedom is preserved within agreed social bounds. Different behaviors are inevitable among human beings, and so are different implementations of "democracy." Democracy gets into trouble when some deny the hard work of compromise. Let us put away the obsolescent terms "Culture Wars" and get back to the human practice of dialogue. It is more important than new science. It is the comparable social discipline, conversation. Compromise is an intellectual endeavor par excellence. It is hard work. Its incorporation into the social life of a large population is a remarkable achievement.

Whatever emotional attachments to an issue one may have, compromise is likely to be difficult. The "founding fathers" had a clear sense of this difficulty. They were disciplined "scientists" in the sense Dugald Stewart intended to include all educated people (cf. V.C). And they worried about the relative incompetence of most people in using their intelligence. The power of demagogues is not a new discovery. However, the British had incorporated in their culture the fantastic breakout of public education in the Scottish Enlightenment. Education was generally respected. One room schools were found everywhere. These contributed to citizen responsibility, building on the uncivilized individuality of the Celtic heritage as well as the intellectual background and spiritual wealth of the European culture. This residue of the native intelligence of human beings won out over the anti-intellectual tendency of the Right and the lethargic instincts of our sometimes sheeplike animal nature. The human spirit triumphed!

Here we want to address the peculiar personal role we play in this enlightened culture. It might be called growing into democratic responsibility. A hole, a lacuna, has persisted in our social responsibility which is now becoming critical. Our improved communications allow everyone to know more about many things which never touched them in the past. Our capacity to sift through this information intelligently depends on our expanding intellectual ability. But the anti-intellectual strain produced by American's early "can do" attitude neglected development of the mind. Education (perhaps necessarily) became a teaching institution rather than an educating one, to lean on an important distinction. We have appropriated education to produce technicians and mechanics rather than people acquainted with Plato and Augustine – just two of our predecessors who used their heads. Masses of Americans have not been challenged to persist in the life-long struggle with self-development beyond their "can do" comfort level. This is not a critique of individuals or particular occupations. The results show up in the frequent votes of large numbers of people against their self-interest. Because of their limited critical capacity, they have been persuaded by ideological leaders to vote for candidates who reflect the perennial comfort of people with the status quo rather than for those who will contribute to the advancement of the people. This huge gap in our culture is due to be severely challenged by the "new mind" emerging among us.

This failure in critical thinking leaves us without discernment, with limited understanding, and encourages a reversion to emotional feeling rather than a thoughtful approach to life. It is strangely like the "bicameral mind" Julian Jaynes described in his 1976 classic *The Origin of Consciousness in the Breakdown of the Bicameral Mind.*[247] We have come to call the "rational" effort of this later version of the bicameral mind "rationalism." It engages in "rationalization" and an unwillingness to discipline our personal, independent judgment about those to whom we turn for leadership and encouragement and those we elect to lead us. We have discovered belatedly in the U. S. Congress how seriously it immobilizes government. Discernment requires time, information, and reflection to distinguish bad leaders, by which I mean those who encourage and perpetrate contentious social patterns. Failure of discernment interferes with expression of human intelligence. And it is those blind to the new mind emerging among us who are also blind to their enslavement to the obsolete culture we must leave behind. We have noted how readily they become demagogues – or follow them.

Skill in selecting leaders is not something that has developed substantially in our history. Democracy in practice is still very young. Like our over-long practice of letting little children raise themselves (finding out who they are by elemental "natural" trial and error), failing to encourage the thinking of which they are already capable, we have neglected *education* of the populace. Education that is not just training would encourage development of the ability to discern which leaders have the creative capacity to refine our marvelous form of government wisely. "Schooling" meant learning the "A-B-Cs" and counting, adding, and subtracting. Memorization of passages of prose and poetry of "great" people was supposed to broaden young minds, and sometimes did that well, when parents and teachers had the good sense to encourage further education. We have depended on the common sense of voters to choose our political leaders without realizing that "common sense" derives from the intellectual capital accumulated by previous generations. We have neglected education while training people "to make a living" which has come to mean material accumulation rather than modest comfort, decent food and freedom from basic want while pursuing one's self-understanding and becoming a discerning citizen.

Materialism is a poor substitute for intellectual development. With modern communication, the result is exponential multiplication of the numbers of people who have been trained but not educated. Institutions of higher education have utterly failed to stem this tide. This does not mean, as antiquated iconoclasm would insist, that colleges and universities have failed. They have produced thousands, even millions of thinking citizens; the human spirit will break through the barriers encountered if given half a chance. But they have not been leading students persistently to think, to expand themselves to encompass larger and larger worlds as they go through life. Education cannot stop with a diploma in hand, as fine an achievement as that is for many of us. The great Americans who have not bothered to pick up such documents on finishing undergraduate work is not large, but it is significant. For them, "education" is but a beginning.

Lawyers are surely among the "best educated" of Americans, but "Jack" professes on his blog to have become disillusioned with the way law is practiced and has stimulated a variety of sympathetic reactions:

> Oct 31, 2008 8:18 AM CST
> BRAVO Jack! You absolutely have my admiration. I just wish that I had your guts. I have thought countless times about doing something like you have done but I have never had the ability to close my eyes, hold my breath and take a flying leap of blind faith and quit it all. And now as I near 55 years of age 30 years of law practice I wonder if it is too late. The practice of law is definitely not what I imagined it would be. Long hours, nagging clients, moral compromises and constant sacrifices of one's personal life. We start out with high hopes of making a genuine change in the World then after years of practice find that we have only been treading water for years. Professional courtesy, respect and decency no longer exist in this profession as "win at all costs" has become the legal mantra. A prime example is some of the posts regarding this story. Get a grip people...we all make our own personal choices in life. Jack has made his and for that he has my admiration. Atta boy Jack! [248]

The problem is one of *culture*, not just the educational enterprise, government, or religion. We are stuck, according to the cynics among us, in a downward, conservative path in which the highest value is preserving what we have. The current backlash, fortunately, happens when we have one of the brightest and most sensitive presidents in recent history. We also are living when the academy is open as never before to the world beyond rationality. And between blogs, Facebook, and half a dozen new electronic wonders anyone can speak his or her mind! For good or ill, electronics also remove us to a degree from the constraints of community "standards." To the good, this means that the "good" words entered are to an unparalleled extent expressions of the minds of persons; less and less are they mimicry. Though these voices are often not well-disciplined, we are not too proud to figure out their intent. Credit for speaking up accrues to everyone.

Still, we are confident that human beings inherit a very ancient capacity to discriminate, to compare things. Primitive people learned to differentiate animals in order to survive. In contrast, in our comfortable world discrimination requires a determined effort that many people are unwilling to give. Our educational system has not grasped the task of helping people to manage their minds. It means bringing our minds to work hard, to examining carefully, and to deciding thoughtfully. In reference to potential leaders, the new mind will ask persistently, "Who has the ability to use his/her head in strong, positive leadership?" Behind this question is our ability to discern, to see others as they are clearly. It is a question that we learn to deal with in early childhood as we establish our self-understanding in relation to other people with similar and different behaviors and thoughts. The Theory of Mind is one of the most important developments in modern psychology (cf. II. B). We are no longer like sheep.[249] Only recently have we begun to learn parenting and educational skills to help young children build sound judgment into their self-understanding. We learn, very young, to assess others' intentions and motives. And these learnings become firm habits. They stay with us throughout life.

While careful use of our minds increases among us we must expect to be confronted by the continuing specter of poorly selected leaders. Unfortunately, the people we need to lead us are inclined to be reluctant to accept the challenge to public office; they will continue to be confronted by "unreasoning" amplified by the media until the new culture has become more dominant. Misanthropic leaders are exemplified by anti-intellectual sloganeers. While the pundits pontificate, some people respond uncritically, some disagree without dissent, and a few, tired of the harassment, again create liberal voices which sounds to these conservatives like strident adversaries. As usual, the extremists on either side stop listening to others -- or appear to do so.[250] Sophisticated people of the late twentieth century had learned to take sensational language with "a grain of salt" and their central, balanced orientations continue to grow. But American reticence to converse still impeded progress by stifling dialogue in the larger population. The new mind will not be so easily distracted.

Carried on for forty years, the failure of communication within the Presbyterian Church was almost universal.[251] The vast majority of people adhered to the old restraints to preserve "peace" while the vociferous minority commandeered the media. We have noted how this attitude disallowed talk about religion and politics; these were divisive topics, and we had come from a past which taught us (at a very high cost) to avoid challenges to the fragile peace of the common life. We note that this reluctance to tick off antagonism was purchased at a very high price. For thousands of years, aggressiveness was rewarded in our embryonic Western world. Its persistence was one of the things culture perpetuated. And its growing prevalence into the early modern period produced a strong cultural reaction. But opinions were just as fixed as the tendency to aggressiveness. It seems that we did not have sufficient self-confidence to hear others' views without feeling either affirmed or put-upon. Recent events have helped us over this bump in our road. It is possible that the explosion of conservative voices in recent decades was needed to break loose this log jam. The middle voices began putting aside their avoidance of involvement, rediscovered the language of conciliation and became energized.

The problem we face is to learn to speak helpfully among those seriously seeking resolutions of differences between us. This is a special effort, especially after our long reticence to engage others. It requires our *initiative*. We must learn to participate in serious discussions with those who differ. Again, this necessitates taking the initiative. We must learn not to use language which inflames passions. It is a duty of human beings to encourage participation. We must learn to listen to others carefully and to address their concerns from our own understanding, not simply to parrot our own positions, or just as debilitating, to repeat stock answers. In short, we must use our brains. We must embrace the self-discipline of thinking – and opportunities to take the initiative.[252]

Unfortunately, having adapted to our present circumstances, we are apt to fall into a lethargic satisfaction. That is part of what got the dwellers in the early cities into their predicament with oligarchy and what kept them under the thumbs of harsh masters for many centuries. Whether or not Julian Jaynes' notion of the dominance of the "bicameral mind" lay beneath this propensity, we can take seriously the social problem posed by a lethargic lack of intelligent initiative. Lethargy among the people tends to perpetuate the status quo. The hunter-gatherers of all time are people who choose to avoid the effort and the arts of settled life. They spend their lives moving to where the food is. Bonobos and other advanced animals became acclimated to the lush food-rich forests of their habitat. We humans now find ourselves attempting to preserve such habitats for animals unable to adapt to another locale – and we ourselves can vegetate in our comfortable, separate cultures if we choose. Fortunately, there will always be some among us whose genes and experience make them move us all elsewhere.

Human beings are hypersocial. Our sociability is what got us into cities, and has driven our imagination and inventiveness to keep us growing and adapting ourselves and our environments. Thinking people cannot rest comfortably without seeking remedies for problems. Governance has become complex enough to challenge us all to share in our own ways. Our readiness to grasp problems and adapt our selves and our use of our environments to resolve them may be the major factor in willingness to share in the elected offices of governance. This includes a readiness to be changed ourselves with thoughtful awareness of possible effects of such change on others. It is the persistent adventure of human life.

Our understanding of government has come a long way in the modern period, but our efforts have yet to find any ultimate solutions. Change has been occurring at an increasing rate. Our libraries are full of books detailing this change in the past fifty years. The pace does not promise to slow.

172

Just as individuals responded to the new environment of the earliest cities and produced a blossoming of human inventiveness, the inability to govern the huge territories the Romans had conquered created a social vacuum as they failed. This gap in authoritarian control provided opportunity for individuals to demonstrate their own talents. In the Renaissance, in Mercantilism, in the Reformation the residual pattern of oligarchy was increasingly challenged by the response of people to their new freedom, however limited it seems to us to have been. Wherever this freedom was felt, people produced innovations. Awareness of it is, in retrospect, called humanism.²⁵³ They began to recognize the need to break reactionary conventions with a heightened acceptance of personal responsibility (also our projection back). These individual efforts, after many more generations, contributed to opening America to a final break from oligarchy, even in the form of monarchy. The high fences erected by oligarchy were tumbling.

With the evolution of the human mind, the world has become a village. The world -- according to Thomas Friedman -- has been "flattened," that is, we have all become neighbors, almost family, through electronic communication.²⁵⁴ Fences are coming down. Creativity, we learn from Whitehead, is the formative element. When people's minds are freed they create, and overwhelmingly they create good things. The natural self-image of human beings is cooperative and caring.

As this is written we seem to be emerging from an unusual sequence of demonstrated illegal economic ventures, and some political chicanery to match. In this process we have found an array of persons whose selves maintained their integrity and balance in the midst of the turmoil, as well as many who should have been more alert and more critical taking more initiative to correct mistaken management. We humans have not stopped learning from our mistakes. This experience should lead us to expect that many more have relearned or reinforced the values of integrity and responsibility to the enrichment of our culture. They are finding themselves freshly within sight of us all making us part of the emerging new culture.

The abortive presidency of the United States at the beginning of the twenty-first century confirmed our worst fears about the poverty-stricken orientation of the far right population. Hiding behind archaic loyalty to individualism and rationalism, they tried to turn the clock back, and succeeded in many ways. But their victories roused the largest silent majority in world history. It was beginning to move. The Presbyterian Task Force and its report in 2008 blazed a path for American ingenuity to bloom again through extended, open, honest conversation throughout the country. The new mind is inescapable. A few years after this report, increasingly in the church, vocal advocates of responsible sharing in guilt and governance are coming out of the woodwork. It demonstrates that it is time to get serious about our conversation in the culture as a whole.

Perhaps this openness can blossom even, most especially, in the halls of government. But there as anywhere the most important component of this opportunity can easily be escaped. We must be serious enough in our search for truth to include in our conversations people who differ from us. This is critical. Americans have in the twentieth century desegregated and resegregated themselves. Our wealth and large numbers have enabled many to resegregate by choice. Open housing and civil rights raised consciousness of differences and rattled ancient parochial attitudes to produce white flight to suburbs. Few of these replicated the ethnic neighborhoods of earlier years. There we began the cultural pattern of conversation severely restricted to people who are like us. It may be that the American amalgam benefited from the comfort zones this created for people in a century of cataclysmic change. Now we must take fresh steps toward enjoying the diversity America represents. All of us must open ourselves to a wide range of relationships.

It is up to us now to find ways to open every conversation to diversity. That may mean simply learning not to squelch those whose views do not conform to ours. Squelching has become standard operating procedure even before others begin to speak.[255] Watch behavior as people first engage in open conversations and learn how to be "open." We can choose to communicate our readiness to hear others' opinions if we are truly open to them. Scientists have shown us how much we communicate to others without a word. Posture and facial expression are two methods embodying hundreds of signals. But communication is far more complex than even that. We must learn to be honestly open. The rule of deceit in public discourse is finished.[256]

Most of us today can understand how we ourselves can best participate in implementing the new mind among us. As we grasp the importance of how we talk about things and participate in everyday life with a fresh sense of generosity and accommodation, this mind will energize our twenty-first century culture. It is the way human beings have changed our culture massively in the past. Now we must again free the human imagination to change some unhelpful and unhealthy social patterns.

Our culture will benefit from the whole of our effort without war and conflict. The pattern perpetrated on humanity by the kings of ancient times was to destroy, only to rebuild to their own glory. Such destruction is a thing of the past. Our first step, of course, is to "swear off" all destructive methods of social change. They are no longer necessary.[257] The new sense of self produced by thousands of years of human struggle enables us to enjoy the participation of all human beings in the evolution of our culture.

X. REBUILDING THE SOCIAL ORDER

We have been talking throughout of a society built on primitive experience. The early elements of organization, of technology, of the government and of the military are significant aspects of our culture. All have very ancient roots however sophisticated they may have become. But culture carries forward both progressive and regressive inventions of people, and much of our history has been the slow and inefficient learning of a pre-critical humanity; it took most of 4000 years to work our way out of oligarchy. We have still to free ourselves from the presuppositions and the force of cultures spawned in the childhood and adolescence of humanity. Now the makings of maturity are here. We now have perspective to appreciate the past without embracing regressive particulars. Our European-American culture has broken open our enslavement to that past. But we are still caught in its residue.

There was a time when a mature civilization was considered past its prime. No more. We understand so much more than our predecessors; we understand *process*. We have grasped the social nature of true humanity, and a better understanding of our selves, our faults and our need for discipline, our strengths and our need to use them wisely. A "mature" culture now means "another development" not "overripe." It means embracing the constantly being-renewed mind of humanity. There will be other cultures following what we shape in the formative years at our disposal. How they will differ from ours depends in part on how well we build. In each period of these thousands of years there have been people of vision. We have tried to see that extensive evolution in these pages. Now as we sense the emergence of a new culture being shaped among us, we must grasp its wholeness and potential with courage and care.

As we progress in the emergence of our twenty-first century culture, we will necessarily still practice and develop skills inherited from our past. The military might of the United States will continue the new trajectory already begun toward a humane, peaceful force, no longer the raping, pillaging, exploiting military that shaped many views of our history. That violent orientation built empires and was inherited by the institutions that developed in recent history. Now our control of military power will increasingly guide it toward less use of force, constrained both by situation and by need, but most of all by our conscious choices. The time has come when the internal propensity of more military leaders will absorb and develop the attitudes and techniques useful in a world no longer afraid of itself and ready to contribute to the happiness and welfare of all. The term "military" itself may undergo the sort of transformation that we hope will characterize our culture, making it a term meaning highly disciplined care and consideration, instead of "war."

National service will increasingly be a training ground for well-rounded, effective intelligence, including restraint and constraint in emergence into adulthood. It will teach basic skills. Instead of a teen notion of growing into adult "freedom" we will enable young people to take charge of themselves as responsible members of society. They will learn early what has taken a lifetime for most humans to learn, that our freedom is fulfilled by responsibility. It is constantly choosing between desired and valued possibilities. Karl Jaspers tells us that we find reality in acting out of our own "freedom rooted in spontaneity and connecting through communication with the freedom of others."

Though it is difficult to foresee a time when a military replete with sophisticated armaments will learn to operate without instruments of force, it is a worthy religious aspiration. It can change a culture over time. At the disposal of a newly sensitive national service, old methods of social enforcement will be replaced increasingly by more humane techniques of restraint where needed and by skills of enablement. Such a new culture in which helping others to grow is a dominant virtue will contribute to the maturing of young men and women. The military will become an impressive part of the educational system which fills the need for young people to learn self-discipline, to express camaraderie, and to explore what personal independence in adult community is about.

The age-old tactics of gaining wealth at the expense of others will also undergo transformation. Tribal peoples of the world still exercise the lively art of haggling and the demonic practice of extortion. Like the ancient end of *lex talionis*, bribery and "influence" for private gain must come under effective social control.[258] People must move easily on the face of the earth across all of our artificial borders, without the exploitation now evident, for example, in the sex trade. Women everywhere will be equal to their male companions in status and rights, free to contribute to our culture as whole human beings. All children deserve the fruits of hundreds of years of human learning to nurture and prepare for productive and joyful lives.

A. The Pleasure Principle

We have several times identified the modern capacity of human beings to keep more than one thought in mind at a time. It is quite likely that one of these days researchers will discover that some people are able to entertain several concepts concurrently and deal with each one intelligently. In a narrow sphere of mental activity like the game of chess, adept people have been able to engage many different games concurrently. Has the effective magician not for a very long time been able to "put one over" slower thinking peers? And with an aging population, some unscrupulous people will exploit opportunities provided by slowing mental processes. Perhaps many of us are able to handle several concepts. But if we try to speak of more than one at a time our thoughts tumble over one another and we are apt to become incoherent. So it will be until our daily language evolves to provide for still more complexity.[259] Is it not like music? Interweaving themes and key changes are fairly common. Dissonance and atonality still surprise us. Until these were mastered, musicians tended to simply abhor such sounds. We will shortly examine John Caputo's suggestion of a playful rationality (chapter XI F) that recognizes the variety of approaches that can contribute to examination of a topic. In recent days it has been refreshing to find scholars speaking of a playfulness in their work. More than admitting their mistakes, they are even able to laugh at themselves. Our humanity benefits greatly from humor, from laughter, from a good "belly laugh." The one thing correlated with brain size in evolution, scientists tell us, is play.

Music may provide another good model for our thought as we approach rebuilding the social order. Michael Gazzaniga tells us that in our primitive centuries

> Music may have acted as a social bonding system, much like language, that synchronized mood and perhaps prepared the group to act in unison, thus binding coalitions and groups.[260]

I think this is clearly the case. It is fun to sing/dance together. It always has been, and still is. Obviously, it does bind us together at many levels. We enjoy it, and in the modern world it is enhanced by fantastically high-quality musical reproduction. The question about why people listen to music alone is a no-win question; it is a pleasure. When a lone shepherd played his pipe it was a pleasurable activity that provided self-expression and helped also to fill the time -- and some who sang could dance at the same time. The Phrygian cult in early Greek history produced artful sculptures of satyrs, often playing cymbals while tramping on a rhythm instrument in a contorted, dancing posture.[261] And children sing and dance at a very early age.

Play and music are probably as fundamental to our intellectual development as any activities. In them our ancestors explored our senses and themselves and learned to deal with our environment. This ability to learn in many ways has always been an advantage for humans; "Pretend play, such as hide-and-seek, can develop skills that are better learned in a play situation than when they may need to be actually used. It would be fitness-enhancing to learn to hide or run from a predator, or stalk and search for food, before one actually needs to do it for survival".[262] It also teaches us to decouple reality and pretense. Joseph Carroll, (English, U. of Missouri, interested in Darwinian theory), points out that we are not captive to "instinct" (very early learned behaviors). It has been suggested that the brain has a "driver" to direct it. We are able to choose or edit (Leslie Brothers) or interpret (Michael Gazzaniga) a vast array of ways to perceive and to react to stimuli. Carroll points out that E. O. Wilson observed that the arts also contribute to our learning to adapt:

> There was not enough time for human heredity to cope with the vastness of new contingent possibilities revealed by high intelligence.... The arts filled the gap.[263]

In these acute observations we find the rationale for increasing our involvement and support in the arts. The arts expand our world. In our information-full world, we have the opportunity to be acquainted with all kinds of situations without experiencing them firsthand. All of them contribute to our development as human beings, increasingly self-conscious, alert, adaptive, creative, and realistically capable. The uniqueness of the human self rests in the mind's flexibility. We can rejoice in the biologists pursuit of biological explanations of living phenomena. But ultimately, the freedom we enjoy to choose living rather than dying is a privilege of the human spirit. Artists frequently express that spirit though, try as we may, it is rarely caught in words.

It adds up to corroboration of the basic principle behind Francis Hutcheson's philosophy in Glasgow early in the eighteenth century. Not an original philosopher, he was, nonetheless, a popular lecturer whose humanism was influential in the development of the Scottish Enlightenment. Jeremy Bentham is often connected with what is now called "utilitarianism," but we can attribute to John Locke its first articulation. It is the notion that we are primarily motivated by our pleasure which may come from contemplation, participation, creative activity, association with others, or almost anything. Russell suggests that even a masochist can attribute engaging in self-inflicted pain to the pleasure it gives. But to recover the practical orientation of the early eighteenth century (leaving out of this equation such later intellectual considerations as Russell's), pleasure was seen as consistent with social approbation. And we may restrict our use of the principle to this orientation also, avoiding excess.

Beauty has given human beings pleasure for a very long time. Gazzaniga describes the work of John Tooby and Leda Cosmides. They note a general principle that sustained sensory attention to beauty cued our ancestors to elements of their environment that would have been advantageous. Beauty, of course, applies to everything from gender, to assessment of game animals, to the exhibition of intricate skills. "There is no other unifying principle in appreciation of beauty except that our evolved psychological architecture is designed to motivate sustained attention through making the experience give us pleasure, to make contemplating things themselves intrinsically rewarding."[264] Relegating pleasure to the artistic dimension has reduced the role of beauty in everyday life and thus diminished the contribution of contemplation to our self-development and culture. It is a case which demonstrates our primitive instinct to organize our environment extended to the sophistication of classifying things. Classification allows us to ignore things – like beauty – when, as with art, we can relegate them outside our sphere of attention. Our instinct to enjoy beauty is one we should take care not to lose.

B. The Inevitability of Suffering

This is not to foreclose the reality of suffering in our world in every age, no matter how optimistic, how pessimistic, how productive or how degrading. Natural disasters will occur and some people will continue to attribute them to a vicious and brutal God however inconsistent that sort of god-concept seems to us. Disease has begun to yield to human intervention, but new strains of flu perennially remind us that in this effort we are doing battle with flexible, living tormentors. The truth is that the number of influences on human life is extensive. Life itself is complex. The human being is an extraordinarily complex being. Some have identified the possibility of life with a very narrow range of possible conditions on the surface of our earth. This reminds us of our tendency always to over-simplify. Non-oxygen life forms have been found in sea volcanoes. Reality is not simple. We are, as an influential educator about 1960 called it, part of a "web of life" that may include unknown strands. "Web" has always been a symbol of inexplicable, intertwined complexity as has weaving.

The existence of suffering in the world has always been of concern. The book of Job is one of the oldest of all recorded stories. Buddhism has taken a particularly narrow position in regard to evil, claiming that denying its existence gives us relief from it. Nirvana is the state in which we are totally separated from the material world in which evil causes suffering. This is to oversimplify for the sake of making a point. What this tells us is that our brains are indeed wondrously flexible things! Shocks like the 1755 Lisbon earthquake (in which tens of thousands died innocently) raised European wariness of the classical explanations of suffering.[265] The Reformation had taken a stance different from Augustine and Aquinas who had with Plato considered evil to be non-being which God turns to good since it is an absence of good. The classic dualism, with roots in the East, is represented by Zoroastrianism and its later derivative, Manichaeism in which God is in conflict with evil in a cosmic battle. In the modern era Idealism sometimes gave evil an aesthetic interpretation, suggesting that without the dark colors in a painting our pleasure in the whole would be sacrificed. But life contains tragedy, not melodrama in which good vanquishes evil completely. Karl Barth refused to discuss the problem of evil; the clay cannot judge the potter. Gustav Aulen in *Christos Victor* affirmed Christ's victory over evil, but this is a religious interpretation not a philosophic explanation of evil. Modern process theology has returned to the concept of a limited God overcoming a disorderly world.

Douglas John Hall points out that human beings are free to choose wrongly rather than rightly, to choose evil rather than righteousness. This is our "creational birthright." "Once chosen, evil contains its own logic and necessity."[266] We will leave the question of natural disaster to others. Our attention is on the human quotient. In our view, suffering is not simply "bad." Suffering is a name we have given to the human struggle to cope with hurt, disease and disaster. We hurt for many reasons and pain is not pleasurable. But we have coped with the tragic, and we have gifts to cope with it. The remarkable truth is that, not infrequently, this path brings us a new depth of life. The tragic is another of the many stimuli to extend our attention, our knowledge, and our appreciation of life.

We recognize with wonder the achievements of persons with serious disabilities, for example, Jessica Cox, a 26 year old born without arms. As a child she did not understand that she was born with a rare congenital disease. "It was difficult to be different," she says. "My mother told me that I could do the things I wanted to do.... My father was my base during difficult moments (growing up). It was he who formed the person I am today." Jessica holds a degree in psychology. She drives without special aids, and pilots a plane alone. She says:

> Sometimes fear starts from the lack of knowledge of the unknown... There is a universal fear, that of the lack of confidence in yourself.... Our great fear is not to measure up. (But) we are stronger over and above all measure.

This strength has been evident among those who have suffered the indignities of the ages. When *talis lexionis* ruled the world suffering was constant and fearsome. As Europe matured, some people became Interested In applying sclence to health problems and the ability of modern medicine to help and heal has made life a pleasure for most of us in America. Pain and death (the last "enemy") have been reduced greatly. Since much of the rest of the world still suffers without such blessings of human intelligence, no description of the human situation can ignore suffering.

C. Differentiation in Our Culture

Granted the importance to us of pleasure and the ubiquity and functionality of suffering, beyond them perhaps, the most difficult aspect of sociality is conquering other fears. We fear losing pleasures of course and fear suffering pain. These are evolutionary developments of the basic instincts to survive and reproduce. So ancient is this that we have as yet no idea how humans transmuted fear of loss into almost universal avarice.

Human society today contains the inevitable spectrum of differences among us. Civil Rights as defined mid-century have not cleaned house for us as we wished it might. Discrimination still abounds, not to say great strides have not been made in fifty years. While discrimination continues unfortunately, the culture has been greatly altered; laws have made a difference, correcting some egregious problems. Jim Crow is dead. The persistence of the residue of the old culture is due at least in part to the very nature of the human creature. Evolved from ancient predecessors of apes, the human brain is unique in every individual. Shaped from birth by environment each one thinks differently from any other. Only recently have we grasped our individual responsibility for choosing our paths not as free and independent individuals but as responsible creatures who love others.

While no two brains work the same except within the framework of some learned discipline, all persons who grow up in proximity will share a mental orientation (or a version of it) which we call "rationality." It is evidence of what we call culture. Culture carries among us the many ways in which we have been relating to each other. It is full of the common assumptions people share, of the common disciplines which children pick up in living with us. Culture also carries forward what we call polity which governs us (our polite habits of sociality). We try to teach these things to children before they are misled into other paths. Only recently have we grasped that much of this is incorporated into the thinking of children before the age of three, and a massive amount (some say more than can be absorbed in the rest of life) by age six. Every person also carries in memory sensory experience which is never quite the same as anyone else. All together one creates himself out of all of this embodying this self as her own mind, interpreting it all and choosing who to be. This mind uniquely interprets the culture as it impresses him or her. (Thus, one might say we are doubly unique.) Part of that mind is its grasp of the rationality of the community.

This is why democratic decisions are often thought to be mistaken from the point of view of some people, inevitable for other observers, and laudable for still others. Bryan Caplan focuses on economic issues to demonstrate the title of his book *The Myth of the Rational Voter.* But his point is applicable to democracy generally. Is his "myth" just another misunderstanding of human rationality? Our rationality does not yield a unity of "rational" perceptions. The point is not that the community rationality (mind) is usually "right," but that democratic self-discipline enables us to accommodate the diverse views of others; this capacity is central to American "rationality."

Winston Churchill was right about democracy being the worst form of government except for all the others that have been tried. Where the democratic process operates, the people are free to express themselves. Being free, they can choose to take responsibility

181

in it and to own decisions with which they do not wholly agree. Owning these they put forth their efforts within the system that protects their "freedom." And perhaps they learn from the experience how to change the system more to their liking. The result is the most persistently vibrant human community humankind has yet constructed. And, the promise for the future is that we have learned to tweak our rational institutions persistently to remedy their shortcomings.

Thousands of years learnings, not even noticed at first, stimulated the evolution of this flexibility. But for a very long time in the development of our civilization the threat of chaos brought forth memories of mayhem, slaughter, rape, pillage and burning. The chaos before civilization began was spotty, no doubt, but anger knew no bounds. Chaos was truly fearful. And the result was to reinforce the natural tendency of animals to enjoy what is stable, provides food, and gives pleasure, in our culture, the *status quo*. Stability has remained a major social goal for us and learning to adjust without constantly opening new "loop holes" in our systems to misanthropic exploitation has eluded us. The founding fathers were right: demagogues have in a degree ruled our nation while the people have avoided developing the essential democratic discipline: discretion. Like all disciplines this too takes time and attention, but the product is persons of greater humanity.

Before the city, polities of individual chiefs ruled thousands of diverse tribes. Starting at least 6000 years ago some leaders of increasingly complex societies attempted to control bottlenecks in the trading routes that had emerged. Some anthropologists consider these trading patterns to be evidence of the accumulation of wealth and the desire for "luxury" goods. Bandits and other skimmers could settle down at these points and live comfortably. This happened all over the world. One is tempted to think of the current global economy as a repetition of this phenomenon. A direct line runs from the spectacular plumage of some birds to the costumes of Aztec rulers and Moulin Rouge cabaret dancers. Throstein Veblen and others, perhaps tongue in cheek, have suggested such "trifling" consumption as the engine of civilization.

We might summarize: *human beings have gradually learned to live socially satisfactorily.* This does not mean that there are no serious problems. In fact current unrest in the world is a clear indication of the misanthropic distribution of wealth. From earliest times some people could not constrain their avarice, their appetites, and their impatience with village life. Human variability will always enable these to be multiple thorns in the flesh of the rest. Finally the democratic process has emerged that allows us persistently to change the ways we control the excesses – giving people some social control without violent revolution,[267] and assuring over 300 million people the personal freedom to be their best selves.

From the emergence of cities until the construction and maintenance of our country, "government" has been refined over and over. The greatest revolution in all history was the acceptance by human beings of responsibility for their own government – and necessarily, with it, embracing one another in all their diversity. This is what democracy is about though it was hardly in the minds of very many a few years ago. Democracy has changed character just as has culture. This in itself suggests the appropriateness of the democratic concept to human variability. But democracy has not solved the problems of human variability. Nor has it resolved sometimes extraordinary failure to disseminate culture. Pirates, terrorists, and plain thugs grab headlines, but ordinary dissimulation, financial chicanery and oligarchic treatment of workers has persisted in spite of cultural learnings. Corruption is a broad term that too often misses the obscenity in some human behavior.[268] Cultures have clearly identified such.

In the twentieth century the talk was all about freedom. The public mind was convinced that this amorphous construction was the essence of democracy. Way back when slavery was endemic, freedom did mean exactly that, not being under limits imposed by others. We have answered the puzzle of why people allowed themselves to be enslaved by postulating the evolution in historic time of human self-consciousness. But as the twenty-first century opened, philosophy, psychology, sociology, and history all changed the color of the scene. Instead of escape into gaudy color from the black and white past, the gray-tone became sharper and clearer, the need for excitement quieted, and the bright but boring sameness of self-images became subtly less conforming and more accurately ourselves. The self-reliance, the braggadocio, the loud self-promotion of public characters began to fade into a new world about to shine forth. We had succeeded in discovering ways to live in peace, though peace still eludes us, as avarice and race and sex and power, misused, still persist.

Nonetheless, we understand ourselves, interwoven worldwide, better than our predecessors. There were many of them over millennia who had visions and dreamed dreams and wrote majestic poetry anticipating our anticipation which is emerging today in the sight of those not trapped in our immediate past. There are many loose ends. Some will become unraveled in spite of every effort to maintain and perpetuate the best we can imagine. Increasingly many opinions can be brought together in public dialogue allowing us to arrive at a consensus – though seldom agreement among all of us – to guide our leaders in their constructions and implementations of programs of public value.

Then the integrity and public awareness of these leaders allows them to govern more intelligently (not necessarily more "rationally" by varied standards) than they are likely to have done otherwise. To the fruits of dialogue, each leader must bring his or her own basic human (intelligent) intuition. After all, "government of the people, by the people, and for the people" captures the essence of democracy – a total reversal of oligarchic government – but we still rely on (intelligent) persons' perceptions and insights. We are not leaderless, but our leaders must not be individualists. They must be sufficiently part of our culture to understand the story we have been telling. Rational? Yes, within cultural bounds. Individualist? No.

The trouble with Libertarianism is exactly its basic premise, rejecting authority, which fails to acknowledge the history of humanity in seeking appropriate and agreeable rational controls called society; real democracy exercises authority in a new way. In the twenty-first century we are no longer concerned about the privileges of persons with authority. Gradually, all persons who exercise authority are increasingly recognizing their necessary limits in our culture. Some of us it seems have escaped the learnings we have noted leading to personal responsibility. And, like all other traits, responsibility will not elicit uniform behavior in us. A philosophy which abhors authority has no place in the real world. From the beginning of sociality, authority of some kind has played a significant role.

Much of the past five thousand years has been squandered in oligarchic forms of leadership that have proven themselves incapable of managing the society as population grew, uncontrolled. As the years passed, the modern institutions of medicine, religion, education, business and law grew naturally out of the social flux. As we enter the twenty-first century all of these function around the world in many, sometimes inconsistent, forms. All of them are subject to some sort of governance and that means subject to *appropriate* authority.

Worldwide recognition of the truth in democratic organization is demonstrated by the regular meetings of nations at Davos, Switzerland. In the current economic messes involving many of the nations of the world, Davos provides a needed forum. Each nation retains sovereignty, but influencing one another they become more rational than they could ever be separately.   The context for Davos is an international community which has assented to a peaceful evolution of authority. While words inform such meetings of persons who carry the authority of their nations, being together allows for additional means of communication. Daniel Lord Smail and Andrew Shryock note that stress response (which Davos delegates surely feel) is closely tied to reward systems in human thought and have internal concomitants in the effect of dopamine in the brain. Thus it is not just the intellectual activity of conversation that we should credit for growing capacity to govern, but the whole human business of being together, about gathering, about *meeting* to communicate. Democracy is the evolved system of people meeting in varied responsibilities to communicate about the nuts and bolts of daily life in mass culture.

Our differences persistently cause difficulty. Perhaps it is the apparently inevitable differences in wealth which is most obvious.   This difference is demonstrated in style of living, in expense of purchases, and often also in political opinion. The comforts provided by wealth have perennially led to support of the status quo, and to hoard wealth, often to be unloaded in ostentatious public projects. This is unfair to those in all ages who have contributed to that wealth but usually suffered without much if any discretionary income – for example, crafts persons, blue collar workers, clerks, artisans, strategists and managers. Is it not this difference which is the rub even in our wealthy, egalitarian nation?

And it is another persistent behavior that makes it unlikely that a solution to this inequality will be solved anytime in the foreseeable future. It is segregated housing – segregation by economic character. Governed by another assumption, we build housing of like expense together because to mix quality of housing degrades the more expensive. And it is inevitable that people who cannot afford expensive homes will not live next to their equals who can. One of the most permanent aspects of culture, housing, stands in the way of the kind of interaction between unlike people that is required to overcome human differentiation.

It seems that as the new mind emerges, some wealthy people share in this evolution.   There seems to be evidence in the ways in which these distribute sizable portions of their wealth to contribute to the welfare of others.[269] Wealth will increasingly be an embarrassment. But such acts are not sufficiently radical in our new world. History shows how our various institutions have contributed to the public good. But, less only than war as such, economic enterprises have been handmaidens to it and introduced misery as instruments of avarice. Marvelous architectural wonders have constrained human suffering very little. The emergence in the Enlightenment of enterprise capitalism is built on the foundations of ownership of property. Like the accumulation of foodstuffs in the granaries of the first cities, large amounts of property under control of individuals soon raise avarice to a fine art. And the skills involved have grown beyond control. The twentieth century produced massive schools of management science supporting these burgeoning economic structures.

Today business institutions are setting themselves up for a radical revolution. Rana Foroohar in *TIME* magazine points to the Apple corporation whose products are made largely in China,[270] thus, on the profit motive, sidestepping American protections for citizens. Apple (in its corporate anonymity), whose executives say they are absolved of obligation "to solve America's problems," nonetheless expects the United States "to protect intellectual-property rights and to keep waterways safe so that it can deliver its made-in-China products."[271] Apple, of course, is only one of the extraordinarily profitable American corporations. Today corporations are so large they can afford the litigious world in which inadequate American controls struggle to fulfill our antiquated laws. Thus it is more than just the huge financial organizations causing trouble today; they represent in accounting terms the ownership of property. They are part of the for-profit corporation complex that has achieved supra-national self-control in an interdependent world. Again, one can too quickly see a parallel to the trading networks of ten thousand years ago.

It is the descendents of those who have chosen to exploit ownership of property who today require radical, new control for the public good. The early corporation in the twelfth century was an educational institution. Its whole purpose was public use of knowledge. So far Western Civilization has failed to manage its economic systems with similar care for the public good. Governed and governing have used economics to sustain the institutions and their constituents. But the direction of evolution I believe is for the profit making corporation, now apparently beyond the control of accountable individuals, to be made part of our inter-personal world. The cancer of oligarchy is gradually coming under the control of human rationality and it will lose its tendency to accumulate wealth for the benefit of those few.

We note that it was those who exploited the natural resources of America one hundred years ago who stimulated the gradual accumulation of governmental controls on American corporations. One hundred years of coal-dirtied cities and particulate-filled unbreathable air forced the regulation of the public environment. And it has take most of another hundred to make the global environment a sufficiently public concern to force the political functionaries in our culture to be serious about pollution. The demanding effort to learn how to regulate the ever-changing economy lies before us. "Economics" is not only an academic discipline, it is the way in which we responsibly share resources for the good of the people. Our culture must find ways to add the economy to the institutions which support the common life.

In the optimism of this book, we surmise that there has been an increase in the numbers of those persons of wealth who have sought to control their avarice and make their good fortune into tools for good in the world. We guess that this number is growing in a fundamental and just way, that in time will overpower the forces of greed. No doubt, in a world of human beings, there will probably always be some whose avarice is beyond their self control. A word for that is "cupidity" and it produces opulence and obscenity. But counter-forces are at work to make a serious generosity fundamental in our culture.

No doubt, what we have called the Third World will gradually learn, evolve and grow in ways which contribute to the wealth of the people. There will be more people who seem to others to be "wealthy." We can hope that the number of people using wealth beneficently will increase. But ultimately, the solution to maldistribution of wealth will require better balance involving governmental controls as well as personal discipline. The solutions will transform our culture in very important ways affecting everyone.

The current dilemma of wealth is illustrated in the political tensions which are exploited by wealthy demagogues to support the status quo. The way things are, in a major way, has always been sustained by those who most benefit from the way it is. When laws were first codified, the scribes saw to it that their security was well taken care of; they made themselves indispensable. Even as the power of people emerged and crystallized, the aristocracies of every age have provided well for their own interests. We have no reason to think the near future will be different – except for the growing evidence of the emergence of the new mind in a new culture.

One of the chief benefits of this new mind among people who have been poor will be their appropriation of ways of living in which they develop their self-confidence as elites have sometimes had the leisure to do. The difference the new mind makes is its accommodating orientation. The ancient world developed laws prescribing ways of living together. The medieval world increasingly found that laws have limited utility; they are not necessary nor desirable for all useful controls Principles, values, and the virtues, helped to shape the growing self-confidence of Europeans. The emergent mind discovered to our dismay that aristocracies of wealth and power have consistently institutionalized the stress which civilization imposes on people. "The poorer you are, the more likely it is that you suffer from chronic stress."[272]

We have also found that aspects of our society have been mishandled, particularly because the very rich have not proved themselves socially responsible in regulating wealth for the common good; it seems that this is impossible. Our long history of acquisition and self-indulgence has not been overcome. Presumably, the wealthy, imbued with the new mind, will no longer persist in amassing wealth which could just as well be disgorged from their control to benefit society, to be spread more evenly among many others, to raise the capability and opportunity level of those who have not enjoyed them. Why should wages be kept at subsistence levels when workers contribute to profitable productivity? I once worked for a company in which profit sharing was taken for granted. The man who started that company always lived generously.[273] There must be many ways in which the wealth produced by human beings can be spread more evenly among them. The new mind will ferret them out.

The new experience of opportunity among the formerly poor will enable them to contribute more to our culture thus enriching us all. How many inventions of our materialistic culture have been the work of ordinary people! For all of us, including both elites and the downtrodden, *the new mind will give increasing numbers of us a new capacity to pay relaxed attention to what is important.*[274] Distinguishing the mundane from the significant is one of its gifts.

Grasping this distinction will allow us to enjoy what we never before recognized as significant. When we see in a flash some element of truth – even in a half-baked demagogue -- we often get excited out of proportion, an excitement which transmits itself to others to create the sometimes inappropriate but very real phenomenon of the popular expression we call "a movement." As the new mind fills more and more of us, movements will take on the basis of fresh meaningfulness, and we might hope an intelligence which contributes less error and more truth in our culture.[275] As this occurs, differences will separate us less, becoming more significant as indicators of shared responsibility. Absurd and disproportionate compensation for socially valued activities will be replaced by something more rational and equitable with general approbation. The obscene amounts currently paid to celebrities and top corporation officials will again become rational.[276]

D. Baby Steps into Tomorrow

Today is yesterday's tomorrow. The first steps into tomorrow were taken a long time ago. In the long view, all contributions to the culture are small. The things which become our indicators of change are inevitably amalgams of thousands of "baby steps." The human self has been free for most of the human journey in the sense that individuals would not notice any change they personally made. That is a legacy most analysts forget because they look seriously only at the past 10,000 years or an even shorter time span. Their window on our civilization tends to show us only what accumulations of personal contributions have produced, the big steps that get named: pottery, clothing, knives, scrapers, walls, aqueducts, swords, and more. Initial steps toward these may well have taken place even before that arbitrary date. My personal list of these includes celebration, song, dance, grunt & show communication, elemental family language, and then dancing and singing of exploits (the earliest story-telling), religion, development of villages (elemental social organization). Long before the city began, people had domesticated animals, tilled the ground, made baskets and clothing.

The early villages were undoubtedly incorporated into hunter-gatherer wandering, following herds and seasons. We can imagine tents of animal skins, scraped thin folded and transported on donkeys. In occasional meetings the people learned skills in relating to other people which eventually led to to the city. Each step probably took hundreds of years – and very likely occurred in unique patterns all over the globe. As we unearth evidence and build suppositions, these "steps" are likely to be found to be sets of smaller learnings.

Most of the steps which we identify as the beginnings of our civilization took place within the past five or six thousand years. They were themselves the products of generations. What we (and our recent ancestors) have done with ourselves in this period, is miraculous though such changes as we sketch here seem painfully slow. But in terms of the vast stretch of earlier evolution of animals and primates (like ourselves in so many respects), the development of our civilization has occurred in a remarkably short time. It is the product of the evolution of the brain, providing for the emergence of people like us who have been shaping up cultures preceding our own. Miraculously, their many ways of living culminate today in a moment of shocking *realization among us* of our power to decide what the culture we are shaping will be like. From our inheritance we can consider an array of errors (from our point of view) that we can to some extent remedy. We are very like those before us in that we will not be able to see the mistakes we make until some years pass.

What has changed is our human capacity to embrace and accumulate knowledge and invent ways not only to cope but to expand our capabilities. Our perspective exceeds theirs as the core memory of my first Kaypro computer (5k?) is truly minuscle beside our buildings full of computer memory devices. They have been holding more and more every year and retrieving it in unbelievable *milli-seconds*. Much of the content is available to any of us. And so the scope of our potential insights is far greater than any people before us. If any generations have been able to influence their cultures, it is those of the twenty-first century. It is our turn to take some baby steps.

The small steps we will contribute will contain positive and negative pieces. Our culture perpetuates learnings of which we know nothing and builds on mistakes as well as hopeful possibilities. We have arrived at the point where we are sufficiently self-confident, pleased with much of what we have done and critical of the rest, that we can now take an (almost) objective look at what we must do to carry forward the task of becoming truly human. There is a sense in which the long road behind us is filled with baby steps and missteps in this direction. Missteps, of course, often prove to be the better teachers, but that requires our thoughtful consideration. Now we feel ourselves self-consciously called into tomorrow. We are shaping the culture into which our children and grandchildren are initiated.

The idea of being drawn into a future different from today was also sensed long ago. I like to think of it in terms of Whitehead's "prehension" which I have suggested even the early homid Ardi may have demondstrated. Today we recognize this phenomenon, not as a divine voice "calling" but as the mind seeing (as the prophetic "seers" *saw*; cf. chapter V. B). We have observed the gradual development of human skill in ancient leaders seeing their cities as greater than others, or perhaps seeing them as more grand than earlier. Now our options for peering into the future vastly exceed those available to our predecessors. As we have more options, we have more need of dialogue to clarify, consider, judge, and choose. We are no longer in a society that attributes final answers to individual leaders. Even scientists, philosophers, and pundits depend on one another's views. We listen to many for contributions to our insight – or at least to several whose orientations and opinions vary. We have tried in previous chapters to tell the story of how seers used their human capacities to examine what they could know. As today we recognize genius, so have people before us who did not possess it. We have tried not to be judgmental, but to lay out our hominid character helpfully. We have, inevitably, been selective; many other scenarios will be considered by readers. The issue is to try to come to a fresh and hopeful understanding, as open and thoughtful a view as seems helpful for us, corrected by one another's insights.

Our reading is that the present is a great, important hinge for us to hammer into place. The great gates on the cities of the past have long been gone. We have a very different situation today than has ever existed before. All sorts of explorations of the past will continue and intensify. We will judge the past as we cannot help doing, judging in the creative sense of looking for what we can learn from those who have preceded us. In the historical period, though we find violence, with some reflection we discover that we may have gifts and strength to expand our world beyond the mind behind the old city gates.

Perhaps the most important hopeful element in our past is our long-term effort to understand how we can live together peacefully. The search began long before cities, of course, as people wished only to be left alone in the wide open spaces of deep history. But as populations grew and interpersonal conflicts multiplied, peace could only be achieved in baby steps. What is the first escape from animosities that were bound to occur? Separation. Even in biblical times, distance was a convenient deterrent to pursuit. People went their separate ways, as did Jacob and Esau. Eventually our expansion populated almost every island as well as the huge continents of the globe. Today there are those who would anticipate colonizing distant celestial bodies, apparently oblivious to the enormous portion of earth's limited resources that such an effort would require. There are others who feel compelled to spend huge portions of our resources on armaments to protect ourselves from other human beings. These views are remnants of the perpetual cynicism and the nihilism of our recent past. To view the world negatively, as a place from which we should escape, is to fall into one of the oldest traps of human conceptualization. It is far easier to extract oneself from an unhappy situation than to seek its resolution. But the time came when there were people everywhere and we had to begin facing up to the problem of human society: How can we best live together? Most cultures neglected the immense capability of humans to adapt to and to change the conditions of conflict. Again, like Jacob and Esau, we discover that human beings are kin. We pine[277] for that relationship.

As distance evaporated with modernity so did separation. But our human ingenuity had taken on the multiplication of languages faster than disappearance of tribes and villages could lose vernacular language. The accumulation of knowledge had created a new flood of languages. Inside the many emerging disciplines, pride and focus required many special words invested with their own meanings. One effect was to reduce contact and communication with other disciplines; concentration of attention tends to narrow the horizon. It contributes to isolation, and the focus on specific disciplines reduced attention to the broader concerns of the arts, history, and philosophy. This confusion of tongues contributed to distrust and wrangling in the political process, often straining at the use of specific language, coded to archaic notions. In the twentieth century we learned to distrust language in earnest. Belatedly, by the beginning of the twenty-first century, this was correcting itself. The mid-twentieth century interest in Esperanto subsided, and digital expertise developed means for instantaneous electronic translation. But more importantly, we began a struggle to gain trust in our fellow human beings.

189

We also had learned that the ancient habit of confusing our mental constructs with reality could cause us a lot of trouble. Language was frequently misused. And manipulation of public opinion became endemic most noticeably, of course, in politics. Under the pressure of obsolete philosophic notions left over chiefly from the Enlightenment, these errors continued to pervert the popular vote against the best interests of the people. We have laid the current blame for this largely at the door of Protestant Fundamentalism which blossomed and withered largely in the 20th century. But the truth is that we had marginalized philosophy and history so that we lost our grasp of the corrections they were entering into our culture. Both facticity and hope suffered. The best hope of overcoming this anti-democratic trend is in individual discretion, small steps of people who think.

Throughout the centuries, the power of language had been growing persistently. Even among the repressed thousands in the early cities, language kept increasing in scope and vocabulary. Family and tribal languages gave way to regional tongues and the languages of nations. More and more people understood related tongues. People used the language at hand to grow out of the roots of story-telling into the more flexible poetic language, and eventually among the Greeks into philosophy. The Greeks and the Jews developed the story form into early history. The beautiful simplicity of alphabetical Greek provided a universal language among elites earlier and more widespread than the Latin of Rome, though chiefly in the mid-east. The Jews appropriated Greek to codify their historic writings for Jews spread throughout the current world.[278] Human linguistic ability grew bit by bit.

Plato and Aristotle were widely studied in Europe and their influence is immeasurable. Beginning with Descartes, the formulation of ideas in writing consumed many bright people and became endemic before the beginning of the Industrial Age. One of the earliest of these was Baruch Spinoza (1632-1677) whose ethics drew on Descartes and the political philosophy of Hobbes. Leibniz (1646-1716) introduced a realism with a transcendentalism which influenced Kant later in the eighteenth century. In the nineteenth century Rousseau's romanticism claimed Schopenhauer and Nietzsche. The flood of philosophic work has not abated, another way of viewing progress step by step.

In the twentieth century our attention is consumed by a virtual flood of baby steps. Three philosophic lights stand out among many: Martin Heidegger, Alfred North Whitehead and Ludwig Wittgenstein. Heidegger focused his attention for most of his life on the nature of being. He understood the human self as the person who animates and understands and creates out of our surroundings. Whitehead grasped similar ideas and fashioned a fresh and bold philosophy still resonating today, and confronted the menacing loss of confidence in religion with speculation, clarity, and an astonishing range of knowledge. Wittgenstein contributed incisive thought about language, bringing philosophy "up short," in other words, calling philosophers to task for their use of language. His critique marked the end of the long worship of words and the beginning of the development of a discipline appropriate to philosophy. All of these people gave their lives to their "small steps" toward a new tomorrow.

190

E. RECOVERING DREAMS AND VISIONS: THE ART OF CONVERSATION

With a maturing in all spheres of intellectual activity, the turmoil of the twentieth century begs for recovery of the art of conversation. Conversation is the nemesis of deception. The capacity to deceive, to take advantage of others, to exploit human beings, and to manipulate the public mind cannot overcome the capacity of people to speak what they know. Once oligarchic repression was left behind, the human self was able to learn to express itself. This is why private networks in the modern world increasingly thwart the dictatorial control of discourse. Though we can maintain cultural controls on language which will guide children and youth to use language helpfully, the future depends on nurturing them to express themselves well with discretion. As important as improving self-confidence is, the increasing ability to express diverse and sometimes deep thoughts in the speaking-listening encounters of personal relationships gives each of us the power to participate in our increasingly social world. One of the joys of life is hours spent in conversation. When conversation is natural, not constrained by authority or culture, people will eventually express their aspirations, their dreams and visions.

The maintenance of personal advantage has been a major function of language. That has been aggravated by an overly individualistic cultural predisposition that has also fostered extreme competition. No doubt language, flexible and individually exercised, will be used differently, misused and abused; that is part of the human equation. We come to understand and use words well by experience as well as education. With more intelligent nurture of our young people and effective adult attention critical of dissimulation, we can clean up public discourse as well as private conversation.

By 1500 correspondence and travel were commonplace among scholars. So it was that, while there had been communication earlier, by the time of the Reformation it had become frequent enough to allow for scholars to read and reflect regularly on one anothers' works.[279] The earlier Greek transition from story to question-response gave the West a marked advantage, and Europeans found their philosophic discussions close at hand in freshly translated Latin. The rapid dispersal of Erasmus' texts demonstrates the immense value of Gutenberg's introduction of movable type. Increasing numbers of bright people felt the urge to write and discuss ideas. Though the bias remained firmly in place, the mechanistic orientation of the Enlightenment was followed shortly by more expansive thinkers, among them Hobbes. Within the next century the art of conversation among knowledgeable people was developed and exercised diligently. The number involved grew beyond a simple listing of names, and the Enlightenment soon encompassed thoughtful conversation about every intellectual subject. The ancient constraints on the human mind were broken, at least among the elites of Western society. Words took wings like the art of falconry: speakers sent them off to obtain responses just as the falconer diligently trains his birds to return with prey. The art of conversation requires the careful hearing we call "listening."

The leadership of academia in developing our culture has been established. But listening can lead wrongly. Academia in the twentieth century veered off the classical pattern toward vocational training. This may be attributed to the turmoil in all disciplines as a revolutionary expansion of knowledge produced "paradigm" changes. Name any discipline and you can find major changes in it, philosophy and history included. As the twenty-first century began, these seemed to be taking effective new forms, and it is time for academia to reconfigure itself to include building the capacity for critical conversation. Wittgenstein told us in his *Tractatus*, "The object of philosophy is the logical clarification of thoughts. Philosophy is not a theory but an activity." We call it a discipline.

Wittgenstein continued, "The result of philosophy is not a number of 'philosophical propositions' but to make propositions clear." Critique of the form which language has taken has become the new and pregnant role of philosophy. Philosophy thus takes a new place in the academic panoply as highly disciplined as any science. It is not a new orientation, the advance of civilization has simply given it new tools and a new mind with which to function. This has occurred to philosophy before. When the Greeks began to shape this discipline, sages soon found questions and discussion preferable to age-old story-telling, but they continued to try to straighten the path of common wisdom. It was the beginning of what we will call "critical thought" – not truly the beginning, but evident. After the light of self-consciousness began to burn more brightly in the Renaissance communication among all people became more self-conscious and better informed. People continued to explore the world with increasingly critical tools. The Scottish Renaissance demonstrated the value of breaking the long hiatus between educated elites and common people. Fees at the University of Glasgow were low, permitting many more to participate in higher education and the effort was begun to make scientific method – critical thinking – the core academic discipline. The effect on the culture is demonstrable in the nineteenth century. Innovations in curriculum sought better education, as always. In each case, the function of academe was enhanced. As professors, teachers, leaders, and ordinary people paid more careful attention to their words, the culture reflected a heightened character.

Of course, not everything was gain. Changes in the economy were not easy. There was no master plan. Free competition had given way to cutthroat competition. The Scot experience was not unlike the transition elsewhere from feudal semi-slavery to landless peasant. By the beginning of the twentieth century the emergence of the new mind we are tracing extended the slow moderation of excesses. We have already pointed to them. Utilitarianism fought out the ground with idealism and pragmatism. Positivism and linguistic philosophy rekindled the age-old task of policing misuse of language – and beginning a cultural correction of demagoguery. Mathematics reached great heights and was soundly brought under control. Even the sacred market and righteous industry faced regulation for the public good. As the century progressed, the inherited humanism (embodying Judeo-Christian anthropology) gradually won dominance and growing respect for every voice. Conversation was being returned to its preeminent place in society.

This is not to say that the art of conversation has been perfected. But we are rapidly approaching a time when we can share open critique of all aspects of culture in our daily conversations. It is a hopeful time. Individuals can again dream dreams and see visions and gradually we will recover the natural relations in which we share these for review with friends. It is unlikely that their conversations about these will sound much like those so long remembered in the recent past. We had been wriggling free of Scholastic rigidities and constrictions on human imagination. Each person on earth was gradually being recognized as an individual with both mind and voice. Following the crowd like bleating sheep would eventually be a thing of the past.

F. The Current Challenge to our Humanity

A spate of books in recent years has discussed the implications of American world dominance and the rise of nationalism among weak nations. One of these was written by Fareed Zakaria, a native of India by birth, who has traveled widely and serves as editor of *Newsweek International*. He argues that in "the rise of the rest" the less developed nations of the world pose a particular challenge to Americans. We are proud of our own nation, but hesitant to acknowledge the pride others have developed in their national identity. It seems that it is time for us to recognize that nationalism is here to stay. It is another worldwide work of humanity. The nations provide a regional identity. In them people with affinity increasingly develop and recognize who they are. They choose their own governments. And these people, who increasingly share with us worldwide evolution, will increasingly become participants in developing the eventual world culture.

Zakaria writes that currently Americans are out of touch with the real challenges of the new world of the twenty-first century which includes the "winners" -- the growing countries like China, India, Brazil, Russia, South Africa, Kenya, and many more. The losers like terrorists and people still worried about security and immigration are secondary at best. Zakaria outlines the contemporary diffusion of power. This is "the rise of the rest." In this world the role of the United States should become more the honest broker than the power center. "It must seek to share power, create coalitions, build legitimacy, and define the global agenda -- all formidable tasks." All of these must be undertaken more as participants than as Western Fathers.

Humans in the past have always responded to new environments. That is what this global system represents today. If we fail as yet to find much evidence of the new mind in the Third World, this suggests only that the "rise of the rest" still has not broken through our consciousness. Evolving everywhere, it is obscured by the dominance of the past, the residue culture. It is possible, of course, as was clearly the case in America before the turn of the century, this may be because the past was strongly individualistic . We had not then been looking carefully – or we had been looking with blinders for our proud American sense of "new." Our social science is maturing, but still young, almost non-existent in many parts of the world. And Americans have not been in the habit of observing others with appreciation for their own views, their own values.

Unfortunately, as others become more self-conscious of their own pride, they may also become less willing to come together to solve common problems. It is a primal challenge to be overcome by the new mind, and history demonstrates that this evolution will take place. Zakaria says,

> As the number of players -- government and non-government – increases and
> each one's power and confidence grows, the prospects for agreement and
> common action diminish. This is the central challenge of the rise of the rest -- to
> stop forces of global growth from turning into forces of global disorder and
> disintegration.[280]

Those world leaders already embracing the new mind will demonstrate not only
helpfulness in the transitions underway in less developed cultures, but they will exhibit the
patience and forbearance which will support and encourage its development. The
dominating international effort expressing the new mind of the twenty-first century has
become working with the elected government of Afghanistan. It is a country which still
includes nearly the complete historical array of human communities, each fixed in its own
status quo. But it is becoming evident that the human mind is evolving among those still
living in these more primitive societies.

Though long fixed in their habits, the minds of many Afghanistan people are
developing the necessary compromises with the past which will enable them to move
forward. The evidence accumulates slowly day by day as tribal chiefs gradually come to
terms with the new realities of life. At the same time, the powers-that-be in that nation are
learning how to avoid simple reinforcement of antiquated mores. Nonetheless, history
makes clear that it will take a long while for new behaviors to replace those which are
antiquated. The result in any case will be a new, more contemporary culture that fits into
the international family of nations more effectively, with more important roles. The difficulty
of composing an Afghanistan cabinet acceptable to the West has demonstrated the
immense gap between a tribal-modern society and a Western democracy. Exercise of
bribery, graft, and favoritism are endemic. Not yet adjusted to the "rise of the rest," an
international level of tolerance finds this nearly intolerable, notwithstanding the level of
corruption that Western nations themselves accept.

As far back as John F. Kennedy, we find a perception of the necessity of self-
determination by all people, then the Vietnamese.[281] So, Friedman suggests, it is
essential for us to realize that in 2010 it is the people of Afghanistan who must take control
of their destiny. This requires a readjustment among us that does not harken back to a
now obsolete experience with American relations to "foreigners." We must accept that

1.   Singular leaders still play a crucial role in nation-states.

2.   Solutions engineered by the current/past players (the world powers) have always
     produced their own sets of problems often fomenting disorder and disintegration.

3.   The only solution is open forum, open international relations, open borders,
     without the obsolete arrogance of the powerful.

Only through total patient, thoughtful respect for each and all national players can
we hope to keep the residual antagonisms from breaking out into open hostility. They have

been simmering under the surface of globalism. Nothing, I suspect, would be more likely to cause such an outbreak than treating any nation-state representative as backward or inferior. The language of Samuel Huntington's term 'uni-multipolarity,' and the Chinese "many powers and one superpower" reflect the messy reality. The emerging order is new; we are likely to live with the present messiness for several decades. The U.S. occupies the top spot in the emerging system, but it is also the country that is most challenged by the new order, and its people will most benefit from their sound, adaptive behavior in the great panorama of evolution.

XI. A PHILOSOPHY OF PRAGMATIC IDEALISM

Our journey has taken us rather nebulously from the most primitive times of human life, even from species preceding *Homo sapiens,* through the degradation of the early city into the ancient world of written history, into the Middle Ages and modern times, leaving us now in what we have no name for yet, the post-modern world. In spite of modern awareness of thousands of years of human endeavor to build a more human environment, the modern expectation hangs on hope that we might bring to birth a paradise of our own making. Recent experience in some of the most primitive areas of the world are bringing forcefully to our attention that the new world will be very different from the old, and we in the West will definitely not be the only brilliant ones contributing to it.

The chance is that from early days in the forest on we have never lacked confidence for long that tomorrow might be better somehow than today has been. Plato, I guess, began calling it the idea of tomorrow, though I don't know that he used those words. But our fascination with abstracts led to the enlightenment idea of the ideal and before long someone dubbed a point of view "idealism." But for us here we simply want to identify our point of view "pragmatic idealism" or perhaps "realistic idealism." The first option seems preferable for a handle, but it doesn't touch the naming of this next period of Western history, the post-modern times. It will be a period that takes human aspiration seriously, the idea of an ideal for which we can reach. Hope seems to lack the depth of anticipation suggested by "aspiration."

Aspiration contains another tantalizing aspect for us. That is hope that is patient, that is practical in its anticipation. It is entirely possible for us to become so anxious to achieve a goal that we take steps that are ultimately self-defeating, steps that are wrong-headed, that lead to unhappy consequences. This sort of thing is to be avoided by thoughtfulness. We also recognize that talking with other people about our aspirations is a way of seeing their practicality. Thus aspiration which is kept to oneself is untested dreaming. But use of our imaginations is a hopeful capability. But for imagination where would inventions arise? Our brains associate imponderable numbers of things, observations, concepts, constructions, words, colors, acts, behaviors, habits, etc.. Aspirations (which come to our attention as we reflect or when we are stimulated to make a new association), aspirations lend themselves to hammering out practical steps toward fulfillment of good ideas.

Our hypothesis is that we can demonstrate the evolution of the human self to a present state of substantial self-consciousness. By its very nature this includes our awareness of others to be both unique in themselves and also as human as we ourselves. In this blessed state the epochal struggle of humankind to adapt from severely individualistic beginnings to satisfying social existence might allow humanity to live peacefully and productively in balance with the earth. This new culture will be sustainable only by our intelligent living, in which we share in evolution of the universe. What shall we name this new culture?[282]

A. TO END A PERVERTED INDIVIDUALISM

We have learned that the many aberrations which have impeded emergence of our new consciousness are largely of our own making. It is fitting that our most sophisticated religion persistently holds to admission of complicity in the great errors of human society. In the twenty-first century we can appreciate contributions of the same people who have in the past been blamed for great mistakes. Often they were not "wrong" in some cosmic sense. They were, nonetheless, people of their own times subject (like ourselves) to their inherited cultures. This is not to say that evil does not exist beyond ourselves; we have been duped more than once. But neither does "evil" encompass our human errors and mistakes which are not motivated by turpitude. Mistakes are not necessarily "evil." Nonetheless an overarching emphasis in Christendom on "sin" has focused the problem of evil in the world on the sins of individual persons. Many were driven to add the existence of supra-personal evil as a force at odds with God in order to explain what lies beyond personal explanation – and the power of an "almighty" God.

The universal belief in sin may have been Europe's best bulwark against humanity's self-righteous tendencies. From the viewpoint of the twentieth century "sin" may have been overemphasized. It succeeded in inducing a nearly psychotic sense of guilt to open the "therapeutic culture." The church maintained rituals of repentance and penance absorbing much religious fervor. Failure to separate "sin" and "evil" surely contributed to the developing reaction to the Church. The long history in the church of guilt and repentance was often ignored by intelligentsia as the nineteenth century progressed; many considered them archaic notions. Material progress seemed to wash out attention to sin. At the same time complexity in doctrine and piety seems to have washed over many leaders without a trace of remorse for their pride in rationality.[283] But this mistaken trashing of humility tended to deny our sociality and to over-emphasize individual satisfaction.

Humans are social beings though our individual nature must not be denied. We were all once the savage warriors who destroyed others' cities only to rebuild them to our own glory; we condoned such egotism. We have blamed others when we probably should have accepted our own roles in such errors. We ordinary people burned the heretics; it was not just the famous people whom we have often blamed for narrow-mindedness. While the notorious Inquisition was essentially a legal procedure carried out by an elite, the many pogroms against Jews in popular uprisings are a blot against people themselves. These were virulent in Eastern Europe in the late nineteenth and twentieth centuries.

The time was when evil was referred to as a cosmic battle, making us helpless in its wake.[284] As we have awakened over the centuries to a sense of responsibility our human "can do" sense has proven over and over that we can do much to ameliorate these conditions. In the rather sophisticated world of modernity, sin is recognition of our complicity in error, and our sincere acknowledgment of the ubiquity of sin is protection against excessive pride in our own achievements. It is, no doubt, this universal reality of error which produced the identification of sin in the ancient world still remains evident today. But in the gift of a new mind, we own our calling to resolve what evil we can manage and to help the victims of those circumstances we cannot change.

There is a significant difference between ancient and post-modern attitudes toward sin and evil. The ancients often fell back on polytheisms and dualisms and sometimes failed to separate human and natural causes of suffering. We do not any longer lump natural disasters with the effects of human turpitude. We have just discussed the inevitability of suffering (chapter X. B.) We now acknowledge the participation of all of us in error. We admit that life challenges our inherited Enlightenment concept of the independent self which tended to remove us from any responsibility for our neighbors. "Self-reliance" may have been a necessary step. So also was the "social gospel." Now "human being" has taken on a new sensitivity that was neglected in modernism: We recognize that we are finite animals who have the magnificent capability to help one another in trouble, sickness, and sorrow. Our focus has shifted from the negative "sin" to the positive "help" (whoever has a need beyond their capability). It is a demonstration of our social self-confidence.

Our commonality is particularly demonstrated in one particular skill of humanity, in language. As we started congregating beyond groups of family and friends, we expanded our ability to sing and dance, to shout and communicate -- though we have no idea how extensively. Nor do we know when words made their debut. There was probably a long period (thousands of years) in which various sounds became standard representations of various things -- calling for mother (mamama) and father (papapa) among them. Naturally, every human group developed its standard vocabulary differently over time, quite unconsciously. As soon as one such group rubbed elbows with another one, human beings began developing the skills to understand others' language. Long centuries of pre-lingual signs and symbols may have helped to bridge the new language gap between humans. Very early in our language development we found it convenient to adopt words others had created. Similarities in their tongues very slowly developed into families of languages. The earliest languages we know emerged in the Indus Valley in Pakistan. After traversing the great mountains to the north, those people spread across the Asian plateaus and eventually into Europe where their languages dominated older populations. The family name of these languages is "Indo-European." This fact of language is a powerful demonstration of the intricate way human beings are inter-related. None is an absolutely "individual." The development of humanity in the East was not the same as in the West; the differences will continue to differentiate us for centuries.

The vaunted art of rhetoric was a necessary development. Surely long before villages began to coalesce into towns and cities, we Homo sapiens learned the first lessons of rhetoric, addressing our peers to persuade them to engage in projects with us, first perhaps in hunting parties and defense against animals, eventually in farming large plots and in harvesting crops together, then many other projects. Language became the prime indicator of our humanity, not shared by any other creature. And we were, undoubtedly, a little proud of the power to talk and command, and to persuade at times, but most of all just to communicate, to express human troubles and joys, to display learnings, and musings. We imagined that when we named a thing we had power over it – after all, enlistment of a hunting team would be much easier if a harassing predator had a recognizable name. All the time, nonetheless, we were individuals related to our primary families and few others. All of us were different from "others" over the mountains. At the same time, our primitive selfhood was gradually modified by socialization which nibbled at the hard edges of our awareness of ourselves.

Leaders-to-be gradually learned from watching those before them both in successful persuasion and in failure. Every generation experimented and learned. Eventually, some used their persuasive skills to achieve their own egotistic ends. The rotten emperor may be the most perverse demonstration of individualism, and rhetoric was the first tool of empire, followed by use of force. That coercive pattern was emulated by "authorities" as late as modernity.

When cities emerged, the whole people were made up of aristocrats and peons. Not all came under the extended tyranny typical of the Middle-East-Mediterranean region.[285] But people all over the world submitted to oligarchy. Leaders everywhere spawned growing hierarchies of aristocrats and many were vicious and selfish. The peons submitted to slavery. Some people submitted earlier than others. We note that even under such conditions people grew in their ability to relate to others. They lived next to one another and submitted in the same ways. When there were celebrations, it was their neighbors with whom they danced and sang. Even tyranny could not stamp out humanity.

Over those earliest centuries of the historic period the people learned how to behave in subservient ways so as to avoid being abused as disrespectful; under their overseers, they could no longer move and work as they chose – as people had for thousands of years. They learned to be submissive. They learned to shade the truth, to avoid blame, and to reduce hurt -- requirements of social relations. It was part of the lengthy process of learning to give and take as socialized human beings, that is, as individuals who can live with neighbors (near and far) peaceably, even under repression. An interesting adaptation to their oppression in biblical times as the population grew and the intimate control system broke down under the Romans was, as John Dominic Crossan calls it, a "broker-client" economy. From the point of view of ordinary people, everyone served the king, but over the centuries people learned how to exercise knowledge and talents so as to gain some control of their livelihood.

By the end of the Ancient period people had begun to seek their own welfare and understanding. The primitive experience gradually had taught us that, like ourselves, all were persons whether or not we liked one another. While the oppressive cities had taught us acquiescence and obedience within our "kind," the animosities which leaders fostered toward "others" – building on primitive survival self-protectiveness – developed into fear and hatred. We might fear that the primitive learnings of empathy and cooperation which contribute to living together were lost. But even in this, their emergent self-awareness evolved in the midst of the human community. The complexity of modern life was already visible in such social tendencies. People continued to develop skills in arts and crafts, in hunting, stone work, and farming, and in the all-important matter of sociability. They had learned to use their minds while serving overlords as necessary to survive.

Even under oligarchy, basic human creativity was preparing for the expansion of the entrepreneurial mind in Mercantilism. Beginning about the Renaissance, sea-worthy ships had become common and navigation by the stars was familiar to sea captains. The nations became aware of the importance of trade and increasingly regulated aspects of it. Taxation had been a practice from ancient times. But the ingenuity of people engaged in reaping economic benefits from trade challenged rulers to gather their share (or more) always out of the increasingly archaic orientation of oligarchy, by force. It was a natural ground for developing resentment of authority in the face of growing self-consciousness. They were regaining their native independence. However, their sense of community had to be built freshly on an extraordinarily obtuse base.

It should be obvious that Descartes' "I think therefore I am" was radical. It is often cited as the beginning of individualism. But we have seen the decline of primitive individualism in the ancient world. We might say, decline in the natural state of man as it has been characterized, in the ancient period when, nonetheless, human beings learned a variety of extraordinarily important things. Perhaps most important among them, while the long process of socialization continued, we incorporated in our psyches a self-discipline necessary to the eventual development of responsibility. This was a very long, slow process through the Middle Ages. In the Enlightenment, awareness of self became self-conscious. Learning came to be understood as a role of the freshly understood individual, emphasizing the "I" in ordinary life. The necessity of community support in individual learning of important social lessons was not understood, though cultures continued to shape the emergence of children into adulthood. People believed that it was as Individuals that people learned the occupational and the social skills necessary to a "disciplined" life. The successful were more highly disciplined than others and rose on the economic ladder.

In the two hundred years following Descartes this overemphasis on individuals fostered a destructive pride that established itself in the increasingly individualistic Western culture. Those originally involved – Descartes, Hobbes, Lock, Newton, and a host of Scots – held fast to the hard-learned sense of community of their past; they themselves were not individualistic. Education of the individual required high self-discipline. The seed of this highly disciplined individuality hatched in the eighteenth century, outspokenly, in Rationalism. It was a natural progression out of Neoplatonism and Scholasticsm and in the next two centuries it developed into the perversion of educated people thinking of themselves as independent and free. And many absorbed by this rampant individualism thought *everyone* should be so able to take care of themselves, self-suffient and self-reliant.

By the twentieth century individualism had produced one of the preoccupations of academia. It emerged as the dominance of nature over nurture. Still generally valuing education In sociality. While masterful men needed education to earn an Income, the role of women had become outspokenly the raising of children, and needed enough education to teach children the alphabet and numbers. The argument emerged that our native individuality assured the perennial competitiveness and aggressiveness of human beings. Education was only a window dressing over this, necessary, perhaps, but not "reality." The Hobbesian description of an animal nature continued to popularize the half-truth. And the parallel determinist view it engendered was shortly to be capsuled in American Fundamentalism. But the culture was still strongly educational at that point and it was not until the twentieth century that reactionary observers would transmute individualism into an anti-intellectual phenomenon.

We call the overemphasis on separateness and independence *individualism*. This may indeed reflect something of the Celtic spirit. But the Celts were still part of the old world in which the early products of community, signs and symbols, played an evident and valued role. Writing and reading came naturally to them as they had learned the value of commonality – as did the rest of the world. Then the American Revolution demonstrated the capacity of people for responsibility. It seems that in the demonstration of successful independence (I am in control) and even prowess internationally, people forgot those hard lessons of community. Resentment of authority superseded fear of anarchy and was aggravated by the braggadocio of the Western spirit and a belligerence in interpersonal relations. The belligerence was a natural outgrowth of the cultural habit of aggressiveness. The language of vituperation was basically the cultural expression of confrontation.

This is reflected today in inconsiderate language which foments division. Adherents of the Right seem to neglect our common responsibility to nurture commonality; their language tends to be abrasive and divisive. The neglect of accurate and respectful language is an affront to our own history. We will continue to suffer its effects for some time to come though cooperation is too deeply embedded in our culture to be displaced. Now this perverted individualism demands to be laid bare, to be exposed, and to be defanged. Confrontation is rapidly giving way to appreciation. Hans Kung finds the cultural change in the model of complementarity.[286]

B. ENABLEMENT OF SELF-DEVELOPMENT

In every age it has been easier for many simply to fit into the world as they found it, rather than to try to make it more habitable. The primitive pattern for such people is simply to acquiesce to the familiar status quo. It seems that the instinct to be lazy (to conserve energy, perhaps) has yet to be conquered. It seems that years of historic servitude – even if a child so perceives his or her childhood – can become an excuse to relax when we are not driven by necessity. Centuries of didactic education perpetuated the distaste. One might, following some contemporary biologists, talk about a "lazy gene." One would think that the physical demands of contemporary sports might teach our young how to incorporate in life a predisposition to use time and energy productively, but that does not always happen. Today it is essential for us to develop discretion in our use of life to overcome the many opportunities we have constantly to "goof off." The evidence mounts that it is challenges that help us to grow – and grow wiser.

Others in every age have heard the call to use life helpfully. They have responded and led forth. To retrace details of our intellectual evolution after the ancient period is a very lengthy process. We will leave that to the scholars. We turn our attention to the development of corporate responsibility. We speak here not of economic corporations, but of society. We call it "corporate society." The difficult lessons of the Industrial Revolution were marked by peoples' rebellions.[287] Western humans had learned that the ultimate corrective of misguided governance is in their own hands. No doubt this was for many simply a rebellion against being forced to change generations of extraordinary skills practiced in familiar circumstances, inside the homes of weavers, for example.

But the larger picture was different. Others saw rebellion against emerging farming and factories as a protest against human inventions which returned them to virtual slavery in a degraded environment. England turned black with coal dust. Miners worked unprotected from new hazards in deep mines. Seamen were still at risk from vagaries of weather and sea but shipbuilding advanced toward mastery of the seas. We had yet to grasp the significance of unanticipated consequences of the Industrial Revolution. Neither owners of the emerging enterprises nor society had experience with worker welfare. The Enlightenment had provoked the development of conditions of living that were as devastating as our own exploitation of the natural environment. The unanticipated consequences were born largely by the poor. In our time the ecological crisis threatens the resources of nations. We have depleted the resources of the "inexhaustible" earth. Even the oceans have been pleading for regulation. And we have begun to count and map the debris our space programs have left in the sky.

We are learning worldwide how to govern our huge modern populations. The "game" here is to keep basic urban services working for the health of the people. And the innovations must be commensurate with the challenge. Increases in population can be identified with past surges of human creativity. Current growth will do no less. But the carrying capacity of the earth, we have been warned, is not infinite. And so, we have been heartened by self-controlled population growth in many places. The Chinese have imposed severe restraints. We are struggling to keep up. Degradation of our environment has proceeded far faster than our awareness of many needs for controls. One need only mention global warming to identify the many impinging concerns. Those who remind us of global cycles out of our control may be correct, but if heating and cooling of the globe affect sea level, hundreds of thousands of habitations are at risk. If dumping man-made chemicals into the oceans and into the atmosphere (and a new island in the Pacific made of plastic and other trash) produce toxins in living bodies, we must be alert to possible connections with modern illnesses. Such things are beyond any individual's capacity to understand. Regulation seems to be essential to human community.

Fortunately, in the twentieth century human minds turned toward acceptance of democratic regulation of the common life. We are painfully moving beyond our inherited fear of government. It is a propitious moment as we belatedly recognize that the opportunity for self-development should extend beyond the able-bodied to other members of society who have been systemically neglected throughout history. Currently we call these the "disabled." Government is now seen as a responsible agent to provide curb cuts, regulate building codes for safety and accessibility, and a variety of steps to enable self development not only of the "normal" person, but of those disabled by whatever cause. What has been called others' "misfortune" is now recognized as "unfortunate" in any human life.

Self-development was introduced in the twentieth century to identify our new capabilities, our new choices, our new opportunities to contribute to healthy living and to our common life, our culture. We have only belatedly come to a general recognition that self-development includes responsible participation in government. Human society, so varied and unpredictable as people are, does require over-arching government. We are fortunate that our own government, "for the people," not only emerged but has proven itself. It goes without saying that we must persist in its refinement to contribute to opportunity for every person to make the best of his or her own life.

C. A NEW HUMANITY IS A THINKING HUMANITY

Philosophy has taken a lot of hits in the twentieth century. Some have called it defunct, over, finished. Others simply continue the same kind of systems development that Enlightenment philosophers indulged. Nonetheless, an encompassing view of the universe in a systematic philosophy has become increasingly difficult. This revolution was led by philosophers in the nineteenth century and mathematics trailed proving it impossible even in the ultra-cerebral atmosphere of that discipline to proceed without making prior assumptions. Physics has proved it. Some biologists seem yet to understand that the human mind will have to wait another day to understand the whole of Creation. That is no longer a task even for the philosopher. In the past hundred years philosophy has overcome the power of abstraction and reentered the world as it is. It has rediscovered the centrality of our dependence on language while overcoming our obsession with words. We must redefine philosophy, perhaps not drastically, but significantly. We call attention to two reasons for this:

First, in the period we call the Enlightenment, since the Reformation, we have largely left behind the culture in which people generally needed to be told what the score is in life. The "sheep" mentality was completely dependent on authority, and Europe developed in its trail. The Church took up the same mistaken view of human life. But as we have rethought our humanity we find imaginative, creative persons behind all that we call progress, behind the development of every aspect of our civilization, and pre-eminently in the the shaping of our culture. The previous world was shaped by individuals (emperors and philosophers among others) on a model derived from oligarchy: the dominant individual spoke the truth for the time. That was the orientation of philosophy all the way through the nineteenth century when we see the first clear signs of change. We will explore some of these signs of change.

The second reason for redefinition of philosophy is the emergence of what we call a *new mind* among us. The new person is a thinking person. The old mind, while wrestling with the power of ideas and abstractions, was still largely trapped by appetites, by feelings which eventually yielded to the power of abstractions. Even Augustine worked over the nature of love, recognizing the power of attraction to objects which provide satisfaction. Hannah Arendt grasped his notion of the nature of time: God's time is an eternal present (cf. Introduction, Section B). She recognized "that every thought was a glance backward, an afterthought, a reflection on earlier matters or events. Any reader of Augustine's *Confessions* will know that this was true for him too."[288] Each person we call genius shows advance in thinking over time.

Arendt's love affair with Heidegger began as an eighteen year old's infatuation. We might say that it was a giving in to the powerful feelings which young people in our culture must learn to master. Heidegger was thirty-five at the time and a highly respected intellectual figure. But neither grew up in a culture which understood these elemental biological drives, and therefore it had not incorporated the early childhood training which is today gradually becoming a significant new force in the development of people's minds. Appetites, "drives," and desires, it was thought were givens, essentially uncontrollable natural tendencies. But we have begun to recognize that humans have been learning to control instincts for as long as we have been advancing beyond the limits of the world of animals. The distinction of "human" belongs to "thinking," and thought gives us self-control, self-discipline, and the recognition that by guiding our tiny children to learn how to control themselves, they need not spend their lives enslaved to any appetites – just as each one masters gluttony and elimination.

These developments make a world of difference in seeking to grasp the new function of philosophy. Wittgenstein told us in his *Tractatus*, "The object of philosophy is the logical clarification of thoughts. Philosophy is not a theory but an activity. The result of philosophy is not a number of 'philosophical propositions' but to make propositions clear." All his life he was tortured by thoughts of his failure, because the mind of the early twentieth century was not yet free to think outside the box of the past. It is still hard for many of us to grasp his thought.

Wittgenstein opened up what Kung called the difference between a philosophy of confrontation and a philosophy of complementarity. Scholars still had not adopted the lessons of Thales, and of the Scot Enlightenment, that rather than debating propositions we should critique, explore, test, and encourage others. In a public that thinks, everyone seeks to complement or enhance what is understood, and to seek clarity rather than hiding difficulty in comprehension.

Critique of the form which language has taken has become the new and pregnant role of philosophy. The facile use of language pleads for informed critique. People have assumed that they communicated, and the listener was too proud to admit that he (more often than she) did not understand. The new philosopher must continue in the role of an erudite, thoroughly thoughtful scholar. But, the human being taking on this role no longer attempts what the twentieth century finally concluded is impossible: The construction of the ultimate world-view. Philosophy is one of the precious tools of our civilization, as it always has been, in the panoply that includes mathematics, all the hard sciences, the social sciences, the humanities, and all the arts and crafts of human invention. All are first and foremost *thinking*. (We pause to note that we have specifically excluded mention here of religion. Religion is "something else" to be explored shortly.) Our point here is to emphasize the intelligent use of the human mind. But the new philosopher must learn from the lesson of the Second Reformation: the erudite must learn to speak helpfully to the public if the public is to grow intelligently. Philosophy no longer exists in an erudite ivory tower. There are windows. And the philosopher must gaze out of the antiquated castle, go downstairs and out into the exhilarating atmosphere of public discourse seeking to lend the gift of intelligence to the culture in which we live. The Second Reformation demonstrated the effectiveness of this way of changing the culture. (See chapter VIII.)

204

Perhaps that is the answer to the apocalyptic mentality. The Church has not been of one mind in this. The best scholarship in the Christian world (and there has always been some of the best) speaks clearly of the absurdity of modern appropriation of this ancient story. Too many are trapped in the past, and the failure of contemporary education to move into the post-modern world has slowed the learning of the skills of conciliation among the erudite. Christian "end times" have been articulated as the bodily resurrection of people to spend eternity in joyous union with God. This is not a vision of gross death and destruction of creation; that view emerged from a particular social/political context representing the views of those who had given up hope in a culture which for generations had seen conquerors destroy what they conquered. This misreading has made the word "apocalyptic" useless. There is no place for hopelessness in Christianity. Revelation is simply viewing the commonly *unknown*, not a hopeless answer to our lack of knowledge.[289] Apocalypse is not instantaneous union with God at the point of death, or shortly thereafter. Paul's vision of seeing clearly at death what during life one can see only as in (an ancient) mirror dimly (cloudily, fuzzily) is as good a description as one can yet find of the condition of death. Paul grasped firmly the Jewish sense of humanity as creaturely, limited, human.

Whatever one thinks about life after death, it must be recognized as a religious concept. Western religions on the whole have found it an important part of religious belief and so it will be for some time to come. Its roots are very deep in history. Though Plato did not originate the idea, his endorsement and development of eternal ideal types fixed the eternal in the mind of Augustine. It has proved to be immensely helpful to many people for a very long time. But it is not important to many others who find other ways to deal with such ultimate concerns. From Heidegger's viewpoint it became a diversion from the difficulty of life itself. "He argued that Plato's conception of ideal forms ... had carried philosophers away from awestruck appreciation of the existing world in favor of nonmaterial ideals that exist only in the mind. Heidegger preferred the pre-Socratics because their thought focused on actual existence...."[290] From this point of view the doctrine of life after death is not fundamentally about eternity; it deals with the difficulty in all human existence of the universal experience of losing a loved one. If we think about it, we see this as a gift from the past to the present which we may wish to project into the future.

Our energies are required to deal with the difficulties of actual existence. In the twentieth century we achieved a new level of our capacity to gather, store and transmit knowledge. It is time we put brakes on the promiscuous hunger to know more. We have indulged a pursuit of knowledge as if our quality of life still depended on it. Our shot gun method to discern how to spend our lives must be replaced with techniques which now permit us to use high-powered aiming devices to refine our ability to discriminate. Increasing self-understanding will enable young people to choose vocations appropriately, avoiding later wandering innocently this way and that. It is no longer a problem of personal fit or capability alone. It is a social problem of seeing the difficulties of life to which one may address himself or herself.

People have always hungered for life, quite without our materialism – witness the joy of the remaining tribal people in their way of life. Our human adaptability enables us to enjoy whatever condition of life we find – with exceptions for the most inhumane conditions. We have dreamed dreams and they have led us forward, but they have also provided us with escapes from the hard work of living with human intelligence – witness occasional worship of "golden ages." Enjoying the persistent satisfaction of human curiosity, and asking what we need to put behind us of the unfortunate parts of the legacy of our past, let us build on positives, on thoughtful considerations. Science must be more than we have made of it by digging ever deeper into detail.[291] Let us learn to think of wholes, to examine the larger view. Let us grasp the redefinition of "science," not only as the methodology of precise measurement, but as our best current, disciplined assessment of how to wisely use our brains in any given circumstances. We must learn to apply our minds to selected difficulties in our common life.

The sheer volume of human knowledge exceeds the capacity of any one brain to grasp the whole. This is parallel to our inability to plumb the purpose and complexity of the universe. It is no longer possible to endorse the vanity that in time we will unravel the whole thing. In the twentieth century, philosophers came up against the limits which have long stymied their traditional work. We have discovered how little we know. And yet we do learn. By the time Alfred North Whitehead, Ludwig Wittgenstein and Martin Heidegger were born[292] the ground was ready for their revolutionary thinking. And when Mitchell Feigenbaum and Benoit Mandelbrot first identified characteristics of non-linear mathematics, it was in a world that was prepared for this extraordinary development. It appears that the new mind evolving allows us the privileges of prescience when we exercise our minds as responsible social beings.

Wittgenstein's singular book (perhaps 500 pages) was not published until 1921. He had trouble finding publishers who would advertise not Bertrand Russell's misleading introduction but the work itself, the *Tractatus*. Written in the trenches of World War I (he served in the German army), this had been his Ph.D. thesis in 1921 under Russell's tutelage. A second book, probably his more important work, *Philosophical Investigations*, was published posthumously in 1953. He died in 1951, leaving for his impending visitors a message: "Tell them I've had a wonderful life." His biography (three of four brothers committed suicide) makes that a witness to his faith, adopted, finally, with a seriousness not evident in his long years outside the church, but with a life-long awareness of the whole of life. He was dazzled, we are told, not by his own brainy thoughts, but by "life's irreducible variety." He told a friend, "I am not a religious man, but I cannot help seeing every problem from a religious point of view."

Wittgenstein grew up a Roman Catholic but he was told in a period of depression that joining a monastery would not meet his needs. All his life he was tortured by thoughts of his failure, though he had earned medals on the W.W.I battlefield. Later, he wrote: "Wisdom is cold and to that extent stupid. Faith on the other hand is a passion. ... Wisdom is grey. Life on the other hand and religion are full of colour." Wittgenstein studied briefly under Gottlob Frege who provided the foundation for modern mathematical logic. (One of Frege's contributions was the first ever adequate definition of "number.") Frege urged him to read the work of Bertrand Russell who had discovered some contradictions in Frege's own work.

Most of Wittgenstein's work was in logic and mathematics, but he lived on another plain. He was pressed to join Adolph Carnap's Vienna Circle in which "positivism" was formulated, but he distanced himself from this group. He is said to have used everyday language intentionally to avoid the "charm" of mathematical logic. D'Evelyn tells us:

> (Ray) Monk's portrait is of a philosopher who forced himself and others to turn from the 'how' and 'what' questions (those science would answer with precision) to the 'why' questions: Why is there something, rather than nothing. For Wittgenstein, after science is done, the deep problems remain.[293]

Wittgenstein's work created a space for new problems and mysteries to appear. He is said to have anticipated a future culture "which treated music, poetry, art and religion with the same respect and seriousness with which our present society treats science."

While Wittgenstein was battling new philosophic problems of math and language, Martin Heidegger was focusing on an age-old problem. Eventually it turned out to contribute to the development of post-modernism. Heidegger felt it was our primary duty to define the word "being." He spent most of his life doing so. His reputation was secured by publishing *Being and Time* in German in 1927. He felt that the Greeks had forgotten "being" in their preoccupation with "substance." Aristotle believed that his classic category of substances represented the natural structure of reality, and "substance" remained the central term in traditional ontology for over two millennia. It became Heidegger's main challenge. Dorothea Frede points out:

> In his study of Medieval philosophy, Heidegger discovered that Christian doctrine was leaning heavily on Aristotle. Its influence is felt even in Kant and post-Kantian philosophy. Heidegger was convinced that the key to meaning cannot lie in the empirical observation of the actual psychological processes that constitute our thoughts. This was the basis on which he adopted Husserl's phenomenology.[294]

Our *selection* of options ought not be confused with the *meaning* of what is judged. It is necessary to explore the content of thought if we are to understand what our thoughts are about, not the operation of the brain as a physiological organ.

The Enlightenment had taken us from preoccupation with the fortunes of empires and nations to grapple with the very nature of human beings and their thinking. Human sociality is no longer simply a matter of getting along with one another, but of understanding ourselves and our participation in evolution of culture. Martin Heidegger, once trapped in the oppressive Nazi culture, found himself called to examine the philosophic concept of being in a depth that was impossible earlier. Only man is aware of Being and of the nothingness that surrounds it, and only man can ask such questions as "What is man?"[295]

In a series of lectures on Neitzsche in the years between 1936 and 1940 (not published until 1961) Hannah Arendt saw a significant change in Heidegger's orientation from the first volume of *Being and Time* to the second. Once trapped in the Nazi culture, he found himself called to re-examine Being freshly. He apparently recognized the Nazi will to power as a kind of original sin of which he found himself guilty. Arendt concluded that he had turned against the "self-assertion of man" which he proclaimed with bellicose pomp and enthusiasm in his public comments while serving as the Nazi *Rektor* of Frieburg University in 1933.[296] Neitzsche and Jaspers had been working in him, trail-blazers in their own right. While we recognize Heidegger as a flawed human being like everyone else, we also find in this change a prescience which opens doors for us today. Daniel Maier-Katkin identifies the point we leave behind from which he departed:

> Only Nietzsche and Jaspers [Arendt wrote] had used the fact of death as a starting point for a life-affirming philosophy in which man's existence is not simply a matter of Being, but rather a form of human freedom, not something given so much as an ensemble of possibilities. For Jaspers "man achieves reality only to the extent that he acts out of his own freedom rooted in spontaneity and connects through communication with the freedom of others." Man has the capacity to make choices, and becomes himself through the decisions he makes in each moment.... Arendt made clear her preference for the "playful metaphysics" of Jaspers over Heidegger's embrace of death as the guarantee of each man's individuality.
>
> Heidegger's self-centered egotism replaced the Kantian notion (and the fundamental principle of the French Revolution and of modern democracy) that each man represents humanity and that the debasement of any individual debases all, and misses completely the fact that man inhabits the earth together with others. Humanity, she argued, is not a collection of atomized individuals coexisting on a common ground that is alien to their self-centered nature.[297]

Such are some of the precedents to our entry into a post-modern culture, still reflecting the confusion of the time, but moving irretrievably into post-modernism. The new world and the new mind build on an anthropology Europe inherited from the Jews.

To grasp the positive contribution of Heidegger in philosophy (without attempting here to plumb his depths) we turn to a qualified commentator, John Haugeland, of the Department of Philosophy in the University of Pittsburgh. In an article in *Heidegger: A Critical Reader* Haugeland discusses the key issue of what Heidegger means by "disclosing." This is a fascinating exploration in which Haugeland succeeds in revealing Heidegger's intent in his use of the pivotal German term "Dasein." In most philosophical literature such terms continue in use, part of the peculiar language of philosophy. But Haugeland makes clear not only an interpretation which makes sense to me, but also the array of Heideggerian language about disclosedness. *Dasein* was an important contribution to our twentieth century understanding the human being and culture. Haugeland

> ... interprets Dasein as a "living way of life," a being lived way of life: Thus, the Polynesian way of life, surviving (though not unchanged) on many Pacific Islands, is Polynesian Dasein. ... There is academic Dasein, modern western Dasein, swashbuckling fighter-pilot Dasein, and so on. By contrast the Aztec and ancient Egyptian ways of life have died out -- there is no more Aztec or ancient Egyptian Dasein. Like natural languages, ways of life evolve slowly through the years, and vary gradually across the landscape; like dialect, lingo, and professional jargon,

many ways of life can intermingle and overlap in a single community, and even a single individual.[298]

We will neglect much of Haugeland's philosophic discussion. Our focus is on this current, lively identification of Dasein with a way of life. A common term for our way of life is "culture." I will make the assumption that we can equate his interpretation of Heidegger's *Dasein* with our use of the term "culture." Undoubtedly, this is a vast oversimplification of a somewhat puzzling and complex philosophy. Nonetheless, the fit seems good for our immediate purpose.

Haugeland notes that when Heidegger introduces his account of understanding (as projecting in terms of possibilities) he speaks first and foremost of *self*-understanding. On Haugeland's reading, self-understanding would be casting oneself into roles. One might see himself as a chess-player (Haugeland makes much of this analogy) or a school-teacher. Such roles tell us not what but *who* I am. And they are community determined. Roles account for how we behave in them.

> A teacher who deliberately missed classes, or a chess-player who deliberately broke the rules, would be culpable and blameworthy. To cast oneself into such a role is to *take on* the relevant norms -- both in the sense of undertaking to abide by them and in the sense of accepting responsibility for failings.[299]

Heidegger has helped us understand our individual relationship and participation in our culture with the proviso that adopting these roles is a choice, and when chosen they still do not *determine* our behavior. As with all choices not forgotten (producing habits) we have already hinted at the complexity of culture, but the detail of disciplined philosophical exploration is extraordinarily revealing and this one short article can help considerably with understanding my thesis: Our individual selves are heirs of evolution and ours is the opportunity to understand that we are each individual persons, selves of our own making, dependent on lifelong strings of hundreds of thousands of personal choices in human communities where our adoption of the norms associated with our existing cultures have intimately shaped us to live. Is this not "Dasein"?

When this understanding of humanity began to emerge in my mind,I had long neglected modern philosophy. But gradually, through the labyrinthine ways of my disciplines, I have emerged into an exciting world thoughtfully constructed by humanity over the entire existence of *Homo sapiens*. Defining culture has eluded many bright and able people over the centuries, but, granted the insights of innumerable modern thinkers, we realize that culture is not the product of any faddish, current human self-indulgence, nor even of powerful long-term community biases (like solving problems through warfare), but of individual human living in community. It is not produced by "great thinkers" but is the work of all human beings: the sum of the way human beings live, evident in innumerable local, regional and global manifestations. The whole thing.

Wittgenstein not only helped in the birth of analysis of language, he did it out of his birth into a wealthy family of extraordinarily broad and extensive cultural experience. Still the underlying religious training he received shaped him, not to become a churchman (another in the long string of bright and even erudite Christian scholars) but as a human being. He valued art and music, deep thought, self analysis, and repentance. For all his extraordinary gifts, he never gave himself to pride but gave himself unstintingly to exercise of his mind with a heart that in the end could be grateful for the eventful, productive, articulate life he gave to us. He was not a saint by church definition. He was a saint by acclimation. D'Evelyn says "The way Monk tells the story it's as if a minor figure in a Dostoyevsky novel haunted the landscape of 20th-century thought. In his own eyes, Wittgenstein was something of a failed saint...." For him his life was "the duty of genius." We are no more called on to emulate his self-denigration than that of the ancient urban thousands or the Middle Ages' millions of peasants, but out of such humility our culture proceeded on its tortuous growth to our present self-consciousness. William James considered Wittgenstein that sort of whole human being – a highly disciplined, thinking human being. The new humanity is a thinking humanity.

D. THE END OF THEOCRACY

Though ordered by the sixth century Roman law and British common law, ours is a world largely formed by the fortuitous joining of Greek and Jewish cultures. This discussion so far has focused on how the modern person has emerged from the confusing cacophony of voices of the ancient world largely intended to keep most people in peonage. Once established by Constantine, the Christian Church played a substantial role in the intellectual history of the West. The Christian canon, once established, served as an anchor for 1500 years. As Christendom crumbled under the duress of unparalleled intellectual growth, diversity replaced the monolithic Roman Church built on its Roman heritage. The many forms of Roman and Protestant Christianity have played important parts in the formation of our world. They witness to the diversity of humanity itself, and to the gradual evolution of diverse people into innumerable comfortable communities.

As the embodiment of the religious heritage of the West before the growing cosmopolitan religious explosion of the twentieth century, the success of Christendom requires an explanation. To rehearse: the Church built a viable structure on the hierarchical principles of the ancient world. Its earliest efforts were to assure the transmission of a true Gospel in the face of pressures from all sides. In that mind, dedication to the memory of Jesus was primary, not the practical questions of polity. The onslaught of animism, dualism, mysticism, gnosticism and other religious ideas assured ongoing religious debate. The confluence of the two distinct cultural strands brought with it a variety of other challenges as well as the marvelous expansion of our use of our brains. Early Christians included many brilliant people who wrestled with these to produce orthodoxy over the centuries. In that world the tension between religion and government was fought not over sovereignty, but over authority. There was only an incipient separation of powers as yet, and the notion we call theocracy lurked constantly in the background. Ultimately, in the West, separation of powers has won out over theocracy.

While its extraordinarily slow metamorphosis continued, the Roman Catholic Church has been a constant reactionary presence in most of the West. While Europeans were refashioning themselves as Christians, the Church maintained its steadfast dual orientation to maintaining its authority and to preservation of the Gospel. This is not to say that it should have ignored these concerns, or that it failed in the compassionate care of the sick, in the study and preservation of the Scripture, and in maintenance of the worship of God. But under the pressures of many diverse formative influences the Church found its major mission in assuring its power to protect the Gospel as it was defined in the first few centuries. This conservative motive dominated it. It did not pay attention to the changes taking place in the culture or the emerging new mind. We have tried to identify these chiefly, as pride in intellect and fear of losing what has been gained. Indulging these, the Roman Church failed to grasp the universal law of change (quite apart from Darwin), the constant change which has always characterized reality and was one of the earliest of philosophic topics among the Greeks. Incessant turmoil had reinforced this inordinate preoccupation with stability and all authorities sought to maintain the status quo.

Nonetheless, the Church spread its influence to every corner of the world providing worldwide Christianity with a basic form with arguable wisdom. It has often hung onto antiquated ideas, mistakenly thinking they were necessary to Christian orthodoxy. The tragic intertwining of philosophy and theology was part of the development of the European mind. The Church appeared to tenaciously guard its circumstantial primacy just as the oligarchs had done before it. Occasionally, especially in the cultural upheavals of the twentieth century, the Church has reentered the human community, regretting some of its past.

At least in our journey here, we can credit Christianity in Britain (St Patrick, St. Columba and St. Aidan in the fourth through seventh centuries) with laying the foundations for the conversion of the Celts in Britain who infiltrated the original inhabitants early in the Christian era, prior to Alcuin of York and the Norse assaults in the eighth century. Rome's failure to dominate the British Isles may have played an important role in the emergence of the United States. Not unlike the protection of Greece by its terrain, the separateness of Britain from the Continent no doubt contributed to its rather different development. Nonetheless, we do not forget that the intellectual vigor emerging in Europe in the second millennium touched even the monolithic Roman Church and restrained its lust for power from perpetuating the error of theocracy. The work of such persons as England's Wycliffe demonstrated as early as the fourteenth century the human capacity breaking out of old constraints as the Continent seethed in frustration and revolt. The British culture, free longer than most of Europe would provide the seedbed for flowering of the Enlightenment.

The quality of British education in the first millennium still focused entirely in monasteries was reflected in such personages as Alcuin who carried his educational philosophy into the court of Charlemagne. This was evident, too, in the prominence of Irish education early in the second millennium when nobility from the Continent sent children to Ireland for their education. But the antiquated hierarchical form of the Church became especially onerous in France and contributed to both the Reformation and, later, the insurgency we know as the French Revolution. The first French thrust at education occurred in the 1630s but those early efforts were motivated largely by the same reactionary concern for preservation, in this case of the French language. At that very time, Scot education was producing the most creative minds of the Enlightenment and the culture of the industrial revolution. The French failed to grasp the development of the mind.

The effective role of Christianity in the emergence of the modern human being of the West is demonstrated by the influence of John Knox in transforming Roman Catholic Scotland into Protestant Presbyterianism. In the sixteenth century, under the tutelage of John Calvin, Knox initiated the education of Scottish people throughout the country. This prepared Scotland for its significant role in "inventing the modern world" as Arthur Herman terms it in his helpful book.[300] Soon thereafter, the English also began public education. Scottish people were reading the Bible in their homes a century before common education was begun in France. It is not strange that to this day literacy began in many places with reading sacred scripture. This educational thrust has paid us the immense dividend of helping to develop a sense of responsibility new to the world.

The role of education in shaping society had long been recognized. We have already noted specific attention to education in the eighth century school of York. And much earlier, in the Biblical period, the Jewish culture encouraged thoughtful people to read. The Greeks had begun writing about the same time as the Jews and successfully adopted the alphabetic version of their language as early as the sixth century BCE. In the fourth century BCE Alexander spread the Greek language throughout the known world. We credit Gutenberg with the invention of movable type in the fifteenth century CE which no doubt contributed to the spread of literacy in Europe and the emergence of Europe as the dominant culture worldwide following the end of the threat from the East.

But we cannot credit education itself with the development of a world culture in Europe. Chinese and Persian cultures had immense head-starts. But the Chinese culture has always been handicapped by its extraordinarily extensive development of picture-writing[301] and an insularity which disrupted progressive steps. Persia suffered unfortunate diversion toward renewal of autocratic social patterns after its auspicious start in philosophic and scientific works. One wonders if the extensive allegorical emphasis in fiction and poetry in the East -- as well as a distinctly oriental orientation in religion -- did not divert attention from practical matters and interfere with development of the sense of responsibility. It is one explanation for the reactionary theocratic governments of much of the Mid-east.

The Greeks and the Jews formed something of a permeable wall between the East and the West to stop the spread of eastern religions. The Greeks might easily have adopted oriental religious forms evident in their classical cults, but their intellectual, fact-oriented mind-set probably interfered with that direction. They focused on understanding humans and the nature of physical reality. And the Jews had long ago broken their intimacy with the middle ease as epitomized in their stories of Abraham and Moses which drew them back into the everyday world of physical realities. Judaism has always struck me as a gutsy religion, closely tied to the realities of living. Together in the developing European culture, these two orientations maintained a practical religious thrust which filled a cultural void as Rome lost control. Embracing both intellect and feeling, it modified the intellectual Greek orientation. Grasping gutsy conviction (we are the people descended from Abraham favored by God), it held self-discipline and passion together with belief in a God concerned for each person and their relationships. In melding into the new European culture, the Greek and the Jewish cultures both supported control of the environment inherited from thousands of years of earth and water manipulation but added a new element, the critical mind – not individual monads in time and space, but people sharing life with others in a fantastic world.

This pragmatic orientation began in the most ancient pre-historic times as *Homo sapiens* spread over the entire earth. In different environments, people found it helpful to build dams, drainage ditches, walls, and granaries, and eventually walled houses and cities. Modification of flood and storm, wind and rain became excuses for projects in which masses of human beings were the machines for land moving. They quarried rock, cut it, finished and inscribed it. They built long inclines (ten miles long for the recent Taj Mahal) to move stone to the tops of towers and pyramids. Cities required constructing aqueducts and sewage drainage systems. In Europe, the many and varied populations struggling against population pressures developed practical minds which extended to every aspect of life.

That same inventive spirit was applied to learnings about law and order of several thousand years' evolution of society. At the same time, skills of the years developed into crafts, and the professions consolidated gains in caring for the sick, sharing and teaching one another as only highly developed language can do.[302] In Rome's shadow the coalescence of Greek and Jewish cultures at the beginning of the Common Era was appropriated by the emergent Church. Aristotle's logic ruled the development of thought, and Aquinas, Duns Scotus, and William of Occam finessed the rigid theological system called Scholasticism at the root of Western theology for hundreds of years. Unfortunately, this strain of thought contained a rigidity which froze personal development with answers just when the capacity to see questions was burgeoning. It was not destined to provide a base for the emergence of democracy without the important modifications of the Reformation.

It seems to me strange that the Jews, having adopted the ways of the world in the Iron Age, seeking government by a king ("like all nations" I Samuel 8:5), ignored warning by the prophet of the dangers of consequent subjection to oligarchy. Their unique self-consciousness as people responsible to a personal God had failed to defend them against the sophisticated Philistines. Theocracy had failed; they had no king. Practically, they felt the need for a commanding defense. They turned to their current religious leader, Samuel. It is remarkable that Samuel's agreement to their request for a king was couched in terms of what the people wanted: "Listen to the voice of the people." It was the primitive charismatic leadership of the past, early populism before anyone thought of such a thing. Samuel is referred to variously as priest, seer, judge and, once, as prophet. It was a time of transition about 1000 BCE.[303]

In spite of Samuel's uneasiness about the people's desire – he understood his responsibility to warn them of the likely fruits of oligarchy in subjugation – one reads of no suggestions to the people of another path toward realizing their own government except their long unsatisfactory experience with what we call "theocracy." Samuel reminded them of the likelihood of war under a king, "...and you shall be his slaves." It seems incredible that they forgot their own story of origins in which Moses led them out of slavery. In that ancient Jewish culture, the seer could grasp consequences but not options. It seems to be proof that the evolution of the mind was not yet advanced enough to analyze the situation as thoroughly as we might do it today.

In spite of their unsatisfactory experience with monarchy, the biblical Jews held onto a theocratic vision, a governmental option many now agree is obsolete. Zionists are one of the groups which perpetuate it, failing to learn from human experience of its failed history. They are still living with a view alive and well before the Common Era.[304] Surely we have learned that replacing an aristocracy of power with an aristocracy of the religious may well be no improvement. While even Christians may aspire to an ultimate ideal kingdom, the human mind has -- at least in the twenty-first century -- begun to grasp how we can separate ourselves (our self awareness) from our understanding of others, of our conditions of life, our society. We are aware of ourselves very differently, and this enables us to become "objective" (in a sense) in our grasp of reality. It seems that this sense of self simply was not possible for human beings in the Biblical period nor in the formative years of European culture. Inability to do this left the people at the mercy of the culture. They had no means to critique it, to ask it questions, to inquire into improvements. They simply, as we say, "followed their noses." That is, they saw what was going on among their neighbors and, as adolescents typically do, they copied. Samuel's insight that the people had a right to speak for what they wanted was an acquiescence, it was the way leaders were chosen, it was the way celebrations were conducted, it was the way political decisions were made. They lacked the sophistication to challenge the power of their culture.

Since religion had long been appropriated by rulers to maintain unity, what we call "theocracy" became a fixed part of religions just when they were becoming sophisticated enough to perpetuate themselves into the future. The human capacity for planning was yet to be developed. Theocracy (our word) simply emerged. It was not designed. It is unlikely that we will ever uncover an ancient people who understood the self-government option. It is unlikely, I think, because the human mind had not evolved to a point at which people could be sufficiently self-conscious to grasp their capacity to govern themselves.[305] For the Jews being God's chosen people guaranteed them God's governance. A grasp of the reality of separation of religion and governance would require three thousand years. When that developed, the critical mind that would discover it also was becoming critical of the religious institution dominating Europe because of Constantine's empowerment in the fourth century. Samuel had seen a glimmer of the separation over a thousand years earlier. But Constantine still operated in the culture which confused the two.

Religion began to differentiate itself from government but the old paradigm lacking differentiation (theocracy) still remains embedded in the minds of some people today. In the twenty-first century the number of us whose minds have matured has grown to be a sufficient portion of the population to be persuasive in the civil arena and to bring new light to such intractable issues as the Palestinian problem.[306] In this century, too, we Americans are at least learning to apply our critical minds to our own current problems: that human society requires self-regulation and compromise. Some among us are better able to grasp such insights than others of us, but we no longer subscribe to the illusion that religious people are wiser than others – the only justification for theocracy.

Theocracy also embodied the mistaken notion of "being right" over against others. We are entering a time when we the people can talk with one another about things without feeling assaulted, attacked, and competitive. The time of gross competitiveness among human beings is coming to an end. Before we began to undrstand ourselves, the alternative to theocracy was conflict. The notion that democracy is a clash of ideas requiring conflict is reminiscent of antiquated antagonism. Our survey of the evolution of the human mind demonstrates that all minds can contribute to understanding. Nonetheless wisdom requires discernment. Someday, the ideal of populism might become practical. But it will require a far greater spread of the new mind among us. A number of the Fathers of the United States were worried that demagoguery would make our government impossible. At the same time they were determined not to fall into the pit of replacing ancient oligarchy with a new theocracy of equally reactionary religion co-opted in the distant past by power. That is not a path to the future. The close tie of religion to government produced by ancient oligarchy clearly proved itself mistaken.

E. FORMING A NEW POLITICAL PHILOSOPHY

Introducing Jurgen Moltmann's "Meditation on Hope," Alistair Kee notes that after a century of demonization of Karl Marx we have learned to engage in a new dialogue with Marx. The opening of our dialogue to Marx, Kee says, is because of the recovery of Marx's early humanism. There is no wonder that many Americans have recognized in Marx a brilliant and prescient voice. "The reason why Christians and political humanists find themselves so often together in common tasks is that the languages they speak spring from a similar passion and point to a similar hope...." It is what Paul Lehmann called "a passion for and vision of human deliverance."[307] Kee quotes Marxist Ernst Bloch: "What is decisive – to transcend without transcendence." Politics is the way humans regulate their social commonality at a given time and place. It is clearly particularistic. Like culture we can describe it at a moment, but it is constantly subject to the changing minds involved in it. Its problems present to us the necessity of transcending ourselves as social beings as intimate parts of communities. Unfortunately, one of the legacies of our past is confusion about ourselves tending toward individualism.

This confusion, like others before it, also must be transcended. "In most civilizations known to us," Mark Lilla writes, "in most times and places when human beings have reflected on political questions, they have appealed to God when answering them." Lilla ascribes the escape from "political theology" to the devastating wars of religion in the sixteenth century. From Thomas Hobbes to John Locke, to David Hume, thinkers who agreed on little else agreed that politics had to be separated from religion.[308] This is a lesson from centuries of struggle to find alternatives to oligarchy. We can understand as ancient people could not, their entanglement of religion as a device in the manipulation of people by the oligarchs. They had set the stage to demean and subvert religion in the Western world and we are still digging our way out of the mess this caused.

While most Christians today live outside of Europe and the United States, Philip Jenkins notes that even those from Africa have largely been Westernized. John Sentamu in 2005 became archbishop of the ancient see of York (founded in 627 CE), second only to the Archbishop of Canterbury in the Church of England. This appointment transcends not only the colonialism of the West but other of its errors as well. Sentamu is Ugandan by birth and practiced law there until he had to flee persecution under the regime of Idi Amin.[309] Sentamu shows the universal effect of the evolving mind on our new culture. Though the staying power of culture is great, human beings have the capacity to remodel it to fit their new world. Sentamu found moving to England the best way for him to transcend a particularly vicious regime. The evolution of the human mind is not western.

Sentamu was familiar with the endless cycles of violence in Africa. For long ages, the innumerable African tribes, without severe natural barriers, from time to time suffered the primitive aggression familiar in tribal life thoughout the world prior to the emergence of cities. Of oppression and slavery there was plenty, but never the prolonged and intensive total control of large populations familiar in the ancient Middle East. Thus, after the relatively short period of colonialism ended in the twentieth century, Africans have slowly gathered themselves together and leap-frogged over much experience of the West. The capability of humans to grasp the significance of such experience without repeating it is one of the great gifts of our humanity. We have already discussed its genesis in the native capacity for reflection in the contribution of beauty to evolution (see chapter X, section A). We can expect increasing evidence of a twenty-first century humanity worldwide.

In his usually acute mind, David Brooks of the *New York Times* wrote of the nature of economic responsibility. He noted that, after indications of a strong egalitarian bias, President Obama in a speech at Georgetown University charged that the traditional economic assumptions have been broken down "by irresponsibility." It is a sign of the end of the rule of an ideology based on a primitive selfishness. To repeat, this also is a failure to transcend the self. Some of us misread the emergence of the United States simply as independence from monarchy. It was the genesis of the continuing illusion that is what "freedom" means – absence of controls. It has taken two hundred years more to convince Americans that society requires controls.

Unfortunately, past surges of proud analysis of sociology and psychology, of politics and organization have reinforced this notion of freedom and misrepresented the lessons of our own past. The Republican Party is currently in disarray after a disastrous presidency. Captured again by reactionary tendencies it is making all the expected noises about that sort of traditional value. In spite of expressions in terms of small government and severely limited government spending, its politicians have been spending money lavishly. For the Grand Old Party to be trapped in such thinking in the twenty-first century leaves the GOP floundering in the past, divided. Conservative minds will press it to extremities. It awaits the wisdom of the burgeoning of new minds in the most unlikely population. Fortunately, some of us have seen the necessity of governmental control and regulation of many social functions – of intelligent, not ideological, government. Three hundred million people cannot be governed the way and at the cost required for small populations.

We have begun to understood global economics – government, organization, regulation, and control require public financing. And we understand freshly the old dictum "all politics is local." Politics is the current expression of the people in relation to governance. The use of per capita analysis is a helpful technique to demonstrate economies of scale and to gauge the existing sense of responsibility. It is the dawning of a new political philosophy recognizing the individuality and lack of unity in any population.

Obama, Brooks says, is building a new leadership class. It is made up of expert teams giving short-term service to broken systems. Instead of careers in public service during which anyone will gradually learn the current "ropes" people come forward to exercise their own strengths to meet current needs of government. In one articulation, the method is to "restructure incentives in order to channel the animal drives of the marketplace in responsible directions." Brooks points out that the danger "of course, is that the teams may not be as farsighted as they believe." Surely he is right that it may not be possible to out-think the market which is made up, like culture, of a multitude of independent influences. But we are moving in the right direction in tailoring governing efforts to the variety of people and in obtaining effective groupings of people to engage in the fresh conceptualization of solutions through dialogue, a new way to apply our minds and hearts to government.[310] The Far Right and the Far Left will undoubtedly exist interminably. But the overriding human desire for peace and love will prevail. Again, we see path correction as a major human tool to improve the circumstances and regulation of life together.

That is the world of the future. Who can imagine in the year 2100 the kind of self-righteousness that is still evident in our legislatures today? In an account for *Newsweek*, discussing what partisans might well call "waffling," Hirsh and Thomas suggest that we are seeing now how "smart people are not dogmatic -- stuck in one narrow ideological groove -- but rather open-minded, flexible, and intellectually alert, able to change with the times."[311] Brooks adds one important point: The integrity of the person we elect to be president of the United States should be clear and consistent. "Economic responsibility starts at the top."

Similar things are being said in many places. At least from biblical times, the changing of minds among leaders has been noted time and time again (Moses, David, Josiah). The Christian belief is that we are put where we are to participate there, to listen and read and speak out of that context. We recall the post-modern notion that the present is best defined as full of possibilities. People who dream about being elsewhere, in different circumstances, may well miss the opportunities in their present locations because the sigh is truncated by the dream. And people who think they must serve some wisdom of the past are subject to the error of reading into the present situation the view embodied in the past as well as the ubiquitous error of reading the past as if it were the present!

While it is possible for the wisdom of the past to be well-applied to a present circumstance, to be bound by such ideas means living in a time past. For us that was a world when people believed that knowledge was permanent and secure, and our rationality corresponded to the natural order. In that world everyone feared the disorder which brought on civil terror thus supporting the status quo (which itself never brought permanent stability). But in a world that we understand requires our intelligent correction and productive effort, the order of the day must be to transcend that chaos and the present itself and move intelligently into the future.

F. THE NEW RATIONALITY

In the twentieth century we fought off several devastating bits of common wisdom, like the economic philosophy of the old Republican party. Our life together required government functions for a nation moving rapidly north from one hundred million people about 1900. In its first one hundred only years we had only begun to learn how to govern huge populations. In another hundred years, when the population of the United States passed three hundred million people (close to the population of the whole world in 1000 CE), that popular economic thinking was still governing many Americans. The same problem of being trapped in antiquated thinking exists all over the world. Some cities are ruly gargantuan, much larger than our biggest. But even in smaller places we have not solved perennial problems of sanitation, health, education, and poverty to name a few problems. Raising children is difficult. Crime flourishes. Class segregation is rampant. And slavery continues.

And yet we contemplate using our limited resources to conquer space as if we were still living in the recent past when we thought open spaces were inexhaustible. The startling fact is that the same problem of learning to live together that challenged the earliest villages, the first cities, and all the nations of modernity too, is still our own. Our natural inclination is self-centered. But humans have the capacity of transcendence. We chose to live together for a vast array of benefits that accrue to common life. And for the most part we solved the attendant problems of interaction as a practical necessity. Occasionally brilliant leaders broke out of old patterns into new ones and always carried with them errors of the past as well as learnings. None, alone, could resolve all the many problems of human beings growing into their true socialized humanity. We can see that even the Greek and Roman forums were only an early step toward legislatures and these, too, have not yet solved all the problems of governing effectively. We were and are still driven by the problems of large and diverse populations.

Persisting in habits of Modernity will not suffice either. Technocrats and biologists often tell us we must extend humanity to other planets to preserve human life. One must question such grand ideas when we have failed to address human needs adequately. Shall we squander our available resources to send a few thousand people to the moon or Mars? Sending *six thousand* would be one hundredth of a percent of the world's present population. How does such a goal contribute to the fulfillment of human life? Do we still let the instinct to reproduce our own species dominate our culture?

The major domains of society have long been controlled by an obsolete capacity to use our intelligence. Many leaders in commerce, government, and education are only beginning to recognize the obsolescence; those who do often find their way lonely. As

Martin Heidegger, recognizing the change late in his career and within the confines of his world, began to speak of humans communicating in community; so must all leaders. The speed of population growth and the the velocity of change now require it.

Jurgen Habermas came to the same understanding early in his career. Witnessing what he called the failure of the German culture to understand or criticize National Socialism, he began to reconceptualize public reason. It saw ahead a "concept of public opinion-formation 'that is historically meaningful, that normatively meets the requirements of the social-welfare state, and that is theoretically clear and empirically identifiable.'" He went on to say, such a concept "can be grounded only in the structural transformation of the public sphere itself."[312] Is that not a reference to culture? The time for gross expansion is over. We are approaching seven billion human lives right here on earth and most are far from fulfillment. We need to increasingly use the considerable rationality embodied in these millions to solve real problems of real people in difficulty who continue to constitute the vast majority of the world population. The poor are not just those outside our gate. They are everywhere, and, after all, they are brother and sister human beings.

Our position in these later years is not unlike that faced by the early city dwellers uprooted from their tribes adapting to the increased sociality of cities of several thousand. Undoubtedly, the miracle of our dominance among all animals depended on our *adaptability* not only to still larger cities, but recently to a global world. We do indeed make our future. Being adaptable means being open to circumstances. Among our earliest ancestors, listening was instinctual and our ears are still turned on most of the time. But we long ago developed the capacity to neglect some inputs to our brains. We can turn off the products of sensory perception and the modern world of concept as well.. The story is told of a competent critic warning the powers that be of the danger lurking in the global derivatives market of many, many trillions of dollars in value. The authorities capable of thinking about that chewed out the warning voice in their fear of adverse world-wide reactions. Years later one of these experts candidly admitted they were wrong, they had this warning, and didn't listen. "Listening" is more than hearing; it is paying not *formal* but *real* attention. Our capacity for adaptation has been growing.

Perhaps the greatest wisdom made plain in the past hundred years is not any of the obvious stupendous discoveries: linguistics, theory of relativity, Godel's proof, Heisenberg Principle, particle physics, chaos theory, astro-physics etc.. It is rather that the situation in which each of us finds ourselves carries clues of boundaries which may need to be addressed and their significance and opportunity for elimination in our time and with our talent. In other words, listening, looking carefully at all evidence, using our brains carefully will lead to adaptive behavior which is helpful and supportive of human relations. The proviso is that we use our minds as fully as we are able and attend to listening to other voices. We have learned to turn off those voices which speak from points of view we still relegate to enemy status in our lives. As long as we do this we will sacrifice our future to governance that may have been appropriate sometime in the past. We will fail to adapt to a present in which these other voices are also our brothers and sisters.

The human mind is now reaching a maturity in which we can choose to be partners. We all can benefit from the combined wisdom residing in sharing our many insights. In various ways and patterns we have long been partners to one another, first to spouses and children, then to villages and tribes, and cities. Recently we have learned to be partners across the ancient bounds of race and nation. In doing so we have been learning to make politics our servant rather than ourselves its slave. And now we are rapidly learning to partner with the earth itself, as the ancients called it, "God's footstool." We are being called across all remaining boundaries.

The most recent cultural revolutions have given us mastery, first, of our natural environment and, second, of our selves. Our scientific capabilities are giving us control over our living patterns. Our spiritual sensitivity evident in religion -- though often hidden beneath exploitation and misguided celebration -- has triumphed and will triumph increasingly. The world religions also are coming to look at one another as brothers and sisters. Our native rationality will find ways to see beyond all our differences into the heart of humanity. Climate change (the current mystery for a humanity largely dependent on food-growing weather) in calling urgently for our partnership and our new self-consciousness, is giving us the power to choose to be partners. The result of needed changes will be a new humanity enjoying the fruits of a balanced existence, rejoicing in diversity, enriched by one another, and satisfied in ourselves and our three or four score years without remorse. But that does not mean we can proceed without admitting our complicity in the shaping of the culture we leave behind.

I have now progressed in reconstruction of an excellent education in philosophy, Bible and theology. I had the good fortune to include work in many other fields and a lengthy exposure electronic technology in research. All together it has led me to a grasp of our human situation in which I rest comfortably. World class philosopher Karl Popper, a realist, played a significant role in my retirement re-education. In *The World of Parmenides* he speaks what seems to me to summarize our intellectual position. With such a title, one may be sure his focus is on the Greeks.

Beginning with the pre-socratic thinkers who became known as philosophers Popper traces our intellectual history back to Thales and the Ionian Tradition. Thales recognized in a nephew's impertinent questions a better way to teach, through questioning. In the dogmatic culture of the time, this perception was extraordinary. Also in Ionia some two generations later, Xenophanes recognized his own thinking as purely conjectural, that others might come who would know better. Popper credits Xenophanes with putting us on track to gradually learn what now seems perfectly clear: *The truth must be approached by means of critical discussion*. Heidegger also found these pre-Socratic thinkers' focus on such realism to be more inviting than much later philosophy exploring abstractions.

Unfortunately, this way seems to have been lost, perhaps due to Aristotle's prominence and his doctrine of *episteme*, a certain and demonstrable knowledge. Western thought became distracted by our fantastic capacity to abstract. We are capable of construction concepts of infinite variety and are still wallowing in the assumption that this is the way to think. Heidegger notes that from Socrates on, philosophy misled the West by focusing on such abstractions. It has been a long path through Western history to recover a balance in our dominant patterns of thought. Popper says, "(The Ionian way) was rediscovered and consciously revived in the Renaissance, especially by Galileo Galilei."[313]

In spite of the popularity of Aristotle's *episteme*, Popper insists that the significance of observations and experiments of science "depends *entirely* upon whether or not they may be used to criticize theories." This is the basis of scientific reason, scientific discipline.

There are just two ways in which one theory may be shown to be superior to another. One is that it explains more. The other is that it is better tested. "This, I believe," Popper says, "is the true theory of knowledge....though there are many scientists who still believe in the Baconian myth of induction, the theory that knowledge proceeds by way of conjectures and refutations." He sites two men who clearly understood this difference: Galileo and Einstein. The earliest ancient philosophers had prepared the ground for Socrates' ethical rationalism, "his belief that the search for truth through critical discussion was a way of life."[314] But in the modern period the role of dialogue was badly compromised reverting to *episteme*, and with it the Western mind focused on rationality so that the popular mind has been easily regaled by demagogues appealing to emotions attached to antiquated ideas.

From its beginnings in the twelfth century to the nineteenth, the university was a boiling pot of diverse ideas. As we left the Middle Ages behind, our culture converted conflicting ancient ideas into a competitive game and fell under its control. The super-rational Scholastics set rigid rules to the game which have been refined for centuries. Here the limits of the old mind are plainly evident. In the modern period while the development of science benefited from this game, the competition played out as conflict in the religious community. Rote learning had worked against our grasp of the emerging critical mind and its natural expression in conversation. The result was to substantially divide members of most communions.

In the nineteenth century the emergence of a new critical historical methodology – application of the scientific discipline to history – began an unnecessary career of frightening many pious people. Some well-educated leaders who mistakenly embraced the rigidities of rationalism led the West into a pervasive reactionary philosophic theology. Rationalism was quickly embraced by ordinary people to reinforce their antiquated theologies and this soon regenerated the ancient psychology of fear of an enemy. It poisoned human relations. In a defensive posture, such people developed rationalistic tests of those they could count as friends (like "shibboleth," a biblical word to distinguish foreigners). This rationalism became the bulwark of their reactionary positions. We have recounted the institutionalization of this Fundamentalist mentality. Jesus' "I am the way, the truth and the life," was rewritten as "Jesus is what eighteenth century orthodox Christianity said he was." The antagonisms prevailed and interfered with the process of learning to listen to one another which was proceeding apace in American culture. It was reminiscent of the early centuries of the Common Era when words became weapons.

But in what was perhaps the more debilitating development, the now entrenched university assumed the role of watchdog of rationality. One of the unsung seers of the twentieth century, John Caputo, tells us "Neither Kierkegaard nor Nietzsche could have survived, could have written as they did, could have created as they did, could have taught as they did within the university. We have draped reason with institutional authority."[315] As with Henry Moore's "Reclining Figures, Draped,"[316] it is difficult to recognize the underlying form. Caputo says, "The play of reason is arrested by the principle of reason; the free movement of reason within the university is checked by its institutionalization." "Reason" has been poisoned and we must administer an antidote. Not only must philosophy not be given up but people must everyday seek to be clearly rational. The antidote is intelligent, rational conversation. Caputo says we must not

J. Kuckuk 2009

Henry Moore "Reclining Figures, Draped"

... simply abandon the notion of "rationality" as another case of metaphysical seriousness.... I want to argue...[that] **we are trying to restore the difficulty in life, not to make [life] impossible.** Far from undermining the idea of "reason," this radical hermeneutic issues in a postmetaphysical rationality.... Reason is not undone by the foundering of metaphysics but liberated, emancipated from metaphysical prejudices.... [317]

As this post-modern rationality becomes the normal practice, the problem of fear will subside. Demagogues will be corrected and their influence will be meager, for the people will be thinking. When the ultra-rational Heidegger was "frightened half to death" in 1945 by the entry of atomic bombs into the arsenals of the nations, he became shrill (not unlike Russell a little later). His cry was like Nietszche's against the mess human beings were perpetrating. He was convinced that science, "even in its most theoretical moments remains a *praxis*," that is, a practice and a way of thinking, not a controlling ideology. And thinking is not science. Thinking is our mental activity and we consider it ourselves and subject it to our scrutiny. Science is made up of particularly restricted rational disciplines. Each one is beholden to one or more communities of highly disciplined people whose judgments determine the current practice, and whose insights tend to restrict the reach of the minds of their graduate students. As tightly scrutinized as scientific disciplines are, it is not hard to understand the ease with which a popular sense of science considers it stable, unchanging. The truth only confirmed in the past century is that science, like all human knowledge, is in constant flux. We no longer fear this change, since we grasp both our own adaptability and the flexibility of our culture.

That science has become the major cultural discipline of a powerful democracy may be fortuitous. The especially American ingredient of personal freedom has made the international culture of science more democratic than science might be anywhere else on earth. This demonstrates again how people are always influenced by their cultures. Those who would have been indoctrinated into their particular sciences in some national cultures would have been far more restricted in imagination than they currently are without the American influence. This peculiar American freedom has proved contagious. Its influence on science contributes to its spread.

As with all human beings, the scientist cannot help but be shaped by culture. Those who grasp the new nature of rationality will, however, find their minds liberated to an extent from even cultural influences. And then, science becomes a vast collection of rational disciplines tailored to specialized examination of aspects of this complex world. And one of their critical common characteristics must be openness, humble awareness of the limited reach of human reason.

Culture embodies the contemporary rationality, but nations cannot control either. Like ancient nations, the institutional embodiments of the current culture are subject to fundamental revolutions, and institutions *will* take steps to forestall them. The high sin of treason has deep roots. No doubt slaves who had been brutalized in their home city sometimes became allies of outside aggressors; their treachery found out would lend them no mercy. Our institutions are no longer so oligarchic, though many tend still to be aristocratic. And so the academic institution does have some control over rationality, and the church has some control over culture. But today both are as much subject to these basic social realities as they are in control.

The tendency of all institutions is conservative, to be bastions of the prevailing culture. Radical innovations in powerful schools may not be funded by minions of the status quo. Unfortunately, Heidegger lived in Nazi Germany. He was stifled in his public voice, and was tempted by his early (and immature) critique of culture to join Nazi reactionary forces. Heidegger had to struggle to shed his German and Nazi sympathies. We know that this is always a difficult struggle for anyone, to shift basic allegiances of the human self. But it is not only possible, it is often called for by our new minds. In the United States people like John Caputo and others we have already noted have been free to speak. Caputo reminds us that rationality as he sees it "is not an exercise in nihilism."[318] It is time for American academia to end its aristocratic subversion of rationality, and I believe steps in that direction are evident.

Caputo suggests that the battle rationalism has set up is unbefitting the university. Revolutions have never been entirely squelched. And it is those people within the institutions who must instigate their deliberate adaptation to new realities. It is not strange, then, that late in the twentieth century, Marxists were mostly to be found within universities. But a change is occurring in tune with the new mind of humanity. Change will not be done by subversion or violence, but with a playful candor. While the free play of reason has been arrested in the past, first by narrow-minded oligarchs, later by institutionalization of the principle of reason, in the twenty-first century it is incumbent on those sharing the new mind to support the role of a newly playful rationality; It is our job to keep the game fair. Primitive honest tactics of cajoling and persuading will replace those of an unkind pressure to go along and certainly coercion. Faculties and staffs of universities will gradually join the assemblage of new minds, joyfully, playfully.

The mistake of many smaller schools associated with religious bodies was to fail to keep the playing field level. The antiquated but popular twentieth century rationality effected what counts as "knowledge" and what went on the classroom. Students not yet acclimated to this rationality could attempt to provide for student expression of religion but with little accommodation by the school. Religion departments were minimized and secularized, often out of a sense of "objectivity" toward less familiar religious traditions. Sometimes such objectives were laudable. But the net effect was to marginalize religion and ethics. This mistake, now visible, might have been avoided if more seers had recognized the end of the modern period and resisted the onslaught that put its obsolescent rationality above reason.

XII. PIETY IN THE NEW WORLD

In our vocabulary, piety contrasts with pride. We have already identified pride as one of the key human errors of our era, that is, an undue intellectual pride. Actually pride has also had a positive contribution to make to our culture: pride in workmanship, pride in crafts, in creativity, in satisfaction given to others for work well done. But the negative kind of pride has gotten mixed up with the legitimate in one of the most important of all cultural characteristics. That is the danger of feeling oneself above the highest expectations of human beings, a pride of insight superior to that of the great religions of humankind. Whether we are active participants in an institutionalized religion is beside the point. Each of the religions which have survived centuries of testing in the crucible of life contains some truth worth holding high, above ourselves. While others may hold exalted views also, the great religions have institutionalized their views and thus assured their perpetuation in their cultures. They thus contribute to the shape of the present world culture, no matter our personal views. That in our post-modern views they have perpetuated proud misconstructions must be understood as part of the human equation subject to question and correction.

Human beings are the highest form of life, no doubt, but that does not set any of us above the highest and best aspirations of the human mind. People together have been able to articulate (always with those before them) visions of hope. These are by their nature transcendent. They reach beyond the every day world to express human beings' highest expectations and aspirations – and to address their immediate, earthy, needs. We are blessed with minds that can envision what is beyond present achievement. These sometimes exceed all hope of achievement. This is a positive hope, not cause for cynicism; we are not children who "want" something. The hopes have been shared, humbly and often in nebulous images, by a huge cloud of "religious" persons. In our present culture it is incumbent upon us to acknowledge the incompleteness of our achievement these and to reconcile ourselves to our personal limits. However unpopular, here we call this "piety."

A. CLEAR ERRORS

This view of religion is probably not familiar. For a long time religion has been seen as a set of rules, propositions, and dogmas. That was the character of the world in which our Scholastic roots took shape. Worldwide religious practice has been circumscribed by rites and rituals. In our experience religious institutions have usually had an organizational structure and a hierarchy of officials. But religion as it first emerged had none of these. This is not to impugn any. But it is time now to understand this more elemental sense of the religious in order to contribute to a faith appropriate to the twenty-first century. From this point of view, we should call the many manifestations of religion in our world by the word "faiths," the word denoting individual commitment of one's self to a socialized understanding of our world. This overcomes the mistaken objectification of both "religion" and the expressions we call "religion." Faith as we shall see (chapter XIV, D) is closely related to the deep personal views we call our convictions.

It is likely that the earliest behavior we might comfortably call religious (not religion) was simply reflection. Reflection remains a central aspect of religion for the foreseeable future. Reflection is a term applicable to thinking things over. It is something most of us do in solitude, though when we are not alone we can momentarily reflect on things we bring to mind. Our culture is so busy, so tuned to filling our time, that we have neglected the ancient art of rumination. The brain, in fact, is tuned to perpetual reflection which may actually consume eighty percent of its work. By paying attention to this activity in our heads, we make our ruminations conscious and we may discover our own ways to understand them. We figure things out in this process. Religion holds persistently before us this capability to transcend ourselves without neglecting our interdependence. And in the gradual emergence of this awareness over the span of deep history some of our exceptional ancestors have conceived images which have captivated and transported them and others beyond their previous conceptualizations. As socialized human beings, modern people are again acknowledging their own limitations. In reflection we explore our minds to help us live with these limits and to expand our minds beyond them. In reflection we may discover our own interest in exploring and practicing life beyond the limits imposed by our cultures.

Human knowledge can encompass that which is not yet and may yet be. It seems possible, in spite of the limited nature of our foresight, that the time might come when we can actually transcend our time-honored acquiescence to the wholesome wisdom of generations elaborated in our many religious institutions. But the diverse religious landscape among human beings hardly suggests emergence of a unitary, universal "religion." Our new mind acknowledges that we carry a lot of baggage into our formation of a new culture. And that baggage often perverts our present efforts as well as enabling us to build on the shoulders of those before us. Since religion is reinforced by deep convictions, it is unlikely that anytime soon the institutional forms into which religion has been poured over the centuries will not continue to shape the cultures of diverse people. But as the new mind evolves among the huge populations in each of these forms, we can expect that gradually changes will take place. Emerging new shapes are unpredictable.

Our religion today carries into our present a deep history. Without it we would be totally ignorant of much of our past, in spite of the baggage at which we chafe. The preservation of magnificent visions in the great faiths is accompanied by the history of their formation in which we find equally important constructions of previous cultures. Our "baggage" derives from such pasts. Nonetheless, until more contemporary forms work into our consciousness, we need to honor the religious communities which maintain the wisdom behind ritual and dogma. Neither language nor drama has ever been adequate to religious expression. *Ceremony* utilizes celebratory forms of the culture in which it develops. But *rituals* are of the religion, intended to capture aspects considered important. They contribute to religious expression at its best, in common celebration of high ideals, our transcendent perceptions, and our most creative visions.

227

It takes a bit of grit in the face of the recent history of human invention of ideas (as well as material things) to swallow pride in stellar new insights and inventions – in religion as well as elsewhere. Each innovation is cause for celebration of human ingenuity. The long string of inventions and innovations tells us that creativity is characteristic of humanity. Our pride in it has blinded us from recognition of our strong tendency to err and therefore to the legitimacy of correction. Pride led us in the past into so many destructive courses that we can see that it is now time to set it firmly under our intelligent control.

Of course, invention of all kinds begins in people's minds, however much it may be a trial and error process. Particularly in the past two thousand years, inventions have flowed through our culture at a dumfounding pace often producing similar developments in diverse cultural settings. Strangely, It is still too easy for us to overlook the contributions of predecessors back to the very beginning of human life.[319] But we will no longer strut and primp our achievements as if they belonged to us as individuals.

In the twentieth century religious knowledge fell on hard times. The easy certainty of fundamentalist and scientistic pundits corralled public attention in the first half century and undermined progress in the adaptation of religions to their new context (i.e., new views of history and of the nature of scientific certainty, and specialization). Technical education infected liberal education in the second half of the century. Popular knowledge of Western literature tumbled, including biblical literacy, and scientists paid less and less attention to religious sensitivities until late in the century. No doubt a correction of "liberal" education was needed for the same reasons as effected the religious sphere; after all, they had both come out of the as yet undifferentiated culture of the eighteenth century. But the loss of respect for religion by some intellectuals produced extreme results which also needed correction. So we have Arnold Toynbee, for example, acknowledging Judaic roots of Western civilization, but missing the significant contribution the biblical heritage made in confronting the increasingly cynical heritage left by the Greeks and Romans . The Greeks defied the degrading sheep-view of man and exalted humans to have no master but themselves. It was a proud and productive view, though it led, Toynbee says, beginning as far back as the fifth century BCE to the disintegration of Greek systems of government. The human psyche was not yet tuned to the nature of responsibility.[320]

The most important contribution of Judaism was more ancient, embedded in its basic anthropology. While the rest of the Mediterranean world suffered enslavement by the aristocracies rampant under the various emperors, with the aid of their prophets and the reiteration of their stories, the Jews persisted in claiming to be a chosen people – a people chosen by their God. While other peoples, including the bulk of the Greek and Roman populations were slaves, the Jews, however oppressed, still thought of themselves as "somebody," as we use that term. It was a basic part of the emerging new human mind. We are not basically beasts, nor slaves, nor selfish competitors. We are unique human beings, every one of us.

Arnold Toynbee, interestingly, considered the Greeks pessimists because they saw man marooned in an unfeeling universe whose ways were not man's ways. The Greeks also had misgivings about their declaration of man's sovereign independence in the universe. Though they had ceased seriously to believe that the universe contained anything superior to man, they could never shake off an ancient feeling that their deification of man was impious and that any human being who behaved as if man were the lord of creation was courting retribution and disaster.[321] Toynbee was sure that their downfall was the result of their worship of their city-states. In the mid-twentieth century, even after the beginnings of the new United Nations, he postulated that contemporary nations had revived this Greek error and was pessimistic that they would be able to avoid the tragedy that fell on Greece. Toynbee concludes this discussion with words of the brilliant and cynical Emperor Marcus Aurelius: "Any moderately intelligent man who has reached the age of forty will have experienced everything that has been and is to be." Like him, Toynbee was essentially talking about the self-assured intellectual elites.

The Jews also had been holding onto a mistaken view. Until crushed by the powerful empires, they persistently thought that they could establish a Jewish state with its temple worship. Like the whole ancient world, they misunderstood their love of their independent existence; that was their nostalgic "golden age." But there was something more important for them to contribute to humanity. It was a commitment to a triumphant view of people. Their rich analogy of children of God preserved hope and individuality in their community. It drew on the deepest history of humankind in the development of parentage and the family. This anthropology was appropriated by Christians.

While the Greeks lionized human intellect, the Jews maintained the humility of children of God. No Jew and no Christian could assent to Marcus Aurelius' dictum. For him life was short and forty years of difficulty was all that could be expected. The anthropology introduced into the new European culture by the pregnant biblical orientation gradually overcame the cynicism of the mistaken Greek world view. But the culture was oppressive. The people were still psychologically like sheep, and the Church adopted the mistaken cynical view of human beings even while it witnessed the gradual disintegration of the ancient world in the Early Middle Ages.

As the sense of personhood developed, the long-repressed individuality of people began breaking out. Scholarship developed and in the twelfth century the first universities were chartered and became, perhaps, the first of the great institutions of the West. Among them Paris became one of the preeminent centers of intellectual development. At the same time, the works of Cicero and Quitilian were recovered, just when then city-states of Italy faced a dramatic increase in administrative and bureaucratic work and the rise of new class of people who were professional rhetoricians. Even ancient Cicero had recognized the individual variety in audiences, and the power of language in shaping society. Language "does things" – to contrast with Plato's notion of language as a static system of signs. Rhetoricians made considerable progress in adapting to the variety of listeners everywhere. But at the height of the development of Scholastic theology in the twelfth century, the Church had not caught Cicero's prescience and retained its autocratic stance. It would be three hundred years before the new mind evolving in Europe would revolt. In the meantime, Europe would experience the Renaissance, evidence of evolution of the human mind.

B. THE UNIVERSALITY OF GOD'S GRACE

Edward A. Dowey, a leading twentieth century biblical scholar, tells us that in the thirteenth century the great Thomistic Synthesis rationalized the relationships between faith and philosophy, ecclesiastical authority and civil authority, theology and ethics into a structure that helped hold Western civilization together for over three hundred years. Aquinas might be counted as a forerunner of the Protestant Reformation, but he did not see the larger issues with that sort of prescience. The brilliant Roman Law had produced a culture in which the study of law overshadowed the progress of rhetoricians toward paying attention to the variety of people. Aquinas worked in that legalistic structure, and produced a legalistic theology. Dowey points out that by the time of the Reformation this expression of antiquated authority had brought legalism front and center making it a time for change. The rebellion had been boiling for a long time.

Calvin it turns out proved to be the sixteenth century bridge in the revolution. His early education was to prepare for the priesthood. Calvin was a boy when Luther publicly questioned the right of the papacy to levy indulgences. In those years he was untouched by the controversies and he was imbued with the aging, deteriorating theology of the late Middle Ages. But when his father fell out with the Church over a business deal (he was a cathedral notary), he pulled his son out of study of theology and sent him to Orleans and Bourges to become a lawyer.[322] Calvin was still a very young man, and the exposure to the liberal world changed his views substantially. Later he looked back at his early life and said, "I was obstinately devoted to the superstitions of Popery." He had mastered Latin and the Nominalist schoolmen of Sholasticism but neglected the realists like Aquinas. He later referred to his early learning as twisted sophistry, a kind of esoteric magic When his father died, he returned to Paris (and Erasmus) for the life of a writer and humanist scholar. He became a rhetorician of some reputation.

Calvin mastered law but explored the sources in Greek literature in a stimulating intellectual atmosphere full of speculation. He was opened up to a new world and expanded use of his mind. "The spirit of the Renaissance filled him with the spirit of free inquiry, accurate scholarship and good writing; the spirit of Greece and Rome, of Erasmus, Jacques Lefevres, Reuchlin and Montaigne who loved the manner of writing equally with the matter." Sometime before 1532 Calvin was converted to the Reformation. He left no memoirs, but remembered the lack of study of scripture in his early life. He believed as he had been taught, but found only terror. Before long he was wholly committed to reform. He was a close friend of Nicholas Cop, Rector of the University of Paris. Cop attacked the Paris theologians and they ran him out of town – and Calvin with him. His wanderings began. In Basel Calvin settled down, learned Hebrew, read Augustine and much else. He saw himself as a writer of theology, but soon became a Reformer.

Dowey tells us that all these influences lie behind Calvin's construction of a theology which became the landmark of the Reformation emphasizing the grace of God.

The chief problem of the Reformation regarding piety and theology was, as it had been for Augustine and Paul, the relationship between law and gospel. For Luther there were two "uses" of the law. First, the civil use, which means the role of the Old Testament law as a basis and guide for order in society.... Secondly, the law was for Luther a means for the conviction of sin. He called this the "theological" use which he considered to be the chief function of the law for the believer. But ... for Luther the liberty of the Christian person was precisely freedom from the law.

In Calvin we find three uses, beginning with Luther's theological use as a convictor of sin. His second use was politically equivalent to Luther's civil use. His third use ... was to show [to] the Christian God's will.[323]

Calvin saw freedom not as civil liberty, but as responsible humanity. The third use of the law was plural, that is, about laws. When we think of the law we mean primarily the moral law. Calvin's treatment of the law in the Institutes is preceded by three general interpretive principles. First, *inward observation must accompany outward behavior.* The Old Testament does not differ from Jesus' Sermon on the Mount requirement of complete harmony. Calvin rejected the popular notion that Jesus added inwardness to the observance of the law. What he did was to make the law clearer.

Calvin's second interpretive principle is to be understood by *synecdoche* (sin-eck-doe-key). This term comes out of rhetoric, Calvin's forte. Simply, it means a part stands for the whole, and it is usually used in reference to literary figures of speech. Dowey says thus a single law such as "Thou shalt not kill" is by synecdoche to be understood as only a partial statement of what is meant by the law.

All of it Calvin summarized as love, the third interpretive principle. This is a positive affirmation of love and not the negative form stated in the Ten Commandments. There is an orderliness in Calvin's conception but it does not violate the freedom of spontaneity. Law never means a series of rules governing all of nature and restricting human freedom as would soon be advocated by some philosophers. Dowey says:

> If we understand law as God's universal orderly will for all his creatures, and the human conscience as the subjective awareness of law in the heart of humans, then we can see how both have been violated by the sin of man. Sin separates man from himself, from his own nature, from the world at large and from God.[324]

"Sin" had long since become an essential part of Western language. But we find that the Reformation turned the widely used idea of sin upside down with a wholistic, positive theology based on grace.[325] Unfortunately, both Calvin's Geneva and later Calvinist societies tended to identify the particular laws of their communities with the law of God itself. But, again from our perspective, we can also appreciate how the widespread influence of Calvin and his brilliant *Institutes* set the development of Europe on a new track. This track is positive, progressive, compassionate and responsible (meaning thoughtfully responsive to the circumstances and conditions of life). It is definitely not cynical and not deterministic. Calvin gave "self" a new twist propelling it forward.

A previous brilliant Christian, St Augustine, saw this sense of the individual as "a private, inner, non-spatial 'place' in which we can find God." Ellen Charry (theology at Princeton Seminary) notes that "Phillip Cary is not sympathetic to this view yet is clearly awed by it."[326] In his *Invention of the Inner Self*, Cary argues that Augustine invented this idea of the self (for him, the soul). This appears to be consonant with the view of this paper. Though Augustine's theology moved away from the participation and involvement for which we argue, we note again that in almost two thousand years the mind which he explored has matured in a large number of humans, and the culture has changed stupendously. Cary tells us that in the third century Plotinus took Aristotle's identification of knower with the known and turned it inward. By the fifth century, "it is the notion central to Augustine that wisdom requires looking into the self. 'Know thyself' became the gateway to truth itself, to the eternal truth that is God." "For Augustine, finding God and finding the self are one and the same quest." Again, we find the residue of our past in our present.

We have before noted the importance of the residue of the Celtic culture in the British Isles and in northern Europe. The entire area from the Isles to the Caspian Sea had been settled by Celtic people by late in the ancient period. In the Iona community[327] the influence of early Christian evangelism is still evident in a variety of devotional literature based on it. In the preface to *Celtic Benedictions*, J. Philip Newell claims that early Irish, Welsh and Scottish writings reveal an immense spirituality. It is marked, he says, by the belief that what is deepest in us is the image of God, and a belief in the essential goodness of creation. "Not only is creation viewed as a blessing, it is regarded in essence as an expression of God.... The Mediterranean tradition, on the other hand, has tended toward a separation of spirit and matter, and thus has distanced the mystery of God from the matter of creation."[328] We have already noted the dualism of the ancient Mediterranean world. We may only need to be reminded that the northern European world into which the Protestant Reformation burst in the sixteenth century was made up largely of Celts, progenitors of the Germanic people. They had not fallen into the dualistic trap. The Romans conquered their southern reaches but the Celtic spirit farther north was never subdued by Rome.[329] Its independent and individualistic culture, and perhaps these spiritual leanings noted by Newell, contributed more than we have acknowledged to the strength of the Reformation movement.

The Reformation break with Medieval Christianity provided Europe with a robust and dynamic faith largely defined by grace. It espoused a faith in which the unity of grace replaced the degradation of dualism. Woven cloth has often been used in Christianity as symbolic of the relational nature rich texture of the faith. The "everlasting pattern" in Celtic art, in which one strand is woven together inseparably with another, points to the belief in the interweaving of worlds, of the divine and the human, the angelic and the creaturely, of darkness and light. We might be inclined to speak of their unity rather than their "interweaving," but this term is far more graphic. "Never," Newell says, "are the spiritual and physical torn apart. The interlacing designs are sometimes drawn into human flesh while sometimes animal limbs are entwined about the lower parts of the body." The unity of God's world and all creatures could not be better distinguished from Mediterranean dualities. It is a faith full of grace and hope for all people. It was among such people that John Knox forged the new Protestant Scotland, prepared by a thousand years of Christian missionary efforts dating back to Patrick and Ninian (fifth century). It was outside the

Mediterranean orbit.

For Calvin, the human person is governed by the intellect and thus is capable of penetrating the real structure of the world and making responsible decisions even though the will has been bent by pride. Calvin saw the intellect as having a distinctly moral character which demonstrates his affinity for the anthropology of the early modern humanists and their preoccupation with those aspects of the intellect that influence one's social action and shape one's disposition. Calvin further identified the intellect as capable of "knowing" God (in the sense of directly relating to God) and therefore of attaining the highest form of truth and happiness. Of course, the intellect also has the capacity to make choices, and Calvin recognized our ability to follow or reject whatever the Intellect deemed good or bad. Choice makes us free. With Petrarch, we affirm that "it is better to will the good than to know the truth."[330] "Will" remains our cultural description of the faculty of choice. And piety is the guide to the will, not an independent "conscience" but our very selves aware of self, others, our world, and God.

For Calvin, this freedom – responsible exercise of humanity – should induce piety: "I call 'piety' that reverence joined with love of God which the knowledge of his benefits induces...."[331] In Calvin's vision our world is full of grace, all things contribute to our pursuit of knowledge of God, our piety. But we must use our heads as well as our hearts (Calvin's word for our wholeness). Piety is the disposition to seek, to see, to believe, and to behave in accord with God's love and grace. Piety is true godliness.

C. JOHN CALVIN: A SIGN OF THE NEW PERSON

Calvin, knowing both Aristotle and Augustine, begins the *Institutes* by raising the question of whether one should begin thinking with the knowledge of self or with the knowledge of God, since he considered these two to be the basis of all wisdom. At the end of chapter one, the reader is left with a sense of ambiguity. Some theologians find this difficult. Our exploration here suggests that we always begin with ourselves, not egotistically, but simply because we are creatures, individual persons whose whole life is a reshaping of the self of birth, relating oneself to others, to other things, and pre-eminently to God. Emil Brunner suggests that divine wisdom begins with an inward glance while Karl Barth vociferously disagrees. But Calvin opens up the debate. Serene Jones, President of Union Seminary, NYC, tells us, "He uses his discussion of the primacy of self-knowledge as an apologetic gesture aimed at converting the reader to a disposition in which divine knowledge alone is normative."[332] She quotes Calvin:

> For until men recognize that they owe everything to God, that they are nourished by his fatherly care, that he is the Author of their every good, that they should seek nothing beyond him – they will never yield him willing service. Nay, unless they establish their complete happiness in him, they will never give themselves truly and sincerely to him.[333]

Translated into our culture, everything we know, see, feel, love, and grasp is given us. We are only to be responsible, to respond with humble intelligence.

Using the opening chapter of the *Institutes* as a proof text, "Paul Tillich describes the way in which human experience presents human beings with questions that divine wisdom in the form of revelation is able to answer. Thus Calvin seems to hold the two approaches in tension."[334] While the theologians probe their minds, we simply pick up life anew, daily recognizing our humanity, related closely to the animal kingdom, but stunningly different, rejoicing in our capacity to see far beyond ourselves and our world though very intimately related to them. Recognizing the limits as well as the brilliance of our minds, we know that our world, including ourselves, cannot be godless. Jones points out that:

> This assumption of self-interest is in direct line with Cicero's teaching, and it gives further insight into aspects of Calvin's anthropology that are not addressed in his more explicit discussion of human nature, but nonetheless informs his understanding of the motives and tensions that shape the human will and hence shape his rhetorical attempts to persuade this will.[335]

It seems that the ambiguity did not bother Calvin. And I suggest that Walter Scott and F. Scott Fitzgerald two hundred and three hundred and fifty years later, respectively, were able to see more evidence than Calvin could perceive, that the new human being gradually becoming dominant is able to "hold two inconsistent ideas at once."[336] Calvin seems to demonstrate that. He had an uncanny sense of the emerging capacity of the human being. In his first chapter, knowing the limited sense of self in his time, he involves his readers with words of inclusion: "we" and "ourselves." Elsewhere he sets readers off with the direct "you," but here he uses "I" to keep us tuned in to the human person writing. Although he was constantly lecturing, his writing was for *readers* like ourselves. Jones tells us:

> This identity created between the work and its author immediately distinguishes the rhetoric of this text from the more disinterested textual presentation of "the philosophers" and the dreaded "Scholastics" whom Calvin opposes. In sharp contrast to Medieval Scholastic literary conventions, this personalizing of the act of writing reflects the Renaissance humanists' conviction that the true meaning of a classical text resides in a blending of the author's mind and the ancient source.... As the rhetorical handbook of Cicero teaches, the use of the audience's positive assessment of the speaker's character is one of the most effective forms of persuasion. If Calvin had completely effaced his authorial presence in the text by writing in the third person, he would have sacrificed the persuasive power of his reputation, a sacrifice that a skilled rhetorician would most assuredly avoid.[337]

This identifies the new mind of humanity which Calvin intuited. It was hardly to be seen in the days of the Scholastics. It is today becoming ever clearer. This new mind is respectful of others, indeed, it is egalitarian. It considers human beings to be intelligent, whole, persons with feelings, emotions, instincts, preferences, predispositions, sensitivities, weaknesses, strengths, disabilities, skills, discipline, and personal appetites (including laziness). It accepts responsibility but does not promote itself. It is the harbinger of a sea-change in human culture. No longer do we repeat the shibboleth that we have to have an enemy.[338] That is pure nonsense. What we must have is one another.

Recent research supports this view.[339] Bishop Tutu uses the African word *Ubuntu* to describe the foundation of his belief. It means "a person is a person through other persons." We all belong to one family, humanity.

Calvin intuitively understood life compassionately. His impact on Geneva was as important to the secular order of hygiene and sewage disposal as it was to religious life. He transformed the secular order. True, he left Geneva under threat of death early in his career, but he was received back openly and hopefully later. Theologians often write in the midst of social conflict (e.g., Augustine). Calvin used his major theological work to address the conflict in which he lived. He is disposed, inclined, to "tease forth" the sympathies of wealthy skeptics, and reinforce the resolve of the persecuted.[340] Chris Iosso suggests that today he would probably accept government subsidies (he urged Geneva's leaders to expand the textile trade) but he would also insist that banks and corporations serve the common good. He might even favor salary maximums and minimums. And he would applaud the end of unlimited consumption and compensation.[341]

Calvin's involvement in the secular order is true to the nature of the "evangel," the good news otherwise called Gospel. The transition from ancient Jewish religion through the liberality of the spirit of Jesus' life and teachings, through the filter of Greek and Roman cynicism (among other things), led the way into a new European culture, best expressed in the United States; indeed, it seems for now proved to be a new *world* culture. But we caution, the world will not simply replicate the culture we see here. The spirit of liberality will allow people everywhere to express themselves in interesting new ways.

Of course, neither John Calvin nor any other individual alone was the initiator of the new culture. But Calvin combined the highest skills of his world, the rhetoric already highly developed in ancient times, and law. With roots in the Mediterranean world, Roman law was brought to a new level of sophistication by Roman emperors, especially Justinian, whose sixth century codification of law was promulgated in dozens of forms in hundreds of small communities over the centuries. It is in the nature of all cultures to be works in progress with more hands sharing in their development than we can ever enumerate. This is not to say that these skills had been perfected, but to emphasize that Calvin himself exemplified the high skills and self discipline he urged all people to use in their daily lives.

And, finally, we note that Calvin effectively grasped the essence of Christian religion (as did many others before and after) and articulated a new orthodoxy we call Protestant Christianity. This orthodoxy has been tested and twisted but in its finest form is not a continuation of ancient ritualistic religion. Liturgy and ritual have a place, and Calvin would celebrate the Lord's Supper much more often than most Reformed churches do today. But "having set aside the dubious project of seeking God through knowledge of the self, he has unveiled the glory of divine wisdom and called the reader to enter a world where all things are shaped against the straightedge of revelation alone."[342] In this world the believer is illuminated by the light of true piety. Calvin's intention in the second chapter of the *Institutes* is not only to describe this piety, but to elicit piety – to evoke a disposition to live piously rather than proudly -- i.e. to live constantly in the knowledge of God. This can be an impediment to minds which are not yet able to appropriate Calvin's prescience: pride in piety. Enough instances of this pride are evident in history that we need not review them. Pride, we are aware, sometimes perverted Calvinist communities, and even Geneva

This revelation is hardly what comes to mind out of Christian orthodoxy. It is the ancient person's voices of God, certainty of hearing, conviction of a calling to action. We have long named it God's call. Boiled down to contemporary language, it is what Bernard Lonergan calls "insight." We have identified revelation with the foresight of carefully tuned, alert, bright human minds, highly disciplined and unrestrained either by self-imposed predispositions or by outside circumstances. In chapter two of the *Institutes*, Calvin delineates this as a *knowing that has a purpose*. It is here that many philosophers stumble and fall. This knowledge is functional. It is practical. It "tends" toward something. It is useful. It is distinctly dispositional. That is to say, this knowledge reshapes and reorients lives. It encourages individuals to be disposed to see "higher things." Minds are not focused only on earth and stars, but on fulfillment of life which is God given. It strengthens the community of faith. This knowledge is called *religio* or *pietas*. Instead of the Scholastics "conceiving" and "knowing," Calvin portrays a religious knowledge that grasps us and shapes us.

"In contemporary treatments of this chapter, the peculiar quality of this knowledge has been seen frequently through the lens of existential phenomenology. It is thus characterized as deciding knowledge or practical knowledge." Jones says, however, that in the light of Renaissance humanism it is a "decidedly effective and active form of knowing." The purpose of all knowledge is to enhance life. "It is a knowing that involves the dispositional reorientation of the one holding it. When *pietas* is viewed in this manner, one cannot help but hear the echoes of Cicero and Petrarch reverberating..."[343] The shameless appropriation of wisdom from the past is characteristic of the new mind, also, acknowledging our indebtedness, endorsed by many minds. Calvin's insights have received this endorsement. Far from a characterization as a wizened curmudgeon, Calvin shines today as a man ahead of his time. Though perfectly adapted to his time, he was trapped to far less an extent than many others by the time in which he lived. Nonetheless, they all contributed to the formation of the modern West. It seems clear to me that this is what Whitehead called "prehension."

D. SHAPING THE NEW CULTURE

Time has honored the thinking of many people. We are not surprised to find that early in the twentieth century a mathematician-turned-philosopher anticipated many conceptualizations that have proved durable and fortuitous. Alfred North Whitehead at Harvard in 1929 (earlier a colleague of Bertrand Russell in England) published *Process and Reality*. While Heidegger sorted through the philosophic implications of being, philosopher Victor Lowe tells us that Whitehead had forged on to a conception in which "the being of any kind of entity is in its potentiality for being an element in a becoming."[344] His philosophy has stood the scrutiny of the twentieth century, and Whitehead emerges as the new world's pluralistic metaphysician fit to guide the development of twenty-first century religion. It has been said:

No one has created a process of metaphysics as complete, comprehensive, and as suggestive for future developments as Whitehead's. The sheer greatness of *Process and Reality* necessarily makes his philosophy the primary locus of modern process philosophy....[345]

Whitehead's orientation is prescient of the position we have found in this exploration. Lowe says:

By way of initial orientation, let us say that Whitehead's universe is a connected pluralistic universe. ...nothing in the world exists in independence of other things.

The ultimate character pervading the universe is a drive toward the endless production of new syntheses. Whitehead calls this drive "creativity." It is the "eternal activity," "the underlying energy of realization." [346]

Delwin Brown and Ralph E. James, Jr. tell us that "Process philosophy" is basically a metaphysical position, the view that reality is fundamentally both temporal and creative, and therefore that "becoming" is more fundamental than "being."

Defined very broadly, process philosophy can be detected in much of Buddhism, at least in the *Theravada*, (and) in obscure fragments of Heraclitus.... Some would find it coming to bloom in the idealistic philosophies of Hegel and Schelling. Certainly Bergson, Alexander, Peirce, and James can be called process philosophers. More recently Berdyaev and Teilhard de Chardin.... Recently, however, it has come to mean especially the philosophy of Alfred North Whitehead.[347]

Without going into process theology, we must conclude this exploration with just a few observations about the direction of our contemporary transition. That direction may be capsuled in a recent book by historian Barbara Taylor and psychoanalyst Adam Phillips, *On Kindness*. They speak practically, pragmatically. Phillips says, "One of our fundamental ideas is to care for other people. 'The kindness instinct' is an attempt to formulate a phrase that could capture the way in which kindness might become as elemental as sex." The popular focus on a sentimental solution to social problems obscures "our recognition that we are all vulnerable, interdependent beings who find in sympathy and fellow feeling some of our greatest pleasure."[348] The biblical record and contemporary realism both focus on this real world. Unfortunately, our inheritance includes such a long separation of mind and body that large segments of our population still operate on the basis of this obsolete idea. This has led us into a morass of sentimental attachments to antiquated ideas and notions about ourselves, one another, and our world which have been severely challenged in the twentieth century. One of the most difficult challenges before the American people is to achieve a predisposition to kindness to replace the raw, aggressive, "cut-throat" individualism of our past. It has been gestating for centuries.

For Whitehead, as for Calvin, acts of kindness would be an application of our minds to life situations. It is a focus on *experience*. Modern psychology is concerned about "consciousness," and we have identified self-consciousness as our major concern. At the beginning of the twentieth century Whitehead agreed with William James who in his famous essay of 1904 "Does Consciousness Exist?" attacked the notion "that the existence of a conscious subject ... must be assumed in the discussion of experience...." They were not attacking consciousness but asserting the real existence of the world about us, like our own, independently but in relation. There had been a tendency among some to consider everything mental – George Berkeley, 1685-1753, for example, to whom "matter" was nothing but a complex of sensations. These asserted that what is not in our consciousness does not really exist. Whitehead's method is realistic, not idealistic: He remarks that instead of describing, in Kantian fashion, how subjective data pass into the appearance of an objective world, he describes how subjective experience emerges from an objective world. This is true to our understanding of how our world emerged and produced us: Over some thirteen billion years the world has evolved, perhaps from a "big bang." In this, twentieth century intellects often have thought they saw ahead a "unified theory" behind that to explain everything. But, as Stephen Hawking says, "Even if there is only one possible unified theory (to explain this), it is just a set of rules and equations. What is it that breathes fire into the equations and makes a universe for them to describe? ... Why does the universe go to all the bother of existing?"[349] Why does he call it "a bother"? Victor Lowe points out that for Whitehead consciousness is "so far from being essential to every drop of experience in the cosmos that it is not even present in every human experience."[350]

Whitehead uses the term "prehension" to describe the mental sense of the mind grasping – the basic meaning of "prehension" -- grasping a significant relation. It is the unconscious emotional feeling by which one responds to realities encountered. Before we express a thought, we are aware of the germination in our minds of the forming idea, "prehension," a grasping at that which we will express in our words when we are confident that we have grasped it. We do not know exactly what we will say, until we rehearse it (after grasping it) or actually speak or write it. A prehension is not so much a relationship as a relating, a recognizing of our thought. It seems to me to be a synonym for "insight."

In the normal course of living, we will discover the whole scope of prehension as we express it in words. Whitehead said "experience" is the "self-enjoyment of being one among many, and of being one arising out of the composition of many." Each enjoyment of something is a "feeling" or "prehension" (a grasping) of that. "The process of composition (the putting together of an experience) is a ... (growing together) of prehensions. Thus, the subject-object relation is the fundamental structural pattern of experience." In *Process and Reality* Whitehead

> ... was writing a theoretical transcript of the fact that you feel this moment of experience to be your very own, yet derived from a world without. By taking that elemental assurance at its face value, he was able to accept a primary rule of modern philosophy -- that the evidence for an external world can be found only within occasions of experience.[351]

So we have a germinal concept embedded in a rounded philosophy on which to build our concept of self. Since we are inclined to build, prone to structure ourselves and our environment, eager to order our understandings of ourselves and our environment, we need to begin even before words, and before singing and dancing. Phillips' "kindness instinct" touches the fundamental nature of humanity. James was right, there is something more fundamental than experience. Whitehead named it "prehension." We name it the elemental selfhood of persons aware of revelations. Lowe reminds us:

> Whitehead's amazing philosophical achievement is the construction of a system of the world according to which the basic fact of existence is everywhere some process of self-realization, growing out of previous processes and itself adding a new pulse of individuality and a new value to the world....[352]

One can debate whether the earliest known human, "Ardi," who lived 5.4 million years ago, had any self-consciousness. But it seems to me likely that she had prehensions of all kinds of things. Out of such primitive mental ruminations she built (composed) operative notions on which she acted, preserving herself and her children and relating to her male partner. Perhaps it is not too difficult for us to grasp the unity of mind and body Ardi represents. And perhaps we can appropriate the openness Ardi had to have toward whatever life presented to her so that we do not lazily choose a comfortable status quo rather than the joyous life of modern, querulous, cooperative, creative human beings.

We humans are creative – sharing in the Creation – creatures. Ourselves created, though we are unlikely to figure out just how anytime soon, we have the capacity to revise our environment and ourselves as well. Whether physical evolution of the human being continues can be debated. But there is no doubt that we ourselves choose directions for our self-development. Every choice we make contributes in its small way to the shape of the new culture always emerging among us, in which we ourselves and our children will live. As our self-consciousness increases, we will be more aware of the prehensions of our own creativity, better able to consider them thoughtfully and better prepared to move into the future to which they contribute.

XIII. EASING INTO OUR NEW CULTURE

Though their exact dates are not coincident, we recognize that this is a noteworthy anniversary of the births of some world-shaking persons. Others might well be added, but for our purpose here, we note the 2000th birthday of Jesus of Nazareth, the 500th birthday of John Calvin, and the 200th birthday of Charles Darwin. Darwin bears the burden of our use of the concept of evolution. Calvin bears the imprint of our concept of religious self-determination. And Jesus, of course, is the father of Christianity. All of these signal important changes in our cultural heritage.

We do twist things a bit as time passes – our culture is influenced by hundreds of thousands, millions, yes, billions of human beings and enough national cultures to make a long list. Darwin's claim to fame is in his explanations of the *reasons* for evolution (evolution had been in the air for a while); they were natural selection and random variation. Calvin is railed against for his strictness in interpreting the providence of God, suggesting the unpopular notion of predestination. But his claim to fame is his eloquent, rounded, progressive Augustinian theology in which grace and love are paramount.[353] And Jesus, of course, has probably inspired the world's record number of alternate concepts of God and how to be faithful. Jesus inspired varied interpretations of his life and work, but the view that prevailed, (whether or not it was more accurate than others) has proved to be so open to a humane humanity that he still inspires extraordinarily varied interpretation and productive involvement in our world and culture.

Only recently have we begun to really appreciate the cultures of peoples replaced by our own. Here native Americans suffered first from the diseases we brought from Europe, and then from the vicious culture we inherited from our European past. Far back, we have only opened the book on the the Sumerians, Persians, Babylonians, and Assyrians. This negect extends to many other peoples in Africa, Asia, and the Americas. The glass sculptor, William Morris, has done much to open our understanding of such distant cultures. An American writer with Chilean roots, Isabel Allende, writing a foreword to a volume of Morris' works called *Mazorca: Objects of Common Ceremony* says: She writes of a visit far south in Chile with an uncle who raised a rare breed of sheep where she heard stories of her heritage:

> The first time I saw William Morris's idols, I felt an electric thrill ... because I recognized them. It was like finally finding myself before the intangible beings I had been looking at all my life, that I had glimpsed in dreams and invoked in my writing. These mystical creatures had been with me always, but they were formless until Morris converted them to glass and blew the breath of life into them.

> Morris spends long periods of time alone in nature.... He also travels the world to submerge himself in other cultures and establish connections among diverse peoples and times.... But his restlessness is never satisfied because the primordial essence of the human condition which is what he seeks, is elusive.[354]

Morris does not try to replicate ancient artifacts. His restlessness is shared by more of us as we recover our balance from the frenetic modern period. Most of us still tend to see everything as reinforcement of our present dearly held views which not unlike the deep attachment all people felt when life, in spite of its harshness, was less hurried. It appears that modern *Homo sapiens* is driven by ideas, by concepts, which modern culture reinforced persistently. It seems that over the whole distant past this thoughtfulness was stimulated by the basic reality of death, life that seems fairly short as it comes to an end. The Chilean culture of Allende impressed her childhood consciousness with the stories of her predecessors and conveyed the depth of their belief to her. The difference between primitive humans and ourselves is that we have much larger stores of ideas inherited from the past plus all those that keep intruding on our consciousness day by day. The human brain has evolved to handle more ideas than it did in the past.

Allende's surprise at the beauty of Morris's glasswork touches the reality of culture in the human community. In her early life she absorbed parental tales and they dwelled in her deeply. The way we hold onto past ideas is usually not so much a conscious choice of options, but rather it is this sort of visceral feeling. Allende's sense of primitive gods was not unlike the "rational" constructions of seventeenth century thinkers who felt confident that they could articulate ultimate reality. They were all, after all, mental constructions of human beings. And as such they must be revered. Morris' sculpture achieved a modern interpretation of these which in Allende's eyes was fulfilling. Though we too may respect past constructions, we may or may not find them fitting to our present.

The experience reported by Pals in *The Victorian Lives of Jesus* (see chapter *VIII*) confirms that even large populations can change their views consciously and do so, quite contrary to our tendency to think of people as intellectually immobile ("stuck in the mud"). These are instances of our culture changing within historic time. Out of the Enlightenment, critical thought emerged in ever fuller dress, until in the twentieth century its bounds burst and the glimmerings of a post-Enlightenment world began to take form. It would, inevitably, be filled with new ideas as well as revealing reinterpretations of the past. As this new mind arrives among us, fewer of us will be so recalcitrant. We too will change.

Our memories are fantastic holding devices. Nonetheless we have been arguing here that we *choose* to pay attention to things, and choose to incorporate them in our conscious minds. Some of us do this more and better than others, but we all do it. So we do change our views here and there, especially if we find that our peers share a different view or are interested in it. Comparing 1900 and 2000 we become acutely aware of changing views. Views of race, gender, and religion have undergone major changes in the United States. In that span, James Flynn reminds us that Western people have incorporated science into their minds. The immense scientific progress of the twentieth century caused no great public reaction, but corrected misconceptions and extended awe and wonder deeper in new directions. This "represents nothing less than a liberation of the human mind."[355] We have pressed the boundaries of our minds, and in review the changes appear startling. Neglecting this heritage exposes us to repeat the old mistaken patterns again.

Perhaps the most important observation we can make today is our kinship with the primitive origins of much of our culture. Such primitive cultures as Allende poignantly describes demonstrate our widening, deepening perceptions. We can feel them, a bit removed (we often and wrongly say "objectively" but we mean "viscerally"), without adopting them. They confirm us as whole human beings. As we come face to face with our own origins, however, we can feel a reticence to change, but still must expect them to reshape a new culture among us. They will stimulate among us new ideas as well as ideas we recover in their pristine sense through adroit reinterpretation. But ideas there will be. And it is our privilege to work them through our consciousness into our new culture.

A. THE MAJOR CHANGE OF THE COMMON ERA

Two major strains of development of the ancient world came together in the formation of Europe. This new culture was produced by the confluence of Jewish and Greek cultures. Both of these two remnants of the ancient world left us treasures beyond measure. They were dead as sovereign entities at the time when Rome itself began to crumble. This last of the classic empires proved conclusively with both brilliant and demonic leaders that the existing patterns of governing large populations were no longer viable. The prevailing view of humanity in the Mediterranean world was demeaning. Though the mind of the people was breaking out of its severe oppression, aristocracy was well established, perennially gaining new supporters by the ancient methods of beguilement, deceit, and small reward. The aristocrat parceled out food, water, or some other necessary commodity to peons as a service to his superior. It was a corrupt bureaucratic system modeled on the privileges of the oligarchs that spread in the necessary hierarchy as an easy way to control people by an insidious gratuity. But the oppressive controls proved itself less and less viable. At the same time these two cultures of the ancient world grew together in Europe enabling human intelligence evident in them to flourish.

The Jews had maintained for over a thousand years that they had escaped slavery and had a special relationship to God. This freedom was a gift to Europeans experiencing the failure of Roman rule.[356] The Jewish flirtation with monarchy had been as abortive as was Europe's similar flirtation over the next two thousand years. They continued their adoration of David in spite of failure, just as other ordinary people have grown accustomed to leadership and reveled in the status quo. But there is a difference. The Jew's view of humanity (their "anthropology" in this text) rejected the view of aristocrats inclined to think themselves superior. Jews rejected the demeaning view of people endemic in the Mediterranean culture, in which both Greek and Roman cultures indulged, supporting slavery. Adaptable human beings everywhere had succumbed to maltreatment but continued evolving, gradually learning in larger and larger numbers to express their own strengths and talents productively in the available economy – a version of the patronage system in its transition to mercantilism. The confluence of the Greek and Jewish cultures provided the conceptual context in which the early Europeans of the common era increasingly recognized themselves and claimed their human identity.

Many persons outside the Jewish faith (the "pagans" of eastern Europe, essentially in Turkey and Greece) where Paul and others did their initial work, adopted Paul's views and left previous religious notions behind them. We understand that their world was a depressing one, a world in which oppression left most people in misery. These downtrodden people recognized their condition with growing obstinance but were coerced by that culture into subservience while chaffing at the way things were. Often early Christians were people who had risen in the pecking order to be patrons of at least a few others and who, therefore, tasted a little bit of freedom. In their early-Christian humility, their sense of freedom became an attraction to others. At first, these were not members of the aristocratic class. Perhaps this small change in personal identity was critical preparation for a major change in their religious orientation. There was at any rate an awakening of people increasingly to resist slavery. But they carried with them the coercive methods of interpersonal relations developed to finese in that ancient world. More primitive and accommodating methods of disagreement had long been submerged beneath violence. Gradually, this culture would decline as freedom assumed a new shape.

So also, one may see the extraordinary contribution of the Greek philosophers as prelude to Paul's brilliant synthesis and the emergence of Christianity as a world religion. Plato saw beyond the prevailing religions of Greece but only far enough to provide a rational base for thinking about humanity and the world that was adaptable to further interpretation.[357] Like most educated men of the time, Paul was familiar with the Greek world, but uniquely saw through their views and his own heritage to a pregnant and teachable synthesis. His message of hope with a just God in charge of the world was a welcome antidote in that cynical world. It was a synthesis of centuries of experience in both of the two contributing cultures – a new idea reinterpreting their situation.

In a parallel way, the English experience with "lives of Jesus" had been preceded by almost four centuries of reading and talking about the Christian scripture. The English biblical scholars who recognized a lethargic public attitude toward religion were familiar with the emergent view of history. In the nineteenth century they began to introduce new views of the New Testament. But different from their German counterparts who caused an uproar on the continent, they chose to prepare the people for the huge change occurring in critical scholarship. Hume, Rousseau, Kant, Kierkegaard and many others contributed to this change. The writing of the "Lives" was not only a tactical choice to advance the general appreciation of modern historical scholarship, but an evidence of the new mind of humanity. English scholars' liberal humanism recognized the common obligation of humans to help one another adjust to our increasingly sophisticated world. It was evidence of the correctness of the impulse we call "egalitarian." Acknowledging that every human being is different provides a basis for our accommodation of differences and enables us to help one another move on.

The modern experience with the "lives of Jesus" in Europe remnds us of the deep roots of most of what goes on in our world. The new historical consciousness emerging among scholars in the eighteenth century was exciting and gave ammunition to those who were skeptical of a variety of religious beliefs. But their awareness of differences between the various New Testament documents was documented long before. The *Diatessaron* of the second century was probably the first parallel version of the gospels. A few others followed many centuries later. Then in the eighteenth century Hermann Reimarus (1694-1768), a German scholar of Hebrew and Oriental languages, a prolific author, wrote "The Intention of Jesus and His Disciples" (published posthumously). As Albert Schweitzer noted, Reimarus began the critical quest for the historical Jesus.

In the nineteenth century, another German, F. C. Bauer (1792-1860) established the Tubingen School noted for its view of Christian history. Bauer heightened interest among scholars. Another Bauer (no relation), Walter Bauer (1877-1960), published *Orthodoxy and Heresy in Earliest Christianity* (1934), arguing that early Christianity consisted of a variety of competing minorities and divergent forms distributed widely across the Roman Empire. Bauer saw the early Church as the scene of power struggles, not just differences of belief. But Walter Bauer's book was not translated into English until 1971. Since then, scholars have considered his analysis and conclusions overdrawn. They have responded with further analyses which make interpretation more problematic.

Walter Bauer's book was published in English two centuries after Reimarus' ground-breaking work. In the intervening time, there was a lot of give and take among scholars. Pals' analysis suggests that the Germans were less inclined to consider the impact of their work on the public than were the English. This contrast seems to fit the pattern of humanist anthropology which was taken seriously by the Scots (Locke, Hutcheson, Reid, Hume and many others). It was transmitted through the Scot culture and emerged in a vibrant Britain. There the habits of mind of people at all levels from scholar to plebeian had created a conversational culture which demonstrated care of others. It was a step toward the accommodating culture now emerging in America.

This is different from the scholarly debate which had become the pattern on the Continent. These two patterns of give and take over two or three centuries by scholars in Germany and England was a proof of the effectiveness of dialogue in developing our culture. The British habit demonstrates, not the aristocratic notion of elite scholars transmitting their great learning to less privileged people, but rather a fundamental process of democratization, a dialogical process which respects the way things develop with participation of every person regardless of his or her credentials in academia. In a culture in which the modern characteristics of openness and sharing predominate, the progress toward a balanced view need not take two centuries.

Though there still are huge numbers of people who do not begin to comprehend the new world rapidly emerging in our culture, they are not to be forgotten in the enthusiasm of discovery and advance in understanding. Instead of plunging ahead in speaking the most advanced criticisms of our culture, those blessed with insights are obligated by their humanity to seek sympathetic steps into the future which are *conceivable in the public mind* and will contribute to the people's grasp of current changes. People not among such elites thus are to be included and invited to participate in the reformation of the common culture. We humans are naturally part of our societies. We are our brothers' and sisters' helpers who know, conclusively, the vast range of our fellow humans' minds. Our complex, multi-layered culture lends itself well to such thoughtful dissemination of ideas. We are increasingly able to utilize a variety of electronic aids to communicate. It is not that advanced theories and information should be withheld from anyone; but we must accept responsibility for communicating sensitively and thoughtfully in popular pieces. There are places and channels for academic credits but those who receive them must not think of themselves as too busy exercising their skills to avoid their responsibility to share generously and helpfully.

B. THE IDEA TRAP

When the Scots grasped the humanitarian reinterpretation of orthodox Christianity, instituted schools, taught reading, and held up words as the connection with the roots of their faith, they were still bathed in the light of Plato's elevation of ideas to supremacy. Among the Scots, the ideas of their faith were reconstituted; they became practice. They destroyed what they could of Roman Catholic vintage, and required strict conformity of behavior. It would be another two hundred years before the idea trap was laid bare.

On Heidegger's eightieth birthday, Hannah Arendt (one of his ardent admirers and critics) spoke of him as having been a great thinker. Following Plato, Heidegger identified meditative thinking with the potential to lead toward understanding of existence. It is a step beyond the calculations of everyday life that persistently determine the safest path to assure primitive survival. The world is the focus of meditative thought. It is basically experiential but it seeks truth beneath the world of appearances. Nonetheless, Heidegger taught that "Plato had turned away from awe-filled contemplation of the actual existence of things toward an abstract metaphysics of ideas and ideal types, which are at best indirect, derivative, and secondary manifestations of being."[358]

Plato and before him Socrates (and Aristotle after him) had left the initial impetus of the birth of philosophy in Thales and other pre-Socratics. These had sought to understand through perception, reason, and intuition without recourse to mysticism or theology. They worked within the ancient oral tradition, close to everyday life, close to gutsy reality. The birth of Europe occurred with the explosion of written materials. Plato brought a new richness to written philosophy, and his writing proved itself a durable vehicle of ideas. Plato's approach led Western thinking into abstraction. His pre-Christian belief in eternal ideal types and the unity of the universe made him especially attractive to Augustine as he sought an intellectual basis for Christianity. Words had become more powerful than ever and have remained so. The power of abstraction, it seems, soon lost touch with everyday reality. And Heidegger and others, understanding the importance of words as they embody experience found the abstraction increasingly unacceptable. He lies closer to the pre-Socratics, a matter of feeling and mood more than to abstraction.

It is interesting that Aristotle's attention to empiricism which created the Enlightenment returned the development of critical thought to experience, feeling, everyday reality. But the excursion into abstraction introduced by the later Greek philosophers had demonstrated the growing capacity of human beings to think outside the primitive box necessary for survival and reproduction, the common sense of our most ancient predecessors. The combination catapulted medicine out of that early empiricism (epitomized in phrenology) into the work of William Harvey, Edward Jenner, and John Hunter.

But Plato's influence is evident in the blossoming of abstract philosophy in the seventeenth and eighteenth centuries. As the glow began to fade from the Enlightenment at the end of the nineteenth century, William James recognized two types of reasoning, association and true reasoning. A century later Daniel Kahneman of Princeton redefined these and in true scientific fashion giving them the names "System 1" and "System 2." The first is the sort of thinking that prevailed for most of our past. Our most primitive ancestors probably began comparing their successes in food gathering and learned quickly to compare habits of their prey. But gradually, beginning before we can know, in small increments, critical and deliberate thinking increasingly enabled humans to adapt to new circumstances. Stephen Baker tells us,

> When it came to intelligence, all humans were more or less on an equal footing in the ancient and intuitive System 1. The rules were easy, and whether they made sense or not, everyone knew them. It was in the slower realm of reasoning, System 2, that intelligent people distinguished themselves from the crowd.[359]

The nature of analytical thinking began to clear. Abstraction and generalization emerged out of simple comparisons. Deduction among the Greeks and induction in the Enlightenment found roles in thought. Quite unconsciously, words took on meanings with only tangential relationships to concrete reality and allusions blossomed. Late in the ancient period constructed ideas became mental realities and people ascribed to them the same magical power that words had taken on – only moreso. The development of ideas in the Common Era was mind-bending, baffling, confusing. Late in the nineteenth century thinkers began a struggle to free themselves from the resulting morass.

Hannah Arendt was enthralled with Heidegger whose preoccupation as professor was to get students to think. But Heidegger had stretched his biases for Germany and for the earthy reality of the pre-Socratics to connect the two, and, some have thought, opportunistically began drifting toward the early Nazi supporters. He was a flawed character, persistently deceitful. "He was an anti-Communist, liked good order, and was drawn to German 'ways of being,' often thought to contain a degree of authoritarianism."[360] By 1933 he fell into disfavor with the Nazis while still thinking of himself as a National Socialist. Remembering that Heidegger was then alienated from the Nazis and had never been part of the killing machine, Arendt, a Jew, loved his mind and his magnetism more than his character and forgave him the flaws.

Heidegger's support of the pre-Socratic appreciation of human capability fit the emergence of phenomenology and he published his famous "Letter on Humanism." Arendt believed he had turned against the "self-assertion of man" which had dominated his talk as Nazi *Rektor* of Freiburg University. His critique of Platonic ideas stood. He began emphasizing Being itself rather than the being of man. Existence. He has been paired with Karl Jaspers at the origins of existentialism.

When the prolonged development of the human capacity to think clearly became evident in the late twentieth century, we could begin to understand the archaic tendency of Enlightenment people like the two unrelated Bauers. In the nineteenth century the battle for truth often still involved demonizing opponents. Scholars felt it incumbent on them to speak out of their "authority" what they thought their roles required of them. (Heidegger surely carried that chip on his shoulder.) We remember that "authority" had a respectable, even honored place in Western culture and accrued to academics for centuries. Now we can look back fifty or one hundred years and recognize the biases many of them shared that led to misunderstandings and misconstructions. Like many other bright human beings, the Bauers both were inclined to think that the long-standing, dominant Christian orthodoxy rooted in the ancient and Medieval worlds was proved wrong in their new, enlightened world. Their ideas of "right" were heavily weighted by the dominant role they gave to human reason. Humans, they thought, were capable of understanding the world definitively. Rationality was the modern savior.

The intellectual revolution we have tried to trace through the twentieth century now challenges such modern preconceptions of certainty. One of the most noteworthy of our recently tested ideas was the assumption that an objective view can be achieved by human beings. It was related to the long history of knowledge. Beginning with the Greek philosophers the attractiveness of our mental processes and their products entrapped intelligent people. Mathematics was especially beguiling, with its characteristic of internal consistency and presumed universality. That view was, however, a cultural misconception conclusively proven in the twentieth century. Even mathematics requires its own unprovable assumptions. Morris Kline was quoted in 1981 saying, "In the end, we just don't know why mathematics works as well as it does. We're faced with a mystery."[361]

For at least a century objectivity has been under attack, especially with the contributions of Jaspers, as psychology developed. It seems a little strange, now, that even with the nineteenth century revolution in understanding history, intellectuals assumed that their newer views were valid, objective criticisms of the past. Secure in their insights which seemed to disprove the old presuppositions, they faulted earlier views. But those who took them to heart ultimately were like the rest of us, human, quite incapable of "objectivity." The Bauers and many others joined the rationalistic frenzy without grasping that they were influenced by their own cultural presuppositions. In the case of the nineteenth century, the proud rationalism developing on the European continent was very much in evidence everywhere. Until psychologists set the record straight, the universal role of emotion and the ubiquity of unexamined presuppositions were easily ignored. We have already noted the decisive blows dealt to rationality in the field of mathematics. Godel delivered the final blow in the 1930s. That was in a sense the last gasp of the long intellectual "trip" pride took throughout academia and the scientific community. Still it continues. In fact it will be some time before the cultural damage from pride gradually diminishes and younger scholars will no longer have older falsely proud models to pervert the humility of their common sense.

It is likely that of many mistaken paths taken by human beings over the millennia, the age-old pride in personal insight, invention, and accomplishment will prove to be the most persistent. Ideas are the priceless possession of the mind, evidence of our creativity. Hanging onto them has been considered a personal right for a very long time. It is when pride has detrimental effects on our common culture that we need to rein it in. Like hanging onto the idea of masculine superiority; the time comes among human beings when women invoke their right to an equal place in the sun; democracy, we who enjoy it suppose, cannot be far behind. But democracy is not a static idea; it is not the ultimate, the final, the good in itself. When democracy happens, history demonstrates that in the modern world the whole culture moves in the direction of egalitarianism and kindness. Women's participation in politics enhances democracy and will transform it. Democracy is the common name for a form of society which allows personal freedom to develop the self, to follow personal intuition, to express oneself, to participate in political discussion and action. But it was not built out of air (or fire or water, to enjoy the innocence of ancient philosophers). Democratic societies recognize the need for some constraints, for example, on inciting to riot (yelling "fire" in a crowded auditorium) and treason. Freedom we have painfully learned requires responsibility. Responsibility requires insight and discretion. And sometimes it is necessary for the good of all involved to invoke constraints on our vaunted freedom. Freedom is also not a static idea and certainly not an individual right. It is our practice of our cultural story.

C. THE SCHOOL FOR DISCERNMENT

Again, the influence of the Jewish experience on our cultural development seems clear. The Holiness Code, long considered a prime implementation of the Jewish concern for being faithful as God's own people, was a peculiarly Jewish version of a deep religious impetus toward divinity. The pre-historic people who conceived of divinity were subconsciously convinced that they and their world were subject to some superior power. They could not exist without some sort of supra-human agency – a being at least as intelligent as themselves, but more powerful – able to shape mountains and command winds. Whenever a person encountered an event with extraordinary consequences, the place would be named something meaning "sacred." We have demeaned this sense of the presence of God in representing moral and spiritual qualities with the notion of sacredness. But "sacred" is more than cultural values. The word is the best translation of the frequent Old Testament word (in Hebrew *Kadash*) and denotes a relationship to God. To grasp the difference is a matter of discernment. We have sophisticated guidance for living in persistent discernment. The Holiness Code was a construction to that end. It appears that America has become a great school for discernment. It is fudamental to democracy.

In the Jewish conception of God, holiness would embody what the Greeks conceptualized as "perfection." Holiness meant seeking purity, being uncontaminated with whatever was considered "impure." Again, our ancestors discovered very early the dangers latent In human waste. The transmission of illness was surely grasped early to segregate human elimination. Ancient cities have been uncovered which had both fresh water and waste disposal systems. The imperial destruction of conquered cities undoubtedly lost many such inventions and in Medieval times people had to learn again how to manage waste in large populations. Surely the widespread practice of immersing oneself in the river was originally a matter of cleansing the body. Purity is deeply embedded in our psyche. "Unclean" apparently included infestation by "leprosy" and later by an evil or diseased spirit (the ephemeral thing easily blamed for derangement).[362] The biblical stories of curing lepers of their illness by immersion fit this pattern.

Certainly there must be a connection to our concepts of right and wrong, to vigorous and unhealthy. No doubt the dichotomy fit ancient times. Oligarchy in all its manifestations led the way to dichotomize social conditions beginning with social class. From jesters to kings, lower and higher, the expanse of persons included all parts of the spectrum of humanity, including the demented and the crippled. Yet aristocracy became the highest aspiration of many people and was dismissive of the others lower in the hierarchies. In all its forms, oligarchy tends to encourage seeking private advantage, holding close such knowledge as one discovers, listening closely only to those above in the hierarchy. Such habits work against creativity. They slow cultural development, and they contribute to divisiveness, to conflict, and to degradation of the culture. Politically reactionary people sometimes hold such views. The libertine often appears to be such a conservative, but in reality is little more than selfish, often just proud of holding an idea.

The conservative mind is an important part of the culture but is as easily perverted as any other. The same mind which worked to sustain the oligarchic orientation still appears as admiration of pseudo-aristocracies of similar people. These bureaucratic groups have served within the memory of such conservatives and thus are part of the status quo they tend to favor. This is apparent in the present climate in America; the aristocratic mind can think nothing but derogatory things of those others whom he or she calls "liberals." This is not to say voices from the far left may not be equally obtuse. In either case, misuse of language contributes to corruption of cultural meanings. But the real problem is in people's failure to discriminate. The truly thoughtful person thinks carefully, weighs things meticulously, and participates to aid the developing culture.

We are at the point in Western culture when that self-discipline is becoming critical. Currently, many people are trapped by *laissez faire* capitalism, or by equal self-righteousness, the libertarian persuasion. But these mistaken frames of mind often substitute poorly conceived, ahistorial economic ideas for thoughtful critiques. (This too is "impurity" in an antique language). Such a mind is in need of the challenge that conversation could supply, carried on among unlike people. It demonstrates a need for the critical mind with a strong component of listening ability. We generally term the discriminating mind one of critical thoughtfulness.

Over the past 5000 years we have gradually been learning how to think critically. Without an important self-consciousness of this necessity, we have too often been subject to the persuasion of those we call demagogues. Such leaders may use rhetoric well. They can be very persuasive. "Demagogue" has historically meant something like "agitator" and is usually looked upon as such by those they fail to persuade. We remember that persuasion was probably the earliest form of political talk.[363] A prehistoric hunter or the early chief persuaded his comrades to his tactics. In the historic period persuasion became the first skill we might call academic and it remained preeminent reaching to both Augustine and Calvin (a thousand years apart). Rhetoric is so basic to our sociality that we know that we will never be free of need for the arts of persuasion. They are as important today as they ever were. The demagogue might be seen as a contributor to the culture even if he or she attacks it. Raising questions, even unpopular obtuse questions, can contribute to dialogue. Polarities often clarify discussion if they are not used to stifle it. All of these are aspects of critical thinking. The result, unfortunately, is not always constructive. We are after all human beings engaging the complexity of society.

Unfortunately, demagoguery has too often taken the perverse path of the "false prophet." In democracy the antidote is the critical thinking of people who might be persuaded. When people recognize the anti-social character of such demagogues, they leave their company. It is an evidence of human common sense. It is the futile wish of many demagogues to stifle such common sense. But the experience of the Moral Majority in the 1980s in stimulating emergence of the voice of silent conservatives should serve as a warning to them. The paths of false prophets lead to disgrace. Common sense has often triumphed over their error.

Unfortunately, people often embrace such perversion; lacking discrimination, they are mislead and jump on board mistaken vehicles. Nonetheless, the stimulation of dialogue contributes to the thinking of the people who are not trapped by popular errors. Popular opinion imposes a powerful personal conflict which must be overcome by self-discipline. The instinct to learn from others, the base of mimicry, remains strong throughout life.

Unfortunately, the human cost can be great to those who stand against negative demagoguery. Claude Williams battled a desperately reactionary stance in the 1940s and 1950s and suffered for it. He was called to be industrial chaplain in the Presbyterian Church in Detroit where race riots soon erupted (1943). Soon he faced the inflammatory rhetoric of Gerald L. K. Smith, a fundamentalist demagogue who managed to get Williams into the files of the Un-American Activities Committee and he was unfrocked by the presbytery for heresy.[364] Fortunately, the people belatedly gathered their wits against that era of hate mongering. Its decline began with the end of McCarthyism. Common sense has corrected many proud and mistaken intellectual positions over the centuries. It is again becoming apparent at the beginning of the twenty-first century.

The problem of political dialogue is the ancient one of speaking the truth in pursuit of political objectives, not of persuading the public to embrace a false agreement. However we may have mastered the art of persuasion, we are required by our humanity to exercise our skills unselfishly. Unfortunately, truth does not lend itself to easy definition, and the narrow-minded demagogue will never cease considering his rants to be honest and truthful, however false they may prove to be in open dialogue (which in our culture usually includes scientific evidence). The Jewish prophets admonished the people to discern the false prophet and to follow the true prophet. This is still the rule. We the people must grasp our responsibility to discern truth.

The capability of discernment is in the individual person. If you are inclined to follow the guidance of a speaker, you must decide what is true and what is false. You will be aware of whether the presentation supports common sense or not, and whether it is good or bad. To this task each of us brings what we call "discernment." The brilliant

Roman Catholic philosopher Bernard Lonergan calls this "judgment." He notes that Descartes thought that "as a general rule, things which we conceive very clearly and distinctly are all true." Unfortunately demagogues often seem to produce clarity where we see only muddle. This calls on us to seek insight into our muddle, not simply to agree with what seems apparent, then to make a judgment discerning what seems to us true. Lonergan tells us that insight is based on information, "a number in arithmetic, a correlation of measurements in physics, or the name of a 'unity-identity-whole' in common sense."[365] He adds that insight is also regularly followed by reflection; it is less than the whole of knowing. We ask ourselves, "Is it so? Is that true? Are you sure?" This is our opportunity for discernment. At this moment we stop and think. In science the insight is understood as an hypothesis and is regularly followed by experiment. The urgency always invoked by demagogues deters such reflection.

But common sense has no explicit method as do the sciences and it is not strange to feel at a loss in seeking insight . For Lonergan, the method of common sense is to withhold judgment "until all the evidence is in." In summarizing him, Terry Tekippe says, "Common sense as well, then, knows that insight is hypothetical, grasping a possible relation or pattern." But, he adds, insight must be checked out. A reasonable method would be habitually check up on our common sense through conversation with diverse people. To converse only with those who share our orientations is only to ask for reinforcement (and we all need some of that). To engage in dialogue with people with limited understanding of our concern is to share generously or, perchance, to reinforce ignorance. Such interchange is not very helpful, but may help to "keep us grounded." Rather, we are obligated to discuss important views with informed people who differ from us. Here we maintain that this capability recently has been evolving noticeably. So, many of us now have the capacity to listen attentively to views with which we may not agree. With care in considering such views, we can learn new insights, adjust our own, and come closer than we were to truth. What we must recover is the predisposition to reflect. We must relearn how to engage ourselves with our minds. Disciplined reflection must become a habit of mind. We must again, as in less frantic times, incorporate reflection in our self-understanding.

In the twenty-first century we will do well to work into our lives more reflection than our culture allowed in the recent past. The frenetic pace of modern life reduced the time any of us spent in ruminating. I felt forced in my own professional life constantly to run fast, to work long hours into the night, to subsist on absolute minimal sleep. All of these work against reflection. Recently, science has corroborated the ancient wisdom of thoughtful reflection. Lack of sleep is detrimental. Frenetic rushing to and fro, double-timing, and misuse of leisure have interfered with fully functioning brains. We have often thought that we were fulfilling our "multi-tasking" capability when we were essentially working within very narrow constraints of our talent. Perhaps one day we will find that this experience has enhanced our capacity for complex thought, but it has also seriously undercut the depth of our grasp of our calling to function intelligently here and now.

Here is another opportunity for us to recognize the most recent work of neuroscientists. Sharon Begley recently called to our attention the work done by Marcus Raichle of Washington University, Alvaro Pascual-Leone and Randy Buckner (both of

Harvard). These researchers think that mental "idle-time" long considered resting by scientists, is actually time spent by the brain in reworking the neural connections and building new neurons to replace old ones. Begley says, "This default activity is no mere murmur in the background of a loud symphony. It is the symphony, consuming 20 times as much energy as the conscious life of the mind...." Begley compared the discovery to the mystery of "dark matter" making up the greater share of matter in the universe. By reflecting, we tap into this neural gold mine to enhance our memory, imagining, and appreciation of others' perspectives. And, most probably, engaging in reflection helps to reshape our memory and thus our self in what we call "cogitation."[366]

About the same time, Amy Goodman wrote of the U. S. Social Forum in Detroit, Michigan, when over ten thousand people gathered to advance a progressive agenda. This event exceeded the size of conservative Tea Party gatherings of the time but hardly received attention, probably because it did not feature demagoguery (using the term for spectacular oratory). Rather it reflected the broadly appreciated style of Martin Luther King who had (two months before his fabled speech at the Washington Monument) delivered the first "I have a dream" speech in Detroit on June 23, 1963. The quiet of this gathering of the Forum belied its future. The people who gathered were the totally diverse group who make up the new world. They were celebrating, but not noisy. They laughed, and ate, and talked. They were engaging their own and others' expectations in exploring and reflecting the realities of our world. New progressive alliances were made, and the next World Forum is the more promising for this fulfillment of the dreams of the first American Forum in Atlanta in 2007. The *Tikkun* reporter said,

> If we focus on appreciating what we agree with, and creating the communities of joy and caring that people want to join, we turn the tables around. We have to focus on empathy (even with enemies!), healing, vision, and building caring communities. (This) is an analytical approach and set of practices, with their attendant language frame. That is pioneered most fully by the spiritual progressives.[367]

Late in the twentieth century the media which harbors both truth and falsehood left behind a definition of news that focused almost exclusively on trouble and catastrophe. Some of our media have sought the same popularity on which false prophets thrive. They encouraged the least scrupulous, the wildest sort of demagoguery. Eventually some media discovered what people know in their guts, that many of us seek to know what good occurs in our world or at least to see it acknowledged by way of illustration. We believe that such behaviors are hopeful – and people have a deep need for hope. "Human Interest" stories are now sprinkled among the horror tales. They will not go unnoticed by a discerning mind.

This is a part of modern culture which to a degree replaces the ancient market place chatter that emphasized the bizarre and was the chief form of information for people through the Middle Ages. In highlighting the negative, the evil and the bizarre, the media supposed they were satisfying "what the public wanted." We call it pandering. What the public wanted, as much as such stimulation, was encouragement (and information) to discern true and false. The common pandering of media was vocal demogoguery and its translation into the more modern vehicle of print. This surely highlights the problem of populism. We have noted the fear of some of our nation's founders that the public would be led unwisely by demagogues. They were hesitant to trust the democratic process. America proves that people are inclined to exercise sound common sense, given the opportunity, and it will triumph over wrong -- though sometimes our patience as well as our vigilance are sorely tested !

Unfortunately, there is no way to predict discernment. It is private, presumably best reflected in the secret ballot. The individuality of discernment defies prediction. Recently, the tennis star Andre Agassi published a book in which he claims to be honest about himself. Presumably he proved this by admitting to use of a drug called crystal meth. But the better proof is that Agassi understands that speaking is often a self-exploration, a discovery process. He admits that at various times what he said publicly was motivated by fear. His fear late in life was different from his fear early in life. In this he was more like our primitive ancestors than most of us would like to admit. For them fear was a major component of survival. But the point here is that discernment begins with this sort of admission. When we are willing to admit our own short-comings, we may be better able to see the good around us. We must leave self-righteousness behind.

The sin of self-righteousness is probably the world's greatest problem. Primitive humans no doubt acted on their own perceptions of their situation. It was necessary for their survival. But we are socialized human beings, not divinities, a fact of life willingly ignored by religions which make our god-likeness into a construct of self. The Jews assiduously avoided this pitfall. The conviction that they were chosen by God to be his people was a strong support for humility. [368] Here we argue that our minds are evolving in capability to put aside the fictions we easily and almost instinctively construct. Psychologists tell us that everyone has lied and stolen sometime. We are all familiar with Agassi's problem. It is truly remarkable that we can see ourselves emerging from self-centeredness in spite of ourselves! We are blessed with powerful mental capabilities. Perhaps the reflection required to write his biography was an indicator of the high value of such self-discipline.

In this new mind we no longer feel compelled to defend previous lies that are a long-way behind us. But we are inclined, still, to pile lie on lie in the near term. Increasingly, we are learning to be honest with ourselves and to admit we make mistakes. But this still does not reveal truth to us unless it is the truth that we are as the Psalmist said, "less than God" which is not a bad place to start. It helps to develop our minds so that lies are no longer natural.

Americans are ready for a new beginning in construction of a new culture for this new century. In a recent poll a majority said it is important for them to be involved with their community. In this recent poll, ninety percent of Americans said that community is at least "very important." [369] Electronic gadgetry seems to be fraying the depth of human relationships; long letters between friends and family members have disappeared. But I believe the instinctual social nature of human beings will counter our fears and reconstruct our new culture around responding to one another more often and more deeply. It is part of *responsibility* to engage in the art of social response. The new mind will not be so hesitant as we have been to share concerns and thinking. And our sharing will respond to kindred spirits in distant places who know only other languages, since technology can translate most common language into almost any written language in the world. We know with a modern certainty that community is more than family, more than language, more than national identity. Community is the family of humankind. As we again find our conversational voices freed from past constraints, we will construct a new culture in which honesty and trust dominate, and lying and deceit are dethroned.

All of this reminds us of the complex nature of our egalitarian democracy. We are aware of the need for organization and a controlled hierarchy of authority (including a national military force controlled by civilians and oriented to peace). We must make allowance for a huge variety of people. This means not only people with impaired capabilities but people who have chosen anti-social paths. Perverted "mass killers" erupt periodically even in a free country where we presume everyone may make a creative contribution. The ancient terms "pure" and "impure" seem to us useless outside religious ritual. Nonetheless, the variety they have always implied is a clear reality; it is not a dichotomy. The time is past when neighbors often disparaged others because they seemed to be somehow less than themselves. Gradually, over thousands of years, we have learned to respect one another, to put aside residual animosities and revenge, and to value both what we can learn from others and their very humanity. Our human variety seems to increase and in it we must rejoice. And while we rejoice, we must learn to differentiate truth and falsehood, especially in the tongues of those who seek to influence us.

D. THE PATH AHEAD

Our prime twenty-first century role in Western culture is threefold: First, to adopt the cultural habit of seeking truth and admitting error: *humility.* The second is to cope with the common task of adequate social control of some resurgent primitive instincts: It might be labeled *sophistication.* And the third role is to open our minds to the inevitable variety of human beings and their varied interpretations and understandings: *openness.* Opening our minds has become a preoccupation recently, so much so as to reawaken Lamarkian ideas of evolution, to add layers of scientific reality in particle physics, and to challenge the old orthodox religion with fresh vigor in post-modern modes.

Our long preoccupation with accumulation of knowledge has resulted in almost complete control over our environment. It began, probably, with irrigation, diverting streams and damming holding ponds for spring overflow. Now we need to divert our attention from this frenetic effort to learn, to overcome the unknown. With hunger among us still, it must be conceded that we *know* enough to feed everyone; the frontier is no longer the mastery of nature, but mastery of our focus on the things of human life that have finally come to a primary place on our agenda: hunger, health care, education, yes, and ecology, peace and justice.[370] This is not to suggest that we stop learning about anything. There is a sense in which we cannot know enough. But past preoccupation with pushing the frontiers of knowledge may now give way to a more measured pursuit. Our knowledge provides the opportunity to choose wisely how to apply ourselves to things of life.

I say this with a certain winsomeness. The evidence is that human energy and acumen do not exhaust human time and energy. A few exceptions here and there prodigious people make my point. All people have time and energy for play, for education, for entertainment, for frivolity, for decoration and celebration. Most of us need to prod ourselves to be intelligent about our lives. We need urging and encouragement to stretch ourselves to contribute to our societies all we are able to do. It does not matter whether that is in athletics, scientific pursuit, leadership, invention, crafts, music, entrepreneurship, human services, visiting the sick and the prisoner, or any other pursuit; all of them impact our culture. Our great human diversity facilitates our application to an almost infinite range of contributions and pleasures. Perhaps exceptions would be the driven people who follow paths of self-gratification. Theirs becomes the unhappy condition of satiation; but they cannot be satisfied; it is a failure in self-development. Multiply this equation by the billions of us on the face of the earth and it quickly becomes evident that we can discipline ourselves better. We have the available intelligence, care, spirit, and muscle needed to control our drives and to extend the benefits of our knowledge to all (or most) people. What is not clear is how we may gather our wits about us and encourage one another toward that goal and govern society to that end.

Having highlighted our creativity, the world of perception opens before us. Having been beguiled by ideas, we have discovered that ideas are wonderful and cheap. The human mind is more fecund than the womb – and look how we have over-populated the earth! When we have an idea that strikes us as especially bright, it is hard to not see it with a real sense of ownership. The attractiveness of an idea is no less beguiling than the invention of a mathematical formula, the composition of music or the authorship of a book. It occurs in the same world in its fundamental components as that in which our primitive ancestors tested their growing capabilities and learned to be social in ever larger contexts. But there is a difference: We have an immensely larger world of ideas and experiences to deal with. As we rapidly expanded our perception and control over matter, pride in our rationality grew out of proportion to reality.

Ancient sensitivity to humility may have been stimulated more often by lack of knowledge than it is today. Humility it appears was finally lost in the euphoric and often proud Enlightenment. Since then, the expansion of the human mind has seemed to signal the end of all limits; given time, all things will bend to the human intellect. That assumption has proved itself unworkable, to say the least. Was it necessary to the development of the mind? It was pushed to the extreme in the eighteenth and nineteenth centuries, for which the ground was laid, at least as far back as the Greeks. It seems that the rewarding climb out of antiquity made pride inevitable. It must be noted that Christianity was always skeptical of the assumptions of such ascendancy. The Jewish insistence on the creaturehood of humankind provided roots for humility in Europe, but it was easily neglected. The creativity loosed in European development overshadowed them. Humility must be a significant component of our embrace of the future.

We have noted previously that the Celts in Europe escaped the long enslavement experienced in the Mediterranean world. That does not mean that they escaped the scourge of oligarchy, only that the extremity of long oppression did not pervert their

355
555

psyche as it did among their southern cousins. Their journey into history apparently followed a more natural development of leaders with a continuity that concentration of power did not vitiate for so long as in the Mediterranean world and therefor did not so oppress the people. The more primitive approach these northern ancestors maintained was never lost so completely, we surmise.[371] The Romans expanded into the north very early along the Atlantic coastline, reaching England in the fir was called to be industrial chaplain in the Presbyterian Church in Detroit where race riots soon erupted (1943). Soon he faced the inflammatory rhetoric of Gerald L. K. Smith, a fundamentalist demagogue who managed to get Williams into the files of the Un-American Activities Committee and he was unfrocked by the presbytery for heresy. But hest century CE. There they encountered the Celts much earlier than on the Continent. But on the continent the push north came at great price, and Rome eventually lost to these northern tribes.

While the Romans were debating their ideas in the Senate, these tribes were living in the more primitive, less sophisticated world of what we have long called "common sense." While Europe was transfixed by adulation of their Greek predecessors, the Celts were still engrossed in their myths of heroic individuals, still primitive spirituality. But the evangelical drive of the early Christians converted them to Christianity and they soon became productive members of the Roman empire: The Gauls (France) and the Franks (Germany). The Gauls capitulated early, beginning with Julius Caesar (first century BCE), but the Franks retained their independence until the middle of the first millennium CE. "Common sense" survived quite well in the ancient world, but as Europe began its gradual conversion toward modernity in the late Middle Ages, the surviving common sense was submerged in the strong currents of rationality.

The Franks, a proud combination of Celtic individualism and the emerging rationality, became the most fiercely rationalistic of all. If this trend began with the Greeks, one must also say that the evolution of humanity made it both possible and necessary that eventually, after a thousand years, the Germans became the masters of Western rationality, turning common sense out almost completely from its natural place in use of the mind.[372] Of course common sense was still operable among the people. Elite Germans could not entirely squelch it. There were always those who maintained their common sense in the face of cultural challenges. Culture does not enslave us; it only establishes the major directions and patterns of the life of a people.

The persistent mental activity we have labeled "common sense" is a natural outgrowth of the primitive, innate mental activity of comparing one thing with another and organizing our impressions in a way with which we feel comfortable – one rock outcropping Is not exactly like another, and there is a way to the top by which one could escape a ravenous predator. The hunter-gatherers accumulated their knowledge of the terrain near their abodes and organized it so as to satisfy the hunger and safety requirements of survival. Their communities consisted of a relatively few human beings and that turf. Our detailing of their activities and the opportunities to think begins to uncover the amazing adaptability of the early human being. "Common" among us moderns has come to mean all kinds of sophisticated things related to community. The most obvious applications of "common sense" were indeed common to all people (as "the commons"), and our use of the term has always retained that sense of commonality. It derives from the common mental activities of comparing and organizing to fit our needs. So common sense encompasses, without specification, thousands of ordinary human activities. The "common sense philosophy" of eighteenth century Britain and the United States began with an immense backlog of established commonalities. It was the rediscovery of a fundamental human capability we call our "rationality" not to be confused with the proud rationalism of recent memory.

"Common sense" as applied to philosophy was sometimes given an anti-intellectual twist, but it is anything but non-intellectual. In fact it denotes beginning with our native mental activity, observing and comparing, with an orientation to think about practical aspects of life and thought, to range far and wide for alternative approaches to things, and to keep one's feet on the ground. It is common sense to observe, reflect, and wait for relevant pieces to fall in place, but the waiting does not suggest lethargy. It is active reflection on observations. Common sense, quite distinct from instinctual leisure, is energetic, ready to put into action. Quite different from being persuaded to act, rather, common sense often means waiting for the formation in our minds of what action one should take, about which one will decide when it forms. It is patient, inimical to knee-jerk reactions. Did the Psalmist not remind us to "Wait"?

Common sense thinking was not natural either to man or beast when food supplies were satisfactory; that too often is when instinctual leisure took control. Our argument is that during the gestation of the city, human beings began a long, difficult journey toward an awareness of their mental capacity and eventually of their common sense responsibility. Our ancestors discovered that they could enjoy activity far more complex and more demanding than food gathering. They accepted the coercive leadership of the oligarchs partly because we could then depend on their fair share of the crops raised by the common effort but also to enjoy dancing and singing, and to engage with others in the initiative required for construction projects. Elements of common sense and rationality became intertwined. When philosophy matured we separated out things like rationality and made them the whole. But common sense never ends. It is the natural condition of the human mind – curiously considering options and weighing our choices. Our future will reflect this fundamental thinking of humanity.

And our culture built on it as we will in the future. As people became more aware of themselves increasing numbers of them found it possible to undertake specialties like basket-making, pottery, arrow and spear making (and production of armaments has remained a major industry in civilization).[373] As our ability to raise food supplies improved, there was enough so that everyone did not have to be involved in food production. Barter – and the late introduction of coinage – allowed specialists to obtain food and accumulate wealth by exercising their initiative. So today we have the knowledge to produce plenty of food for seven billion people, but we have yet to grasp the necessity of finding new ways of shaping our commonwealth for the common good.

Today we are again discovering the wisdom of enabling people to exercise common sense albeit with new appreciation for discretion. It is closely linked to initiative and as we again learn to appreciate the capacity of people to innovate, more and more people will accept their responsibility in using common sense with discretion to make themselves useful members of society exercising creativity and adapting to new conditions of life. It is what our civilization is built of. Today the scope of our understanding is gradually expanding to benefit the great mass of humankind currently pressing the boundaries of the earth's "carrying capacity." We have been slow to control our instinct to multiply. Now we must increasingly use common sense to limit human reproduction and to adopt policies in our political processes which encourage common sense reduction in populations. "Growth" has captivated Western culture as a mistaken economic principle. It is another of our good ideas gone viral.

It was a significant discovery in the twentieth century that people who are able to exercise their own creativity naturally reduce their fecundity. We rediscovered that women are particularly disposed to common sense, having from ancient times reduced the number of pregnancies by succoring children longer,[374] and always had a major role in managing food and household. In women's propensity to nourish and nurture children, humanity has always been blessed. Throughout our new world, women are achieving educational and occupational equality with men. Together with women, men are learning to rein in their excessive sexual drives (which were long misunderstood as validation for paternalism).

In the mid-century panic over population growth, the natural increase was still dangerously high. Since then the number of children borne by the average woman has decreased significantly. And the aging of the world's population as the birth-rate declines will continue to demonstrate the capacity of people to control growth of population. Still, the seven billion of us will grow for some time. Some day soon we will undoubtedly breach eight billion. By then we should have achieved the cultural intelligence to displace our insistence on growth with common sense.

The desirability of growth is another of the mistaken assumptions we have perhaps innocently adopted, especially in the economies of the twentieth century.[375] The time has come to reconsider this idea. Growth is natural, but not necessarily good. Surely, the monstrosity of cancer in the human body has brought that forcibly to our attention. The long growth of the armament industry throughout the world, with all its adjunct arms and tentacles into our economy is a monster, "an elephant in the kitchen." The perverse nature of such growth is evident in the absurd argument that all we need to do is destroy the atom bomb and the capability of producing such weapons of mass destruction. Millions of mouths are fed in our world by the money paid by common consent to weapons researchers and suppliers. Common sense insists that we use our native ingenuity to create new ways for people to earn their bread and shelter – but more, to live life as the biblical phrase has it, "abundantly." Common sense is no longer just applying muscle to sometimes arduous tasks like mining.[376] The trades require common sense for application in modern America, and the trades person who can think about alternative problem solutions – who is free to adapt to the situation – is the one who will excel. Ultimately, common sense requires better and better use of our brains as our civilization becomes increasingly complex. We will rid ourselves of the specter of economic growth though we may find that we simply have appropriated the wrong measures of our economies.

Another sort of specialization occurred inside different cultures in the development of language, so that when the cities developed, peoples from different language groups found it necessary to translate words. A translator is required to interpret. There was no assurance (there never has been) that a word or phrase chosen to substitute for another language actually denotes the same thing. No doubt translations of the names of the variety of cats in the world produced quite different reactions in different languages – "cat" may mean tiger where they wander at will, but lap cat in an urban apartment. But within one language, the time soon arrived when generalized concepts gained acceptance so that no one expects "cat" to mean precisely the same thing to all hearers.

All of this points in just one direction, seldom acknowledged: Humans are destined to be more and more diverse, more varied and different from one another while they simultaneously manufacture increasing sociability and commonality. We want to be clear that, while we have traced the increasing socialization of human beings at least from the early city five thousand years ago, we have not wished to imply that this meant sameness. Society is magnificently diverse, varied, richly textured, not a homogenous thing. It might be thought of as a mixture, but not as a solution of like atoms. There are many kinds of mixtures, and sometimes people take on habits, patterns and characteristics which appear to make them very much alike. But they are never actually, completely, thoroughly alike. We live together not as cyborgs[377] but as human beings. In the future we will not only acknowledge this variation, but embrace it as a richness we share.

So also we have talked of religion as if it should be singular. We have imagined a time (a "golden age" when we talk of culture) when everyone believed the same thing. Indeed, from outward appearances, one might say this was characteristic of medieval Europe, when everyone presumably belonged to the Roman Catholic Church. That was, of course, an illusion, desperately desired and sought by some, in the face of real differences among neighbors, not only nations and nationalities. The great variety of understandings of Jesus' life and teachings coming to attention today never ceased, in spite of appearances. It might be said that this ambiguity in our Christian roots has served well, encouraging innumerable interpreters to make their contributions, thus enriching the whole long story.[378]

It is time for us all to rejoice together in our diversity, while embracing one another for the richness we share and the amazing capabilities which enable us to grasp, to understand, and to enjoy views we do not share, skills we do not possess, lifestyles we do not engage, and even religions, allegiances, and nationalities which are distinct. Much of our most heinous history would have made us a very different people had we not reveled in the illusion that we should all be alike. While all language is metaphorical, we no longer embrace allusions as if they were realities. This means, of course, that we now put behind us the idea of enemy, the language of conflict, and the actions of belligerence.

This view also recognizes that the realities of our human world include a great variety of oral constructions, some of which appear to some of us as realities, while being to others only figurative expressions of communication. What appear to some as inanities of the past are variously regretted, not understood, and even lauded by various ones of us, and some of these will not be understood among many of us. So also our exaltation expressing religious wonder may be easily misunderstood by other people. These social realities lead us further into enjoying our human diversity and to persistently inquire of one another. Now we understand disinterest in others' constructions as a social error we can correct that was perpetuated over millennia by the adversarial mentality we inherited.

Our diversity calls forth our patience. Patience was in the past a word applied largely to enduring evil or to exercising forbearance. In a world not too far behind us, life was dreary and full of trouble. One often had to grit one's teeth. But patience has another connotation focused less on evil and more on simple persistence. In a bureaucratized society there are many times when we pass on to an appropriate bureaucrat ideas or knowledge that could change living conditions. We may find ourselves pressing our ideas on people over long periods of time. Or, to change the nature of the problem, we may make what is more than a suggestion to a child, a student, or a colleague once, twice, even three times. Most of us will not press on after a third time. But sometimes our impatience can break through protective shells and ingrained habits but it must never produce overt anger. Every discipline requires patience.

In international relations, diplomats have long exercised restraint in their anger. They have developed ways of showing their disagreement without outbursts of anger, but often, still, with too much evidence of aggression. Anger is too often unconstrained, the expression of the instinct of rage issuing in aggression. But we can control our instincts, including anger; we have already moved decisively to control rage. Our evolving sense of responsibility requires it.

In the aggressive world of the past, people found ways to relieve the tension in their lives. Many smoked various weeds to change the chemical balances of the body. Even religious leaders within the past century have found relief in nicotine, part of the most recent American health battle. The arch conservative Gresham Machen said cigar smoking was his "idea of delight." He once wrote (presumably of cigarettes),"When I think what a wonderful aid tobacco is to friendship and Christian patience I have sometimes regretted that I never began to smoke." Others who did smoke include C. S. Lewis and Reinhold Niebuhr. Dietrich Bonhoeffer mentioned in a letter from his prison cell, "I am very grateful for any smoking supplies." The time it takes to finish a decent cigar is a respite from a hectic schedule. It is time set aside for backyard meditation or contemplation. So who can say that it has not served us. But in our world, discovery of the dangers of nicotine make it necessary for us to leave this solution to tension behind. People will create new means.

We Americans have been slow to accept the evidence with which my father insulated me from joining the ranks of my smoking teenage friends. Though he had a life-long habit, long before science uncovered the consequences, in reflective moments Dad called cigarettes "cancer sticks." Reflection has suffered a severe cutback in our culture as we became white collar workers, and we fell into the competitive regimen of working frenetically to advance and to raise production. "Nose to the grindstone," was the archaic term, "Hustle!" (to push hard reminiscence of slavery). Now this is becoming an archaism of an already dying, pressurized culture. But the residue of past, bossy management styles persisted, driving the mid-century culture under the rubric "efficiency." And smoking, soon to be proved cancer-causing, soared in popularity, a mistaken resolution of these cultural pressures. Our readiness to engage in reflection lost an artificial encouragement.

Self-discipline is a better path to happy living. Recovery of the Medieval practices of contemplation would help us as adults to relearn the art of patience. Patience provides space in life for reflection which can remind us to slack off, to think carefully, to consider options and alternatives. Anyone giving up an addiction must indeed learn to be patient. Once our endemic waiting for things (as in a line of others also waiting) was imposed by authority. Gradually it has become part of our culture; we can even wait with good humor. We stay in lines easily. It will be easier for everyone in a free society to use such time creatively as we adopt patience as a cultural habit while we trust in and encourage responsible authorities everywhere to work at solutions to undue waiting.

The new human mind will grasp the opportunities in life to reap the benefits of patience with those who are in any way disabled. This is a change that fits our better understanding of our common humanity. We do not ordinarily have the privilege of insisting on change. We are called, even when we are deeply concerned, to be patient, to allow ideas to sink in, to amass new evidence of the need we press, and to listen. For all sorts of reasons we have found that patience is a great virtue in society. There is time for pressing on, when people cry out for redress "Singing the song of angry men,"[379] when long-standing injustice requires attention. But in the ordinary press of life, patience is the better route while giving persistent attention to possible change.

In our new mind, we have the ability to see change in a time frame impossible a very few years ago. We know things don't happen in a day. Our appreciation of the age of the earth and the universe may have little to do with life today, but our new perspective recognizes that good changes often take a little time. And what comes out of our own hearts and minds does not always prove best, requiring tweaking. Others also have contributions to make, perspectives to share, and needs to address. Together, sharing patiently as we are able, listening carefully, and habitually reflecting, all insights can make contributions.

E. OUR OWN CONFUSED PATH TO RESPONSIBILITY

Paradigm changes have confused our culture in the past, and still do today.[380] But above such confusion there has been a gradual working out of a variety of cultural learnings that seem to persist.

One of the accomplishments of civilization is recognition of the essential nature of political organization. Yet, each leader in turn, the primitive chief, the early mayor, the ancient king and emperor and the Medieval monarch proved incapable of ruling the complexity of human society beyond fairly small communities. Assuming that each had done his best, it would take another millennium in the European caldron after the ancient period for human beings to begin to piece together a political system adequate to governing the emerging millions of human beings. Overwhelming success in survival – populating the planet – was not matched by self-confidence among those growing numbers. The limits of early leaders' political capability may well have been tested with cities like Athens and Alexandria reaching over 300,000. By the time of Roman power, the Greek archipelago probably exceeded one million people. The Roman Empire in its full extent may have reached over 50 million people. It would take the European experiment to produce means of governing such numbers peaceably.[381] Acknowledgment of the need for such government has long been part of the common sense of the people. We can think of it as a long-delayed common wisdom.

We must tap that common sense in taking control of development of our culture. It is a layering of current understandings on top of inherited notions, often modifying and correcting them. It may be credited with the energy to adapt to evolving forms of oligarchy through the Middle Ages. For a very long time the power of central authority was thought to be necessary to keep the peace. Though many of us maintain that this was a perversion established by a culture of coercion in the ancient city, the fact of aggressiveness among earlier humans cannot be denied. From our vantage point it appears that the corrective process of socialization has taken an extraordinarily long time. The human beings who emerged from the tiny tribes and villages across the face of the earth had become inured to dependence on oligarchic authority in the growing cities. They had established patriarchal social patterns long before, but many also had already learned that peaceable life was preferable to constant conflict. This learning was trumped by the war-making of warlords, some of whom still operate, especially in some less developed countries. The culture of war was so thoroughly established as to be virtually unchallenged for centuries. That time is over, world-wide. The human self has matured with a magnificent sense of self in a world of others and its common sense will no longer be subordinated to egotistic authority.

Now it is time for the common people to stand up for peace, to insist on peaceable settlement of international squabbles. It requires that we ourselves think in peaceful terms. We now must put behind us the whole "enemy" mentality in which we have often spoken of others outside our circles, the language so easily exploited by demagogs. As long as we easily respond to jingoistic calls, they will be exploited.[382] This is probably the most pressing cultural challenge today. We must think carefully, not only of cost, not only of lives lost, not only of the grief of suffering, but of the indisputable fact that we are actually, provably related to all other people. It is an enlargement of our early childhood learning that others share our own identification of self, emotions, thoughts and ideas. Others are, like us, human beings.

Wariness of outsiders, of "others" than those in humans' closed circles was endemic among many of our predecessors. That is not to say that they treated everyone else as enemy, but the common sense of their times led them to be cautious if not suspicious, probably with roots in experience or stories about the inevitable anti-social nomads of all time; hit and run robbery and wife-stealing may have kicked off this ancient pattern. But we have long controlled many such propensities with legal constraints and more recently by changes in the culture from which children learn what is considered common sense.

The suicide of town doctor James Redd of Blanding, Utah, demonstrates the necessity of taking culture change seriously. A good friend of his, archaeologist Winston

Hurst was born in Blanding and still lives there. Hurst says, "It's just incomprehensibly tragic that anything to do with archaeology should ever drive someone to suicide." Redd killed himself the day after federal agents descended on Blanding and arrested 16 residents for looting archaeological sites on public and tribal lands. Hurst agrees that scavenging history by ravaging archaeological treasures for display to neighbors is not acceptable social behavior. But "busting" a bunch of people who have for generations scavenged and may not even know it is illegal is "nothing but theater." Hurst himself grew up in Blanding collecting artifacts as a teenager. He says:

> I didn't know any better and I was in college taking classes in archaeology before I understood that it was illegal. We just did it. It's something you did like you hunted rabbits.... The challenge is to get into people's heads when they're little kids that in the big picture artifacts are our common history. I know the people here very well and I have absolutely no doubt that if they got it, they'd be perfectly happy to leave that stuff alone.[383]

The arrest tactics in Blanding were, from the point of view of this writing, reprehensible. It is time to recognize that the place of law and government enforcement is not superior to the forces of common sense. What might have been done, instead of the tactic used by the agents, would have to be determined by people related to that agency and their context. But when the authority of democratic government is exercised independently of intelligent educational processes, they are apt to repeat this error time and time again. The exercise of power is one of the beguiling temptations of having learned the value of law and the necessity of governing authority. Now we must overcome that ancient error by the critical use of our new minds.

Perhaps the fall of the Berlin wall on November 9, 1989, is a contemporary example of the importance of patience. The long period of the Cold War (from 1945 to this event and the fall of the Soviet Union) necessitated a civilized stand-off. For most of our past, "cooling off periods" were provided by the slowness of communication and mobilization, and the general pace of life. But in the period immediately after World War II the world became one, and communication across great distances almost instantaneous. In 1963 President Kennedy's rebuttal to the Cuban missiles sent into our borders by Russian lions was stern and dangerous. It was decisive: The missiles were removed and returned to Russia. The new mind had begun to provide evident fruits of peace. Thereafter for almost three decades the "free world," as we called it, stood against the demagoguery of the Communist idea. It took immense patience and endless hours of thoughtful consideration – and communication among the national leaders of the free world. Their dialogue succeeded in reigning in the war-hawks always waiting in the wings, still wielding their power in terms of the antiquated culture of the past.

In 1946 Hermann Hagedorn wrote a long poem he called "The Bomb That Fell on America." It reflected the new mind growing in our culture. His reference, of course, was to the bomb we Americans loosed on the world first at Hiroshima, Japan. The decision to drop the bomb was in part a rational attempt to reduce fatalities anticipated in terminating the war. But it loosed on the world another new weapon so terrible that it is said a full scale atomic war would end human life on this planet. I want to quote the last lines:

263

"There is power in the human soul," said the Lord.
"When you break through and set it free,
like the power of the atom,
it can control the atom.
the only thing in the world that can.
I told you that the atom is the greatest force
in the world, save one.
That one is the human soul." [384]

The residue in the United States of our past self-sufficient, self-reliant, rugged and proud ethos of personal independence can be overcome in the twenty-first century. The emphasis on "rights" in the middle of the last century reinforced a misconstruction of society. The freeing of human beings from the degrading slave posture of the ancient world took a long time. And learning to be responsible participants in the unfolding world of the Enlightenment and modernity has unfolded slowly also. Our native creativity has been impatient with this unfolding, failing to grasp the immense underlying residue of the sheep mentality evolving slowly, unaided by the elite advantage of relative freedom (which elites always carefully protect). Breaking the floodgate of "rights" reinforced the conservative American dedication to "freedom." But this construction was of boundlessness, a profoundly wrong error. The "force" Hagedorn spoke of was the emerging force of people who feel the unity of all people, who respect the humanity of their neighbors regardless of the boundaries society proposes. The freedom to be our whole selves, unconstrained by authorities or ideas and open to the future unfolding in our hands, is a new thing, within the vision of ancient genius, but far beyond the social boundaries of past cultures. Freedom is freedom to be free to be human selves, not life without constraints. This freedom, says Hagedorn, is the greatest force in the world.

The long gestation of "rights" – recognition of the artificiality of gender and race boundaries in our society – finally broke through to establish a new sense of freedom in our culture. All Americans were finally freed from these barriers and such freedom is indeed full of grace and hope. But it is not boundless. Even the churches have failed to grasp the impact of the long spans of time involved in achieving important social goals and therefore neglected to hold ultimate goals and present opportunities together in creative tension. This must now change. They have been free of constraint by secular authorities for long enough to grow out of the residual sheep mentality of overarching authority. slow nature of the evolution of society requires patience. And the persistent danger of neglecting timely change requires attention to the emergent awareness of our common humanity. The survival instinct is always satisfied with the status quo. Religious people have neglected their own teaching about patience and respect for others while often behaving counter-intuitively. We have neglected the freedom emerging out of the heart of literal slavery in Egypt, initiated by Moses three thousand years ago.

But Westerners have inherited the makings of the new mind which have given us the capacity to put braggardly bizarre behavior behind us and to forge ahead with grace and knowledge. As a child in the 1930s I was still being fed on the childhood literature of heroism. [385] The magnificent short stories of Jack London will always be part of our culture but "How to Build a Fire" was of heroism versus severe natural conditions. Unfortunately, the popular mind that translated that rugged individualism into macho activity also demeaned women and seldom acknowledged the gentle art of masculine parenting. Our future holds better alternatives for raising the next generation. Our culture cries out for it. This is a song of people calling for change.

There are always great differences in the intelligence of authors. For some time now they have not been expected to lead. But skills of leadership, as well as those of deceit and subterfuge, of cunning and courage, are calling to the writers who grasp the new understanding of our culture and human evolution. Recently, evidence has been uncovered of unhappy relations with our predecessors the Neanderthals: A *Homo sapiens'* spear point was found embedded in the body of a Neanderthal. But such conflict probably was not universal. Social and sexual intercourse probably took place between species as well as between tribes. That they also sometimes conflicted is consistent; these also were human beings. We must remember that among ourselves some people tend to be belligerent while others are peaceful and cooperative. We can expect such variability across the earth. Nonetheless, the basic drive to reproduce, nurture children, and grow old in peace ultimately trumps other tendencies. It is no longer incumbent on authors to reflect the assumption that men are essentially tough and belligerent. We need more literature that demonstrates this shift. "Macho" is a thing of the past.

The avalanche of hand-held electronic devices in the last few years is challenging the relatively stilted previous level of communication. Email had already largely destroyed the habit of written correspondence, though it did not require the current abbreviated patterns. The new technology is keeping people tethered to the abbreviated culture of the Internet for everything from news to maintaining personal relations. Some think it is changing the way people think, reducing their ability to hold in-depth conversation, keeping them from forming and expressing complex thoughts and developing deep friendships. Harvard psychiatrist John Ratey calls the effect "acquired attention deficit disorder." Many late twentieth century liaisons proved to be based on shallow acquaintance, and marriages often ended in divorce. But this increase began long before these devices; they were not the result of such devices. My career involved "coding" and the development of brief shorthand for organizational detail. It seems not to have much affected my ability to think. The human mind is too big for the internet to stifle it. Is not "texting" just another dialect?

We maintain that digital technology will encourage the depth and complexity of thinking and development of culture; that is the direction of at least five thousand years of evolution. One recalls to mind our survival of the introduction of movable type that put a final end to the role of hundreds of people copying manuscripts. But it gave us a flood of print communications and set the Enlightenment in motion. What will our new tools do for us? To many of us it seems that multiplication of miniature communications devices of the first decade of this century is having the salutary effect of increasing the size of the world familiar to most of the world's people and at the same time, with its images and translation, personalizing these relationships.

From the point of view of this writing, this demonstrates further the evolution of the expanding mind of human beings. In a very short time millions of people have become neighbors. It suggests that increased productivity of people should accompany such expansion.[386] Does common sense suggest that fear of such inventions is just another blip not unlike that of the Luddites of nineteenth century Britain? (They became iconoclastic, destroying machinery while calling attention to the dehumanization of the early Industrial Revolution.) Common sense has often justified the way things are, the "status quo." But common sense can also endorse creativity. California might be taken as a model (if it were a nation, it would be among the top ten in Gross Domestic Product) demonstrating that error. Perhaps California's secret is in its positive, common sense attitude toward change. Along with its massive problems besides budget and taxes, it continues to attract cutting edge business. The culture is of "early adopters." California "voters approved huge bonds for stem-cell research, high-speed rail, and repairs to aging infra-structure while Washington was dragging its feet."[387] Attention to eco-friendly systems has produced the world's largest manufacturer of solar panels. There, failure is appreciated, not stigmatized. That, after all, is the basic human learning mechanism, failing and going on, adapting, innovating and adopting.

The status quo has always enjoyed the residual bias of past cultures. People are always clinging to "what we have and what we know." It was true of the slave cultures of the ancient kings, but its unassailable arguments are no longer called for. In the new mind we can encourage and enjoy what is new. This is a surprise learning of the twentieth century. Perhaps the auto industry taught us this: Americans love what is new. Conservative dedication to the past is an old conservatism, an obsolescent conservatism. True conservatism will seek to solve real problems with imagination and adaptability driving forward what *Homo sapiens* have demonstrated is worthwhile and leaving behind what has become obsolescent.

Population growth has always caused change, and we are now at the crossroads to change the growth patterns of our own status quo. The world population for many thousands of years was constrained only by the food supply and survival considerations. Humans continued their deliberate growth until the Agricultural Revolution. Then a new abundance of food kicked off a population explosion.[388] As we learned to use organization, persuasion, and law with increasing effectiveness, cities (for a while largely independent political units) found it possible to grow past the ancient limits of thousands to tens of thousands. Still, the spaces between settlements, the necessity of interaction for distribution of food and other goods, and the simple matter of human ambition and jealousy, all required effective government with skills in negotiation. Eight or ten thousand years after the Agricultural Revolution, by the year one, world population had hit 300 million. This signaled the end of the era of classic empire. Rome for all its acumen and sophistication was incapable of ruling any large part of these surprising numbers.

Along with learning to live together in large aggregations, we are learning to listen more critically to those who wish to persuade us of their agendas. Orators learned to project their voices to be heard by hundreds are now heard by millions. But the culture has not assured us (and may never) of honesty in public discourse. Our critical listening is essential as we proceed. Again, we should not be surprised that the course of civilization has often been retrograde, stymied by what the Jews called "false prophets." Such demagogues have not always been countered by those who could reveal their errors. Some people choose to ignore them, others to simply be quiet (the perpetrator being a friend or a friend of a friend, or a feeling of incompetence). This is no less true today than in the past. But as the future unfolds, friends will expect correction and difference of opinion so that the human mind may learn and share unconstrained and unsullied by subterfuge. Sara Hacala reminds us that "there is 'greatness' in treating others with respect, compassion, kindness and generosity. With this we can make a difference in the lives of many" – and in our culture."[389]

In a sometimes elusive way, our culture seems to have progressed to favor truth over falsehood. And we recognize, sometimes belatedly, that those who follow demagogues pervert the culture. Another lesson from the Berlin blockade of the Cold War is found in the reply of Nobel Prize winner for literature, novelist Herta Mueller, who was asked whether she listened to Radio Free Europe while growing up in communist Romania. Her reply: "Several times a day, and those who did not do so were idiots."[390] Perhaps not idiots, but unfortunately, people confused by the cacophony of their situation. Increasingly, people are learning to distinguish truth from falsehood.

Speaking the truth to power is still possible, perhaps more possible than ever before with electronic communication. The transmission of free voices in upheavals in the Mediterranean basin will have future consequences that cannot but be fortuitous in the eyes of free people. The other relevant reality is that human conversation is perhaps the oldest social reality in our long history. Where people speak to one another, the truth might eventually win over falsehood. Does recent history not prove that growing numbers of people will eventually free themselves? Some will disagree. And the remnants of cynicism will persist in creating unfortunate contemporary aristocracies.

In a recent column, David Brooks discussed the importance of the stories we choose to explain ourselves to ourselves and to others. Most people, it seems, choose narratives that stress cooperation and goodness. But some choose narrow visions that reduce the scope of their compassion. It is easier, after all, to talk of enemies causing the world's ills than to accept responsibility for a role in remedying them. New stories will come aiding our transcendence of the status quo – new visions, new paths, new solutions.

Even though identifying enemies gives one automatic membership in the club of aggressors, most people who take that route are loners, without a developed sense of discrimination. Truth for them is in cliches, in slogans, in easy targets. But it is important for those who choose hopeful narratives to remain grounded. Common sense reminds us to recognize danger in the grousers. They may be fed by ideologues, by bright people who use their minds to instruct loners in anti-social activity. Their always negative stories test the democratic ideal and our discernment of these significantly impacts our culture.

XIV. FAITH FOR OUR NEW CULTURE

John Wesley is credited with the occasion called the "Wesleyan Quadrilateral" which included tradition, reason and experience in its discussions of authority. We have focused largely on reason and experience in these pages with a tip of the hat to tradition since our concern is to delineate the evolution of the human mind. We have spoken of tradition largely in terms of culture. This is a somewhat more flexible concept than tradition, as this latter term has been used. But our Western culture clearly includes elements of tradition: the Bible, the life of Jesus and his teachings, and of our Western tradition: medieval history, the Reformation, the Enlightenment, and the science. All these contribute to what we have might call the authority of "our faith." While authority was perverted in the distant past to refer to power over others, authority is rather a moving influence in life.

The human problem we have explored is the difficulty of realizing the full potential of the wondrous creatures we are. Our exploration has pointed to a variety of influences from many people which seem to have become incorporated our culture. But this "culture" is a continuously changing tradition which influences everyone. While tradition generally points to ideas and ceremonies, culture includes everything, driving us deeper into the human psyche.

Our physical development produced a fully functioning human being capable of adapting to most any circumstance within the confines of nature itself, modifying them by our behavior. It seems obvious that evolution for some time has been developing the brain, and the development of that organ has provided us the unique capability to observe the evolution of our humanity evident in the human mind. Our powers of observation have extended our capability to converse stretching our experience into the minds of others and over immense stretches of time. Experience, it seems, is always new.

Understanding which had been limited to experience has been extended so that history and tradition have taken on new significance. Ancient views have been extended and revised. The cultures of our predecessors mutated with every generation and now have extended our experience into outer space and inside atoms. We have begun to plumb the working of the brain itself to see more deeply with the faculty of reason, and to utilize our minds more carefully with the faculty of imagination. We are at the point where we can begin to take control of the development of our culture. The maturing of our understanding of history provides a welcome tool. Our view of history must be extended far into the past. The fore-shortened sense common among us is far too short to allow us critical judgment. Demagogues persistently play on this short memory, and our questions to them have too often failed to push them toward greater rationality.

We must pause to note that development of critical faculties now leads us to be cautious in taking things for granted. As this realization began to form in the minds of the Enlightenment we began to scrutinize the institutions of Europe. The Church was, perhaps, an easy target. Governed in the humanists view by ordinary people elevated to positions of authority, the Church had fallen into the same traps as the rest of the culture. Barbara Tuchman called the fourteenth century a time, more than any other, when attention was focused on money and possessions, with "a concern for the flesh the same as any other." Awareness of corruption became acute. The Reformation followed. On the continent a critical bias against the Church crystallized in the seventeenth century and ran through the twentieth.

Sophistication to differentiate the institution from the religious faith did not develop soon enough to check the extension of this bias. The delineation of the limits of rationality began with Kant and it in the nineteenth century independent voices began Kierkegaard, Husserl, and Heidegger. Wittgenstein pursued the slipperiness of language, and a constructive modern philosophy emerged in Whitehead. By then thinkers on the Continent particularly had established their bias so firmly that they neglected the import of Britain's Second Reformation and attention to bringing the general population into the emerging new world. And American analytical philosophy passed them by with its implications for all human intellectual activity: the requirement of assumptions, starting points, even though these are always assumed and not proved. This truth was clinched in the 1930s by Kurt Godel.

Only recently have we recognized that each of our vaunted disciplines, structured around increasingly specific experience, involves assumptions. Without assurance of the truth of such beliefs, for a very long time we created the hypotheses on which our science progressed. Our remarkable brains made it unnecessary for us to persistently remind ourselves of such faith until, again leading the way, mathematicians sought to establish the foundations of mathematics culminating in Russell and Whitehead's *Principia Mathematica*. We had been taking assumptions for granted, but this search led to Kurt Godel's definitive incompleteness theorem.

Today, then, we speak of faith in a culture quite different from our tradition. It is sure to produce new religious concepts in the twenty-first century. This movement is freshly recognized almost daily by one or another thinker. The core if it will undoubtedly be "faith." Christians have long said that their religion is best described as *faith*. It is recognition that throughout history, in spite of contemporary interpretations as learnings directly from God, every religious indication we have was of their faith that they had rightly understood what they believed to be the voice of God.

The word "faith" means confidence or trust. For a very long time, we have identified firm belief in God as faith. It is not well-used to identify any institutional form of religion; these are not illicitly identified with "beliefs." The distinction is extremely important today as fewer and fewer people hesitate to overlook past differences in beliefs, switching denominations of Christianity without much difficulty. So "religion" has been identified with these varied sets of beliefs, with little understanding of the human experience of faith. Nonetheless, our language permits us to say we believe in God by which we mean we have faith in the God revealed to us in human experience. The revelation, however, is not the exposure of God that can lead to endless articulation of beliefs! Faith is the our sense of assurance that this revelation is a valid call on us to be wholly human.

Americans are rapidly waking up to the distinction. In faith, we have long since ceased to try to describe God.[391] The ancient Eastern acknowledgment that God is "ineffable" holds, but "God" is more than an "unutterable" word – we do need to keep using the word! ("Ineffable" is itself a reference to an essential characteristic – God by definition is beyond our grasp.) In our tradition, God has been recognized as "hidden." God is a mystery, and a purist would insist that nothing can be said about God. From a demythologized, deconstructed, and modestly "objective" point of view, God is unknowable. It is said only that people believe in God which is to say, they have recognized the "ineffable" as pertinent to their lives. They hold themselves to be faithful.

Only Moses saw God.[392] We are inclined to trust not in a "thing" (things can be examined by science), but in our grasp of inherited constructions of thousands of years of religious experience. We understand that this tells us that God can best be identified with love and compassion. We see the perpetuation over thousands of years of the magnanimous, generous, loving lives of those who believed, those who held this faith. Socialized as we are, we pay a good deal of attention to them.

And only recently have psychologists begun to elucidate the long-standing recognition that the culture into which each human being is born carries the essentials of his or her lifetime orientation. Granted that we have the capability to shape this orientation, it is likely to be largely a product, their interpretation of the religious orientation of their native culture – some of course hold only a residue of it. This gives every individual a "home" (remembering that all language is metaphorical), and an orientation to respect oneself (unique among all six billion human beings), to be socially responsible (loving and compassionate), and to exercise human rationality (be thoughtful, reflective, considerate). The fundamental human description as *Homo loquens* (man who speaks) recognizes that our interpretations inevitably will reflect our vocal interactions in our dominant cultures, in other words expression of our human capability to speak; we call it conversation. Few people in our world today have the sophistication to choose either their language or their conception of God. But this number is rapidly growing. It will give us new religious expessions as the decades pass.

"Providence" describes my own personal experience of the presence of God. So many occasions which fit my immediate need occur in ordinary life (as well as in pursuing my writing as I have already noted) that I cannot avoid the conclusion that God is present. As Jesus said, "I will be with you." In both cases theology identifies this presence with the Holy Spirit. Seeing persons who have or had such a sense has always been impressive. I conclude that similar experiences have occurred over thousands of years. And the religious impulse flows naturally from these. Why would we not, then, trust in our sense of God as a persistent presence? In my language this is gutsy reality.

The biblical references to the spirit of God eventually leading to the doctrine of the Holy Spirit is a theologically sound way of speaking of the providential involvement of God in our world. Both "spirit" and "providence" are helpful language in the realm of faith. Joseph Haroutunian, my theology professor, said, "There is no faith in the church apart from the recognition of miracle in Jesus' company." It is that awareness that characterized the disciples of Jesus after he was killed. This is another way of speaking of the Spirit of God. Classical theology has ascribed the miracle of our sense of self and others to the work of the Holy Spirit, admitting in the fundamental formation of humanity the miraculous capacity to know ourselves and to relate to others with integrity and respect. This miracle of our minds (called ToM) is intimately part of the world. I trust in the basic rationality of the whole of creation, and there is obvious hunger in our culture today for such faith. But, we emphasize, this is not the hubris of the modern period.

A. FAITH IN CONVERSATION

The road has been rough with many of the obstacles being our own creations. Our solutions to the requirements of evolution itself (survival and reproduction) have also given us institutionalized belligerence, inequality, and disingenuous conditions of many sorts. We have proudly eschewed the humility identified thousands of years ago as a truly human disposition. And today, with much of this baggage still tormenting us, we face the evident necessity of getting hold of ourselves and correcting what we can of it as quickly as possible. We impatient Americans want it now – not to say we understand that. But the wisdom of the past suggests that we slow down long enough to be sure of our bearings. The truth of our present condition is far from universally recognized. It is time to grasp the fact that almost everything we do or say can benefit from sharing and hearing in the normal course of social life. And sharing – and related reflection – take time. Many times our nation has been guilty of imposing itself on others instead of taking time for our dream of a democratic world to take shape. The resulting waste of time, life, and resources is beyond calculation.

Following that advice, let us assess a few of the voices clamoring for attention. Our dominant theme has been human conversation, made possible by the evolution of our bodies and our emerging sociality. Over several millennia each culture has produced its own successor cultures in a continuous line of development, with the contributions of each participant constantly changing and particularizing itself in hamlets and nations and subcultures with an evident internal logic. Our most recent cultures – as many ancient predecessors -- have stifled conversation by imposing restrictions reminiscent of oligarchy on ordinary people. Constrained by working hours, organizational pressure and their own loyalties to conform to cultures of industry and commerce, people have been constrained from going where they wish and associating with others as they choose. Like their ancient slave ancestors, people accepted these restrictions as necessary. In the 1960s the "organization man" epitomized the extension of similar constraints on "working people" to the "white collar man." Fifty years later we found that the clamoring of women to join this regimented life had finally succeeded, and some of them became more aristocratic than the preceding male managers; the cultures we choose to enter change our behavior!

The same hierarchy of associations characterized our leisure and our recreation. In too many aspects of life we found ourselves associating only with people who were very much like ourselves – just as in the business corporation one only heard and spoke the "company line." We reduced the age-old stimulus of human interaction to boredom as we engineered homogeneous communities; like minds use like language and concepts fall to the same error. Failing to recognize our fault, we indulged in the easiest, the most mundane conversation. Civic trouble and sports provided endless trivia and trivia ruled interaction. Rather than take on the difficult business of seeking solutions to troublesome human problems. We were frenetically busy with the details of increasingly sophisticated requirements of industry and commerce. We avoided the real world of human diversity that still existed among us by ruling out talking about religion and politics which then also suffered the plague of the status quo. We ignored our own roles in producing a century of successful challenges to social difficulties. The lazy instinct prevailed. Life again became boring and we were ready for fresh demagogues. It was the end of another millennium. And we had not yet faced up to the individualistic, anti-social nature of our culture.

Over the ages, in occasional interludes between periods of greatest regimentation, as dissatisfaction with the status quo built up, demagogues who reflected our illusions about the "good old times" lulled us into becoming the world's greatest consumers. But satiation soon proves itself boring, too. Fortunately, some of us saw the pitch-man and the car salesman with humorous sarcasm. Looking back we found once more that demagogues mislead us. And some people spoke up reminding us that we are still capable of rebellion. It is a capability that in this country we no longer need to prove to anyone; it is a human social capacity of our evolving selves. We don't want simply to return to the past. From that plague we must free ourselves, and we will do so by grasping the necessity of learning to think critically and to converse openly – all of us.

In this new critical capability, the century also saw the building of new forms of alliance many of them aimed at the world's growing human and ecological tragedies. Non-profit organizations of every stripe emerged and our slowly evolving capacities to organize ourselves for productive social progress (rather than for personal gain) called forth many leaders capable of enlisting us in reshaping our society. It seems that in the larger population, self-consciousness had passed the line between selfishness and social awareness.

Of course, we have always listened to demagogues. It seems we have preferred the personal approbation they regularly use to gather us in, rather than stimulation to use our minds to find solutions to problems. Our failure to discern problems in our everyday lives is obvious. We prefer to ignore them and we use our leisure time to "recreate" rather than to reflect. The demagogue confirms our fears and encourages our self-righteousness. It is pandering. As we spoke only within our like-minded communities, we listened primarily to pundits who reflected our own viewpoints. Our recent increases in exposure to persons from strange places has helped little since most of these came out of communities overwhelmed by our own culture. Those admitted to our circles most often have been through our own educational mills and reflect our own biases. (India may be a good example of this, Afghanistan a poor one, yet even here the smattering of Western culture will contribute to the revolution of Afghanistan culture.) Their joy in American opportunity tends to make them poor critics of our poor thinking.[393] This illustrates the necessity for us to become more astute in our conversation. It is time to pay attention to how we talk with others, to drawing out of them more than surface thoughts, to getting beyond politeness, to extending thinking that occurs during our dialogue. We need to exercise our new found faith in conversation across all boundaries.

Recently, sharing real points of view across human boundaries seems to be contributing to opening ourselves to new points of view. This development has been gestating for many years as demonstrated in the repeated phenomena of Middle Americans being forced into dialogue by ultra-conservative Far Right power plays. We have watched this happen for fifty years. Our psyches have demonstrated the capacity for resistance to undesirable views. We seem to be developing greater ability to discriminate between chaff and substance. In fact it appears that we are finding the stimulation of serious conversation satisfying. So more and more we listen genuinely and try to understand, we ask questions, exchange views; in short, we converse. In this is the hope that we will increasingly learn and introduce into our culture a dominant capacity to see through demagogues and utilize differences in points of view so that we may all grow wiser – and our culture with us.

It is our lack of the capacity to differentiate between thoughtful commentators and demagogues that most impedes the development of our culture today. Failure to recognize the necessity of *public* education among all age groups could prove to be our downfall. Recent awareness of the importance of care in educating the very young is an important sign of progress. Recently, older children and teens have been receiving attention also. This learning continues throughout life. Now, in the twenty-first century we must continue to expand the public mind to think. Learning to think begins early in life, and matures as we persist in learning. We must not any longer short change the humanities in the educational process; especially, history and philosophy must not be neglected. These, as well as literature and particularly poetry, must be understood in the context of deep history, and in that reflective sense, history turns out to be more basic than ever. We must spend enough time in that thoughtful context to contemplate life and intelligence and culture so that we may grasp the newly intelligent world – and participate in it. Then, we expect, people will find themselves enabled to distinguish the demagogues in their experience and converse intelligently.

Having denigrated the "dark" ages, we failed to incorporate into our increasingly frenetic routines of modern life the value of reflection they so diligently encouraged without recognizing the base they laid for our increased self-expression. Perhaps some of us will agree that seclusion, meditation, and reflection were pressed beyond logical constraints in the Middle Ages. But the people who pursued them, disciplined by previous millennia of repression, learned to use time by themselves and in common prayer to explore the limits of the human mind. We have neglected that. Most of us in the West have pressed our capacity to concentrate our attention on tasks at hand beyond rational constraints. And when we relax we have adopted dual patterns of leisure: either we enjoy just being lazy, or we pursue "active" lifestyles. In both cases, we tend to neglect the art of reflection.

Because of our extreme indulgence in frenetic exercise of "our responsibility," we have sleeping time we need for recovery of our physical and mental well-being from our hectic indulgence. It is possible that this sort of American industriousness has interfered with the development of our own selves. This not unlike the effective restraint on self-development of ancient cultures. A remedy is required. With a renewed faith in face-to-face dialogue we may recover the humanity imbedded in our capacity to discern truth.

B. FAITH IN INTELLIGENT REGULATION

The outstanding contribution of the twentieth century to our culture is the acceptance of regulation. Regulation is our name for a new sort of authority. Hammurabi's stele forty-five hundred years ago was indeed a form of regulation, a valid attempt to replace the more brutal law of retributive justice. Mohammad tried again in the seventh century CE. But today we usually mean by regulation not decree but an order governing the critical transactions in our economy in an *agreeable* fashion. We will always have issues around regulation in a democratic society, as we do today in the aftermath of a misguided episode of deregulation. Regulations do tend to accumulate and become redundant as well as onerous. They do need to be reviewed, revised, and replaced. But there is no doubt that regulation is needed. It is a modern kind of authority in a new kind of society. Our government requires agreeable regulation.

It seems evident that economic change has driven Western evolution for a very long time. Ancient trade confirmed productive relationships. The arrival of "mercantilism" contributed significantly to the emergence of a new Europe ushering in what is better named "commercial." Commerce is "communication" transmuted appropriately into trading of goods and now embracing the whole realm of finance. Perhaps in bartering and bamboozling it involved more conversation in the ancient world (as the bazaars still witness). Christendom demonized charging interest on loans, under a dominant rubric of care for the poor. But by the Reformation, this concern for others was reduced from generality to specific care for the poor. And as we have become more sophisticated about the causes of perpetual poverty, there are those who believe that the poor are helped more by a positive approach to economic development than by such negative restrictions. Economic regulation in the past has always provided for the protection of wealth. But today regulation of interest rates persists for the good of all, and we know that if commerce is unregulated, human avarice will undoubtedly produce exploitation. This is no longer acceptable. Culture is maturing. Might the time come when money is no longer the driver?

By the end of the nineteenth century the economic dominance of massive corporations had proved to be exploitative. In 1927 the Supreme Court restored to the government the oil fields at the center of the scandalous Teapot Dome affair and the conviction of Harry F. Sinclair. As governor of New York, Theodore Roosevelt had previously begun taxing corporation finances. In 1901 he became president of the United States when William McKinley was assassinated, and he soon set about "trust busting." His actions were based on the moribund Sherman Anti-Trust Act of 1890 which was a reaction to growing public opposition to powerful corporations. In 1911 that Act was employed by President William Howard Taft to dissolve the Standard Oil Company, and in 1914 it was supplemented by the Clayton Anti-Trust Act under President Woodrow Wilson along with the establishment of the Federal Trade Commission. Attention to this regulation declined until Franklin Delano Roosevelt became president when the Robinson-Patman Act and other legislation vigorously renewed anti-trust action.

It seems that enough had been learned in fifty years to satisfy the public cry for regulation for two decades. It is worth noting that the early regulations were promoted by Republicans (Senator John Sherman, associated with the Sherman Anti-Trust Act, Roosevelt, and Taft). Woodrow Wilson, a democrat, was elected with the support of the moderate wing of the Republican Party when it split. F. D. Roosevelt, of course, was a Democrat. But when they sensed the growing strength of the conservatives in the 1970s, the Republicans took on a different coloration. The so-called "right wing" (we might call those involved in this movement "ultra-conservatives") began exercising its growing influence to shape the political landscape, an orientation Susan Jacoby describes in some detail in *Age of American Unreason*. This Right Wing felt its muscle, enlisting broad (thoughtless?) public support. This block of support was too great a temptation. The Republican party could not resist. The age of american unreason began in earnest.

A serious undermining of regulatory progress in social organization was soon initiated to implement these populist cries. It is instructive to note that this was done by Republican Ronald Reagan and was furthered a short while later by Republican George W. Bush. This is not meant to denigrate the Republican Party, but to demonstrate the shifting currents in American politics. Government for the people is not always moved forward by government by the people; reactionary minds choose reactionary paths. Built on the proposition that people must have a voice in government, democracy is subject to the ebbs and flows of popular opinion, often reactionary, often self-defeating for the populace.

We have pointed out how dangerous many Founding Fathers considered this threat to be, but their faith in human integrity and education outweighed reverting to government by an elite. Unfortunately, some Americans have not yet recognized that regulation is the way we have found for a democratic government to maintain a healthy society. It is a way to assure restraint among entrepreneurs and managers, executives, and CEOs and their commercial interests which too easily neglect the public good.

Deregulation has made it easier for demagogues to exploit a long-seated pleasure of the public in what we call "free enterprise." The breakdown of religion-based morality was the first sign of the rise of secularization. For centuries religion was thought to be the bulwark of morality. The role of what we now call culture was not recognized. The confusion of religion with reactionary religious institutions stimulated the anti-religious atmosphere.

Unfortunately, free enterprise mutated into cutthroat competition under an expansive and greedy nineteenth century morality. Entrepreneurs who had not grasped the nature of "the public good" were learning how to manage the government to their avantage. But "cut-throat" competition produced a public reaction which birthed regulation. We trash it to our peril. As usual, advances in learning to live together as freedom-loving creatures, in fact all changes in human society, are fraught with the need for correction and improvement. We try what seems best to us at a point in time, and then experience unintended consequences and loopholes in enforcement provisions that are exploited by some of our fellow citizens. Apparently evolution does not filter out selfishness and greed, so some such people are always present to produce static in the status quo. In democracy we have found that it is possible through regulation to reduce bit by bit the consequences of destructive social patterns.

The story of twentieth century regulation highlights the current danger of populism, that is, exploitation of people too easily available to demagogues who play on antiquated prejudices. In populations made up of people just like us, currents of opinion have rolled back and forth, especially as modern media were available to leaders who, I suggest, think poorly. Such circumstances have been abetted by a popular "foundationalism." We apply this word to the deep rational tendency to find solid and irrefutable foundations for ideologies. Thinking people have long sought to understand "reality." In the Enlightenment this came to mean certainty about a rational understanding of the world. The social approval of some understandings became foundations, presumably certain realities, assumed to be correct. Once they have become solidly part of the culture, people hang onto these foundations irrationally. They are very hard to change. In modernity, one of these foundations was the too-easy certainty of early modern science. These had become a fixed part of American culture by the early twentieth century. But for a century critiques of this Enlightenment aberration have been growing.

"Correct" ideas have led many to impose their ideas on others, and this went on for so long that people became acclimated to accepting the ideas of leaders, correcting them only with great pain and passage of time. It is a demonstration of our freedom in democracy. The path has been full of pitfalls and mistakes requiring correction. Clearly, we have been learning to do this in Western culture. It might be fair to call these "adjustments" except that we are apt to think too much of uncertainty in such a word. Adjustments are serious "corrections." To enter into the cultural mix, we want to know more "certainly" than that. It helps to appropriate the analogy of space flight "correction" of trajectories with which we have become familiar. In space flight path corrections are understood to require continued tracking to maintain the course of the projectile. So it is true of our society. No longer so certain in our knowledge as in simpler times, we grant ourselves freedom to correct our paths. Our new sense of freedom enables us to change our minds.

The story of regulation in the twentieth century flags how ephemeral populist concerns tend to be. Crowds have been swayed throughout history by powerful orators. Even more unfortunate at the moment is the revival by demagogues (some of them "educated" people) of early twentieth century misunderstanding of science and ignorance or dismissal of the cultural revolution of the nineteenth century. Nonetheless, we have learned that thoughtful and intelligent people will question leaders who exploit public discontent, especially through fear, and this learning should help to move the American public toward a new mind. With the increasing prominence of the new mind, we may be able to surmount the current ultra-conservative binge adroitly.

A word of explanation may be in order about Jacoby's use of "unreason." The *American Heritage Dictionary of the English Language* (2009) defines unreason as irrationality, or nonsense, absurdity. Jacoby focuses on "irrationality" epitomized in the Fundamentalist movement and laments at its capture of the word "conservative." We, too, object to this misuse of "conservative;" at base, conservative means retaining what is good. It seems that those who unreasonably hold to ultra-conservative positions are quite unwilling to listen and therefore often fail to see better ways. When they make feints so as to engage in discussions with "liberals," too often they seem not to hear. Such people have often found "crying" effective in gaining a reprieve for their causes. Such "crying" is a use of cultural hurting and mourning postures for gaining assent; it is sometimes used by little children. George Steiner correctly labeled such posturing as "resolutely strategic." It is a tragic twisting of human emotions to serve personal gain. But we are learning also to discern the difference between "crying" over obsolete cares and true need.[394]

I suggest that the better definition of the unreasoning mentality is "doctrinaire." The people involved have become trapped in ideological doctrine. This entrapment is particularly sub-human in that it means the mind is not free to think creatively. The time is past when we call it idolatry; ideas have become the idols. Doctrinaire means entrapment. It is the kind of thing at which common sense raises its eyebrows and says, "Oh?" Unfortunately, Western culture is so complex that the innate tendency to be lazy plays into freezing peoples' attention. Many people have not learned to discern unreason. In this condition they are easily confused. They are targets for demagogues who care little for intellectually respectable discussion but speak easy answers to complex problems. Doctrinaire entrapment leaves people helpless to seek truth. They seldom face the possibility that their doctrine is untenable.

Today this does not mean "irrational" (a term that reflects doctrinaire Rationalism), and these people often claim to be rational. For example, the standard of living has been tied to the creation of wealth so long, and confirmed throughout the Industrial Revolution, that today's meager job creation of growth industries does not make any impression. Facebook employs only 2,000, Twitter 300, and Ebay 17,000. It takes only 14,000 employees to make and sell Ipods. "In other words, as Tyler Cowan says, many of this era's technological breakthroughs produce enormous happiness gains..." but little cash to employable people.[395] The world is really changing in just the ways doctrinaire irrationalists (people trapped in ideologies of the Rationalist era) most fear. Unfortunately, their rationality is tied so closely to obsolete ideas embodied in their doctrines that most of them are unequipped to wiggle free of this entrapment to examine the problems presented to them by critics. This is "unreason." Gradually it will be replaced by the new mind.

Early regulation represented the liberal tendencies in late nineteenth century politics. The late twentieth century support of deregulation followed the popular ultra-conservative uprising and the primitive power of some conservative pundits deeply entrapped in doctrinaire positions. Most recently, the aggressive antagonism of the right wing has stimulated (in ancient tit-for-tat imitation) the same sorts of rebuttals by the far left. This is a sort of degrading politics. We may be grateful that it has not succeeded in tarnishing the progressive image of democracy in the world.

Again, we are driven to grasp the evident prehension (mental grasping) that American culture has been articulating increasingly for over a century. We refer to this prehension in several ways: human values, humanitarian ideas and concepts, and positions in politics which have been labeled pejoratively "liberal" (being lumped with a variety of disliked ideas beginning with monarchaism, socialism and communism). It is time to end the long enslavement of Americans to such political sloganeering which has been practiced by all parties for many decades. Of course, this will not happen overnight. It will happen only as we reinstate the popular respectability of intellectual attention to our conversations with one another, and pay attention to views which prehension is telling us must grow if we are to further humanize our culture. Jacoby wisely argues for heightened attention to the intellect.

This history reminds us of one more thing: human communities are made up of large numbers of unique individuals. Each one makes up his own mind increasingly as the old mind enslaved by outsiders diminishes and evolves into the new mind. There will probably always be some people who are more like sheep than the new humanity now emerging. Some people may continue to indulge in negativity, popular ideas, and support of the status quo. We can only hope that the human community can mature fast enough to avoid some of the worst ecological disasters now staring at us.[396] We have advocated concerted conversation among unlike parties to seek the solutions of perceived problems. Such models and experience are still young. But if we have faith in conversation, the time and effort required to include diverse people in such conversations will not deter us. Our increasingly educated public contains enough mental acuity to address the most complex issues. Faith in intelligent regulation, especially of the powerful economic forces pummeling us today, can make the difference. Will we apply the immense power of millions of human minds in conversation to find solutions?[397]

In this section we note the importance of regulation of economy. Other regulation is, of course, needed as well, traffic for example and even that can be thought of economically. But perhaps government is primarily an instrument to govern economy. If so, one must be aware of the fox in the hen house. Every person is economically dependent. Therefore those who govern must be disciplined to deal with their tendencies to favor matters for their own advantage. We call it "conflict of interest." In jurisprudence it has long been the practice of judges to "recuse" themselves from cases in which they might be found to have a personal interest. Perhaps it is impossible to define economic interests so cleanly.

Setting additional problems aside, the assurance of economic well-being is its own temptation to favor entrepreneurs, owners, and, perhaps, managers. The problem we currently face is "old wives' tales." For example, the notion that giving rich people tax breaks produces jobs for ordinary people. With employment decisions resting on profits, deploying more employees is determined by complex commercial considerations, not entrepreneur's wealth. In the meantime, income disparity grows and production will increasingly come at the price of human jobs. Society has never controlled wealth effectively and increases wealth in the upper echelons has become meaningless. We have much to learn about how to regulate our society.

It seems clear from recent history to agree that our present American system is in need of a conceptual reworking. The Founding Fathers accomplished their work and gave the world a new lease on life. The many special interests of the people have been identified and untangled from the common good of simpler times: law, medicine, and religion. But the two emergent issues today are the disentanglement of government and economy. It is a problem far beyond our scope here. All we can do is hold up an unequivocal reminder that we as a people of extraordinary capability must apply ourselves to developing a government free of the obsolescent power of money. We have already suggested that the solution may lie in the new mind which is not trapped by the high value of wealth accumulation perpetuated by the rich. Everyone needs and deserves sufficient access to resources to live fully. We all recognize that wealth itself is not a sure path to life health and satisfaction. Perhaps we need to reflect on the admonitions of prescient people of ages past as to how all people might find the means of fulfillment. But there are also those in our midst who have already been testing ways of doing this.

C. FAITH IN RELIGIOUS CONVICTION

For those of us who have found our home in one of the world's great religions, atheism seems impossible, but we are no longer of the mind to ostracize those who who differ. We remember the primitive experiences of religion recorded in our scriptures, and we know that long ago our ancestors knew nothing of our sophisticated systems of belief. Yet that they were religious cannot be doubted. The basic quotient in religion is earnest expression of wonder at what is beyond our comprehension and the inexplicable fact of our human superiority over all other life on our globe. It is a remarkable and wonderful creature that can contribute to the Creation, transforming the surface of the world into habitable and useful bits and pieces, and living in it in increasing harmony.

Before our civilization began, in more primitive days, people's pleasure in relating to other people led them to innocently give up their sense of wonder and substitute submission to leaders who were able to organize them to assure the food supply. Civilization began, and vast numbers of people lent power to the manipulations of governments by their acceptance of leaders' rhetoric. Gradually, evolving human beings lost their individuality in the service of their overlords; they lacked freedom to develop themselves. No doubt this happened innocently. On the basis of a primitive self-image, this produced the overlay of a sheeplike mentality on their intelligence. The individual deficit was swept forward into our time by the immense power of culture. The residue of that sheepishness is still to be fully overcome. And its legacy has corrupted, but not destroyed, our religion.

It has taken two thousand years for Western civilization to largely free itself of this legacy of oligarchy. The dominant religion growing out of the best left from the oligarchic world was nonetheless tainted by that model of government which assumed authority to "govern" large populations. That oligarchic model was exactly what kept people in peonage for over three thousand years. Perhaps one can consider it a contribution to humanity that under oligarchy Western humans learned to discipline themselves in the midst of their growing numbers. In other words, they were socialized as somewhat disciplined human beings. The ancient individual was familiar with living with unrelated other people.

Unfortunately, the self-discipline was tainted by subservience, so that the prevalent view of humanity was of two classes, one masters and the other slaves. The main fault of the Church after the fourth century was in adopting this model for the Church to maintain the work of the Church. This meant neglect of the image of humanity embodied in Jesus' life which the Church professed to hold sovereign. The Church perpetuated the degrading image of a sheeplike people who required overlordship to avoid self-destructive behavior. In addition, the leaders in that late ancient culture were concerned with building a Church which would perpetuate their faith, and this provided the opportunity to create their personal security maintaining their privileged status. The priests, nuns, brothers, and monks became another aristocracy with the bishops at the top on par with nobles.

We can be grateful for ancients' acquiescence to persuasion in order that language might become highly refined. Naming things, description, comparing, story telling and reflection on it all were necessary for the development of the sophisticated language produced in ancient times. It was important to growing socialization. And it provided for the development of the art of rhetoric necessary to all political activity since. The combination of persuasive skill and sheep-like people worked wonders for oligarchs for long centuries. But when Europe emerged, the autocratic formula increasingly fell apart. The populations were too large, too diverse for autocratic government – and for an autocratic church. The coalescence of Greek and Jewish cultures enabled people to gradually gain confidence in themselves. Unfortunately, the new aristocracies of the wealthy and the religious could not see the shift in the human image. The long, slow and wholly natural development of rhetoric gradually kept it flexible and it continued to be an effective tool during the emergence of modernity and for the task of replacing autocracy. Rhetoric may be our most adaptable skill as language itself naturally changes with use by huge populations -- a grand symphony.

The language fit for reformation of first millennium Europe had been developing. It had embraced extensive abstractions and soon would include more words about human beings as humans. A new self-consciousness was being shaped with the help of the less-subdued peoples of northern climes. All helped to shape the Reformation and the ensuing Enlightenment, the two names for the early emergence of a new mentality revealed in modernity. We have reviewed the gradual separation of civil and religious authority in Europe, aided by the more primitive individualism of the northern European people. Before it was tamed late in the Middle Ages, the aggressive, different people of the North overwhelmed the fragile evolving institutions of the South. This spirit contrasted to the sheeplike fears of Mediterranean peoples. It could be fierce. Violence characterized society far into modernity aided and abetted by people we currently speak of as "hawks." The residue of that violent culture still awakened primitive actions against Jews and Muslims at the beginning of the twenty-first century. All the while, human self-consciousness was evolving. It would find expression in the Reformation.

The deep residue of sociality growing more sophisticated over thousands of years helped to harness hearts and minds in a new way to live. Gradually, distinct changes in attitudes emerged in the European psyche. These were shaped by the convictional language supplied by Christianity which was as pervasive as the language of war. The sacrifice of Jesus identified individuals as worthy of the love of God. Reminiscent of the Jews sense of being chosen people, European Christians universally believed themselves to be somebodies. The overlay of ritual and institutional pomp of the middle ages was replaced by the innovative participation of ordinary people in the new Protestant world. We speak of it as a new mind.

The Enlightenment vastly broadened the population excited about use of their minds. The introduction of particular disciplines associated with specific areas of inquiry enabled many people to focus their attention wholly on empirical reality, the subject of science being the sensory world. Philosophers, accustomed to critical thought, dealt with rationality without the constraints of scientific criteria and sought to extend the reach of human reason to all things. Some who ruled out nothing from the reach of their minds came to belittle religion and Christian orthodoxy specifically, finding such things as miracles entirely untenable. Theology had long taken refuge from rational critique by separating "revelation" (by which they meant God speaking to people) from human reason. But some scientists insisted on disparaging such thought, particularly in the early twentieth century.

Reluctance of some intellectuals to acknowledge religious conviction as a significant component of our culture led to recent neglect of the the Reformation as an anticipation of the Enlightenment. It is surprising in the light of the Dark Ages that Christianity not only survived but had been the source of the rebuilding of institutions and European culture after destruction of Roman society. Universities sprung off from monasteries. Church festivals provided for community celebrations. Market morality was constrained by the religious ethos. While we leave behind its pedagogy, we may be grateful that the Greek virtues were expanded by the Church and that they permeated the population. The European culture of the early Enlightenment can very simply be called Christian. While late in the Enlightenment beginning with the Deists, Christianity orthodoxy was questioned, the culture built by Christianity is and will remain a tribute to human intelligence.

The residual belligerence of the ancient world evident in prejudice is more product of culture than of religion, though it cannot be denied that through most of its history, religion has supported violence. This is part of the entanglements of our past. It is not limited to American forms, of course. Aberrant forms of Islam embody the same negativity taking form at the end of the ancient period, after Christianity. Still, the form taken by Islam is significantly different from the American "fundamentalism" which was not violent. All extreme behavior can ultimately be traced back to the antagonism engendered here and there in ancient villages and cities and to the persistence of humans who have not grown out of such primitiveness. It was brought to a vicious and extended climax in the ancient empires and was strongly evident in Europe during much of its history. The problem of belligerence first emerged, no doubt, in unhappy experiences among early human beings, before pacts and codes were developed. It is very primitive, belonging to times before the development of much capacity for discrimination.

Like instincts (also in the background), belligerence is subject to our intelligent choices. Once people generally realize that they are more alike than different, that they can learn from the "others," and that together they can live a richer life with cooperative behavior, antagonism fades. Again, it is evident that the human mind now has the capacity to make more human choices than people often practiced in the past. As the distinction between religion and culture emerged, major religious groupings took on peace-making as an article of faith. Pacificism is a doctrinaire form of this peaceful intention. As such, unfortunately, it elicits reactionary jingoism.

When they recur, belligerent behaviors still impede the development of a religious faith fit for the twenty-first century just as all reactionary behaviors do. Residual American Fundamentalism, its deadly tentacles reaching much of the world as a mistaken orthodoxy, will continue, increasingly submerged, in the new world emerging.[398] Its most virulent expression in the United States is in the right-wing anti-government extremists who feed on the kind of fearful politics now in vogue. Mark Potok in the *Intelligence Report* of the Southern Poverty Law Center notes that the last time the political scene seemed this overheated was in 1995 when we witnessed the bombing in Oklahoma City. "In the days after the deaths of 168 people there, a *USA Today* poll found that fully 39 percent of Americans agreed with the proposition that the federal government had become 'so large and powerful that it poses an immediate threat to the rights and freedoms of ordinary citizens.'" Potok goes on, "Whether or not today's rage on the right is motivated chiefly by racism ... it seems obvious that violent rhetoric leads to violent action. Words have consequences."[399] All leaders who use inflammatory or simply negative rhetoric reinforce this sort of ominous potentiality. It is a persistence of misguided conservatism.

The roots of such belligerence are in fear. It is an instinctual reaction to whatever is dreadful. The Gospel According to Mark makes it a prime target of Christianity: "Do not fear, only believe" (MK.5:36 NRSV). But conquering fear is required of the individual person. It cannot be directed or commanded. The persistence of violent rhetoric helps to keep fear alive. But today fear of the government in the United States is absurd, not that we do not have to maintain vigilance always.[400] But the way in which we keep an eye on authority and maintain our freedom in this country is no longer by vigilante separation, but by alert participation with our hearts and minds. Demonstrations, marches, and sit-ins may be useful techniques today and tomorrow. But in this guise they are simply part of a societal conversation. Though violence still breaks out in reaction, such behavior will continue to recede; the people involved will join the mentality of the mid-twentieth century Civil Rights movement posture of non-violence. The motivation is increasingly recognized as originating in religious conviction.

One of the persistent characteristics of western religion has been the mind-changing aspect of conversion to faith. People who have not been raised in a religious atmosphere, like those who adopt doctrinaire scientism, sometimes open themselves to new recognition of their limits, their finitude, and their creaturehood – in a word, to acknowledge that all human rationality begins with faith in something. Neither should we assume that children of irreligious people inevitably will be like them. Some of the children of hating adults separate themselves from such venom. This emphasizes our belief in the capacity of humans to rise above even deep cultural inclinations, above both fear and misconstructions of their culture.

> Shortly after white supremacist James von Brunn's fatal shooting attack this spring at the United States Holocaust Memorial Museum, his 32 year old son issued a statement to ABC News in which he denounced his father's ideology and described the devastating impact it had on his family.[401]

Charles Stangor who runs the Laboratory for the Study of Social Stereotyping and Prejudice at the University of Maryland thinks the community is a more powerful force for such attitudes than parenting. Apparently intuition may be independent of DNA and culture. Carolyn Wagner, daughter of an Arkansas Klansman who she witnessed torturing a black man, has spent her life working for respect and hope. She suffered the taunts of her classmates all through school when they found out she was the daughter of an outspoken racist. She feared that the Black Panthers would burn down her home. Carolyn discovered herself after freeing a man from the railroad tracks where her father had left him to die. "I felt like I had made a difference when I was able to cut that man free," she said. Fear can be overcome as, in her case, by conviction.

Words are secondary to experience, especially especially conviction rooted in family and community. Still, words carry past experience forward. And the attitude of one's community toward such words carries over directly into our experience. Laws instigated by the Civil Rights Movement proved effective in gradually reducing both vitriolic racial speech and belligerent actions. We can, if we choose, use social controls to increase the viability of the new mind. One of the prime functions of the church in our society is to persistently repeat the words of love and respect emanating from the Bible – telling the story. Even those churches which hold onto early Christian ideas such as the centrality of the bloody body of the crucified Jesus and the atonement for our evil bodies and separation from God, have gradually acceded to those among them who saw Jesus' loving work and message as primary. The Scottish Kirk (stalwart of orthodoxy, not unlike Rome) itself grew out of such a change. The freedom to study scripture raised impatience with the rigidity of Knox Calvinism and stoked movement toward humanism. No doubt the reality of Jesus' physical suffering has comforted many people in distress, but the world in which we live makes our empathy with his grief over human suffering more empathetic as we focus more on his life and less on his death. Like all cultural change, subtle and often small differences in emphasis eventually change our focus. Words and experience have interacted to change our convictional stance.

One of the unfortunate aspects of early Christianity was its institutionalization of beliefs as if for all time. The sense of history was very limited. Throughout the premodern period, reinforced by Platonic ideas, the permanence of accepted ideas was always assumed. The concept of truth was like Plato's "eternal idea." We must credit this ancient attitude with a rigid understanding of the orthodoxy which sustained the Church for a thousand years. Even in the Reformation, the mistake was not wholly understood and most Christians today spring out of that background. But the minds of the Protestant Reformation conclusively demonstrated the evolution of such ideas, making them fit for the emergent world. Interpretation of scripture has been part of our religious heritage for at least three thousand years. The proliferation of theologies which followed the early reformers demonstrates this, but it flows mostly out of increasing understanding of rationality, not out of a better understanding of history. That consolidation would take another century.

Conservative tendencies have a place and contribute to the richness of our heritage. But progressive tendencies have a place also, and our intelligence must guide our adaptations. On one occasion Jesus seemed to put his relation to his disciples ahead of the traditional priority of family. But this intellectual affinity was not meant nor has it usually been interpreted to mean denigration of family. We have the capacity for many commitments and the ability to reorder commitments, however dear they may remain.

The truth be told, as we say, old ideas as well as new ones require attention to the degree that they contribute to our present culture. No denigration of the past fits the new mind. Without Petrarch and Erasmus, Calvin might not have been able to write the *Institutes*. Without Pythagoras, Descartes might not have been able to advance science into the Enlightenment. We know that contributions of our predecessors will not satisfy all our insights, but ours might never occur to us had not others come first. So it is with all culture. In every sphere of human activity, things which came before have contributed and often continue to contribute to human life. Of course there are things better left behind; we no longer need to watch for signs of marauding animals. In the United States for the most part we rejoice in no longer fearing arbitrary arrest or periodic local warfare. But the list of our indebtedness to the past is long and does not need another rehearsal.

This is as true for religion as it is for politics or science. Without the earliest wonder of our ancestors, the mind might not have developed at all. But we now know that wonder is not what really sets us off from other primates. Perhaps wonder led us to begin *constructing ideas*. Such construction also seems to be innate – we constantly construct things in our heads and have for generations imagined them to be real. Or is it *organization* of ideas and concepts that is primary? It hardly matters. Perhaps organization and construction are two sides of a coin. At any rate, we have to guess that as humans pursued their wonder, awe, and conceptual constructions, the idea of outside forces emerged, and they began to think that they might be able to escape misfortune by placating such forces. Even in their primitive state, they could bring gifts to a place at which they had encountered something wondrous or where they had a fearful experience, just as they might do to gain the favor of another person or a chieftan – to avoid further retribution or to demonstrate remorse. But let us assume for now that the earliest such expression was one of simple gratitude, say for escaping a predator. At that place there was no need to think of cause and effect; the person escaped certain death. It was *memorable*! Today we understand that anything that happened relevant to that experience would reinforce the conviction in it.

What appears to us a matter of faith was often the expression of such cultural habits. This is not to diminish anyone's faith, nor the pressures on Abraham to sacrifice his beloved son, Isaac. Abraham had to make the decision whether to follow the settled pattern in his culture. His insightful experience of substituting the ram for Isaac changed the culture he bequeathed to his son, family, and followers. Done with conviction, we see that religion does not remove the difficulty of life, it simply gives it meaning. Sometimes this meaning is so significant that it changes the whole future by changing the culture.

The crucifixion of Jesus fits into the ancient pattern of sacrifice for the common good. Unfortunately, what was good in Roman eyes was executed with consummate cruelty. Minor conspirators were easy to spot and probably not worth much effort. But one who could quietly command large crowds and enlist silent but committed followers around the countryside might also mobilize them into a rebellion. We know from recent events just how quickly tens of thousands of people can join in a rebellion.[402] Jesus was one of those charismatic leaders. He gave uncounted people a new view of life. They talked about it. What the Romans did not anticipate was the energizing of his small band of followers with conviction strong enough to establish a flowering culture which would in three hundred years replace Rome itself. It was largely spread orally among the people, but the culture of writing was also flowering and the leaders among them took full advantage of that burgeoning capability. Conversation was blessed with a new method bound to multiply the effect of their convictions on Europe.

One cannot imagine people of the first century failing to follow the pattern of interpretation long practiced by the rabbis. Allegory and premonition were not questioned by anyone and most alternate interpretations, for example of Isaiah and Joel, used the same limited literary tools. The science of writing history had only begun to develop in the Greek Herodotus. So Jesus fit what they considered the pattern of God's communication to God's people through the words of the prophets. But the followers of Jesus were convinced by more than words, by living with his demonstration of his teaching, and this conviction imploded into southeast Europe. One must remember that these followers were Palestinian Jews who never anticipated traveling and preaching until they came to realize the liveliness of Jesus' continued presence in their lives. It was this conviction that made them move out from their comfortable homes into the larger world.

Combining these and other elements one begins to see how early Christians formulated the theology handed down to the twentieth century. If we see actual events contradicting "prophecies" we need to remember that modern psychology has demonstrated that circular reasoning is the common logic of humanity and whatever events occur are interpreted to support people's presuppositions. It is easy to criticize the past, and those who perpetuated its misconceptions. But without their contributions, our culture could not have developed as it did. "Orthodox" Christianity is the culmination of centuries of profound circular reasoning. It provided a quite amazing rationalization for the appropriation of long-held, highly developed presuppositions we call "convictions."

Ceremony is a social construction which absorbs emotional energy. Without inherited ceremonies, humans would invent other ways of expressing their exuberance. We see such invention constantly in the media. Perhaps that is what "partying" is. But ceremony does this by capturing and molding the imbedded thinking of the time into the patterns of the time before the present that people have in their minds. It can hold onto such memories for centuries, as Christianity demonstrates. Ceremony is not in itself productive of anything but personal satisfaction in group solidarity. It tends to become extravagant, often not representing essentials, but peripheral aspects of the culture. It is often redundant. A ceremony might be repeated a hundred times without challenge or change of routine. Or it might go through a growth process with innumerable revisions over time. Ceremony can stagnate. Gifted leaders have from time to time crystallized ceremony freshly. But still it tends to grow naturally through time, adjusting to the people who also shape the culture. They adapt ceremony to the present and they adopt ceremony which touches their convictions.

Performance is less important in ceremony than participation. People may do nothing but follow along in a procession or observe it, but they are involved. It will, therefore remain an important part of our culture; no one is left out (though today we note the exclusion of at least some of our disabled neighbors and work to include them). Though there are loners among us, our culture immutably makes us social creatures. The shape of ceremony depends on the local culture, local patterns of life, and the past familiar to the people. We note with some surprise the persistence of royal pomp in some historic monarchies, and especially England. As anachronistic as they may seem to Americans these ceremonies are likely to retain their auspicious character as long as they satisfy the public's pleasure in that past. I believe that eventually they will be succeeded by more contemporary forms. One can note in the United States that the ceremonial character of the inauguration of the president reflects that pomp. Were it not for the new mind of President Washington who rejected a crown, we might be saddled with much more show and spectacle in this country. The oath-taking with hand on Bible reflects much earlier pledges of fealty to lords and monarchs. It was modified by Protestantism into the now familiar hand on book. It is an easily forgotten demonstration of the importance of our individual roles in shaping our culture but we also note that Washington's interesting insistence also underlines the residual power of the inherited European culture in the fledgling United States. Some early Americans did not want to sacrifice monarchy in fear of memories of anarchy. The fear was overridden by the conviction of those who saw the future in democracy.

These are largely illustrations of American "religion-in-general" (or, as some prefer to call It "clvll rellglon," a term that perpetuates the contusion ot religion with culture which may be more a reflection of the past than the future). The distinction is fairly subtle and some would actually confuse the civil religion with their religious beliefs. In our culture, deeply held religious beliefs, when explored, usually still reflect the orthodoxy of early Christianity. But increasingly, there is an evolutionary tendency to reinterpret that orthodoxy, an inevitable effect of emergence of our new minds. Culture has been at work reshaping orthodoxy throughout history. But occasionally, conviction trumps culture (as Abraham demonstrated). Such convictional motivation has influenced society throughout history.

It is true that the percentage of Americans who say they have no religious affiliation edges up bit by bit. It is now about 15 percent. Nonetheless, in 2008 76 percent of adults said they were Christians, compared with about 77 percent in 1990. Such a difference is statistically insignificant but acknowledged dwindling of mainline Protestant memberships reinforces our expectation of the direction of change. There is, here, no cause for fear among us. Such figures involve us in evaluating social research and pointing out the difficulty by noting that another survey conducted by other researchers a month later said that the number of Americans claiming to be Christian is down ten percent since 1990, and yet another points out that the present 15 percent without religious affiliation is double the 1990 figure. A growth in Roman Catholic numbers in the Southwest, Texas and Florida is largely due to the influx of Latino people. We note that the Roman Catholic Church in the United States has grown by 11 million people since 1990. But that church has suffered greater loss than others to Protestant denominations and by those who "just drifted away."[403] Its huge size obscures this loss from our awareness.

The picture appears to substantiate the claim that people feel less attached to traditional religious groups than in the past. When we realize that almost everyone was counted in the Roman Catholic Church in Europe as recently as 1500 CE, and that barely five percent of Americans belonged to established churches in 1800, change is not abnormal, but entirely to be expected. People today make up their own minds as they grow to adulthood and some never do settle into a named religious identity. This corresponds to a general decline in membership organizations, and a growing distrust of government. At the same time the number of trustworthy special interest groups has burgeoned; in 2010 the Columbus Ohio *Dispatch* listed about 500 of them (omitting religious groups). If this juxtaposition seems obtuse, perhaps, nonetheless, it points to changing convictional expression. Should those choosing to devote time and resources to innumerable good causes be charged with irreligion? I don't think so. Nor is the distrust of government like the earlier hate for monarchy; people still acknowledge its value.

Our culture has not been one of unanimity religiously, but one of diversity. In fact, the country was founded to preclude the sort of commonality that can only be achieved among people by an overarching authority like the power of the Roman Church in the Middle Ages. Unanimity was hardly a characteristic of very ancient people who gave up almost total independence (within the limits of a patriarchal culture). They became submissive in bowing to authority under the very early kings and emperors. But since gradually coming to a self consciousness about their personhood, people have grown increasingly confident in choosing their own identities. And, in America and Europe especially, as modernity has produced abundant material goods, medical miracles, and personal freedom, the decrease in the difficulty of life has reduced the urgency of religious faith. Religion has become more cerebral though Christianity simultaneously affirmed the whole human being. Ideas became the focus of belief.

Until late in the twentieth century the ideas of orthodox Christianity were the focus of religious believe in the United States. And then, one of the signs of the emergence of the new mind occurred. It was the dethronement of religious ideas in favor of religious experience. The intellectual distinctions of modernity no longer served well to identify people religiously. Recent findings of the Pew Forum on Religion and Public Life indicate that 44 percent of Americans do not belong to the faith of their childhood. If the data were available fifty years ago, it might have been fifteen percent. The expectation that one will retain childhood religious affiliation through all of life no longer holds. Changes among Protestant denominations are easier than across other lines. Marrying a person of a different identity also happens within Roman Catholicism and Judaism, of course, and is believed to be responsible for halving the number of Jews who are religiously observant. When we hear that almost three million Americans identify with groups such as Wicca or Spiritualist, some will be upset and talk about the drastic change in the Christian complexion of the country.[404] And the truth is that the effects of scientism during the past century or more have left many people without the experience of intimate belonging held by Jews for over three thousand years and characteristic also of many Christian churches.

It is true that the monotheism of the Jews arose in the ancient world. Monotheism was becoming an attractive religious idea. Greek intellectuals, in a culture trapped in ancient mystery and fertility cults, largely ignored the long-standing human sense of the sacred and the holy; they were intellectually preoccupied with examination of the world. The Jews, like the Greeks, sought to use their minds carefully and thoroughly but added one important modifier: the Jews sought to maintain the personal sense of sacred and holy. We are not simply intellectual beings. Our emotions are not only important, they are essential to our humanity, and Jewish monotheism was significantly different in recognizing a passionate God who loved them. This conviction is embedded in their story.

The anthropology behind the Christian entrance into Europe grew out of the conviction of the Jews that they are a "chosen" people, somebodies contrasted with the nobody slaves of the surrounding Mediterranean world. Their claim to know the price of slavery can hardly be doubted; slavery was the condition of life among most people in the ancient world. Their tradition claimed that God called them out of slavery and established them as a unique people. That very personal relationship to the deity held sway for most of the past two millennia in the West. It is behind the religious practices of Christians, Jews, and Muslims – theoretically two thirds of the world's people. For a huge portion of the people of the world it has contributed to a sense of being more or less "somebody."

The Christian sacraments in our culture embody a symbolic way of conceiving of the convictional aspects of our story. They require explanation because they are human constructs. They are tied to simple aspects of life (eating, bathing, committing). Their reiteration, explanation, and practice year after year, century after century reinforced convictions and evoked among us emotions which made us want to share in them. Stanley Hauerwas reminds us that emotions are signals that help us remember what kind of people we are. This is still appropriate. It is too easy to forget such things without persistent reminders. In our habits of life we stimulate these signals daily (as in prayer) because we have grown distant from our stories and easily neglect them. The sacraments are our conversation with our religious, our human, past.

There is probably something irrational about conviction, but we seem to be convicted very strongly of some things. For some it is the family, the integrity of the marriage relationship, faithfulness between two people. For others it may be a political conviction in laissez faire capitalism, such as the far right seems to hold. For many years such convictions have been trapped by belief in the rationality of such ideas. Beguiled by the power of the human mind to give ourselves undue credit for creation of understanding, we would commit ourselves to positions in distinction from others. Luther's cry, "Here I stand, I can do no other" may be the outstanding example in our culture. A more contemporary position, saying, here I stand, as long as I cannot be persuaded otherwise, would have been irrelevant to his historical moment. This is an example of the kind of change we have inherited. Some have labeled the more recent position pejoratively "relativism." Such labels should be understood as archaic. We still cry out for understanding that is encompassing and true; labeling tends to ignore the point.

Rationalism demeaned conviction because *conviction* is not alone intellectual. Willem Zuurdeeg (a Dutchman) notes that in German and Dutch the roots of the equivalent terms mean "witness." It was used as a legal term as early as the thirteenth century. The Latin root (related to "conquer") includes the prefix "con" meaning "with" and also "thoroughly." It came to mean proving someone guilty of an error; thus its root meaning has come to be to show clearly, to demonstrate, and finally, to be overcome thoroughly.[405] Unfortunately, the bias for certainty accrued to "conviction" over the years, as if one was not privileged to change his or her mind. But conviction is a matter of decision. It is one's present, personal sense of reality. While all decisions probably include an "element of commitment, even in scientific language the term is used in regard to the whole human being, not just his or her intellect; a person decides to give himself to this...." Traditionally conviction has indicated being so overwhelmed that a person is willing to give her life for it.

We maintain here that in the new world we are free to shape our minds freshly every day, choosing to make changes when our thoughtful, careful, maybe agonizing cogitation calls on us to do so. This is not a negative relativity but common sense. At times in the past, when one could not say "my mind has changed," such changes were characterized as called for by voices in the night that forced the change.[406] Today we accept the blessing of amazing brains that allow us to cogitate, to think, while we continue to care for others. We can still talk of conviction and of convictors, acknowledging that some of our beliefs are so important to us that we give ourselves to them, letting them influence us. We are no longer too proud to cry out for the impoverished and hurting people of the world as Jesus did in the face of the proud Romans and the fearful Jews!

And we join our fellow human beings in the building of a better culture for our children and their children – for all children. In this new context conviction takes on a hugely important new character. This conviction has the character of common sense at once more cerebral and more sensitive than the common sense of the past. It is the common sense of thoughtfulness, consideration, accommodation, straightforwardness, honesty, and integrity. We call it "intelligent" because we have been blessed with brains capable of grasping our own being and the realities of our neighbors, others everywhere, and the world around us. It is caring. This is not conviction in some creed. Nor is it belief in some orthodoxy. It is ourselves identifying our human commitment.

Conviction is no longer something to be defended tooth and claw. It is insight – a grasping of understanding to be shared and examined and explored. It is hope and satisfaction joined in expression of our true humanity as we are able to grasp it and make it our own today, sometimes for the first time. It is putting into words our most basic self-identification. We have faith in such conviction because we are wholly self-conscious of our choices in arriving at who we are.

D. OUR DEEP CONVICTIONS

In his later work, *Man Before Chaos*, Willem Zuurdeeg tells us that "Plato's birth as a philosopher came when he cried out loud 'Being *must* prevail over meaninglessness and death!' " Plato's prowess is not so much demonstrated by his ideas or his intellectual ability as by his conviction. His works follow from this expression of his conviction of the reality of an imperishable fundamental being without which everything succumbs to the threat of chaos. Our study suggests that the deep conviction of the worth of life motivated the people of that degraded civilization[407] to struggle against insuperable odds to surmount their chaotic world. Plato could see a new world, but as all human foresight has always been, as in a fog. His voice has never died, honoring his brilliance. In Zuurdeeg's words, "Western civilization has been brought into vibration by the painful but joyous outcry of Plato."[408] He suggests that the cry "God is dead!" (in the voice of a madman seeking God with a lantern in the middle of the day) came from Nietzsche's traumatic understanding of what we humans have done. The chaos of the nineteenth century signaled to many the final end of Christendom: "We have killed (God)."

But, of course, the failure was in misunderstanding religion and a proud mistake: Rationalism perverted by the misconception of the eternity of ideas. This cry was without hope except in power. Only after achieving power could Nietzsche's superman be magnanimous, a perverse conviction. The confluence of a proud German self-sufficiency with a cultural Rationalism was too much for this brilliant writer; he died of a stroke after a decade of incapacitating mental illness. Society suffered for the same convictions in the exercise of nihilism by the Nazi regime.

We have been slow to grasp persistent evidence of our rational limits. The human construct of God is of the greatest reality, not to be undone by a lack of perception by some critics of religion. Thus the "cry" of human beings for reality as they understand it represents the explosive expression of an agonizing individual (who is part of a crying culture), who becomes an agent of cultural creativity. Plato's cry is a demonstration of the gradual freeing of humanity from the slavery of the ancient period – and from the slavery of misconceptions. Though the cry often was not heard and was quickly muffled for a very long time, its underlying persistence generation after generation helped to shape new cultures which freed others. The fear among autocrats of the cry of the people induces severe repression. It has taken thousands of years of experience for the world gradually to learn how to overcome such misunderstandings. Now it is our deepening conviction that we are on the path toward a brighter future.

In the twentieth century new dimensions have been given to that cry. Not long ago, bright people often felt helpless in the face of the error and degradation of civilization (as Nietzsche). Then the pragmatic minds of people like William James, Ludwig Wittgenstein and Alfred North Whitehead. This burst of creativity began to percolate in the midst of the human community, representing what Christians call work of the Holy Spirit. We might in the context of this work identify this as the gestation of the mind of humanity. Years of development as we have traced them through the Enlightenment had worked the magic of human thinking, or as Christians are inclined to say, the Spirit of God among the people. The century demonstrated, again, the immense creativity of the human being, clearly made central by Whitehead. Wittgenstein brought his genius to bear on the slippery language on which we are dependent. And William James argued for the fundamental wholeness of the human being. Others' contributions in many fields defy enumeration.

Today we are heirs of a century of immense productivity in almost all areas of life, even in religion, we may hazard the guess, though that is only today becoming evident. Among them are the development of innumerable avenues for individuals to participate in shaping their world, not just the physical environment, not just the civil infrastructure, not just the workings of competition and of free enterprise, but the very nature of human community. We have in a sense passed a watershed, the towering mountains of the Enlightenment and our pride in our rationality. These have separated us from others just as antagonism between communities did some time before. We have demonstrated the possibility of undertaking any enterprise and acknowledging our assumptions without enslavement to them. We are no longer of necessity enslaved by any human constraint.

Our conviction of our freedom enables us today to hold our assumptions up to the light of day, to the eyes and ears of our peers and superiors. Achieving a new integrity, we leave pride behind. There is no further need to think in terms of friend and enemy. All people are our brothers and sisters. As long as one hurts, we all may feel the pain. When one cries we are all ready to help. It is a new world. Within 36 hours of the Japanese magnitude 9.0 earthquake our rescue teams were on the way in the air. Only sixty years ago we demonized Japan.

We still embody some remnants of our aristocratic past. We still imagine that some of us are wise enough to create institutions, industries, enterprises, and practices without the scrutiny of the public. So America has had to battle to finally provide the humanitarian medical care of which we are capable to all our citizens. Soon it will become unusual for the popular mind to be twisted against its own self-interest by demagogues. This time has finally arrived, because the new mind sees beyond the past just a bit more into the future than we could before. We can see that it is our calling, our duty, our obligation world-wide to care for one another first and foremost of all our necessary reactions to the needs of our world. Contributions to refinement of our culture arrive from all quarters. We are learning to trust in one another in our common search, through open communication. And the billions of us around the globe have enough brain power to accomplish new miracles in the years ahead.

Zuurdeeg noted that if one really wants to find the ideas that dominate a population we must look for those quietly lurking out of sight as well as those ideas which are commonly taken for granted, which are considered as self-evident and cause for vociferous defense. These two have an important difference. Those lurking out of sight characterize our discussion of culture. We see those taken for granted in the often popular, local and generational "life styles" which include the easy jingoism of war-thought and the popular prejudice of any moment. These are easily stimulated by destructive rhetoric. It is the ideas lurking deeper among us which deserve more of our time in conversation than we have for a very long time given them. Zuurdeeg called the important, self-conscious, and individual portion of culture "conviction." It is the core of our religion. Our difficulty in discussing convictions in conversation now requires our intensive attention.

We will refer to the underlying worldview guiding us as religion. It is made up of our deep convictions. We no longer need to be afraid to talk about that public part (the parts which are taken for granted) without the vituperation common until now. But it may take us a while longer to be open about deeper aspects. They are related to the person we have made of ourselves and therefore we are hesitant to open them up to criticism, but usually they are common in their general outline. We must corral our pride (as with all things which involve us personally), and realize that reactions to our sharing simply help us identify aspects of ourselves which, so far, we may not have examined with sufficient care. It remains forever our own choice as to whether we accede to others' reactions to ourselves. Our religion is our own, however much it may have common, public connections. Our selves are influenced by others about us, but they are our own making.

When we self-consciously think about reforming the deepest aspect of our self-image, we step out of the world of the white-collar man and the man of the gray-flannel-suit that often sublimated the self to the corporation. We sometimes failed to recognize that was the world of life-styles, not the world of which we are convicted in our whole being. We sometimes forgot the commitment implied in the shaping of our selves to more permanent beliefs. Increasing numbers of us have discovered that to be a mistaken path. Though rationalism had been successfully challenged over the early part of the century, at the midpoint the common sense of the times still was overwhelmed by the residue of scientism and rationalism and led to denigration of the flourishing post-war religiosity of the 1950s.

The sociological markers of church attendance and membership showed a contrary and short-lived surge, but common sense, as usual, prevailed and the shallowness of religious commitment demonstrated itself over the next fifty years. Attendance and membership fell off over the entire spectrum of Christianity. Many who had made the mistaken connection of their faith with the populist "common sense" turned to the old placebos of conservatism. They listened to demagogues without recognizing their perverse, destructive orientation.

Fortunately, today our newly evolved selves are better able to distinguish that "life style" view and understand that is not what convicts us. It may, of course, masquerade as common conviction – our language is very slippery. But conviction is far deeper than has been thought in the past. Religion is not a simple-minded residue. In the same ways that religion began in the distant past, post-orthodox Christianity begins now with the same dumbfounding awe and wonder. Struggling to emerged from the fog of religious feelings behind primitivism to numen (Otto), ritual (orthodoxy) and organization (modernity), religion will find its faith again in an intelligent grasp of human conviction.

With the exception of genius here and there in the human scene, until recently, few have been able to see beyond the reaches of acknowledged common sense rationality. We remember the "true prophets" among biblical "seers." These human beings were of all classes and peoples. And they are today as well. That is why it is so very important for us to read widely and carefully of the perceptive thoughts of others. The wisdom garnered from such cogitation is fodder for our weighing of innumerable cultural influences on our inner being.

We are aware that the process of living begins to build our selves in our earliest childhood. Some of it is absorbed from our parents. There are parents who utterly fail in the task of helping children form effective self-images. Some simply ignore the eager child's love and turn off the admiration which normally follows the young child's recognition of self and others. Fortunately, there is almost always a residue of that earliest human experience if the parent was in evidence, supportive, and accepting at the beginning. The process goes on throughout each lifetime.

So it is that Cindy Foster remembers a face at the window in the middle of the night. Because of her father's notoriety as a Klan leader, she feared a threatened bombing by the local Black Panthers. She tried to scream, but her voice failed. Later she discovered that it was probably an FBI agent checking on her family's safety.[409] It is just an extreme example of how a parental failure can undercut a child's development. In the small town where everyone knew him and expected her to share his beliefs, Cindy said, "I just wanted to be me – not the daughter of my race-hating father." Cindy Foster's convictions were quite unlike her father's and demonstrates the diversity of influences which shape our culture through individuals. She attended a Methodist church as a child and discovered a colorblind Christ. "All children are precious in his sight.... I saw that what my father was doing was wrong." In the nature of creation, our universally unique selves are a precious protection against those perverse human beings who occasionally cross our paths. The historic province of the self has been the common sense that, given half a chance, seems so often to grasp the best of our inheritance.

It took evolution of society thousands of years to grow out of the nascent brutality of our ancient history. Zuurdeeg quotes Mircea Eliade telling us, "the restoration of the primordial chaos (during the Babylonian New Year's festival) abolished order and hierarchy and reintroduced universal confusion in order that, as in primordial time, life might arise again out of death, cosmos out of chaos, light out of darkness." It was a cry for life free from sickness, coercion, sin and death. Theirs was a vicious culture which replicated itself in the hands of a growing aristocratic class throughout the Mediterranean world. As that world crumbled, the subdued cry of the repressed, sheep-like people grew stronger. Pride continued to dominate the condition of society.

But the Church was preaching to ordinary people. It kept the human spirit alive while they cried out for justice. Here and there the human spirit triumphed over degradation, finding ways toward independence of the class structure personally and economically. The people woke up here and there, bit by bit. The deep self-awareness of the individual, properly chastised by human error, very slowly achieved its wholeness as a socialized people. In the nineteenth century even philosophers became aware of the cry, and in the twentieth the reputation of a Norwegian artist, Edvard Munch, rested on a single one of his many paintings called "The Scream." As he described a youthful vision while walking with friends:

the "air turned to blood" and the "faces of my comrades became a garish yellow-white." Vibrating in his ears he heard "a huge endless scream course through nature."[410]

We must be grateful that as the scream for humanity coursed through the roots of our civilization, the Greek-Roman analytical culture and the Jewish understanding of the self emerged as the dominant constructive cultural forces. They provide our outstanding Western cultural inheritance. The nihilism of the twentieth century was produced not just by a few perverted leaders, but by endless centuries of self-serving aristocrats who perpetuated oligarchy far past its useful life. Zuurdeeg reminds us that Karl Marx, demonized by an immature society (essentially for perversions of Marx of others), organized powerful revolutions out of his cry that the industrial revolution had dehumanized the worker. Zuurdeeg has reminded us that Neitszche cried out "God is dead!" not because he wanted to kill the idea of God, but because he felt so strongly that it was people like us who by nineteenth century Rationalism and religious ritualization perpetrated destruction of the basic order of the world.[411]

Sigmund Freud cried out that the only way to recover our humanity is to recognize the cry in ourselves. Once-upon-a-time all humans were fairly – though not completely – individualists, and oligarchy had an important role in our socialization. Even before that we had found joy in other people and natural ways of working together in small groups. All of it helped our ancestors learn to discipline themselves, to subordinate themselves to bigger things, and to begin a long journey into organized society. That was modified in earliest times by the necessity of filial loyalty and it is that extraordinarily deep history which still functions to keep the family at the center of our convictions. After all is said and done, it was the family that first introduced each of us to life, to ourselves, and to others. And it is still each of us individually whose cry for peace, justice, hope and a sense of transcendence will shape the culture of the twenty-first century. Unfortunately, Freud became the father of a proud individualism.

Today, we suffer from that mistake. Its long-term development crystallized finally out of scientism in the early twentieth century. Freud and the other great founders of psychoanalysis never doubted the primacy of the individual and of our rationality. Their emphasis on the psyche was part of recovering ourselves from even the residue of autocracy.[412] Freud was right; we had finally to see ourselves as ourselves. It appears that as a people we may, unfortunately, have grasped these insights by the tail, focusing on our individualistic selves as if we were separate from our world, and thus we have, ourselves, contributed to the overarching individualism of the twentieth century and the emergence of the "therapeutic society." But, again, our heritage prevailed. It laid the foundation for the great array of humans who saw beyond their prevailing cultures and formed convictions deep enough to make them articulate in speaking persuasively to us about our basic sociality. We have touched a few of these persons in these pages, but their number is too great to identify all of them in a single work. Nor is it possible to name them all.

One of the characteristics of our New Human Being will be graciousness. Whoever understands the self as we have tried to delineate "self" will be grateful for the contributions of all those who have gone before us as well as those about us, whatever their origins and propensities. We are not proud "individuals" as the modern world has painted us. We are human beings. We love others as ourselves, and therefore we are moving rapidly into a post-modern world. It has been a hard road to the self that grasps itself fully enough to truly appreciate others. Such deep convictions will form the future.

POSTSCRIPT: ON INSIGHT

This book began in a recollection of difficulty in reading. That difficulty was actually more complex than a mechanical use of eyes. It resulted in a difficulty in achieving insight. I see still today it in dyslexic-like occasions that reminds me that learning to translate squiggles on paper into the sounds of familiar words is the bare beginning of the process of modern learning. Learning is the product of all human mental activity but in our world language in graphic form is essential. Being told in childhood what was to be learned helped me only at the surface level of knowing things. Since my school days we have discovered that knowing how to learn is the object of education. I learned that lesson in the college of hard knocks. While insight was familiar to me earlier, learning how to learn has vastly improved my ability to perceive insight.

How is it possible that long before such awareness people experience not only learning but insight? College prepared me for graduate studies in two important ways. First I learned what it meant to study, to drain every drop I was able to squeeze from many hours of lectures and reading. I find it helpful to equate that learning with people's gradual incorporation of self-discipline in the emergent city. Second, I grew in my ability to understand difficult writing (and lectures) with the help of patient professors. Perhaps that is a bit like the cultural development of apprenticeship and academia itself. But it was not until I finished graduate school that Bernard Lonergan published his monumental study of human understanding, *Insight*. And I did not come into contact with this brilliant Roman Catholic philosopher and theologian for another fifty years, until I had nearly completed this book. There I found the insight I had been seeking into how it is we understand.

Insight is the 'aha!' moment – like the story of Archimedes rushing naked from the bath when he suddenly grasped the secret to a problem: "Eureka!" (I've got it !). The early development of our mental capabilities may well have begun when the earliest people found that a familiar environment had been changed by a violent storm, or a congenial and productive home was disrupted by the death of a spouse. Then wonder became reflection.

I found Londergan's words exhilarating. For Lonergan, insight is far down the chain of intellectual activity. After our brains have learned to translate squiggles into the words we are already using as tiny children, we begin to see how they string together in phrases and sentences. That is no mean achievement and constitutes what we call "literacy." But the next step is to grasp the series of sentences as pointers in the direction of what we call a paragraph. The meaning of a paragraph depends on how our brain puts the thoughts together in our heads with knowledge already there. This seems to take shape by the way the brain works; it makes endless connections. This seems to be its major activity waking or sleeping. Lonergan's "insight" is on down the chain of mental operations from this. But even the lowly paragraph can induce insight.

Our expectations are what is familiar. Terrain is always the same. Friend always shows up. Then earthquake changes the terrain; friend has fallen to a predator. Even animals may grieve but respond instinctively. But the human brain became capable of facing the disappointment of expectations and choosing new paths, new partners, behaving freshly; this is the root of our adaptability. At the moment of disappointment even familiar clues change and the human begins to think. First there is a stimulus which piques one's curiosity, almost always unexpectedly -- except perhaps when we moderns are *reading* and we rather hope for insight.

Lonergan notes that such stimuli are outside of us. But there is an inner condition also necessary for insight. Lonergan calls it "a habitual orientation." We have called this a predisposition, an inner commitment to use one's mental capacity. Since we choose to override instinct, we must set our minds on how to respond to disappointment, how to follow up curiosity, how to apply ourselves to surprise. We must be self-conscious about our "habitual orientation" if we are not to be driven by unconscious habits.[413] We choose as we engage in innumerable considerations and as we reflect inside our brains. Very small children can be encouraged to exercise their brains and to aspire to do so. They have a natural tendency to ask questions when they begin to talk. There are so many things they have to get in place in their heads that everything raises questions. The little child whose questions are put down or ignored is not likely to develop the disposition to think. Probably, any answer is better than no answer; a child will eventually sort out the mistakes. But to begin thinking that answers are unimportant is a bad start for learning to use one's head. At any age, fixing in ourselves our intention to use our ability to think is a key to having insight. As early in life as possible we must develop the habit of thinking – and begin discovering how our own minds work.

With a similarity to Archimede's experience, a jolt occurs when one grasps on his own terms the thought of a paragraph. I have often found myself re-paragraphing what I read differently than an author has done and wondering why. And then I *see*. The author's rationality will not be exactly like mine. We are all rational, in the sense that things seem to us to fit together. But it is quite unlikely that any author's style will closely fit our own manner of learning. Each author brings his or her own self to work. The words fashioned by each one will express that person's insight in a way that emerges from her or his own self. I was reminded of translations I read as a student of some great thinkers whose *sentences* went on for over a page, and I took heart. Such a sentence, from our point of view, has got to be confusing.[414] Shorter sentences help us understand and I have begun (somewhat late in life) to see how to write a short sentence. Whatever style we encounter, we are faced with the impossibility of knowing that what we perceive through words is exactly what the author meant us to find. But grasping as well as one can the thought of a paragraph, one is prepared to ask a question or to accept the thought understood and go on reading. Thus we are prepared for insight.

Going back to the uncertainty of human communication, those pesky words nonetheless may lead us to begin a curious journey into the unique human mind. The thousands of volumes of commentary on Bible passages witness to the difficulty of understanding with certainty. The Jewish Talmuds (Babylonian and Jerusalem) both ancient interpretations of the Torah stand as powerful reminders of variable communication. And the struggle cannot ever end. We are bound to communicate with metaphors. We must grasp what we read as well as we are able. It is a blessing that the brain is so gloriously complex that it persistently makes connections of all that enters our awareness. Reflection allows us to mull it all over and over. Often new connections appear. The evolution of the human self allows us, then, to take heart in our comprehension. We may have confidence in our own understanding. As we test it in conversation with others, hopefully we will find that we have understood well. But if not, we have learned to roll over thankfully and try again. We are forever confronting difficulty and learning to rejoice in the encounter for it is in difficulty that thinking occurs.

That means that we can never close out the blessing which is the capability of listening for it may reveal to us some difficulty we have neglected. Listening is the gift of hearing with understanding. Our peers can enrich our grasp. Insight, we would point out, does not come without effort. At least from biblical times speakers were haunted by the difficulty people often had in understanding. People had to learn to apply themselves to listening if they were to benefit from the wisdom shared with them. In Mark 4:11 Jesus emphasized the importance of hearing with understanding. The next verses contain Isaiah's idea that the recalcitrance of people in *not* grasping his intent is purposeful. Perhaps "kicking against restraint" (recalcitrance) is an obsolete concept. Those who do not grasp the message are those who have not opened their minds to hear (or to see) and thus perceive no insights. They have not predisposed themselves to learning. In Lonergan's words, they have not created a "habitual orientation." In that sense it is a purposeful failure to be ready to listen. If they do not understand, reflection may help.

They may look , but not perceive,
and they may indeed listen, but not understand...(Mark 4:12 from Isaiah 6)

We take another tack. Yes, people must make the decision(s) to open their minds, to perceive, to listen and to struggle to understand. Being lackadaisical will never fulfill the humanity available to us. As Isaiah and others have said, "All right, then, if you refuse to see, then you will not comprehend, you will not understand." But post-modern people do not give up. It is a universally applicable lesson of the Enlightenment; we learn from our errors to go on, to continue the pursuit. Even those who are incarcerated must be persuaded to open their minds. We no longer say, "Stop their ears, shut their eyes so that they cannot understand." The decisions we make, as we say, to open our minds and hearts to understanding, are the targets of the rhetoric of Calvin, and of every great religious leader. Calvin tried to persuade his wavering audiences to get on board with the direction and intent of his lectures so that they could understand (see, hear, grasp) the truth. It is a matter of tuning our instruments, our brains, to be insightful.

Everything depends on our utilization of the gifts given us as human beings. Each of us has limits. These are imposed by genes, by birth circumstances, by parental and community nurture, by training and education, but most of all by our individual choices to stay alert, to seek understanding, to reach out into the unknown world. The earlier in life that we learn to extend the rapidity with which we see and grasp the words, the groups of words, and even the paragraphs almost as whole pictures in our minds, the better chance we have of gaining the fruits of insight. And we can work at it. As long as we live, the brain never stops its persistent building of connections. That means that at any point in life we can accept the discipline required to improve our insight. It is not easy to get started.

It takes patience. "Understanding" is a temporary affair, a condition of mind in circumstances which are always new. Since "mind" is our personal product of choices built on inherited culture, experience and the intellectual habit of learning, no two of us think alike. "Soul-mates" are perhaps nearly alike at best, and as they age they will probably delight in their differences. Understanding is our self-conscious grasp of ourselves and our world. Understanding is never corporate, always individual. It you and I who understand, not our churches or our communities. When we say "it is understood," or "we understand" we are presuming on the grasp of insight in our communities. We cannot separate our understanding from ourselves. If we understand something that we do not believe, that, too, is part of our own being. If, on the other hand, we believe something that we do not understand (including God) we acknowledge our limited capacity. We are not God. I also am not a physician, nor a mathematician. I do not understand anything completely, however thoroughly I may explore it. There is always another question. I must be conscious of any impatience I feel. Sometimes it is called for. Consciousness means self-discipline and discrimination.

The current debacle of American politics is in the conservative resurgent blindness to the progress of the twentieth century. The labor unions fought a hard battle for respect for the common worker, largely in the pre-World War II world. The institution of collective bargaining was a major step forward in provision for dialogue between employer and employed and was copied by many not originally part of the struggle. In the post-World War II world, in the euphoria of materialistic exuberance, it is possible that some too-generous provisions were made for worker progress. But that direction of caring for persons who will never have any material "wealth" means fewer poor elderly people today. It means better health and reduction of the social costs of poverty. Growth of the middle class in this period was noteworthy. Unfortunately, such people have always been susceptible to arguments of those richer than themselves, who purport to demonstrate that those aspiring to climb the economic ladder from the bottom nonetheless have more than they deserve. But this lack of insight meant that many in the lower class were left still suffering as a third-class. Whether or not we agree, the reduction and eventual elimination of gross economic inequities is important. In 2011 the myopia of the Far Right broke its reticence to attack social progress, revealing a disturbing failure of insight.

The universal American preoccupation with recovery from the current recession provided a perfect opportunity for the residual resurgent Far Right to exercise its muscle. But the polls clearly indicate that the majority of Americans now see that unions are an American blessing. The mayor of New York, Michael Bloomberg, was quoted across the country saying in a *New York Times* column:

Rather than declare war on unions, we should demand a new deal with them – one that reflects today's economic realities and workplace conditions, not those of a century ago. If we fail to do that, the fault is not in our unions, or in our stars, but in ourselves.

Such perceptive insight is typical of the new mind emerging rapidly among us. Bloomberg continues the use of command language: "we should demand." "Collective bargaining" in its conciliatory role is oriented more helpfully to achieve our cooperative objectives. We can and will now begin to use more accommodating language in all human relations. Another sign of the new mind among us is awareness among the very rich of the unreason in the vast discrepancy between top and bottom incomes. It has been said that American tax brackets were well suited to, say, 1930. Eighty year old insights are now obsolescent.

The twentieth century taught us at long last that government is essential to provide for the common good. The rugged individualist may have been common even in 1900 but rapid urbanization has changed that substantially. Philanthropist Abigail Disney (heir to the Walt Disney fortune) tells us, "The estate tax is the cornerstone of a progressive system that leaves the wealthy heirs with ample funds while providing the government with the resources it needs to build an environment for the common good."[415] Well, to a degree. The people are still coming to terms with the balance of governmental power required for social existence. Such insight recognizes the new reality that government of the people by the people has become the major player in reshaping the environment primarily because it can command the resources necessary to sustain a culture in which the common good is paramount. While guardian of the common good, governments must embody foresight and control sufficient resources to enable seven billion people to live together creatively. Granted, there are still many who survive rather independently in the less developed areas of the world. May there always be such people. Nonetheless, the majority of us will live in urban proximity we create wealth together in different roles. We must rely on government to help use that wealth for the common good. Even most of us who treasure the lonesome out of doors and choose to retreat there from time to time, will live in urban society.

As the new mind evolves among all people, changes in government are both necessary and inevitable. Some change will come only by rebellion as in the past, but more often, rulers who fail to meet modern needs for government will step down and permit the human intelligence of others to restore necessary order. Each person deserves the respect of all and increasingly this will mean the responsible participation of everyone. Whatever I understand, is in a sense mine. My understanding helps to define me and I take a little pride in what I do understand. Whatever I understand is my knowledge, my self-conscious grasp of myself and our world. What is commonly understood is common knowledge and comprises a significantly active part of our culture. Often only segments of the population understand our extensive specialized knowledge, and we have learned to trust those who master it, with appropriate safeguards. This knowledge is nonetheless a social entity though our own understanding is limited. It is I myself who hold my understanding in my own mind, based on my own experience. If I believe that my understanding is mistaken, I most likely discover this as I listen, perceive, and find insight. When my knowledge changes I have new understanding. But common knowledge may or may not change either sooner or later. And government must maintain an intimate connection with the people, avoiding the separate mentality characteristic of aristocracy. Thus governmental change will occur naturally, But it will change, slowly, sometimes too slowly if it has not maintained an enlightened attitude toward constant change.

Heraclitus was more right than those early philosophers who thought that all things have a unitary origin. Change is characteristic of existence. We wind down this study of humanity with comments about the effect of insight on the two key dimensions of society we have explored, culture and religion. Only recently have we grasped the persistence of change even in these two conservative descriptors. It has become clear that while culture is the almost indescribable whole of human life, the way we live, religion is our attempt to share a common expression of it as a cohesive view that embodies not only what seems to us to be real in our past but what our best expectations are. Both culture and religion are deeply influenced by the past, the former quite naturally and essentially unconsciously, the latter with a hightened self-conscious effort to enjoy and make common sense of our inheritance and of our transcendence consciousness.

We conclude that philosophy is now morphing into an analytic orientation. It is the summation of centuries of development of critical thought, in other words, of insights. In those years – in addition to learning an infinite array of skills and arts – we learned to explore rhetoric, law, medicine, the sciences, and how we think, that is philosophy. My intention is not to preclude efforts to construction of wholistic systems, but to avoid the historic trap of idolizing these. Thus Whitehead's system is grasped today, as early theologians and philosophers did, as guides to contemporality – rational discussion of their foci. In the new analytical stance philosophy will examine all aspects of culture and religion with a growing, comprehensive set of tools to help us in two ways. The first is to alert us to what appear today as mistakes, in order to consider these and possibly revise them. The second way is to articulate contemporary understandings of culture and religion. This will increasingly make It possible for us to influence the shape of the culture we bequeath to our grandchildren, and it will help us to keep our religion a helpful and effective influence in their lives. The new role of philosophy will provide more helpful critique of insights and of their applications than in the past.

Culture and religion will continue to pursue paths appropriate to their functions in society, culture shaped by our living patterns which may include revisions of law and order, i.e. of government. The path of religion will be shaped by the multiple convictions held by religious people, by their grasp of intellectual changes in their cultures, by institutional incorporation of such changes, and by the persistent guidance of professional theologians. This is a very hopeful path to constant renewal of culture.

All of it is dependent on language. Our ability to speak teamed with our fantastic brains, allows us, it seems, infinite potential. That may be true. Not long ago we believed that language itself would limit us to development of one universal tongue. Esperanto,[416] which achieved recognition by UNESCO in 1954, is used by very few people today. But recently, Google has introduced a translation capability which permits people to write to one another in their own languages. Based on mathematical analysis of words used by many translators, it makes it possible for practically anyone anywhere to talk to another regardless of their languages. Granted some limitations, the technique makes it possible for everyone to speak for themselves in our emerging one world. Conversation can now take place in real time across language barriers. With millions of Google-capable tiny electronic devices, perhaps human creativity has conquered the most universal divider of human beings – language. Since it is evident that language emerged in the dim, dark past, we are aware of how long we have been on this path. No doubt the technique of conversation is on track to greater perfection. Humanity is not yet completely out of the cocoon – or, perhaps we should say, the butterfly is still unfolding its wings.

1   Priestley, J. B., *Literature and Western Man*, (1960), Introduction, x. This is one of the books in my small retirement library that has been a stimulus and encouragement to complete this work.

2   The concept of culture has befuddled many people. "In the 1940s the celebrated anthropologist Leslie White proposed reducing all human history to a single equation: E x T → C, where E stands for energy, T for technology, and C for culture" (Ian Morris. *Why The West Rules – For Now*, 148). Though Morris reminds us that White was talking about something like "social development" the literature makes my point. We stand by the common sense definition suggested by Emanuel Schegloff in likening culture to the world of microbes. In that realm, as a virus can incorporate bits of another organism's DNA, culture is constantly reshaped by appropriating current elements of human life. Cf. Leslie Brothers, *Friday's Footprint*,143f

3   Ian Morris notes, "The historian Norman Davies has found no fewer than twelve ways that academics define the West, united only by what he calls their 'elastic geography'." The West, "is essentially an amalgam of intellectual constructs...." *Why the West Rules – For Now*, 2010, 41.

4   Born and raised in India, my friend Sanjib Ghosh has opened my eyes a crack to see into the source of our Indo-European tongues. He had learned three languages by age 13 including the root of all Indian speech. He tells of seeing original Sanskrit manuscripts from 1000 BCE which deal with mathematics, philosophy, and economics. The numerous Indian languages all use the phonetic alphabet of Sanskrit. The Vedas were in Sanskrit. This appears to be a very different path of civilization which merits fresh analysis of the evolution of the human mind.

5   Psychologist Robin Dunbar in *Grooming, Gossip, and the Evolution of Language* (1996) proposed that language evolved as a kind of vocal grooming, an efficient substitute for the universal primate use of grooming to sooth, placate, and reconcile tensions.

6   Arius died in 336 CE, but he had many advocates, including Eusebius of Nicomedia. Arius was generally distrusted as one who degraded Jesus. But he can be understood as advocating a hierarchical trinity (Jesus not equal to God) rather than a trinity of unity (three persons in one). It is a controversy which did not die easily and Arianism in various forms was appropriated by Goths and Vandals who would not be silenced in the fifth and sixth centuries – the price paid for the Empire's best mercenaries. But the Empire never became a Christian institution as its successors did. "It adopted Christianity, it never incorporated it."

7   Philosopher of biology David Buller counters evolutionary psychologists' tendency to ascribe human intelligence to evolution in the deep past. He says, "The human mind did not just adapt at some fixed moment in the past. It is, instead, continually adapting." (In Daniel Lord Smail, *On Deep History and the Brain*, 2008, 147.)

8   See Joan Huber's brilliant *The Origins of Gender Inequality* (2008).

9   *Nature*, 2/27/99. *Popular Science* July 2000, 26. Is it possible that such findings challenge our belief in the African origin of all human beings? The orangutan, after all, is native to Sumatra.

10   Remember, the cosmic conflict of light and dark was a very old concept. It was basic to the Zoroastrian religion and was promulgated in the third century CE by Mani (Manichaeism) spreading into Europe. Zoroaster himself (sixth century BCE) tried to reform Persian religion and disliked the introduction of bull-sacrifice. He divided the Persian pantheon into good and bad deities.

11   The idea of evolution is found as early as Greeks likeThales and Aristotle. Church preoccupation with literal interpretation of Genesis resisted development for 1500 years when we find suggestions of it in Francis Bacon, Descartes, Leibniz and Kant. Even Goethe made a contribution. "Social evolution" is much debated and to some discredited, but the basic idea of evolution is not restricted to changing species.

12   As I write this, Senator Edward Kennedy died. During his fifty years in government he consistently moved in paths of cooperation and accommodation, displayed appreciation for the outcast, and love for humankind. In the Kennedy family, two of his brothers did not reach their fiftieth birthdays,. They were cut down in their prime by assassins. But Ted blazed on and reinforced the family culture of public service. We forgive him his slips, his humanity, as it were, for we all, like him, are far from perfect human beings. But human beings are not limited to an animal nature, and all may rise above that five million year old heritage.

13   We omit consideration of thousands of clay tablets of trade records, to focus on history.

14   See Michael S. Gazzaniga, *Human: The Science Behind What Makes Us Unique*, 2008, 212.

15   Marshack, Alexander, "Ice Age Art," American Museum of Natural History.

16   Nonetheless, in a Ukrainian mammoth-bone hut, six different musical instruments made of mammoth bone were found, each with a different tone indicating a specialization among musicians. These surely indicate a cultural development in music and the probability of a role in ceremony as much as do the polychrome paintings in the caves of France and Spain.

17   "Thus says the Lord," is a familiar biblical admonition. If one understands the necessity of persuading people both to listen and to act, we can see how use of such a phrase would carry great weight. The person speaking, convinced that his insight is from outside himself (the artistic inspiration), uses the most effective rhetorical device he knows. Does he believe his words? Of course. The prophets reminded

the people, however, that they had to listen carefully; False prophets can use the same words as those who are faithful. Among the Jews, "thus says the Lord" embodied the early anthropomorphic vision of God. It is easy to forget that they made strenuous efforts to avoid anthropomorphism but they, too, had only the language developed to that time. Much modern theological language would have been unintelligible to them. Even erudite theological students easily fall into habitual use of language as if words were more than pointers. Many verbal devices are embedded in religious ritual. Like language itself, rituals tend to perpetuate antiquated concepts. Some people will carry forward such beliefs. Language expression is part of being human. We can intelligently express ourselves only in familiar words – unless one believes glossolalia.

18   Ibid., Alexander Marshack. More recently, Tom Teepen in his column told about the finding of a five-hole flute in Germany which may be several thousand years older. Teepen points out that ancient people did not think of such art as frivolous, even in the tough circumstances of life they faced. He suggests, "Apparently there has been something in us from the beginning that has felt compelled to reach through the mundane and feel around for the transcendent." (*Columbus Dispatch*, 7/11/09.)

19   John McDonald, a molecular evolutionist at the University of Georgia, attributes this split to bits of "junk" DNA that we probably inherited from ancient viruses. Such "junk" accounts for nearly half our genome. It appears that the critical bit occurred six million years ago, exactly when humans and chimps separated. (Kathy A. Svitil, *Discover*, November 2002.)

20   Such god concepts are often called "oriental" recalling views of oriental despots.

21   One should note that in ancient culture "common sense" counted for much more than it does today. And elderly people's wisdom was, outside the intellectual aristocracy, largely made up of common sense – the accumulated understandings of life.

22   Boehm, Christopher, *Hierarchy in the Forest: The Evolution of Egalitarian Behavior*, 1999 in Daniel Lord Smail, *On Deep History and the Brain*, 2008, 166. .

23   Ibid., Smail, 164f.

24   It appears that adventurous traders circulated far and wide carrying not only trade goods but tales of power and aggression.

25   The concept of evolution is basically "unfolding." Unrolling, to open out, expand.

26   So, American culture has been characterized as that of the Roaring Twenties, the Depressed Thirties, the Tumultuous Forties, and the Fortified Fifties. The new "generations" since World War II have been the Baby Boomers, the Generation Jones, the GenXers. New "cultures" of this sort emerge constantly.

27   A list of late twentieth century wars have added to the millions of murders in World War II. In 1996 the National Defense Council Foundation released a list of 64 hot spots down from 71 a year earlier. The Center for Defense Information held 27 active conflicts and ten that were mainly nonviolent but unsettled. The Central Intelligence agency tallied 28. In 2005 Gwynne Dyer wrote "If nuclear weapons can't change your mind about the usefulness of war, then maybe you haven't got one." (Columbus Dispatch, 5/6/05, A13.)

28   Toynbee, Arnold, *Change and Habit: The Challenge of our Time*, 1967, 19.

29.   Hall's work by that title is worth reading. But his great influence is captured in his trilogy Christian Theology in a North American Context: Thinking the Faith (1989), Professing the Faith (1993), and Confessing the Faith (1996).

30   Before Calvin became embroiled in the tendentious arguments of the times, he was focused on the grace of God and the wonder and joy of the Christian life. As age and disease ravaged his body, he became more irritable and his reputation has suffered accordingly. *The Institutes* reflect the earlier Calvin.

31   While this was being written, the identification was announced of a skeleton 4.4 million years old, nicknamed "Ardi."

32   The diminutive "Flores Man" (three feet tall, 55 pounds) described in *Nature* (Oct. 28, 2004) was one of four human species that existed 50,000 years ago; the others beside ourselves were ? *Homo erectus*, and Neanderthals. Though its brain was smaller than ours, pound for pound the intelligence of Flores Man as judged by sophisticated stone tools was superior. Rick Potts at the Smithsonian noted that within a certain range, it is brain "wiring" not gross size that determines intelligence. Flores Man was probably wiped out by the same volcanic eruption that destroyed the pygmy elephants.

33   Recent research has shown that the great proliferation of art about 35,000 years ago occurred when the most advanced part of the human brain, the prefrontal cortex, was developing. This part is very limited in the Neanderthal. (Gazzaniga, 233.)

34   Gugliotta, Guy, "The Great Human Migration" in the *Smithsonian* magazine, July 2008, 56.

35   Chesley Sullenberger demonstrated this cool mind when he landed disabled US Airways flight

1549 in the Hudson River just after takeoff in January 2009. All passengers survived.

36   There seems to be wide agreement that seven basic emotions shown through facial expressions (fear, anger, surprise, contempt, disgust, happiness, and sadness) are the same in all cultures. However, the same emotion from a specific facial expression may be recognized by a culture, but the same intensity of emotion may not be perceived. (Wikipedia the free encyclopedia)

37   Brothers, Leslie, *friday's footprint: How Society Shapes the Human Mind*, 1997, 100. I owe a great deal of my own post-retirement reshaping of early psychological understandings to Brothers along with insights from Julian Jaynes' *The Origins of Consciousness in the Breakdown of the Bicameral Mind*, 1976. Jaynes is the focus of a 2007 book titled *Reflections on the Dawn of Consciousness: Julian Jaynes's Bicameral Mind Theory Revisited*. Evolution is generally accepted as the "answer" to how we became *Homo sapiens* as Scot Atran tells us: "Chomsky and Fodor as well as Pinker and Bloom fundamentally agree ... on the fact that all of this is uniquely the product of evolution...." (*In Gods We Trust*, 42.)

38   Ibid. 103.

39   Ibid. 106.

40   The King James Bible gradually came to dominate and remained the major religious text of English and American Christianity until the middle of the twentieth century.

41   Calvin's *Institutes of the Christian Religion* were first published at Basel, Switzerland, early in 1536, Its much-elaborated later edition was published in 1559. Thus 2009 was the 450th anniversary of its publication as well as the 500th anniversary of Calvin's birth.

42   Two of the familiar Americans of Scot origin are Alexander Graham Bell and Andrew Carnegie.

43   "Piety" is a word we will try to resuscitate later in this paper.

44   Ibid. Leslie Brothers, 28f. Scott Atran tells us "Barber and Peters (1992) indicate that the defining moment in the evolution of language may have occurred about a half a million years ago, as indicated by the apparent enlargement of the prefrontal region of the *Homo rhodesiensis* cranium...." Nonetheless, Atran reminds us "In brief, almost nothing about human cognition is clear from fossils." (*In Gods We Trust*, 47)

45   Ibid. Brothers, 23. Gazzaniga, 47. who reports that ToM "is fully developed in children by age four to five and there are signs that it is partially present before age two".

46   Ibid. Brothers. 30. Frans de Waal, *Our Inner Ape*, 2005. De Waal notes the emergence of theory of mind experiments as early as 1922 in primate study and illustrates very sophisticated (though not human) demonstrations of self-differentiation among primates. I am indebted to de Waal, who provides many primate illustrations, for his helpful observations and interpretations.

47   As this was written astronomers Pieter van Dokkum (Yale) and Charlie Conroy (Harvard) announced the likely tripling of the estimated number of stars in the universe, accounting for most of the "dark matter" mystery of the mass. (*USA TODAY*, 12/2/2010.)

48   There are innumerable discussions of Godel's 1931 "incompleteness theorems." "The first showed that axiomatic systems like Euclid's exemplary system for geometry could never capture all the truths of arithmetic. The second showed that the consistency of such a system could never be proved by reasoning inside the system" (Peter Suber, Earlham College).

49   The Columbus *Dispatch*, 5/9/05, A8.

50   Ray Brown is credited with coining the term "popular culture" discussed in more than 70 books.

51   The long-lasting detrimental effects of neglect is still evident in the children raised in Nicolae Ceausescu's iron-fisted Romanian institutions under Communism. Raised in filth and degradation, tied or shackled in chairs, many were still, seventeen years after his execution (1989), in similar mental institutions.

52   Ibid. Dunbar, 86.

53   Shure, Myrna B., *Thinking Parent, Thinking Child*, 2005, describes how a parent can begin helping a child learn to think from the earliest months of life. However, we do not forget Piaget's demonstration of the natural readiness to learn as children grow. We avoid "over-parenting" which describes paternalism.

54   Mimicking is a primitive learning technique. It is natural to animals and children. As we mature, parents can guide development and, as a child grows, stimulate replacement of the instinct with discriminating ways to express natural curiosity and habits of exploration. Rabbi Irwin Kula is one of those who persuades us that bad times help us grow, a lesson wisely learned early in life. (*Yearnings: Embracing the Sacred Messiness of Life*.) The biblical story of Job follows a long string of such stories in history which recognized and tried to make sense of misfortune. Americans have recognized the error of "keeping up with the Joneses"

55   "Will" is given two full columns in *Webster's Third International Dictionary of the English Language Unabridged.* It is one of our most-used words. As a mental power or disposition it goes back to Scholasticism and is defined as "the faculty of the soul coordinate with the intellect that determines rational choices ... as distinct from instinct." Such words are verbal constructs which denote huge underlying complexes of behavior. Instincts are buried in the old brain where they are triggered by our senses, if, without self-discipline, we permit them to function. Emotions are of this same nature, complex behavioral patterns activated as we permit them to emerge without calling on them. Our forebears who often used such constructs as substantives did not have the advantage of the past hundred years of exploration of psychology. "Will" has to do with behavior, the actions of persons. See *Friday's Footprint*, chapter 8.

56   Kuhn, Thomas, *The Structure of Scientific Revolutions* (1962,1970). For some years, this was the single most influential book in the philosophy of science. It recovered use of the term "paradigm."

57   Robinson, Marilynne, *Absence of Mind: The Dispelling of Inwardness From the Modern Myth of the Self,* 2010, 118f.

58   "Sanctity" is usually, but not necessarily connected to the holy (Latin *sanctitus*). It refers to that which it would be foolish to deny. "Responsibility" (Latin *respondere*) is to respond. We tend to associate it with accountability for lawful behavior, but we use it here more in the sense of reliability, trustworthiness.

59   Coakley is currently at the University of Cambridge. She previously taught at Harvard where she and Nowak conducted the research noted. The quotation is from the article "Evolution and Sacrifice" in the *Christian Century,* Oct. 20, 2009, used with permission. It appears that the technical, non-volitional "cooperation" of the scientists is one more opportunity for the free and open mind of human beings to domesticate the too-convenient excuse of instinct, like the self-protective readiness to kill and the pervasive drive for sexual gratification. Though parents are inclined to think in terms of cooperation, a baby's overcoming its original selfishness is critical to becoming a socialized human being, we note that two of the social skills a child first learns are to control the flow of urine and movement of the bowel. Nowak has published "Five Rules For the Evolution of Cooperation" in *Science,* December 2006.

60   Laura I. Harris, citizen of the Comanche Nation, native American, tells us that President Obama was given a distinctive name by the Crow Nation which means "One who helps people throughout the land." It was in honor of the President's attention to Native Americans, of course, but we can hope that their vision of the name is as broad as we might hope. ("Obama Reflections," Kirwan Institute for the Study of Race and Ethnicity, The Ohio State University, 30.)

61   Fiduciary is one of the words related to the fundamental notion of trust, of being faithful. We use it to identify a responsibility assumed and acknowledged, usually financial, but not necessarily so. There are a variety of forms of *fides* in Roman law which reminds us that even in ancient times there were flickerings of the new mind among us. Here "fiduciary" is used to indicate preservation of valuable elements of the past.

62   Amitai Etzioni (George Washington Univ.) has said, "the new definition of sovereignty treats it as conditional: a nation can maintain its sovereignty only if it meets its responsibilities to its citizens and the international community." (*The InterDependent,* Winter 2005-2006, 35).

63   "Global Village" was named in 1962 by Marshal McLuhan. In his *The Gutenberg Galaxy* he characterized the ancient village as a place of "panic terrors, exactly befitting a small world of tribal drums, total interdependence, and superimposed co-existence ... Terror is the normal state of any oral society, for in it everything affects everything all the time...." Though that seems badly narrow to us now, he did anticipate Thomas Friedman's "Flat Earth," a new term for the world shrunk by electronic communication. In both cases, we are alerted to the enlargement of the human self. McLuhan it seems didn't see this and Friedman is totally preoccupied with the affects of the flat world on the United States. Broad emergence of the self is a revolutionary shift invalidating all previous definitions of boundaries – especially national boundaries – and sovereignty. The prescient establishment of the United Nations was anticipated by the unique pressures toward globalization forced on us by the Second World War. The continued outlandish race in sophisticated means of destruction following the advent of the atomic bomb raises the stakes against human annihilation. If we have "failed" in the opinion of some of us, we must be reminded that human beings have been learning from failure for a very long time. While we all are aware of many failures, the truth is that the number of major conflicts in the world has diminished substantially, global trade has raised standards of living everywhere, and poverty has been cut in half in the past fifty years. Such facts are argued ably and in depth by many authors, particularly: T. Friedman, *The World is Flat: A Brief History of the Twenty-First Century,* 2005. Fareed Zakaria, *The Post-American World,* 2008.

64   Plato named prudence, courage, temperance, and justice and these are often called "natural virtues," though they were to be obtained by training and discipline. The Roman Catholic Church added faith, hope, and charity. In late Medieval literature these were together the seven cardinal virtues.

65   The Church played an important role in this rediscovery in the 1950s. Hulda Niebuhr reshaped education in the church with the insights of Piaget and others. Ruel Howe carried the banner for dialogical

adult education in the church. Robin Dunbar shows how the emergence of the theory of mind (ToM) "turned Piaget's theories of development on their head." He did not have access to our understanding of how complex society is. But Piaget helped us to move on! Here is another demonstration of the evolution of mind and of culture. He understood how self-centered children are; born without ToM. Cf: Dunbar, 87f.

66   The educational problem this presents is the necessity of teaching every child how to use humor, how to be critical in an appropriate way, when one feels this to be appropriate, as in community skits intended to help an audience laugh at itself. These are skills that can be learned, and the student can be helped to incorporate into her/his self the ability to choose the immense satisfaction of exercising such skills effectively, or taking care to leave them for others more skilled. The art of rhetoric was the great skill of ancient and Medieval intellectuals. Persuading other people has been a highly developed skill in our civilization for a very long time. Our post-modern concern is to rule out deceit and subterfuge from public debate.

67   In the current scene this rhubarb grew especially in the schools of business administration which seem to be more impervious to language and ideas from outside their circle than others. So Walmart has made a policy of avoiding graduates of certain schools.

68   Frans de Waal, *Our Inner Ape*, 2005, 7. De Waal has provided a lucid and helpful work on our near relatives, especially Bonobos.

69   Small, Daniel Lord in *On Deep History and the Brain* credits Stephen Jay Gould with the term "exaptive" describing the application of instincts to behavior which does not serve the original evolutionary cause for their existence. "Sexual desire is adaptive with regard to its procreative function, but many primates have figured out that sex can be fun regardless of whether it produces offspring;" this is "exaptive." This use is unrelated to the evolution of sexual copulation. (127)

70   A curious disconnect, that animals do not associate birth with copulation. So-called "alpha-males" often kill the young of other males when they come to power. And they jealously guard their right to copulate as they please. One might think this shows their awareness of the relation. No such case. They are simply adhering to instincts over which they have neither consciousness nor control.

71   Pieter Bruegel (1525-1569) also depicted the vicious side of the Inquisition in his "Massacre of the Innocents." In spite of such gory pieces, his work generally displays a robust and invincible gaiety.

72   "Libertine" in Roman antiquity referred to a freed slave. In the sixteenth century it referred to the antinomian attitude that the law, and the Decalogue in particular, were unnecessary. Roget's *Thesaurus* gives a full quarter-page of synonyms for loose sexuality without a hint of either previous meaning. It would seem that this demonstrates the perennially changing meanings of words.

73   Leslie Brothers, *Friday's Footprint: How Society Shapes the Human Mind*, 1997, ch 2, "Constructing Mind: A Human Specialization."

74   In *In Gods We Trust: The Evolutionary Landscape of Religion*, Scott Atran tells us "Neanderthal burial sites indicate that by roughly 50,000 to 100,000 years ago the time traveling self was consciously imagining and reshaping its own mind and body as well as the surrounding terrestrial environment, to suit its own imagined ends, (e.g. death as another stage in life, betraying) a keen self-awareness and a concern for the human spirit" (39).

75   Williams, Peter. N., *A Brief History of Scotland*, chapter 1: Celtic Scotland.

76   Raffaele, Paul, "Sleeping with Cannibals" in the *Smithsonian* magazine Vol.37,#6, Sept.2006, 48ff. Raffaele is the author of *The Last Tribes on Earth: Journeys Among the World's Most Threatened Cultures*. The Korowai people live on the island of New Guinea, the second largest island in the world after Greenland. Raffaele reports that elder Korowai are very conscious that their way of life is ending.

77   Mumford, Lewis, *The City in History: Its Origins, Its Transformations, and its Prospects*, 1961. Mumford eloquently describes the attraction of the city as human settlements outgrew their tribal village limits. This monumental work contains a thorough index and extensive annotated bibliography with references as far back as ancient Greece. It seems that "cacoon" is a good simile for that beginning and that socialization describes the emergence of humanity from the cacoon.

78   For a popular and careful presentation of the war-origin of sociality, see Nicholas Wade, *The Faith Instinct: How Religion Evolved and Why It Endures*, 2009. Wade builds on the speculations of scholars who extrapolate from recently discovered aboriginal communities, long isolated from other humans without recognizing that their determined maintenance of unchanging rituals is like the cul-de-sac of the apes. Satisfied with their paradises of plentiful fruits (and isolation from "others") they obscure their evolving human brains. But their progeny are moving to the cities where in another generation they will be little different from those whose aboriginal ancestors are far behind them.

79   We are made aware of the prevalence of brutal regimes over several millennia within historic time on all continents, throughout the Mediterranean world (Mesopotamia, Egypt, Greece, etc.), China, and the

western hemisphere (Maya and Aztec). But that says more about the residual tendency toward primitive selfishness and the influence of culture than it does about heredity.

80   Again, Wade listens to those who tend to interpret everything as survival mechanisms. Primitive people, they say, were forced to institute such things as coalitions to control wild leaders. We maintain that the necessities of social life stimulated human creativity that led to development of such mechanisms to facilitate the common life. Early development of our rational capabilities did not wait for the Enlightenment.

81   In her *Friday's Footprint* (1997), brain researcher Leslie Brothers says: "As the amygdala became more connected with visual and auditory areas, the arrangement of nerves and muscles in the primate face also changed, giving it the capacity for expressiveness ... and all the while primate social groups were becoming more complex.... The transmitting equipment (expressive faces) and the receiving equipment (sensory brain wired to the amygdala) were evolving in step, prodded on by a demanding social milieu."(57)

82   *Nature*, 9/21/06. Scott Atran tells us that "Evolutionary scenarios for the emergence of language tend to range (far involving) bee dances, fish courtship, bird songs, dog barking (and an array of other signaling devices)." (*In Gods We Trust*, 2002, 39)

83   Ibid, Toynbee, *Change and Habit*, 1967, 16.

84   See "The Great Human Migration" by Guy Gugliotta in the *Smithsonian* magazine, July 2008.

85   The music of Greece, based largely upon the acoustical mathematics of Pythagorean ratios influenced Medieval European music. We still use its concept of *consonance*. The Greek forms were undoubtedly influenced by earlier Egyptian music after Greek culture infiltrated Egypt about the 7th century BCE

86   It took until the early nineteenth century before the shape of the modern novel took shape in the work of Sir Walter Scott. Scott was disturbed by the iconoclastic spirit of earlier times and wrote his novels with a clear eye on the actual history of his times to preserve the Scottish story. One of the glaring examples of the iconoclasm was the destruction by Presbyterians in 1664 of the Ruthwell Cross, a marble Anglo-Saxon cross dated in the eighth century. Typically, the pieces lay where they fell. It was restored in 1818 by Henry Duncan. In 1887 it was moved to Dumfriesshire, Scotland, to a specially built apse of the Ruthwell church.

87   Jean M. Auel in her series "Earth's Children" does an interesting portrayal of life about 30,000 years ago, at the juncture of cultures of Neanderthal and Home sapiens. The series begins with the well-known *Clan of the Cave Bear* (1980) in the older culture. The series includes an adventurer's encounter with the ostracized heroine (both Homo sapiens).

88   Such citadels, high above the cities growing around them could well have appeared in memory as great floating ships in times of exceptional floods. Obviously, the lives of innumerable peons were lost in such inundations. Human memory being as faulty as it is might well have constructed stories much later of "Noah's Ark" to explain vague memories of such mass drownings. When that was done, they were put into the only meaningful context available, the work of God to cleanse the earth of sin. But the citadel originally was a safe storage structure for surplus food which came to provide a fortress for priests and kings against outsiders and also on occasion against an angry populace.

89   Popper, Karl, *The World of Parmenides: Essays on the Presocratic Enlightenment*, 22.

90   It certainly doesn't hurt to read and even study secular literature. It has taken us many long years to stop burning books as if secular knowledge was by nature anti-religious -- another holdover from ancient fear of the power of writing. Why did the ancients (most of whom could not read what had been written by their scribes) erect monuments to their mighty selves? They erased previous king's inscriptions so that what would be read in the future was of their prowess. The power of writing has not often been underestimated.

91   William F. Albright in "The Old Testament World" reminds us that Babylonian science not only invented zero and the simple logarithms but in the second millennium BCE explored abstract thinking. (The Interpreter's Bible Vol. 1, 1952, 251.)

92   The period of the Old Testament is approximately this same time frame (1400-300 BCE). Iron is mentioned quite frequently in the Bible. Glass was one of the enduring products of this early iron age, unmatched by any other advance in physical science before the Industrial Revolution.

93   When the Israelites clamored for a popular king as other peoples had, the prophet Samuel demurred, reminding them of the ways kings take advantage of the people. The people persisted, and he relented to the clamor, in the manner of natural leaders in ancient times . Cf. I Samuel 8.

94   Rostovtsev, M., *History of the Ancient World*, quoted in Bertrand Russell *History of Western Philosophy: and its Connection with Political and Social Circumstances from the Earliest Times to the Present Day* 1965, 44.

95   Ibid. Russell, chapter III, 49. Russell's comment might be modified if he had been aware of the achievements in India in mathematics long before Pythagoras was born. Petr Beckman reports in detail the origins of the value of 3.1416 for pi earlier in the Siddharta in *A History of Pi*_(1993) (26).

96   Worship of Dionysius was savage but was spiritualized in Orphism.

97   Cornford, F. M., *From Religion to Philosophy*, quoted by Russell, *History*, 51.

98   The Confederacy was founded near the end of the sixteenth century to reduce intertribal warfare and to eliminate cannibalism.

99   Crossan goes on to say, "From Mark's point of view, (Peter and Jesus) had different visions of mission.... Jesus was ready to move on because he offered an *unbrokered* Kingdom to all who needed him. **The equal sharing of spiritual and material gifts, of miracle and table, cannot be centered in one place because that very hierarchy of place, of here above there, of this place above other places, symbolically destroys the radically open community it announces.** For Jesus the Kingdom of God is not his to offer as patron or for others to broker. The Kingdom of God is a community of radical or **unbrokered equality** in which individuals are in direct contact with one another and with God, unmediated by any established broken and fixed locations." (Emphasis added.) Cf:Mark 1:35-38. John Dominic Crossan, *Who Is Jesus? Answers to Your Questions*, 1996.)

100   In the sixth century BCE the Babylonians leveled the Temple and trekked selected Jews to Babylonia. Soon thereafter the Persian Cyrus, overpowering the Babylonians, authorized the erection of a temple which was surrounded by a wall as were the citadels of all Mesopotamian cities. After a tumultuous century in the region, Herod again rebuilt the temple in 20 BCE to befriend the Jews.

101   Russell, Bertrand, *History of Western Philosophy*, 1965, 295.

102   Ibid. 300. Russell explains that the defect in the philosophy of Plotinus was in encouraging people to look within themselves rather than at the world (encouraging languor), by contributing to the growth of the subjectivity which was to be found in Protagoras, Socrates, and Plato as well as the Stoics and Epicureans. Eventually this view reduced attention to science, (dependent on Aristotle) and the emerging emphasis on virtue (as conceived by Plato) prevailed.

103   Ibid. 432.

104   Foakes Jackson, A.J., *History of the Christian Church from the Earliest Times to A.D. 461*, 1951.

105   Ibid. 145. Foakes Jackson notes Justin Martyr's (100-165) use of the term "Memoirs" of the Apostles. In the 20th century discovery of well preserved copies of ancient manuscripts included The Gospel According to Thomas. Elaine Pagels' *Beyond Belief: The Secret Gospel of Thomas* discusses this second century quandary in detail.

106   Political dissimulation might be understood as a function of language. Michael Gazzaniga, Dartmouth neuroscientist, points out that researchers have demonstrated our capacity to misremember and to embellish recollection to our advantage in order to fit our personal story. Cf. *The Mind's Past* (1998) and *Human: The Science Behind What Makes Us Unique* (2008).

107   Ibid. Russell, 17, 579.

108   Marcus Aurelius, a zealous stoic, was a devoted and humanitarian emperor but continued the policy of Trajan in persecuting Christians.

109   Aquinas' versions of the Greeks were largely those which came through Averroes in Spain.

110   The followers of Wycliffe were called "Lollards" as a reflection of a Dutch heresy. They insisted that the people could read the Bible. Even Wycliffe's formidable reputation could not squelch the popular reaction to his innovations. It was not the first occasion of populist error.

111   Lest one think that burning people was an historic innovation of brutality, we need to consider recently observed practices of the aboriginal Adaman Islanders an indication of their pre-historical practices. The burning of strangers was deeply embedded in their minds. Though they must have evolved, they remained stuck in the past as did most primates. Alfred Radcliffe-Brown who visited the islands between 1906 and 1908 reported that they preserved their ancient ways against all invaders by killing them and burning their bodies. It is probable that in the past they also ate them but cannibalism seems gradually to have passed. (*The Adaman Islanders*, 1964.)

112   Frenchman Peter Waldo, a wealthy merchant, had given his fortune away and went about preaching evangelical poverty as a way of perfection. In Lyon his followers were forbidden as laymen to preach but resisted, objecting to teaching on sacraments and doing good works for the dead. In 1533 they met with Protestants and accepted some of their views. Eventually they were recognized in France and some settled in the United States as members of the Reformed group of Protestants.

113   "Strain" is another English word with multiple meanings. Here we use one of the older ones, indicating descent or heritage.

114   This may not be very different from any people who similarly conceived of God as *their* god. The difference apparently has to do with their increasing perception of themselves as responsive to a god who is superior to their highest expectations. From their beginnings, they understood themselves as responsible people with a growing sense of their responsibility to live with high expectations of themselves.

115   *The Columbia Encyclopedia, Second Edition* 1956, 813.

116   In very early ancient times (possibly before 4000 BCE) the stories from separate tribes were accumulated into the Vedas, the oldest of Hindu writings.

117   Bertrand Russell, *History of Western Philosphy,* 1965, 41.

118   See Oliver Roy, *The Politics of Chaos in the Middle East,* 2008.

119   I surmise that the significant difference between cultural development in Greece from that in the central Asian area south of the mountains and plateaus is that the Greeks were on the sea. Trade was easy and natural, very different from central Asian land commerce. Thus the Greeks enjoyed human stimuli denied to their Asian cousins with its consequent cultural development.

120   Comparisons of Gautama's words on social responsibility and Jesus' words produces long lists of comparable phrases never equaled by similar comparisons with other world religions. Late in the nineteenth century Ralph Waldo Emerson once responded to a clergyman who had said publicly that passages of Christian scripture he had read could not be matched in any other religion. Emerson said, "The gentleman's remark proves only how narrowly he has read" (*World Bible*, ed. Robert O. Ballou, Viking, 1954, 13).

121   Ibid., Russell, 289. Life after death had been in the air for a while. The concept is to be found in eastern religions as well as emergent in the Mediterranean basin.

122   Ibid, Russell, 523.

123   John Dominic Crossan and Marcus Borg have authored many useful inexpensive books in their attempts to spread knowledge of late twentieth century New Testament scholarship. Cf. *Who's Jesus?,* 1996, Crossan with Richard Watts.

124   Ibid., Russell, 482.

125   Ibid., Russell.

126   Hobbes' *Leviathon* (1651) has been a major Western text for 350 years. In this book he argued his mechanistic political philosophy. The view is weirdly reflected in some late twentieth century biological views.

127   Rationalism might be thought of as a sort of extreme nineteenth century kind of reason. In the context of increasing individualism, it was powerful. Beginning with the philosophers of the French Revolution (Helvetius and Condorcet) whose "enthusiasm" was simple excitement by the power of the mind to understand, the rational faculty of the brain was stretched by some to be the exclusive source of knowledge.

128   Hans Kung says, "It was unnecessary for Christian theology and the Church a priori to put themselves in opposition to the insights of rising natural science.... (They) essentially contributed tot he establishment of scientific and political atheism.... It was equally unnecessary that reason should often have absolutized itself (leaving) no room for the meta-empirical...." *The Beginning of All Things,* 2005, 53.

129   Ibid. Russell, 104f.

130   "Humanism" is a name for liberal thought which emphasizes the growing anthropological sense of people with integrity. It implements in the Western World the inherited Jewish sense that people are persons.

131   Herman, Arthur, *How the Scots Invented the Modern World: The True Story of How Western Europe's Poorest Nation Created Our World & Everything in It ,* 2001. 63.

132   It should be evident that I am indebted to Herman for his thoughtful exposition of the effect of the Scots on our American culture.

133   The encyclopedia was not new, however. Pliny the Elder is credited with the earliest one in 37 books in the first century and the most famous is probably Diderot's, engaged in the contemporary war of ideas about the same time as the Britannica began publishing. Britannica's continuous publication since 1771 is phenomenal. Edinburgh had become a bustling publishing center and paper manufacturer. In 2012 the publication of paper volumes had ceased, but the encyclopedia planned to continue electronic publication

134   Stephen Miller, "The Death of Hume," in the *Wilson Quarterly* (Summer 1995). Miller describes Adam Smith's arduous attempt to prevent the publication of David Humes' *Dialogues Concerning Natural Religion* written in the 1750s. Miller is author of *Two Faces of Religion: Johnson, Hume, and Smith on the Utility of Religion,* 1995.

135   Ibid. Herman.

136   Even in Milwaukee, Wisconsin, where I grew up in the small Scottish Bethany Presbyterian church, the St. Andrew's Society was active. The air there was thick with Scottish names.

137   Ibid. Herman, 263f.

138   My own Great Aunt Jen memorized many of Burns' tales and readily spoke them for her grand-nieces and nephews. She was a Kippin, my own mother was a Cameron, of the generations which still carried the pain of hard times. Putting those killing times behind them was aided by the mythology Scott

constructed.

139   A church and monastery were built in 635 by St. Aidan. Its illuminated manuscript of the Gospels written before 700 is called the Book of Durham because a gloss was added in the tenth century at Durham.

140   The first 39 chapters of Isaiah are usually attributed to a prophet or school we simply label "First Isaiah." The rest of the book comes from a later time. Scholars think that additions may have been permitted as late as the second century BCE. The motives for such additions were entirely honorable, and in no way insidious.

141   Simony is one of the many words in our language with Biblical roots. In Acts 8:20 Peter rebukes Simon for trying to purchase the gift of the Holy Spirit. We note that the person **requesting** the mistaken act is rebuked.

142   Ibid. Williams.

143   These eminent names, all persons of importance in Western history, demonstrate clearly that even very bright human beings are limited. The limits seem to be related to the way they have formed their selves over the years, and how they have, thus, developed their capacity to use their brains, including the nature of their cultures. In this evolution of the mind they embody and demonstrate the confusion out of which they themselves emerged, since like all humans they are products of a lagging culture.

144   Ibid. Russell, *History of Western Philosophy*, 1965, 646. Russell maintained that "induction is an independent logical principle ... without which science is impossible." He claims that "Hume's skepticism rests entirely on his rejection of induction." (646f)

145   Albert Schweitzer's twentieth century *Quest of the Historical Jesus* details the German efforts but he seems oblivious to work in Britain. Explorations of early Christian writings has proceeded in the twentieth century. Rudolph Bultmann and some of his disciples contended that the concerns of gospel writers were almost wholly religious or, to use the philosophical term, "existential." The nineteenth century German efforts were largely focused on literal inconsistencies between them in the events of Jesus' life they recorded. They reflected efforts in the earliest Christian centuries to defend the Gospels. In the fourth century Augustine , feeling the force of pagan objections, wrote that the evangelists are not in harmony with each other.

146   Daniel L. Pals, *The Victorian "Lives" of Jesus*, 1982, 9. Pals' summary of the introduction of the Second Reformation (chapter VIII in this essay) is helpful:

> The two styles continued, harmonies and works of devotion, (from the second to the seventeenth centuries). But ... the latter also saw the first stirrings of something entirely new: the modern critical study of the scriptures. It began almost invisibly among outcast thinkers, Hobbes in England, Spinoza in the Netherlands, Simon and later Astruc in France; scarcely crusaders, they began by applying to the scriptures the same literary canons and philological analyses that were used with other ancient texts. By middle of the eighteenth century the literary, linguistic, and historical questions combined with the philosophical skepticism of the Enlightenment to produce a powerful solvent, which for some seemed capable of eroding orthodox beliefs. Its effects were felt everywhere, but the historical application was most evident in Germany, where thinkers like Lessing, Semler, Reimarus, and others jettisoned supernatural beliefs and claimed to find distortion, superstition, and forgery in the scriptures.

> These attitudes were only a beginning. The full consequence of the new historical studies was not to be felt until the nineteenth century , and here again the foremost site of impact was Germany.... Their rigorous frontal assault on the old styles achieved nothing less than the establishment of a third tradition in biblical study, the critical style, which came very near to a total victory over the old ways. The story of these remarkable changes, particularly as they affected study of the life of Christ, has already been told with inimitable skill and perception by Albert Schweitzer in his great survey of criticism from Reimarus to Wrede, *The Quest of the Historical Jesus* (1906). It was during this same era that Great Britain also witnessed a resurrection of interest in the life of Christ. Yet on Britain's quest neither Schweitzer, his successors in the field of biblical study, nor the students of Victorian thought and culture have much to say.... (This) study is at least partly designed (to fill this gap). (Quotation used by permission.)

147   I note that this attempt to differentiate the British and continental intellectual development is not intended to suggest a bad spirit among German and French people. The evidence we have is chiefly about elites in all these locales, except where appearance of evolution is evident among the people. We have tried to identify general shifts in the sense of self at different times in history. From this we have inferred a persistent increase in self-understanding among ordinary people as well as elites.

148   Russell reminds us: "[Aristotelian syllogisms] are ... among valid deductions." Aristotle repeatedly

admitted the importance of induction, though it is less cogent than a deduction and yields only a probability. (*History*, 209).

149   In his *How the Scots Invented the Modern World: The True Story of How Western Europe's Poorest Nation Created Our World and Everything in it* (2001) Arthur Herman details the expansive role of the Scots in the Industrial Revolution ala Alexander Graham Bell. The origin of the frontier individualist has been traced back to invasion of the central mountains by Ulster-Scots who understood themselves nonetheless as part of their community. It is more than amusing to note that the similar-sounding "foraging" (from a different root) well describes an early occupation of American settlers as they settled the Eastern shore. While "foraging" has had unfortunate connotation of pillaging, we use it here to indicate the gathering of food. "Forging" also applies literally – the settlers always had a blacksmith among them to keep the horses shod. One might project that activity into the experimentation with democratic government in the town meetings that gave the early Americans experience with the potentials of government before the Revolution – forging ahead without oligarchy.

150   As a child I lived within earshot of a small drop-forge. As a young man I worked among large drop-forges in a heavy industry which made steel girders for highway tractors and trailers. Their noise and ground-shaking impacts left a deep impression on me.

151   Epithets for people using animals to indicate "dumb" such as "dog," "donkey," "cow," and others are not unlike the "dumpkof" I heard as a child.

152   Ibid. Pals. Pals quotes a delightful ninth century Medieval account of the prevailing attitude toward the Christ child. Such time-bound expressions flicker with insight into the evolution of the human self.

> Then they stepped nearer to the All-Saving Christ,
> Such disciples, as He had chosen Himself,
> The Wielder amid His vassals there. And the wise men
> The heroes, stood all gladly about God's son,
> The war-men most willingly; they awaited His word,
> Thought and were silent, longing to hear
>   what the Lord of the Land-folk
> The Wielder Himself, would make known with His words
> For love of the land-folk.
>   -*The Heliand*, tr.Mariana Scot, n.d., 42

153   Tuchman, Barbara *The Distant Mirror: The Calamitous 14th Century* (1978).

154   Bailyn, Bernard in *To Begin the World Anew* (2003) notes: "(Jefferson) said he sincerely loathed slavery, condemned it as 'an abominable crime,'...did not free his own slaves and is reputed to have fathered children by his slave Sally Hemmings." The vituperative critiques of Jefferson have never stopped. "Yet he was chosen to draft the Constitution because, as John Adams recalled, he was known to have 'a happy talent of composition.'" (40,43.) "Philosophes" was a label attached to eighteenth century quasi-philosophers of the French Enlightenment (Webster's Third New International Dictionary).

155   "Aristocracy" was classified by the eminent scholar Peter Mark Roget in his *Thesaurus of English Words and Phrases*, under "737 Authority." Here we find most of two whole pages of related words. The word aristocracy has been associated with so many discredited forms of government that it may now be useless. We have use "leader" often but it appears that those who at any moment comprise the leadership (i.e. the aristocracy) have an inordinate influence on the formation of the culture which aristocracy has always connoted.

156   Friends uncover from memory their common experience. Somehow, in the relaxed mode of the mind, not under the pressure of "being told," our defenses are not up to reject what seems to challenge our inner selves. Ancient slaves did learn, of course, as we still do from direct instruction. The point is only that in society learning is possible in both modes. The "provincials" were not told to become leaders of a new nation. They observed themselves and their world and responded intelligently. So what we have called "natural" leaders have always emerged as an expression of human creativity. Their skills must include some facility in rhetoric, and enough "charisma" to obtain peer approbation; above all, they have intelligence

157   Ibid. Priestley, 16.

158   Harsanyi, David in the *Columbus Dispatch* 2/19/11.

159   Clark, Taylor, *Nerve*, 2011, 245-249.

160   Jean Jacques Rousseau is considered the father of romanticism though the trend existed before him. He was prolific but his later works were marred by paranoia.

161   The source of that idea must have been the certainty that accompanied the euphoria of early scientific discovery which grew out of earlier Scholastic logic. It does not have Jewish roots. Mark Brettler

who edited *The Jewish Study Bible* points out that "The tradition of biblical interpretation has been a constant conversation (marked by) the diversity of approaches employed and a multiplicity of meanings produced." ix.
Archibald Hodge (1823-1886) was the son of Charles Hodge, both theologians at Princeton.
162   Rogers, Jack B. and Donald K. McKim *The Authority and Interpretation of the Bible*, 1979, 348-353.
163   I am indebted in this section to Mark Stephen Massa, S. J. in his *Charles Augustus Briggs and the Crisis of Historical Criticism*. 1990. 59ff. One should note that not all those who are influenced by Fundamentalism claim the title. Some have simply disagreed with all or part of the credo, and others have their private alternative interpretations. As the culture has become less accepting of Fundamentalism, some of its advocates have simply stopped using the term and some deny their adherence.
164   We note that they are hardly the only ones to claim being "scientific" only to be proved mistaken. Before the end of the twentieth century, Sigmund Freud had joined their ranks. As in his case, there is still much of value in their work, but the unquestioning adulation of Freud in the mid-century proved badly mistaken, as is the case with these two Princeton theologians.
165   Francis Bacon (1561-1626) was the founder of the modern inductive method of thought and the pioneer in the attempt at logical systematization of scientific procedure. Scottish realism came to be known as "Baconianism"
166   Charles Briggs had spent some years collecting the original documents of the Westminster Assembly where the Westminster Confession was written (1645-1647). He found that his colleagues were using a revised version containing Francis Turretin's eighteenth century interpretation of Calvin.
167   Ibid. Rogers and McKim, 244f.
168   This is discussed more extensively in chapter IX, section C.
169   Victor Hugo's novel (1862) traces the lives of some people early in 19th century France leading to the June Rebellion. Music by Claude-Michel Schönberg. Lyrics Alain Boublil (French lyrics). Herbert Kretzmer (English adapt). Book: Claude-Michel Schönberg, Alain Boublil, Trevor Nunn and John Caird,adapt.
170   The American Civil War was exactly that., but in an unexpected way. The leaders of the South in their defeat tried to paint the cause of the war to be states' rights. But that was a cover since the real issue, slavery, was discredited and there was no political gain in admitting this. The truth is that the war proved the power and the value of a centralized government to hold together such disparate elements as those (still) favoring slavery and those who opposed it.
171   "Doyen." One may choose who is "head of the group" of persons seeking through Whitehead's new view of metaphysics a theology which overcomes the antagonistic relationship of the past century or two between science and religion. David Ray Griffin (Claremont School of Theology), who edited with Donald Sherburne a helpful version of *Process and Reality*, has written: "Having long considered 1964 the year in which the term postmodern began to be applied to the Whiteheadian approach, I learned that this (term had actually been used) as early as 1944, when John Herman Randall, Jr., writing of the emergence of 'postmodern naturalistic philosophies,' referred to Whitehead as 'one of the pioneers' of the movement." Its advantage is, in "rejecting the modern, mechanistic reductionist type of naturalism, it overcomes the modern conflict of scientific naturalism with moral, aesthetic, and religious values." Griffin adds that this accords completely with Whitehead's stated purpose.
172   David Ray Griffin, "Reconstructive Theology," in *The Cambridge Companion to Postmodern Theology*, ed. Kevin J. Vanhoozer, 94. Griffin has been of immense help to me in melding the developments in the modern world with Christianity. Charles F. Altieri teaches at the Univ. of California, Berkeley.
173   Jacques Maritain (1882-1973) in "A New Approach to God" in *Our Emergent Civilization* (1947), ed. Ruth N. Anshen, (pp.280-290) described Existentialim as a school for "the work of reason. The act by virtue of which I exist and things exist, transcends concepts and ideas; it is a mystery for the intellect. But the intellect lives on this mystery. In its most natural activity it is as ordinary, daily and vulgar as eating or drinking. The act of existing is indeed the very object of every achieved act of the intellect, that is, of judgment. It is perceived by that intellectual intuition, immersed in sense experience, which is the common treasure...." Jean Paul Sartre is usually identified as the key existentialist of the twentieth century, Soren Kierkegaard (1813-1855) was considered a Christian existentialist with Aquinas (1217-1274).
174   Hubert Dreyfus and Harrison Hall, eds., *Heidegger: A Critical Reader*, 1992, 3.
175   Ibid. Haugeland in *Heidegger: A Critical Reader*, 35.
176   Cf. Introduction, section D.
177   Ibid. 37.
178   Ibid. 39.

179   Richard Rorty, "Wittgenstein, Heidegger, and the reification of language," in *The Cambridge Companion to Heidegger*, 1993, Charles Guignon, ed., 337. Rorty (1931-2007) was a "postanalytic"

philosopher who was the grandson of Walter Rauschenbusch. He considered himself a pragmatist, an ironist, and an atheist. He taught philosophy at Princeton and elsewhere.
180   Gleick, James, *Genius: The Life and Science of Richard Feynman*, 1992. Feynman was a highly respected physicist who worked on the atom bomb and won the Nobel. The point is that self-discipline is the root capacity beneath all human achievement. We maintain that more disciplined use of our tongues will contribute to our development of a more human culture in the twenty-first century, not just to science.
181   We have taken pains to enumerate the slow change occasioned by the advent of cities, the lengthy suffering of most human beings under oligarchy world-wide, the slow and painful emergence of a European culture, and the gradual speeding up of change beginning with the Renaissance.
182   Gleick, James, *Chaos: Making a New Science*, 1987, 2008, 244. I am indebted to Mr. Gleick for his exploration of chaos theory.
183   Ibid. 3f. Before Gleick concludes his book, he will have introduced us to the exploration and development of chaos theory in each of the areas mentioned.
184   Ibid. 94.
185   Werner Heisenberg noted that quantum mechanics could not satisfy Eintein's "conviction that … the hypothesis should be able to make precise statements about the objective side of it." He goes on: "All scientific work is based on some philosophic attitude of this kind, on a particular thought structure which serves as a solid foundation for further development…. But in the course of scientific progress it can happen that a new range of empirical data can be completely understood only when the enormous effort is made to enlarge this framework and to change the very structure of the thought processes. In the case of quantum mechanics, Einstein was apparently no longer willing to take this step, or perhaps no longer able to do so." ("Introduction" to Max Born's *Einstein Letters*, x.)
186   Again, we are compelled to note that this is not an indictment of graduate professors and their schools in general. The sagacity of elders has often appeared to "young bloods" as foot-dragging. It was one of a Chief's sage insights that as American armed forces pushed the Indians out of the land, the young braves often failed to recognize the suicidal nature of armed resistance -- and the older men had no power to restrain them. The leadership of the young into demonstration of their sometimes ignorant prowess has often been a problem. But the opposite has also been true. For generations in Ancient and Medieval worlds young people were restrained by forces in which they could do little more than repeat the ways of their elders. We must open communication to recognize the values of youth.
187   Ibid, James Gleick, 250f.
188   Ibid 197.
189   Ibid. 210.
190   "Jimmy Carter still fights the guinea worm in Sudan," *Columbus Dispatch*, 12/23/2010. Infestation by the three-foot long worm has declined from 50 million cases in the 1950s to 1,700.
191   The Vikings, the Danes, the Norse, and the Swedes -- generically the Scandinavians -- are variously credited with harassing Britain. They were also known as Northmen and Normans; in Russia the Swedes were Varangians. They were known to be extremely cruel in an emerging world where cruelty was about to start its long path toward social control. Their raiding ended with the introduction of Christianity and the emergence of European nations able to defend themselves.
192   There will continue to be much debate over the wisdom of multi-tasking and divided attention. "Texting" while driving a car seems obvious foolishness. But most of us move from task to task with ease.
193   Quoted by Sen Amartya in *Identity and Violence*, 2006, 55.
194   *The Social and Political Philosophy of Jacques Maritian: Selected Readings*, ed Joseph W. Evans, Leo R. Ward, 1955, 326.
195   The German efforts in rational biblical criticism listed by Albert Schweitzer in his *Quest for the Historical Jesus* neglected biblical scholars in Britain who produced the genre "lives of Jesus." The British "lives" tended generally to be popular, predictable, and contributed little to the scholarly enterprise with a few exceptions. But they did induce the people to think about Jesus as a human being who lived as we live rather than as the bloody body and spiritualized divine duality inherited from Medieval Christianity.
196   Pals, Daniel L., *The Victorian "Lives" of Jesus*, 1982, 10f. Pal's "partial success" might seem to relate to the failure of the Second British Reformation to carry over to the United States where liberal historical study of the Bible produced a shock.
197   It is quite interesting that "form," in spite of Plato's strong advocacy, has never become a Western idolatrous idol. We have raised "truth" and "knowledge" to deific heights, but "form" has remained a common noun describing the shape of things. It is ubiquitous, with color, size, density, etc.
198   Russell, Bertrand, *History of Western Philosophy*, 1965, 766f.
199   Ibid. Caputo, John, *Radical Hermeneutics: Repetition, Deconstruction, and the Hermeneutic*

END NOTES – 313

Project, 1987, 77.

200   This handy concept of the "uncanny" has gotten twisted over the years. It has often been used to mean mischievous or untrustworthy. But "canny," quite independently, has meant sagacious, prudent, cautious, skillful and even cunning. The connection between the two definitions seems to be in "cunning."

201   Presentation at the Ohio State University in a seminar on November 6, 2006. It is worth noting that Galileo was in the next generation after Knox, Buchanan, and Calvin and concurrently with Johannes Kepler, the other great early seventeenth century astronomer.

202   This "driver" is of concern to current neuropsychologists who seem to think that the heart of this human capacity to choose and direct the mind is twofold. Gazzaniga tells us that we have a "hot" (rapid) decision system based in the amygdala (which affects the motor system and also how we think in the future), and a "cool" cognitive system based in the hippocampus and the frontal lobes (slower, it deals with spatiotemporal and episodic matters). How the two systems interact seems to depend on age, stress, and temperament. Gazzaniga, Michael, *Human: the science behind what makes us unique*, 2008, 147. In *The Trouble with Neurobiological Explanations of Mind*, 2002, Leslie Brothers disputes the tendency of some neuroscientists' explanations of mind in terms of the individual brain, ignoring the social dimension.

203   "Mathematics and the Good" a late lecture (1940) in *The Philosophy of Alfred North Whitehead*, v.3 in *The Library of Living Philosophers*, 669.

204   Massa, Mark Stephen, S.J. in *Charles Augusta Briggs and the Crisis of Historical Criticism* (1990), chapter 3, describes the "sides" in tension in the northern Presbyterian church which persisted (in spite of a formal resolution) into the twentieth century.

205   Dorrien, Gary, *The Making of American Liberal Theology*, 3v., 2001.

206   Mark Achtemeier presented his new views to the Covenant Network conference at Cleveland, Ohio 11/5/2009, "And Grace Will Lead Me Home." See Jack P. Rogers, *Jesus, the Bible, and Homsexuality: Exploding the Myths*, 2006.

207   Usually these were made of a rough denim with straps over each shoulder and a "bib" in front with pockets.

208   USDA, "U.S. Farms; Number, Size, and Ownership."

209   George Gershwin (1898-1937) is credited with successfully bridging the gap between Tin Pan Alley and the concert stage. His *Rhapsody in Blue* and *Porgy and Bess* are well known.

210   *The Columbia Encyclopedia*, 1950, p.1543.

211   Tween-agers (18-28?) in the past had been hugely controlled by the universal training ground of apprenticeship. By mid-century the proportion of tween-agers who had been through an apprenticeship was dwindling severely and there was no replacement until the community college phenomenon emerged. That may well prove to be a helpful contribution to a solution to tween-agers' immaturity.

212   A megalith is a very large undressed stone like those of Stonehenge in England. My intent here is to characterize the proliferation of stand-alone departments that occurred in the second half of the twentieth century. By 1990 it had become common knowledge that the practitioners of these specialties had (nearly) lost the ability to talk to one another. Their in-house languages were constructed to meet the needs of their specialties and lost touch with their larger context. Their awareness of the problem was evident in efforts to encourage "inter-disciplinary" courses and to facilitate communication. It has been said that schools of business, particularly marketing, listened to no one; one does not meddle with success. It was not unlike the self-satisfied certainty we have noted in the ultra-conservative mentality of Fundamentalism and probably stemmed from the remarkable achievements of entrepreneurs evident in early years of the twentieth century.

213   The invention of the transistor during World War II to enable the military to set cities aflame with thousands of incendiary bombs began the apparently endless process of miniaturization which currently makes switches of molecules. Unaware, this also marks the end of domination of the culture by the mechanistic orientation. Beginning with Descartes thinkers have been enthralled by the wonderful mechanisms which have dominated thinking and analogy ever since. Even biologists have often thought in mechanistic terms.

214   We have not explored the fantastic developments in the field once simply called "'physics" during the twentieth century – nor the stories of biology. Their proliferation of special departments of extraordinarily specialized inquiries into both micro and macro worlds tell another story about the growth of human application of our mental capabilities. But we should mention their eclipse in the nineteenth century by the beginnings of modern psychology and sociology. It may be that the only one of the humanities that progressed in a similar fashion is history with the application of science to archeology and anthropology and its extension back in prehistory. Interestingly, in the nineteenth century philosophy became mired in the misconceptions we have called scientism, with a few brilliant individuals breaking those constraints in the new century to forge recovery of intelligent philosophy and a similar new life in theology.

215   Jesuit scholar Mark Stephen Massa, S. J. put it this way: "In the latter half of the nineteenth

century a profound crisis occurred in the intellectual life of the West.... The underlying metaphysical assumption of (the previous tradition) -- the certainty of the ethical meaningfulness of historical action -- seemed in danger of imminent collapse, and the (prevailing interpretation of Christianity) that rested on that assumption entered a prolonged identity crisis.... The new theory of evolution might have required no more ... accommodation ... than a reinterpretation of the creation story, had not the ancient model of transcendental revelation itself become problematic as a result of the onslaught of historicism." (Parentheses enclose my paraphrases. - jk).

216   The public history of Unitarians goes back to the burning of Servetus in 1553 for his antitrinitarian views. In Poland Socinus carried the torch. Universalists trace themselves back to John Murray who came to the U.S. in 1770 from England. Even simpler than the Unitarians, they believe that God's purpose is to save every person through grace revealed in Jesus Christ. The two bodies joined in 1949. Long before, John Simson, appointed to Glasgow about 1710, had discussed such issues as professor of sacred theology.

217   David Kirp, UC Berkeley, critiqued books by Jonathan Cole (*The Great American University*) and Andrew Hacker and Claudia Dreifus (*Higher Education?*) in *American Prospect* (November 2010).

218   *A Rauschenbusch Reader: The Kingdom of God and the Social Gospel* (1957), Benson Y. Landis, consists of excerpts from "the pen of a modern prophet." This book was published on the fiftieth anniversary of the publication of Rauschenbusch's first major work, *Christianity and the Social Crisis* (1912). The Introduction to the *Reader* was written by Harry Emerson Fosdick.

219   *Confessing the Faith* (1996), 156. This is the third in the series *Christian Theology in a North American Context*. Volume one was *Thinking the Faith* (1989), volume two was *Professing the Faith* (1993). The series is an extraordinary theological *tour de force* Douglas John Hall taught at McGill University.

220   *USA Today*, 1/19/10.

221   "Edward Farley is right in celebrating the 'critical modernism' of contemporary Presbyterianism." (Milton J. Coulter, John Mulder, Louis B. Weeks, *The Reforming Tradition: Presbyterians and Mainstream Protestantism*, 1992, 142.) Thus the best critical minds of the church have begun to recognize the emergence of the new mind of which we speak here. These authors published a series, "The Presbyterian Presence: The Twentieth Century Experience." Caputo argues that "radical thinking" is renewed vigilance about the gaps and differences inherent in our experience.

222   Smail, Daniel Lord, *On Deep History and the Brain*, 137ff. Smail tells us that these modules are understood like computer programs of "vast, interconnecting sets of neurons." Smail reminds us that if such modules exist "they must be triggered by environmental circumstances."

223   Augustine is far more complex than his sharing in the denigration of women suggests. He held, for example that women are made in the image of God, and will be equal to men after the resurrection. He also held the prevailing view that the chief function of women is to bear children and this function is inferior to the activity of men. It is significant that the church engaged persistently in high praise of women in their role as "virgins." The veneration of Mary contradicted the negativity of the inherited culture. Rosemary Radford Ruether, innovative Roman Catholic theologian, details the cultural dualism of the ancient world which infected early Christianity in "Misogynism and Virginal Feminism in the Fathers of the Church." One should note that perhaps the best introduction to Augustine is Peter Brown's *Augustine of Hippo*. It does not explore his theology, however. An excellent introduction to his thought is Carol Harrison's *Augustine: Christian Truth and Fractured Humanity.*

224   Ibid. Russell, Bertrand, 128, regarding Plato's *Republic*.

225   In her article in *Religion and Sexism*. "Equality of Souls, Inequality of Sexes: Woman in Medieval Theology," Eleanor Commo McLaughlin tells us that Aquinas' discussion of the creation (Gen.2) does depart from Augustine's account in an important way: Aristotelian man "is a composite of body and soul, in contrast to the platonized patristic anthropology in which the human being was a soul imprisoned in flesh. [Aquinas] evaluates the body positively as an integrity of body and soul.... This view might have helped overcome the patristic pessimism about sex and the body that always led to a fear and denigration of women. But followed Aristotle and his patristic authorities in their definition so that the body-denying dualism and its associated androcentrism were reinvigorated ... achieved by the operation of the rational soul. Ultimately, therefore, the body is again left out."

226   Herman, Arthur *How the Scots Invented the Modern World: The True Story of How Europe's Poorest Nation Created Our World and Everything In It*, 2001, 65. The word "austerity" is interpolated for Herman's "austere fundamentalism" because his use of "fundamentalism" is inconsistent with our understanding of the origins of this twentieth century Protestant error.

227   An atrophied form of Puritanism in the twentieth century produced, for example, the Prohibition Act, though Puritans were not against the use of alcohol. The influence of the Ulster Scots in the formation of the United States was not unlike the impact of the Puritans in England where the Puritan Revolution helped to bring the constitutional form of monarchy into reality.

END NOTES - 315

228   I think this common expression means that it is our judgment – from our point of view – that in any case in question values that are ostensibly old tend to dominate the viewpoint. It is not pejorative, but a simple description with which all might agree. In religion, it usually means there is an evident emphasis on orthodox ideas and is often intended to be the opposite of "progressive" in the same framework.

229   "Individualism" as I use the term is the nineteenth and twentieth century development of an extreme form of the individuality which is native to humanity. In the West it apparently was focused by the seminal dictum of Descartes that "I think, therefore I am." Carried to the extreme, it betrays our social character. That is essential to our survival, the source of great human joy, and our hope for the future.

230   This, too, is a signal of the change in self-perception taking place in the West. British universities' boards had been largely clergymen when the tide changed and scholars and scientists began taking control. The same change took place in the United States.

231   Madison was definitely not a monarchist, but the tendency hung on to believe that centralized authority was required by human beings to overcome their antagonistic and competitive nature. It contained, after all, nuggets of truth (which are evident in our repeated twentieth century experience) of the need for Federal regulation of the justice system, finance, trade and commerce.

232   Leslie Brothers, *Friday's Footprint:How Society Shapes the Human Mind*, 1997, xii.

233   Let me suggest that it is not difficult to understand the effect of dialogue on our society. It is like the way conversation in a family can alter an individual's self-image. When a young teen tries out a new posture, the family adjusts in various ways, altering its culture, sometimes permanently. We recognize how such changes influence family members. We can gain a sense of the way in which we all contribute to the cultures of our communities, our churches, and other social units. It does not matter particularly whether everyone is aware of the change in the individual. How that person behaves, thinks, reacts to others anywhere will reflect the changes instigated in the family. This simply illustrates a process that is happening constantly as people relate to others everywhere. The result of everyone's constantly changing self-understanding makes definition of a culture ephemeral – it is always changing. It may be more dynamic than the individual person, since it reflects us all and constantly imposes change on each of us. We can characterize it only grossly. Nonetheless, in retrospect culture may be defined for a period, people, or place.

234   Sometimes called the father of modern philosophy, Rene Descartes' (1596-1650) influence was wide. In philosophy his dualism was mechanistic, contributing substantially to the mechanistic thinking of the industrial age. He essentially adopted Francis Bacon's (1561-1626) method of induction (as opposed to the *a priori* method of Scholasticism) with emphasis on rationality. Though he discarded Scholasticism he was substantially in debt to it. He made important contributions to geometry and algebra.

235   Bertrand Russell reminds us that philosopher-theologian Augustine postulated that Time was created when the world was created. In God there is no before and after but only an eternal present. "What then is time?" he asks. If no one asks, I know; if I wish to explain to one who asks, I know not." Then "past" must be identified with memory, and "future" with expectation. Both memory and expectation are present facts. So there are three times: a present of things past, a present of things present, and a present of things future. Time is in the human mind, which, remembers, considers, and expects. To speak of time before the Creation is meaningless. The Greeks had no concept of creation out of nothing, but it is critical to the Judaic-Christian heritage. (*History*, 351ff.) Descartes' *Cogito ergo sum* (I think therefore I am) had been in the air for a very long time. Dualism is an ancient conceptualization tying him to the past.

236   Cf: Peter Strawson, *Individuals: An essay in descriptive metaphysics*, 1959.

237   Shay's Rebellion in 1786 led to a stronger Federal government and assured the success of the American experience in democracy by instigating the Land Act of 1787, a precursor to the Constitution enacted later that year.

238   One must notice that in this make-or-break conservative effort, this movement embraced its democratic basis to engage the public in *conversation*, however its intention may have been simply to *persuade* the public (and itself) of its rightness. Actually, bereft of intellectual rigor, the effort gave little assistance to any who might have been persuaded. Nonetheless, the tension it caused gave Middle America a kick into conversation, breaking its long silence. This can be surmised from noting the publication date of Mark A. Noll's *The Scandal of the Evangelical Mind*, 1994 -- years after the "Moral Majority" came and went. It was more than another decade before the Presbyterian Church (U.S.A.) pushed dialogue front and center.

239   The reader should be aware of Kuhn's *The Road Since Structure: Philosphical Essays* 1970-1993 (2000) ed. by James Conant and John Haugeland. These essays were written and ready for publication at the time of Kuhn's death. The original *Structure of Scientific Revolutions* (1962,1970) has been the single most influential book in the philosophy of science. It recovered use of the term "paradigm."

240   The state of lethargy was named "apathy" in the eighteenth century (meaning an "I don't care" point of view). It may, indeed be just that, but I think generally we should ascribe it to a simple failure to stay alert.

END NOTES – 316

Life requires of us attention to many, many details; many of these become habitual and unconscious. But awareness of our surroundings, of the conditions of life in which we find ourselves, this consciousness is a mental alertness, a disposition, which we may learn and practice always. Hopefully, we learn to stay alert early in life, so that (as with most early learning) we don't have to spend our adult lives reworking it over and over. It is a self-discipline which little children can easily make an ongoing attitude, a way of life (N.B. *Thinking Parent, Thinking Child*). Learning early to pay attention and to think can save untold personal grief and contribute to healthy communities everywhere one goes. Much of the "sheep mentality" we noted earlier ended up being lethargy, lack of initiative, a quiescence, and not infrequently it became a forced obedience that was evident in a servile insolence. It is a source of cynicism, hopelessness.

241   Ibid. Rogers and McKim. Nineteenth century roots of Fundamentalism go back to dispensationalism (1820) differing from both Calvin and the Westminster Confession. Two basic doctrines, inerrancy (this word is more specifically rationalistic than "infallible") and reliability of scripture texts, were supplemented by divinity of Christ, Second Coming, heaven and hell – the "Five Essentials." They were characterized by a personalized view of salvation. Verbal inspiration or literal interpretation of scripture was hung on the hook of inerrancy. It is radically opposed to Roman Catholic insistence on human tradition and to the historical-critical method of biblical interpretation adopted by most traditional Christian groups.

242   Charles A. Briggs' efforts to reconcile the older evangelical world view with the newer, historicist one began from the common orientation of mid-nineteenth century. But he gradually was led by his inquiry into conflict with advocates of Fundamentalist views. These people also illuminate the cultural story of the times. Briggs' insights had shown him as early as 1887 the threat of those who were so captured by Enlightenment certainty that they "sought certainty in very 'un-Protestant' kinds of infallibility" (with roots in the work of Francois Turetin). (See *Charles Augustus Briggs and the Crisis of Historical Criticism*, 1990, Mark Stephen Massa, SJ., 22f, 47.) Presbyterians in 1967 adopted a whole "Book of Confessions" (none definitive, all "instructive") confirming the historical revolution, the Third Reformation.

243   Placher, William C., *A History of Christian Theology: An Introduction*, 1983, 248. Placher died in November 2008, a youthful 60. Induction is the process of reasoning from the particular to the general credited to Francis Bacon early in the seventeenth century which set science into its ascent.. Deduction is reasoning from the general to the particular (credited to Aristotle). Russell suggests that this Greek penchant "misled not only the ancient world, but the greater part of the modern world, also ... For this reason (alone) it is a mistake to treat the Greeks with superstitious reverence." (Russell, *History*, 58.)

244   Marty, Martin Emil (1928-) taught at the University of Chicago Divinity School from 1963-1998. He is the author of many books and particularly *The Fundamentalism Project* with R. Scott Appleby (1991-1995). See also Mark Noll, *The Scandal of the Evangelical Mind*.

245   Like the funding of *The Layman* (beginning in the 1960s), the earlier definitive publication of Fundamentalism had been funded by an oil company mogul. He also was a Presbyterian and a dispensationalist.

246   When Walter Scott produced the celebration for King George IV they insisted that the "authentic" highland costume mandated for the parade must include a dirk inserted in the stocking above the ankle. Carrying a jack-knife with blades safely folded inside was a necessary part of a boy's equipment as late as 1940. In a teen-age killing at a recreational church dance in 1957 such a knife was the deadly instrument.

247   Jaynes wrote that ancient humans before roughly 1200 BC were not reflectively meta-conscious and operated by means of automatic, nonconscious habit-schemas. Instead of having meta-consciousness, these humans were constituted by what Jaynes calls the "bicameral mind".

248   *ABA Journal*. Posted Oct 30, 2008. Typos edited by the author.

249   To be sure, this reference to sheep is in the context of the discussion earlier in this monograph. It is not meant in any way as an interpretation of the biblical or church use of the term in Scripture and liturgy.

250   As this was being written, a deranged 22 year old gunman shot Congressional Representative Gabrielle Gifford and killed six bystanders. Immediately a nationwide debate began as to whether the present acrimonious political climate in the United States caused this incident. A related question is whether this climate resulted from opening up of communication over recent decades.

251   This is not a criticism of the church's use of modern communication. Efforts had been continuous and extensive. All means of publication had been used. Unfortunately, as the controversy hardened, language took on innuendo imputed by the other side and even the efforts, for example, of Peanuts' author Charles Schulz failed to a degree. We are, rather, talking about the failure among us to engage in meaningful discourse as a matter of course everyday.

252   This persistent emphasis on thinking should be understood to mean that sort of self-conscious thought in which we are constantly aware of our surroundings. There are times when we can focus on ourselves alone -- when we are alone, perhaps traveling, in our private times of prayer and reflection. There are times when we must be especially sensitive to those we are with, such as the elder, the hard of hearing,

persons of other persuasions and positions. And there are times when we must be tuned specially to listening, though we must always keep our senses alert and ready to perceive our world. When we have personally adopted the discipline of thinking human beings fit for the twenty-first century, we are ready to participate fully. That is what democracy, benevolence, and love require of us.

253   The first person credited with "humanism" was Italian Francesco Petrarch (1304-1374).

254   T. Friedman's book *The World is Flat: A Brief History of the 21st Century*, 2005, promises more than it delivers. It is a very abbreviated "history" at best, but it makes his point.

255   Chances are that long before much speech had developed among Hominids, strong leaders used a glance or gesture to silence efforts to participate of those who garnered their dislike.

256   It should be obvious that this is not to say deceit is done. Since humans began speaking, they learned to use speech to obfuscate. There are times and places for hedging the facts of a case or our opinions on an issue. The funeral is not a time to press our "correct" views of heaven or life after death. The point here is that we must stop using subterfuge to pervert human society. Certainly, the public forum is not a place for lies. It is exactly the place where responsible speakers must carefully check facts first.

257   This not to say we can foreswear all use of force. We are aware that there are people in our world who will exploit others for their personal benefit. Turning over a new cultural leaf dedicated to better use of our minds will not rid the world of crime or tyranny. The infinite variety of humanity produced by the inheritance of DNA and cultures which have been violent in the past will continue to put among us those whom we must control in order to maintain the peace. For now and the foreseeable future we are likely to need police and armies, too. We may hope and work to reduce the waste of resources in the sort of mammoth and expensive armaments currently in vogue, turn more of these functions into positive, reconciling activities, and literally reduce the need for them as well.

258   Everyone knows of the persistence of vengeful cultures, but this very persistence is evidence of the slow and uneven progress of humanity toward a truly human existence for all. The promise of a new Iraq in which the national legislature will have a higher percentage of women than even the United States bodes well for progress.

259   We shall look at an American philosophers' struggle with Heidegger's German *Dasein*.

260   Gazzaniga, Michael, *Human: The Science Behind What Makes Us Unique*, 2008, 235.

261   A lifesize sculpture is pictured in William Flemming's *Arts and Ideas*, 1986, 61. Fleming suggests that the austere, thinking elite Greeks saw such frenzied dance and music as quite undignified. This cult followed a more sedate musical culture, not unlike the intrusion of Rock and Role after W.W. II.

262   Ibid. Gazzaniga, 224.

263   E. O. Wilson, *Consilience: The Unity of Knowledge*, 1998, quoted in Carroll, J., "The adaptive function of literature" in *Evolutionary and Neurocognitive Approaches to Aesthetics, Creativity and the Arts*, 2007, Petrov. V. Martindale, Locher, P., and Petrov. V.M. (eds), 225f. If more of us had been twenty-first century people during the early 20th century we might have grasped the message of the extensive innovation in graphic art. Yet the innovators had their impact on our culture – and will for some time to come – though for the most part we are unconscious of this influence. Our common language has not kept pace.

264   Ibid. Gazzaniga, 223. A neighbor on the Dodge work force in Detroit in 1962 exalted at the beauty of the new model. It was one of their more graceful models in a power era, I think, but his joy was of ownership – he belonged to the Dodge Corporation. Jacoby reports that after his last performance in Russia, Rostropovich observed, "In Russia, people go to a concert not as an attraction or entertainment, but to feel life.... For us art is bread."

265   As this was being written Port-au-Prince, Haiti was digging out of a 7.4 earthquake and reported perhaps 200,000 deaths. The quake flattened most of this city. Shortly after, Santiago, Chile, suffered a much greater 8.8 quake though estimates of deaths there are well below a thousand. In both cases aftershocks have added to the misery.

266   Hall, Douglas John, *Confessing the Faith: Christian Theology in a N. American Context*, 1996, 321.

267   Perhaps Thomas Kuhn's greatest contribution was the redefinition of revolution as a major intellectual change. In the years following the greatest carnage ever, his book became a major ingredient in college education throughout the world. *The Structure of Scientific Revolutions*, 1962, Thomas S. Kuhn.

268   "Obscene" derives from a prehistoric Latin words kin to "to" and "filth." Dirtied, disgusting, gross.

269   The Bill and Malinda Gates Foundation is an illustration of this today, but there are others. Though their largess is all excess beyond their most extravagant needs, wants, and desires, their use of it is a vast improvement over the ostentatious and self-serving styles of many wealthy people. For example, the gorgeous Taj Mahal, for example, was built as a memorial for the beauteous queen, Mumtaz Mahal, who gave her husband 14 children and died in childbirth at age 39. This exquisite structure does little for humanity other than fuel our pride in human accomplishments. It is a product of a brutal seventeenth century emperor in India. (Prem Kishore and Anuradha Kishore Ganpati, *India*, 2003.)

270   Allegations that such firms exploit foreign workers who have needlessly suffered lifelong injuries have become public information with the advent of electronic communication.

271   Economist Clyde Prestowitz quoted by Rana Foroohar in *TIME Magazine*, 2/13/12, 21.

272   Ibid., *Deep History*, 65, based on Robert Sapolsky, *Why Zebras Don't Get Ulcers*, 2004.

273   This was Harold Bostrom, president of the Bostrom Mfgt. Company in Milwaukee, Wisconsin.

274   Ibid. Gazzaniga, "Being in a good mood increases cognitive flexibility and facilitates creative problem solving in many different settings. It has been shown to increase verbal fluency. People with a positive affect widen category groups by finding more similarities between objects, people, or social groups, enabling a socially distinct out-group to be placed into a broader mutual in-group....", 240.

275   Many movements are ephemeral. But the development of some in America, like Civil Rights and Feminism, can easily be traced to a century or more of commitment by prescient leaders. Although there is a place for forceful articulation of reformed law, the change will inevitably be evolutionary, not revolutionary.

276   These absurd amounts are nothing more than the evolution of the way we mistakenly formed the relationships in our economy. But there are many who also excel who go without notice and we have not figured out how to assure them a comfortable living. Beginning with guilds, brotherhoods, patents, copyrights, unions, associations, and movements we have tried a variety of ways – not withstanding their contributions – all of which are compromised or eventually fall to the pressures of the status quo. Again we note, failure to discriminate often causes victims to acquiesce.

277   "Pining" is a strange old expression derived from penal incarceration, presumably the inevitable hope for a way out. This context clearly identifies an urgency, a very deep hope, and anticipation of the future

278   In the third century BCE a Greek version of the Jewish scripture called the Septuagint ("by 72 scholars in 72 days") emerged as the authoritative Greek version.

279   Wolfgang Amadeus Mozart traveled all over Europe, but never farther than about 900 miles.

280   Zakaria, Fareed, *The Post-American World*, 2008. He wrote the bestseller *The Future of Freedom*.

281   L. Friedman column in the *Columbus Dispatch* 12/5/09.

282   I suggest "Transcendent Period" realizing that our new consciousness is aware that we need not be trapped in any human system, but can transcend them all as we continually grow in understanding. This suggests something else to follow, a reasonable expectation.

283   We have noted Hume's recalcitrance even on his deathbed despite the urging of close friends and associates to admit his humanity. See chapter V. D.

284   See Introduction section B.

285   It is fitting to remind ourselves that eventual entry into modernity and post-modernity was vastly aided by the northern peoples who eventually became significant players in the evolution of European culture. These people had not suffered the lengthy imprisonment in slavery of the Mediterranean populations. The largest of all the ancient empires, Rome never succeeded in forcing its imprint on these free-spirited peoples for more than a short time. Their main difference from southern invaders is that their primitive independence had not been perverted by the lengthy, systematic slavery of the southern peoples. People who came from the south into northern Europe in Roman times all reflect the extraordinary length of tyrannical rule they had suffered.

286   Kung, Hans, *The Beginning of All Things: Science and Religion*, 2005.

287   The Industrial Revolution was from this perspective the culmination of oligarchy. Factories, the instruments of industry, were workhouses in which a new form of oligarchy dictated behavior.

288   Maier-Katkin, Daniel, *Stranger From Abroad: Hannah Arendt, Martin Heidegger, Friendship and Forgiveness*, 2010, 48.

289   Martin Hengel (1926-2009; German historian of religion) tells us that an essential mark of the apocalyptic outlook is the quest for a higher wisdom through revelation. Such thinking is similar to the Gnostic tendency early in the Common Era. The *Revelation to John* remains a part of the Christian cannon. Jurgen Moltmann's *Theology of Hope*, 1967, details the Christian eschatology out of which apocalypticism springs, reminding us that such thinking "led to a peculiarly barren existence" and left thinking about the future "to fanatical sects and revolutionary groups" ("Meditation on Hope" in *A Reader in Political Theology, 1974*, ed. Alistair Kee). Breaking the hold of this sub-Christian orientation is another accomplishment of the twentieth century.

290   Ibid. Maier-Katkin, 27f.

291   I am not suggesting interference with scientific exploration, but a re-education to encourage funding efforts to pursue human needs rather than the overriding focus of the twentieth century on advance in hard science. This focus has led to extension of human knowledge into ever-greater detail (physical science), distance (astronomy, transportation), organization (business, commerce) and extension of life (medicine, etc.). Following the established course has led to gross errors as well as achievements: misconstructions in the social sciences -- such as Freud's unscientific conclusions dirtying up his contributions -- fanciful and

faddish waste of talent and time in innumerable graduate explorations seeking effervescent funding. If this points to a problem in graduate placement, we really should be seeking better solutions.

292   Adolf Hitler, too, was born in 1889. Both Heidegger, and Wittgenstein were born Germans; that intellectual climate has been prolific, but it failed to provide an environment for its nurure. Wittgenstein became a British citizen after his appointment to a chair at Cambridge which he served until 1947. His sympathies had led him in the 1930s to consider moving to Russia but he was opposed to Marxist theory. Heidegger's path was different. In the 1930s Heidegger adopted a neo-Nietzschean stance and attended Nazi rallies. Embraced Hitler he alienated colleagues and scholars. Late in the decade he was disillusioned, and after the war was considered only a sympathizer, though his behavior had been rather strident.

293   Thomas D'Evelyn, in the *Christian Science Monitor* (12/12/90) quoted Ray Monk's biography *Ludwig Wittgenstein: The Duty of Genius*. Monk is professor of philosophy at the University of Southampton.

294   Dorothea Frede in *The Cambridge Companion to Heidegger*, 1993, ed. Charles B. Guignon, 46. Frede is Mills adjunct professor of philosophy at Berkeley. Emphasis added.

295   Ibid. Maier-Katkin,116. Maier-Katkin has been of great help to me in grasping Heidegger through the eyes of Hannah Arendt..

296   This is evident in the penultimate chapter of Hannah Arendt's last book, volume two of *The Life of the Mind*, published posthumously in 1978.

297   Ibid. Maier-Katkin, 166f.

298   John Haugeland, "Dasein's Disclosedness" in *Heidegger: A Critical Reader* (1992), ed. Hubert Dreyfus and Harrison Hall, 35. Based largely in Heidegger's great second volume after his new insight.

299   Ibid. 39.

300   "Knox's original 1560 Book of Discipline had called for a national system of education." "A century later, Scotland's Parliament passed its 'Act for Setting Schools', establishing a school in every parish in Scotland not already equipped with one." This act reinforced one of 1640. The schools were supposedly free to all, though not always in practice. Many were rudimentary, teaching little more than reading and grammar. Arthur Herman, *How the Scots Invented the Modern World: The True Story of How Western Europe's poorest Nation Created Our World and Everything In It*, 2001, 19.

301   It is understood that the Chinese and Japanese writing patterns using thousands of symbols which are actually picture graphs take a child at least four years longer to master than the alphabetic languages. Elsewhere picture writing gave way to cuneiform patterns in the Stone Age. Written forms have been documented back about 8,500 years but spoken language is probably much older.

302   It was not until Vesalius in the sixteenth century that the phenomenal work in anatomy of Galen (130-200) was challenged. Galen wrote extensively and some of his works were still extant in the twentieth century. Before William Harvey (1578-1657), Michael Servetus (1511-1553) and others also contributed to development of medicine. (Servetus was burned in Geneva for anti-trinitarian views.)

303   Samuel sensed the danger of demagoguery in his unsophisticated populace. The danger remains in the West, making populism a dangerous political philosophy, much diminished by the growing awareness among people of their rationality.

304   We acknowledge that there probably are millions of people in the world who still support that point of view. Just as we in the West still held onto many obsolete views far past their time (one thinks of the need for women's and children's Rights), just as almost all of us still understood ourselves to be subservient if we lived in the first century CE, human beings have a capacity for tenacity built into our brains. We now insist that we also have the capacity to learn from our own history – as the Jews learned partially long ago. The maturity becoming evident in our own minds – and long evident here and there among humans everywhere – our own new self-consciousness, allows us to move toward a more accommodating, inclusive, hopeful world community.

305   One might argue that certain prophets had alluded to patterns of government which would not enslave the people. I will welcome such insight. My belief is that alternatives to oligarchy had not had a chance to emerge in the human mind under the oppressive three thousand year rule of the oligarchs who emerged in the early cities. Perhaps, given greater freedom, the consciousness of the pre-historical human beings who lived quite isolated lives might have developed controls on too-ambitious, selfish, egotistic leaders who rose among them while they lived in smaller social units, like tribe and village. By the time cities developed, the rhetorical skills of leaders were undoubtedly developed far beyond the capability of the people to cope with them. Rhetoric (essentially the art of persuasion), we note, was a primary educational field far into our Common Era. It seems to me that given this alternative to oligarchy, our predecessors might have begun development of the critical mind much earlier.

306   Israel declared itself an independent state (1948) with genocidal terrorist activity already an

established pattern. In the middle of the twentieth century, the critical mind had not yet spread that deeply.
307   Alves, Rubem A., "The Dialectics of Freedom" and "Theology of Hope" in *A Reader in Political Theology* (1975), Alistair Kee, ed., 21-29, 35. During the 19th century "humanism" was perverted by aetheism.
308   Lilla, Mark, *The Stillborn God: Religion, Politics, and the Modern West*, 2008. Review by Wm. C. Placher, professor of philosophy and religion at Wabash College in Crawfordsville, Indiana, in *Christian Century*, 8/11/08. Political philosopher Mark Lilla recently left the University of Chicago for Columbia Univ.
309   Jenkins, Philip, "Notes from the Global Church: When South is North," *Christian Century*, 3/24/09, 45ff.
310   Brooks, David, "Economic responsibility has to start at the top," *Columbus Dispatch*, 4/22/09.
311   Hersh, Michael, and Evan "The Reeducation of Larry Summers," *Newsweek*, 4/2/09, 24.
312   Habermas, Jurgen, *Structural Transformation of the Public Sphere*, 1989, 160, 244. For twelve years director of the Max Planck Institute in Starnberg, he returned to his chair in sociology and philosophy at Frankfurt, Germany. (Reviewed by James Bohman and William Rehg in *Jurgen Habermas*, 2007.)
313   Popper, Karl, *The World of Parmenides: Essays on the Presocratic Enlightenment*, 1998, 23.
314   Ibid. 24.
315   Ibid. Caputo, 234.
316   The sculpture is installed in front of the museum of art in Columbus, Ohio. It is a little like seeing a beach party covered with painters' canvases. Rationalization is so common among us that one has a hard time distinguishing reasonable answers from defensive constructions. The need for discretion grows.
317   Ibid. Caputo, 209f. Emphasis added.
318   Ibid. Caputo, 6. While Caputo "never gave up on the word hermeneutics," I have not given up on the word "humanism" !
319   The discovery in 1994 was recently announced of a very early human link in our animal past, perhaps a million years before Lucy, the previous earliest reconstructed person. "Ardi" (*Ardipithecus ramidus* in anthropological terms) was recently dated 4.4 million years ago. She probably still spent part of her time in the trees. But she walked upright and possibly also lived monogamously, and more than likely, cooperatively with a partner. But we are only at the beginning of seeing into this new chapter in our picture. (*Science*, Oct. 2, 2009.) In 1997 *Ardipithecus Kadabba* (5.8 million years old), predating *Ardi. Ramidus*, was uncovered and in 2000 *Orrorin tugenensis*. Found soon thereafter, remains dated to 6 to 7 million years ago named *Sahelanthropus tchadensis* may be homind. (*Smithsonian*, March 2010.)
320   Toynbee, Arnold J., *Change and Habit: The Challenge or Our Time*, 1966. Toynbee attributed the Judaic influence on Europe to the Pharisaic tradition which was heavily influenced by Greek philosophy and was substantially shaped by Moses Maimonides in Spain in the twelfth century. But such mistakes have been common, even though Paul was a Pharisee and it is evident that it was more than this which contributed to his success. He used his head a thousand years before Maimonides.
321   Toynbee, Arnold J, "The Ancient Mediterranean View of Man" in *Man's Right To Know*, an international symposium presented in honor of the two-hundredth anniversary of Columbia University, 1754-1954, 4f.
322   I have often laughed with friends of German background about our experiences with the paternalistic German culture our parent's still reflected.
323   Dowey, Edward A.,"The Third Use of the Law in Calvin's Theology," *Social Progress*, Nov. 1958, 20.
324   Ibid. 25.
325   Sin in the ancient paradigm of a vengeful god was terrifying. A God of love made it necessary to accept responsibility for avoiding sin.
326   Ellen T. Charry's review of Phillip Cary's *Augustine's Invention of the Inner Self: The Legacy of a Christian Platonist* (2000) in *Theology Today*, July 2001. Cary teaches philosophy at Eastern University.
327   Iona is an island in the southern Hebrides off the west coast of Scotland. It was an early Christian center where St. Ninian established a base before 432 CE and St. Columba landed in 563 CE. It is separated from the Isle of Mull from which many Scots made their way out of the country after the closures of the nineteenth century.
328   Newell, J. Philiip, *Celtic Benediction: Morning and Night Prayer*, 2000. Newell explored the two major characteristics noted in *The Book of Creation: an Introduction to Celtic Sprituality*, 1999. The beauty of various Celtic Christian manuscripts should be further evidence of the single-minded spirituality of northern European Christians. The Celtic spirituality encouraged personal responsibility (cf. Note 319).
329   The Salian Franks, southern brothers of other northern tribes, became allies of the Romans. They converted to Christianity and founded the Frankish empire which grew to include most of France. Charlemagne was a Frank (800 CE). Scots were of Irish stock (perhaps originally of the same stock as early British), a ruddy, dark race. Rome never invaded Ireland. Northern Scotland contained many Norse and Danish, the same stock as the northern Continent.
330   Jones, Serene, *Calvin and the Rhetoric of Piety*, 1995, 76.

331   Ibid. 132.

332   Ibid. 114. Jones brings to her academic work an appreciation for the public role of religion in American society.

333   Ibid. 133. *Institutes of the Christian Religion, (1559)*, 1.2.1.

334   Ibid. Jones, 88.

335   Ibid. Jones, 133.

336   Ibid. Arthur Herman, 263. We should note that our interest in the "self" was far from Calvin's mind. At that time, psychology was not envisioned, much less the preoccupation it has been in the twentieth century. Calvin's sense of the self was quite intuitive, the product of a bright and inquiring mind. Four hundred years later, the disappointment of Jean Piaget (1896-1980) in studying various philosophers and the application of logic led Piaget to commit himself to finding a "biological explanation of knowledge" and to psychology. His was a major contribution to contemporary psychology, though somewhat dated already.

337   Ibid. 90. Jones adds this note: "In 1536, when Calvin wrote the first version of the Institutes. his reputation would have been as a young, classically trained humanist and burgeoning reformer. By 1559, however, his reputation had grown as an international churchman and political leader. In both instances ... his reputation would have played a significant rhetorical role in his work." (115)

338   "Shibboleth" was a test-word created by biblical Jephthah to distinguish the fleeing Ephraimites who could not pronounce the "sh." So shibboleth has designated a word to distinguish enemies. Among new human beings there are no enemies. Here, it would be a test of one's jingoistic patriotism, insisting on naming enemies.

339   This is a substantial change from the psychology prevalent through the 1950s, that is, before the present sea-change became evident to many. As I went through school, the individualistic psychological focus on the ego was running rampant through popular psychology. This individualism produced the Me culture that in the Sixties and Seventies swept through the cultural scene in the United States as George Steiner described in *In Bluebeard's Castle*.

340   Ibid. Jones, 190

341   *Presbyterians Today*, December 2009, 4.

342   Ibid. Jones, 121.

343   Ibid. Jones, 124.

344   Lowe, Victor, "The Metaphysical System," in *Understanding Whitehead*, 1962, 45, Johns Hopkins University Press used by permission, Lowe attended Harvard where he studied with Whitehead. He was professor of philosophy at Johns Hopkins University.

345   *Process Philosophy and Christian Thought*, 1971, eds. Delwin Brown, Ralph E. James, Jr., Gene Reeves, Preface, v. Two of the major exponents of process theology are John Milbank, *Theology and Social Theory: Beyond Secular Reason*, 1991), and John B. Cobb *Becoming a Thinking Christian*, 1993.

346   Ibid., *Understanding Whitehead*, 35, 36.

347   Ibid. Brown and James.

348   Review of *On Kindness* by Adam Philips and Barbara Taylor, *The Nation*, July 20/27, 2009, 33.

349   Stephen W. Hawking, *A Brief History of Time: From the Big Bang to Black Holes*, 1988, 174.

350   Ibid., *Understanding Whitehead*, 38.

351   Ibid., *Understanding Whitehead*, 40.

352   Ibid., *Understanding Whitehead*, 34.

353   Calvin's austere predestination seems to represent a drive for thorough logical consistency which was familiar in Scholasticism. One day we may recognize it as a residue even Calvin could not overcome of the Greek notion of absolute which was soon thereafter to feed the misconceptions of determinism.

354   Morris, William, *Mazorca: Objects of Common Ceremony*, 2004, 9f. Allende's foreword is priceless.

355   Shenk, David, *The Genius in All of Us: Why Everything You've been told about Genetics, Talent, and IQ Is Wrong*, 2010, 35f.

356   Aristocracy meant being superior to other people. John Dominic Crossan suggests that Jesus explicitly rejected the patronage system which extended limited privilege to whoever might have a commodity for some clients. If one could broker a service or commodity, others would come to him or her for it. Jesus rejected the offer to become a local healer for whom his family could become agents, that is, patrons to the sick and maimed..

357   "Neo-Platonism" constructed on Plato by Plotinus in the third century was popular in Europe. It was a useful base for Christianity. Early in the second millenium CE a version of Plato came into Europe from Spain, largely the work of Islamic scholars and Erasmus' translations followed in the fifteenth century.

358   Ibid. Maier-Katkin, Daniel, 27. We are reminded that the oral tradition of the pre-Socrates reached on through the middle ages. Erasmus tried to get Colet to write, but Colet preferred his superb oral skill.

359   Baker, Stephen, *Final Jeopardy: Man vs. Machine and the Quest to Know Everything*, 2011, 45ff.

360   Ibid. Maier-Katkin, 76.
361   Kline, Morris, *Mathematics: The Loss of Certainty*, 1981. Kurt Godel (1906-1978) showed in 1931 that any consistent formal system strong enough to axiomatize arithmetic must be incomplete (containing statements that are "true" but not provable). Cf. Douglas Hofstadter's *Godel, Escher, Bach: An Eternal Golden Braid*.
362   A variety of related diseases have been called "leprosy." Some are mild enough to have not interfered with civil participation. Others were truly hideous in their gradual consumption of the body.
363   I am, obviously stretching the modern notion of "political" which has long had to do with government. The point here is that the beginnings of social organization (and politics) are to be found in the ordinary activities of life. The modern complication of society must not neglect these.
364   Claude Williams continued to work for desegregation and brotherhood. (James Aronson, *National Guardian*, September 25, 1961.)
365   Descartes, Rene, *Discourse on the Method of Rightly Conducting the Reason* , in Terry J. Tekippe, *Bernard Lonergan: An Introductory Guide to Insight* (2003), 60f.
366   Sharon Begley wrote "The Hidden Brain: What scientists can learn from 'nothing'" in Newsweek, 6/7/10. Six months later scientists announced the tripling of the number of stars in the universe, thus accounting for most of the missing "dark" matter which Begly compares to the brain's "default mode" (*USA TODAY*, 12/2/2010). Thus both great mysteries were apparently uncovered in 2010. "Cogitate" comes from Latin, "think" from German roots, "consider" from French. "Reflection" moves toward the effects of thinking, with Latin roots meaning to turn, to bend, to recurve. We use "reshape" often.
367   *Tikkun Daily*, 6/28/2010.
368   It should be noted that "conviction" in this paper is a deep psychological state. The Jew's conviction was not what today is commonly called "belief" which increasingly has become a sort of arbitrary and easily changed thing. Conviction is a self-identity which predisposes a person to think and act.
369   "People say they need involvement" in *USA TODAY*, 12/9/10.
370   Ancient rulers were essentially overwhelmed by the growing populations. There is no way without significant changes in government that they could have governed the expanding population. In only two hundred years, the 1800 CE world population has multiplied by seven – from one billion to seven billion people. In spite of our sophistication, the State of California seems perennially to prove itself ungovernable, both by its size and its diverse population. Interestingly, it seems also not to have lost its leadership in innovation. Is it possible that its turmoil has kept it from becoming too proud to allow expression of the human creativity at home there? Cf. *Time* magazine, 11/2/09.
371   Some think that there was a long period in hunter-gatherer culture in which coalitions held the power of overbearing leaders in check, long avoiding the earliest aberrations of oligarchs. Such coalitions are observed in various primates today, especially among females. Perhaps the climate and varied terraine of northern Europe helped maintain the control of the people over their lives.
372   Harold Garfinkel reminds us "that the facts that 'anyone can see' (common sense) are created and perpetuated by people through their talk and actions." "The reality of socially constructed categories is underwritten by circular logic: Their factualness is presumed while at the same time inherently ambiguous events are brought to bear as evidence of them.... It is the pervasive logic of everyday thought." (Ibid. Leslie Brothers, *Friday's Footprint*, 106.)
373   After the broadsword made man-to-man warfare into inconceivable slaughter, gunpowder and the firearm raised the stakes again and then it was not long before the cannon made castles obsolete, again increasing the cost of warfare and the burden on the people. It has taken a long time to grasp this folly.
374   Ibid. Joan Huber. The growing importance of women is illustrated by the Egyptian revolution of 2011 in which Esraa Abdel Fattah Ahmed Rashid and Asmaa Mahfouz rallied the people on Facebook and YouTube. There are many other women who have played prominent roles in the quest for self-governance. (Rachel Newcome in *USA TODAY* 3/16/11. Newcome teaches anthropology at Rollins College.)
375   The common sense idea of growth is the annual renewal of plant life in the spring followed by maturing and ripening. This growth produces food for us and for many animals. But especially in the age of the Enlightenment, economists realized that a growing economy produces wealth beyond immediate needs, and thus more wealth. Gradually in the twentieth century we have proven capitalism to be a productive engine of wealth and we have set before the world this model of productivity in which growth "solves all problems." But of course, it does not, as the growth of trade in sex, in drugs, and in armaments clearly demonstrates. In the Seventies the "Limits to Growth" project of the Club of Rome demonstrated in spades the problem of growth relative to natural resources. Scientism confidently bet on such things as the green revolution to solve the problem of the earth's limited carrying capacity, but it did so only temporarily.
376   It cannot be proved, but I think probable that grovelling for gold may well have been one of the very first labor specialties. Long before cities emerged, the natural attractiveness and malleability of gold made trade for body ornaments worth a good deal for food. Copper proved also to be similarly attractive. And with

the earliest smelting silver then brass and then the bronze produced hard, dangerous work for many ancient people. Remember the source of our alphabet was an opal mine in the Sinai peninsula. So we know that precious stones had long been cherished and thus were inviting to miners also, probably as early as gold.

377   A cyborg is a cybernetic organism (i.e., an organism that has both artificial and natural systems). The term was coined in 1960 when Manfred Clynes and Nathan Kline used it in an article in *Astronautics*, about the advantages of self-regulating human-machine systems in outer space. D. S. Halacy's *Cyborg: Evolution of the Superman* in 1965 featured an introduction which spoke of a "new frontier" that was "not merely space, but more profoundly, the relationship between 'inner space' and 'outer space' -a bridge...between mind and matter." (Wikipedia, the free encyclopedia.)

378   Karen Armstrong suggests that much interpretation narrows understanding. I think that what it reduces or sharpens in orthodox interpretation may increase doctrinal precision but interpretation may also be an enlargement of thought. The Roman Catholic Church persists in trying to maintain a homogeneity and unity which is totally artificial. One may argue that its institutional singleness of mind allowed it to spread a varied but still identifiable church over much of the globe. But it does this only while accommodating or ignoring the real differences between varied groups and people.

379   *Les Miserable* on stage. See Chapter VI. D.

380   We have observed the confusion around the transition from slave obedience to voluntary allegiance and equally difficult learning of humility to replace the pride of conqueror, victor, and discoverer.

381   For comparison, in 1790 the population of the United States was under four million people. By the middle of the twentieth century it reached 150 million people. The U.S. population more than tripled during the 20th century – a growth rate of about 1.3% a year – from about 76 million in 1900 to 281 million in 2000. Shortly after 2000 the 1950 population had doubled (300 million). The United States alone contains six times the maximum estimated population of the Roman Empire.

382   This avenue of leadership was exploited as recently as the second American intervention in Iraq after the 9/11/01 terrorist attacks using three commercial airliners on the World Trade Center and the Pentagon. The "Neo-Con" strategy was not only an archaic reaction, but a counterproductive one which fed the terrorist frenzy in the receptive cultures of the Middle East. We note that, like other reactionary behaviors, this also brought forth positive, healthy, and hopeful efforts.

383   Journalist Keith Kloor met with archaeologist Winston Hurst to prepare "The Looters Next Door" in Archaeology. September-October 2009, 16.

384   Hagedorn, Hermann. *The Bomb That Fell on America*, 1946, 57. The jingoistic use of the "communist scare" in the United States through much of the twentieth century was a classic case of the ease with which demagoguery has stirred up large populations to irrational heights. Voices like Hagedorn's had been speaking with increasing clarity against the mentality that made war an easy option.

385   I remember vividly the plot of a thin volume my father had read as a boy about the frenetic flight from a pack of wolves of a young man on ice skates. My early view of real boys outwitting nature (and wolves) was, indeed, shaped by that book. It is worth noting what a distance this is from the slaughter of the Danish saga "Beowulf" on one hand and the children's literature available today, on the other.

386   This mind expansion may be compromised by the lowered productivity demonstrated by people who think they "multi-task" effectively. A Stanford University study earlier this year found the opposite to be true.n a Toledo *Blade* editorial printed in the *Columbus Dispatch* Nov. 25, 2009.

387   Michael Grunwald, *Time* magazine, November 2, 2009, 26.

388   This revolution was not an unmixed blessing. "It is not as if farming brought a great improvement in living standards either. "A typical hunter-gatherer enjoyed a more varied diet and consumed more protein and calories than settled people, and took in five times as much vitamin C as the average person today. Even in the bitterest depths of the ice ages, we now know, nomadic people ate surprisingly well - and surprisingly healthily. Settled people, by contrast, became reliant on a much smaller range of foods, which all but ensured dietary insufficiencies." Bill Bryson, *At Home: A Short History of Private Life* , 2010, 37.

389   Hacala, Sara, *Saving Civility: 52 Ways to Tame, Rude, Crude and Attitude for a Polite Planet, 2011*.

390   Jeffrey Gedmin, *Columbus Dispatch*, "Forum" November 9, 2009.

391   Hymns, like poetry and literature, being products in a tradition, tend to keep old language alive.

392   Exodus 33:23. Orthodox Christianity has insisted that the obvious "hiddenness" of God necessitates the doctrine of revelation. Until recently our language failed to communicate this revelation as our "grasp" of our experience of God.

393   Remember that Alexis De Tocqueville was a French historian not an immigrant.

394   Please do not confuse this misuse of the human release of emotion in crying with the legitimate cries of people and intellectuals for correction and righteousness such as are discussed in chapter XIV. C.

395   David Brooks quotes Tyler Cowen's ebook, *The Great Stagnation*, the *Columbus Dispatch* 2/16/11.

396   Peter Phillips, University of Saskatchewan, reminds us that not all agree with the World-watch Institute's pessimism that the United Nations projection of eight billion human beings by 2020 will exceed the

diminishing product of scientific improvement of the food supply. The International Food Policy Research Institute concluded that "the aggregate global (food) picture will be relatively good." Phillips concludes that "complacency is not the answer. A solution will come only with greater examination of the options." (Population_Forecasting, Summer 1997 v54, June 22, 1997.)

397   Paul A. Samuelson, first American recipient of the Nobel Prize in Economics, died while this was being written, 12/13/09. Samuelson recognized the need for "regulation, monitoring, and punishment,"

398   This is not to suggest that the conservative mind exported through religion to the third world will necessarily mature into Fundamentalism. The people of the third world did not receive Christianity in the frame of mind that produced American Fundamentalism in the early twentieth century. They have already demonstrated capacity to think beyond us, often with greater compassion than we commonly know.

399   Intelligence Report of the Southern Poverty Law Center, issue 136, winter 2009.

400   The truth was known long before liberty was possible on the scale we know it today: Somewhere it has been written, "The price of liberty is eternal vigilance." It seems that this aspect of the new mind emerging among us has been evident in some rare individuals over millennia.

401   Ibid. Intelligence Report, 23.

402   The massive unrest in the Middle East in 2011, following decades of autocracy, took shape with extraordinary rapidity. It is not a new phenomenon and has always been feared by autocrats. The skill with which it often has been accepted and disarmed represents both modern learning and ancient devices – sowing divisiveness in the public is an old technique. But the new capability of people to communicate with electronic devices gives some assurance that depressed people will be able to disengage from their past more effectively. A history of destructive revolutions have armed us against the brutal and the abusive. Thomas Friedman reports a message to Egyptians from Tunis where an apparently successful revolt has occurred was "don"t burn yourself up, burn up the fear that is inside you. That is what happened here. This was a society in fear and the fear has been burned." (Columbus Dispatch, 2/9/11.)

403   I believe that this continued growth of the Catholic Church represents the hunger in a technological society for ceremony as well as ties to permanence and the past. That many "drift away" is symptomatic of the longl trend away from institutional orthodoxy.

404   One of the strangest was "Rev. Ike," Frederick J. Eikerenkoetter II. who died in 2009. For twenty or thirty years he preached material prosperity: "Close your eyes and see green" he told his 5000 parishioners. (Columbus Dispatch/New York Times, January 31, 2009). Less extreme, but equally aberrant, is the take-over of America's pastime (football) by an extreme form of Christianity which promotes an antiquarian "us vs. them" philosophy. Their belief statement published by "Baseball Chapel" preaches this self-righteous, divisive view. At a time when America has the opportunity to encourage its young to live openly with people who are different, this far right extremism is counterproductive.

405   Zuurdeeg, Willem Frederik, An Analytical Philosophy of Religion, 1958, ch. 1.

406   Joseph Stein gave us a good stage version of this in Tevye's nightmare in "Fiddler on the Roof."

407   This appellation calls for an explanation since Greek society has for long been seen as a golden age. But one must remember that it was still a slave culture in which the vast majority of people served the welfare of the elite. As we have shown, this unhappy past has never stopped the evolution of the human self. Among elites and also among peons, the human self continued to evolve.

408   Zuurdeeg, Willem, Man Before Chaos, ed. Esther Cornelius Swenson, 1968,15f,

409   Ibid. Intelligence Report, 26. An episode in the Civil Rights War of the 1960s.

410   Lubow, Arthur in the Smithsonian Magazine, March 2006, 58.

411   In the 1960s, in a group discussion of "god is dead" with William Hamilton, I was convinced that we were in the midst of rethinking Christianity and doing a lot of thinking in the process.

412   We note, however, that Jurgen Habermas shared the critique that built into psychoanalysis was an asymetry between patient and analyst. This did not represent emancipation and it contradicts the movement out of autocacracy. (See James Bohman and William Rehg in the Stanford Encyclopedia of Philosophy.)

413   In some cultures, the pattern is to whale and cry loudly and incessantly at death of a loved one. The tiny child learns this automatically and will so respond unless he or she chooses to respond differently.

414   Hannah Arendt recalls her struggle (as a German familiar with the language) with the "paragraph-long sentences" she had to read during her educational experience, noting the same difficulty. Unfortunately my habit of compiling phrases into long sentences continues almost unabated.

415   Holly Hall, "A Philanthropist's Case for the Estate Tax," The Chronicle of Philanthropy, 8/31/10.

416   Esperanto was created in the late 1870s and early 1880s by Dr. Ludovic Lazarus Zamenhof, a Belorusian-Jewish ophthalmologist from Bialystok, at the time part of the Russian Empire. According to Zamenhof, he created this language to foster harmony between people from different countries. (Wikipedia)

AN AUTHOR'S CHRONOLOGY

PERIODS

PRIMITIVE			Years Ago
Paleolithic (Pleistocene)		1,000,000	20,000
Early (Java, Peking, Ice Age)			
Middle		300,000	200,000
Great Migration		100,000	80,000
Upper (more recent) Ice Age			40,000
Chauvet Cave (France)			30,000
Neanderthal graves			25,000

ANCIENT

Mesolithic (Old Stone Age; Mousterian)			
Gobekli Tepe			11,500
Agricultural Revolution			10,000
Neolithic (New Stone Age; Fayam, Egypt, Samara)			
Danubian, Swiss Lake			
Stonehenge			5,500
Early Cities (Jericho)		5,000	3,000
Great Pyramids			2,900
Bronze Age		3000	2,000
Iron Age			1,500
Petra			1,200
Iron Age		1500	700

LANGUAGE YEARS BCE/CE

Hindu Vedas (Vedic language, parent of Sanscrit)
Egypt (picture writing) 4,000 BCE
Chinese (picture writing)
Sumarian (Cuneiform)
Akkadian (Semite, Akkad)
Celtic
Turkic Khaganate
Alphabet (Sinai emerald mine to Greece) 800 BCE
Cyrillic 900 CE

MESOPOTAMIA

South: Sumerian (Sumer, Ur)	4,000 BCE
North: Semitic (Akkad)	3,000 BCE
Sargon (blended Akkad and Sumer)	2,800 BCE
Hammurabi	2,100 BCE

MEDITERRANEAN

Minoan (Crete)	2,500 BCE	1,400 BCE
Mycenean	1,400 BCE	900 BCE
Helene	1,200 BCE	
Lydia		
Miletus		
Palestine	4,000 BCE	
Axial Period (Major Religions)	500 BCE	600 CE

GREECE 800 BCE 146 BCE
Solon 594 BCE
City States (Athens, Sparta, Syracuse)

Peloponnesian War	431 BCE	404 BCE
Macedonian Period		
Philip II	382 BCE	336 BCE
Alexander III (The Great)	356 BCE	323 BCE
Helenistic Period	323 BCE	31 BCE

ROME 500 BCE 476 CE

Roman Period – 1	Republic	500 BCE	48 BCE
Roman Period – 2	Empire	48 BCE	476 CE
Constantine		288 CE	336 CE
Visigoths (Africa), Ostrogoths, Franks) 395 CE			527 CE
Roman Period – 3	Byzantium	552 CE	800 CE
Byzantine exarchs ruled at Ravenna			
Roman Period - 4		800 CE	814 CE
Charlemagne at Rome ended Byzantine rule over West			

MEDIEVAL PERIOD (Middle Ages)	6c	14c
Scholastic Period	10c	15c
Universities begin	12c	
Ottoman Empire	14c	16c
Feudalism		

RENAISSANCE		14c	16c
REFORMATION		14c	18c
MERCANTILISM	(superseded feudalism) 16c		18c
ENLIGHTENMENT		16c	18c
INDUSTRIAL REVOLUTION			19c
MODERN		19c	20c

PERSONS AND EVENTS
BEFORE COMMON ERA (BCE)
Arranged in Groups by Century
(by birthdate and date of event)

Hesiod	Greece		700 BCE
Homer	Greece		
Zoroaster	Persia	660	583 BCE
Josiah	Israel	646	608 BCE
Thales	Greece	636	546 BCE
Anaximander		611	547 BCE
Anaxagores		6c	
Pythagores (Geometry)		582	507
Xenophanes		570	480 BCE
Gautama (Buddha; India)		563	483 BCE
Confucius (China)		551	479 BCE
Cyrus (Persia)		529 BCE	
Heraclitus		535	475 BCE
Parmenides		514 BCE	
Anaxagora s		500	428 BCE
Zeno of Elea		490 -	430 BCE
Sophocles		496	406 BCE
Herodotus		484 -	425 BCE
Protagoras		480	410 BCE
Euripides		480	406 BCE
Socrates		469	399 BCE
Leucippus			
Democritus		460	370 BCE
Euclid		450	375 BCE
Xenophanes		430	355 BCE
Pericles		430 BCE	
Plato		427	347 BCE
Gorgias		485	380 BCE
Aristotle		384	322 BCE
Antigonus		382	301 BCE
Philip II		382	338 BCE
Alexander		356	323 BCE
Epicurus		342	270 BCE
Zeno of Citium		336 -	264 BCE
Aristarchus		310 -	230 BCE
Observed movem'nt around sun but Aristotle also claimed			
Ptolemy (Egypt)		308	246 BCE
Euclid (Elements of geometry)		300	BCE
Pyrrho			-275 BCE
Timon			-235 BCE
Sextus Empiricus		225	150 BCE
Posidonius		135	51 BCE
Cicero		106	43 BCE

Julius Caesar	102	**44 BCE**
Virgil	70	19 BCE
Cleopatra	69	30 BCE
Augustus	63	14 BCE

PERSONS AND EVENTS
DATES IN THE COMMON ERA (CE)

Philo	20 BCE	50 CE
Jesus (Christ)	4 BCE	32 CE
Seneca	3 BCE	65 CE
Heracleon		
Dionysius the Areopagite	1c	
Pliny the Elder	23 -	79
Quintilian	35	95
Josephus	37	95
Plutarch	46	120
Epictetus		60
Polycarp	70	156
Hadrian	76	138
Marcion		85
Clement of Rome		88
Justin Martyr	100	165
Ignatius of Antioch		110
Marcus Aurelius (Stoic)	121	180
Irenaeus of Lyon	125	202
Ptolemy (Last ancient astronomer)	127	151
Bar Kokba		135
Galen	130	200
Clement of Alexandria	150	216
Tertullian	150	230
Origen	185	254
Lucian		2c
Tatian (Diatesaron)		2c
Plotinus	204	270
Mani (Persia; manichaeism)	216	276
Porphyry	233	304
Eusebius of Caesrea	263	339
Constantine the Great	288	336
Athanasius	293	373
NICEA		331
Arius		336
Ambrose of Milan	339	397
Eusebius of Nicomedia		342
Jerome	347	430
Augustine	354	430
Pelagius	355	425
Patrick	385	461
Gaiseric	390	477
Aleric		410
Ninian		432
Attila (King of the Huns)	433	453
CHALCEDON		451
Zeno of Narsia	474	491
Adoacer		476
Boethius (Boece)	480	524
Justinian I (Codified Roman Law)	483	565
Clovis		496
Columba	521	597
Cille, Colam	521	597
Dionysius Exiguus		545
Iona (Scot Inner Hebrides; Columba landing)		563
Mohammad		560
Gregory the Great	590	604

Aidan (Irish; Lindisfarne Scotland)		651	
Charlemagne (Charles the Great)		742	814
Ignatius of Constantinople		800	877
Erigena, John Scotus		810	880
Avicenna (Ibn Sina)		980	1037
Anselm		1034	1109
Abelard, Peter		1079	1142
Alexius I (First Crusade)		1081	1118
First Universities		12c	
Averroes (Ibn Rushd; Cordoba Spain)		1126	1198
(Muslim scholar, Arabic interpretation of Aristotle)			
Maimonides (Rambam; Cordoba and Cairo)		1135	1204
(Moses ben Maimon, Jewish scholar in Arabic)			
Dominic, St.		1170	1221
Eisai (Founder of Zen)		1187	
Francis of Assisi		1181	1226
Manus, Albertus		1203	1280
Bacon, Roger (Eng.,Franciscan,science)	1214	1294	
Kublai Khan		1215	1294
LATERAN COUNCIL		1215	
Aquinas, Thomas		1227	1274
INQUISITION		1233	1820
Marco Polo		1234	1324
Dante, Alighieri		1265	1321
Scotus, John Duns (Scot Scholastic)		1274	1308
Occam (Wm of Ockham; Scot)		1300	1350
Petrarch, Francesco ("First Humanist")		1304	1374
Boccaccio, Giovanni		1313	1375
Wyclif, John		1328	1384
Tamerlane		1336	1405
Chaucer, Geoffrey		1340	1400
Huss, Johan		1369	1415
Gutenberg, Johan		1397	1468
Valla, Lorezo		1435	
Lombard, Peter		1435	1515
Columbus, Christopher		1451	1506
GLASGOW UNIVERSITY		1451	
Leonardo da Vinci		1452	1519
Colet, John		1457	1519
Erasmus, Disiderius		1466	1536
Machiavelli, Niccolo		1469	1527
Copernicus, Nicholas		1473	1543
Michanlangelo Bournaroti		1475	1564
More, Thomas		1478	1535
Virgil		1478	1555
Luther, Martin		1483	1546
Mair, John		1540	
Zwingli, Ulrich		1484	1531
Cranmer , Thomas		1489	1556
Bucer, Martin		1497	1551
Rabelais, Francois		1490	1553
Loyola, Ignatius		1491	1556
Menno Simons		1496	1561
Knox , John		1505	1572
Buchanan, George		1506	1582
Calvin, John		1509	1564
Servetus, Michael		1511	1553
Versalius, Andrew		1514	1564
DIET OF AUGSBURG		1524	1524
Elizabeth (Queen)		1533	1603
Montaigne		1533	1592
Suleiman (Ottoman Empire)		1535	
ABERDEEN UNIVERSITY		1536	
Brahe, Tycho		1546	1601

Bellarmine	1542	1621
COUNCIL OF TRENT	1545	1563
Spenser, Edmund	1552	1599
Bruno, Giordano	1548	
Bacon, Francis (Inductive method)	1561	1626
Schakespeare, William	1564	1616
Galileo, Galilie	1564	1642
Nashe, Thomas	1567	1601
Kepler, Johannes	1571	1630
Donne, John	1572	1631
Harvey, William	1578	1659
Ussher, James	1581	1656
EDINBURGH UNVIERSITY	1583	
Grotius, Hugo von	1583	1645
Hobbes, Thomas	1588	1679
Descartes, Rene	1596	1650
Cromwell, Oliver	1599	1658
Williams, Roger	1603	1683
Rembrant	1606	1669
Milton, John	1608	1674
THIRTY YEARS WAR	1618	1648
Shaftsbury, 1st Earl	1621	1683
Pascal, Blaise	1623	1662
Turretin, Francis	1623	1687
Cromwell, Richard	1626	1712
Dryden, John	1631	1700
Spinoza, Baruch	1632	1677
Locke, John	1632	1704
Pufendorf, Samuel	1632	1694
Buxtehude, Dietrich	1637	1707
Newton, Issac	1642	1727
PURITAN REVOLUTION	1642	1649
WESTMINSTER ASSEMBLY	1645	1647
Leibniz, Gottfried Wilhelm	1646	1716
Carstares, William	1649	1715
William III	1650	1702
HARVARD	1650	
DeFoe, Daniel	1660	1731
ROYAL SOCIETY	1662	
Vico, Geovanni Batis	1668	1744
Shafsbury, 3rd Earl	1671	1713
Watts, Isaac	1674	1748
Berkeley, Bishop George	1685	1753
Handel, George Frederic	1685	1759
Law, William	1686	1761
ENGLISH REVOLUTION	1688	
Pope, Alexander	1689	1744
Montesquieu	1689	1755
WILLIAM & MARY COLLEGE	1693	
Hutcheson, Francis	1694	1746
Voltaire	1694	1778
Reimarus, Hermann	1694	1768
Bach, Johann Sebastian	1695	1750
Kames, Henry Home Lord	1696	1782
YALE	1701	
Edwards, Jonathan	1703	1758
Wesley, John	1703	1791
Wesley, Charles	1707	1788
ACT OF UNION (Scot-Eng)	1707	
Johnson, Samuel	1709	1784
Reid, Thomas	1710	1796
Hume, David	1711	1776
Rousseau, Jean Jacques	1712	1778
Diderot, Denis	1713	1784
Helvetius	1715	1771
Witherspoon, John	1723	1794
Smith, Adam	1723	1790
Kant, Immanuel	1724	1804

Lessing, Gotthold	1729	1781
Washington, George	1732	1804
Haydn, Franz Joseph	1732	1809
Priestly, Joseph	1733	1804
Watt, James	1736	1819
Gibbon, Edward	1737	1794
Paine, Thomas	1737	1809
Boswell, James	1740	1795
Condorcet	1743	1819
Jacobi, Friedrich Heinrich	1743	1819
PRINCETON	1746	
Bentham, Jeremy	1748	1837
Goethe, Johan Wolfgang von	1749	1832
INDUSTRIALISM	1750	1950
Madison, James	1751	1836
Stewart, Dugald	1753	1828
COLUMBIA	1754	
Mozart, Wolfgang Amadeus	1756	1791
Burns, Robert	1759	1796
Schiller, Johann Christoph F. von	1759	1805
Fichte, Johann Gotlieb	1762	1814
Malthus, Thomas Robert	1766	1834
Schleiermacher, Freidrich	1768	1834
Beethoven, Ludwig von	1770	1827
Scott, Sir Walter	1771	1832
Hegel, Georg Fredrick	1770	1831
Mills, James	1773	1836
Schelling, Friedrich von	1775	1854
GREAT AWAKENING	1776	
DECLARATION OF INDEPENDENCE	1776	
CONSTITUTION OF THE UNITED STATES	1787	
Schopenhauer, Arthur	1788	1860
BEGINNING OF FRENCH REVOLUTION	1789	
Bauer, F. C. (Tubingen School)	1792	1860
Hodge, Charles	1797	1878
Comte, Auguste	1798	1857
Maculay, Thomas Babblington	1800	1859
Darwin, Charles Robert	1802	1882
Feuerbach, Ludwig	1804	1872
Disraeli, Benjamin	1804	1881
Tocqueville, Alexis de	1805	1859
Mill, John Stuart	1806	1873
Napoleon Bonapart	1808	1873
Strauss, David Friedrich	1808	1874
Tennyson, Alfred	1809	1892
Greeley, Horace	1811	1872
Wagner, Richard	1813	1883
Kierkegaard, Soren	1813	1899
Bismark, Otto von	1815	1898
Thoreau, Henry David	1817	1862
Marx, Karl	1818	1883
Engels, Friedrich	1820	1895
Spenser, Herbert	1820	1902
Renan, Ernest	1823	1892
Hodge, Archibald Alexander	1823	1886
Ibsen, Henriok	1828	1906
Brahms, Johannes	1833	1897
Dilthey, Wilhelm	1833	1911
Carnegie, Andrew	1835	1919
Moody, Dwight L.	1837	1899
Briggs, Charles	1841	1913
James, William	1842	1910
Nietzsche, Fredrich	1844	1900
Wellhausen, Julius	1844	1918
IRISH FAMINE	1845	1849
Bell, Alexander Graham	1847	1922
Frege, Gotlob	1848	1925
COMMUNIST MANIFESTO	1848	
Tchaikovsky, Piotr Ilich	1849	1893

Freud, Sigmund	1856	1939
Durkheim, Emile	1858	1917
Curie, Pierre	1859	1906
Bergson, Henri	1859	1941
Dewey, John	1859	1952
Husserl, Edmund	1859	1938
Inge, William Ralph (Dean St. Paul's)	1860	1954
Rauschenbusch, Walter	1861	1918
Whitehead, Alfred North	1861	1947
Mead, George Herbert	1863	1931
Matthews, Shaler	1863	1941
Weber, Max	1864	1920
Wells, H. G.	1866	1946
Otto, Rudolph	1869	1937
Troeltsch, Ernst	1865	1923
Gandhi, Mohandas Karamchand	1869	1948
Lenin, Vladimir	1870	1924
Russell, Bertrand	1872	1970
Jung, Carl Gukstav	1875	1961
Schweitzer, Albert	1875	1965
Bauer, Walter	1877	1960
Buber, Martin	1878	1965
Einstein, Albert	1879	1955
Stalin, Joseph	1879	
Pope Leo XIII (declared Thomism official)	1879	
Keller, Helen	1880	1968
Asche, Sholem	1880	1957
Teihard de Chardin	1881	1955
Picasso, Pablo	1881	1973
Maritain. Jacques	1882	1973
Keynes, John Maynard	1883	1946
Kafka, Franz	1883	1924
Jaspers, Karl	1883	1969
Rank, Otto	1884	1939
Modigliani, Amedeo	1884	1920
Bohr, Neils	1885	1962
Muste, A. J. (20c pacifist)	1885	1967
Tillich, Paul	1886	1965
Barth, Karl	1886	1968
Ferber, Edna	1887	1968
Chagall, Marc	1887	1985
Marcel, Gabriel	1889	1973
Wittgenstein, Ludwig	1889	1951
Heidegger, Martin	1889	1977
Albright, William Foxwell	1891	1971
Polanyi, Michael	1891	1976
Northrop, John Howard	1891	
Carnap, Rudoph	1891	1970
Niebuhr, Reihold	1892	1971
Langer, Susan	1895	1985
Gershwin, George	1895	1937
Fitzgerald, F. Scott	1896	1940
Piaget, Jean	1896	1980
Hartshorne, Charles	1897	2000
Mead, Margaret	1901	1978
Heisenberg, Werner	1901	1976
Popper, Karl	1902	1994
Gehrig, Lou	1903	1941
Rahner, Karl	1904	1984
Montague, Ashley	1905	1999
Rand, Ayn	1905	1982
Sartre,Jean Paul	1905	1980
Bonhoeffer, Deitrich	1906	1945
Arendt, Hannah	1906	1975
Godel, Kurt	1906	1978
Carson, Rachel (Silent Spring)	1907	1964
Eliade, Mircea	1907	1986
Sewall, Richard B.	1908	20

Zuurdeeg, Willem Frederich	1909	1966
Ricoeur, Paul	1912	2005
Camus, Albert	1913	1960
Ramsey, Robert Paul	1913	1988
Bohm, David	1917	1992
Schlesinger, Arthur	1917	2007
Feynman, Richard	1918	1988
Hook, Sidney	1920	1989
Jaynes, Julian	1920	1997
Kuhn, Thomas	1922	1996
Lindbeck, George Arthur	1923	
Becker, Ernest	1924	1974
Chagal, Marc	1887	1985
Mandelbrot, Benoit	1925	2010
Segal, George	1926	2000
Kung, Hans	1928	
Hall, Douglas John	1929	
Steiner, George	1929	
Habermas, Jurgen	1929	
Bloom, Alan	1930	1992
Derrida, Jacques	1930	2004
Rorty, Richard	1931	2007
Portman, Neil	1931	2003
Searle, John R.	1932	
Berry, Wendell	1934	
Goodall, Jane	1934	
AUBURN AFFIRMATION		1934
Peters, Karl E.		
Caputo, John	1940	
Kripke, Saul	1940	
Gomes, Peter J.	1942	2011
SECOND VATICAN COUNCIL (Pope John XXIII)		1963

Alphabetical Index